BRITAIN AND THE CONQUEST OF AFRICA

BRITAIN AND THE CONQUEST OF AFRICA

The Age of Salisbury

G. N. Uzoigwe

Ann Arbor
The University of Michigan Press

*Published with the assistance of a grant
from the Horace H. Rackham School of Graduate
Studies of the University of Michigan*

To my father and mother

Preface

About the year 1878 less than 10 percent of African territories were under European rule; by 1900 the whole of Africa had been conquered by the imperialist powers of Europe. Only Abyssinia (Ethiopia) and Liberia retained some sort of fragile independence. This development must rank as one of the great historical movements—perhaps the greatest historical movement—of modern times. W. L. Langer's vision of this age is both perceptive and revealing. He writes: "Centuries hence, when interests in the details of European diplomacy in the pre-war period will have faded completely, this period will still stand out as the crucial epoch during which the nations of the western world extended their political, economic and cultural influence over Africa and over large parts of Asia. The tide of European control has already turned and we are living now in an age of retreat and retirement. The tremendous outburst of expansion and the almost complete victory of Europe was, therefore, crowded into a couple of generations, the peak of the movement being reached in the last decade of the 19th and the first decade of the 20th centuries. During that score of years the competition in the acquisition of territory and the struggle for influence and control was the most important factor in the international relations of Europe. We cannot avoid giving it some special attention." (*The Diplomacy of Imperialism, 1890–1902*, 2d. ed. [New York: Alfred A. Knopf, 1951] p. 67.)

The feuds of historians as to the motives behind the European conquest of Africa have become proverbial in African and European history. This book has been written as a contribution to the understanding of this crucial phase of Afro-European history. Although it focuses on Britain as the premier imperialist power of this age, it has not failed to take into consideration the general problems of European international politics as they related to the conquest of Africa. One intriguing aspect of this study is that it is—incredible as it may seem—the first effort by a historian of African origin to attempt a general interpretation of this period. The existing studies are either national or regional in orientation and emphasis. Indeed, the only other general interpretation of this period in recent years is the highly reputed *Africa and the Victorians* by Ronald Robinson and John Gallagher—a work published over a decade ago and whose provocative thesis inspired this book. Our theme, then, is not only an important but also a controversial one. I hope that readers of this book will agree that I have investigated my sources as broadly, thoroughly, and critically as possible; that I have presented my arguments in a fair and historical manner; that my conclusions are based on my comprehension of these sources; and that these conclusions have shed light on a theme characterized by its elusive complexity. Those readers anxious to be confronted by another one factor theory of historical explanation in the tradition of Robinson and Gallagher will be thoroughly disappointed. I do not subscribe to that school of theorizing. Finally, I hope that this book has dealt with some fundamental historical issues without a thorough comprehension of which developments in twentieth century Africa, and to some extent in twentieth century Europe, will become unintelligible.

This book has been a long time in preparation. It is based on nearly a decade of intensive and careful research in British and African archival sources. And employing these in juxtaposition with private papers, oral traditions, parliamentary debates, parliamentary papers, periodicals, newspapers, diaries, memoirs, memories, autobiographies, and biographies, this study shows that the motives behind the European conquest of Africa were complex and oftentimes contradictory, and breaks new ground in methodological and conceptual terms by discussing the intellectual and socio-politico-economic problems of the second half of the nineteeth century against the background of European diplomacy and African history. It also reevaluates the role of Robert, the Third Marquis of Salisbury (1830–1903)—British Prime Minister and Foreign Secretary for most of the crucial period between 1878 and 1902—in the conquest of Africa. Salisbury, whose name hitherto has appeared in small print in the roll call of imperialists, emerges no longer clad in the garb of the lugubrious and reluctant imperialist drifting against his better judgment to acquire African territories and maintain the integrity of the empire, but rather as the *eminence grise* of European imperialism, sophisticated, sensible, practical, level-headed, cleverly adjusting to the realities of historical developments as befitted one who saw himself as the "trustee of the British Empire." He invites comparison with Bismarck in scope although the latter had not the same interest in European expansion. In British imperial history this period may rightly be called the "Age of Salisbury" for he largely shaped—albeit in a quiet sort of way—the character of British expansion overseas.

Indeed Salisbury's claim to historical fame lies not in foreign policy so-called but in his management of the conquest of Africa. This study also analyzes the character of African resistance to the European intrusion; reveals the Africa and Britain not found in the official records; argues that the scramble, partition and conquest of Africa is as much an important episode of European history as it is of African history; and shows how the foundations of the modern multi-nation states of West, East, Central and North Africa were laid.

In the course of producing this book I have been greatly indebted to many scholars, institutions, governments, and friends without whose help it could not have been undertaken or seen through to publication. I am particularly indebted to Dr. A. F. Madden of Nuffield College, Oxford University who, as supervisor of my doctoral thesis, introduced me to the intricacies of historical research. His remarkable knowledge of the British Empire and the location of primary source materials in Britain as well as his good humor, patience, and understanding were of tremendous assistance to me. Special thanks also go to Professors John A. Gallagher (formerly of Balliol College, Oxford and now of Trinity College, Cambridge) and Ronald Robinson (formerly of St. John's College, Cambridge and now of Balliol College, Oxford). They listened to and read with patience, understanding, and respect my criticisms of their works and offered me, in turn, valuable criticisms and advice. I still do not accept their interpretation of the partition of Africa, but their influence on my development as an historian has been substantial. Other scholars who read my manuscript either in part or as a whole and contributed in varying degrees to whatever value this book may have include Dr. Colin W. Newbury, the late George Bennet, Dr. Bueno de Mesquita (my tutor at Christ Church, Oxford), Professors Gerald S. Brown, John Bowditch, and Bradford Perkins. To all of them I extend grateful thanks. I should also like to thank the dean, the late Dr. Cuthbert A. Simpson, and the Students (Fellows) of Christ Church for the help and encouragement they gave me during my studies at Oxford. I wish also to acknowledge here the benefits I have derived from discussions of the ideas contained in this book with my graduate students at both the Universities of Makerere and Michigan.

Lord Salisbury kindly allowed me to make generous use of his grandfather's papers (housed at Christ Church Library, Oxford University) which form the backbone of this book, and Dr. J. F. A. Mason of Christ Church, Oxford offered me every help. To all of them I am most grateful. I am also very conscious of my gratitude to all those who made available to me other private papers under their charge. These are: The librarian, The Joseph Chamberlain Papers (Heslop Room, University of Birmingham Library, England); the Duke of Devonshire for use of the Papers of the Eighth Duke of Devonshire (housed at Chatsworth, Bakewell, Derbyshire); and the executors of the Papers of Sir Alfred Milner, Viscount Milner (housed at Bodleian Library, Oxford). Other important private papers which were of great help for my work include those of Lord Arthur James Balfour, Sir Charles Wentworth Dilke, Sir Henry Campbell-Bannerman—all deposited at the British Museum Additional Manuscripts, London; The First Earl of Cromer, Lord Thomas Sanderson, The First Marquis Curzon of Kedleston; Lord Francis Bertie; The Fifth Marquess of Landsdowne, Sir Edward Malet—all deposited at the Public Record Office, London; and Lord Frederick Lugard (Rhodes House Library, Oxford). To their families and archivists of their papers I extend grateful thanks. Nor should I neglect to thank the librarians, archivists and staff of the Foreign Office and the Colonial Office Libraries (Public Record Office, London), the Colindale Library of the British Museum (for newspapers), the Bodleian, Rhodes House, and Christ Church Libraries (Oxford); and Entebbe Secretariat Archives and Makerere University Library (Uganda) for all their help. I must also extend my acknowledgements to the publishers of many important works from which I have made extensive quotations.

To the Federal Government of Nigeria and the British Government I am beholden for a Commonwealth Scholarship which helped to finance my studies at Oxford. The Research Grants Committee of the University of Makerere, Uganda, funded my researches in Uganda, and the Horace H. Rackham School of Graduate Studies of the University of Michigan, Ann Arbor, contributed generously toward the cost of publishing this book. To both these institutions I am indeed very grateful. I am also grateful to the Center for Afro-American and African Studies, University of Michigan, for financing the cost of typing my manuscript; the typing was expertly done by Mrs. Aida Dorrity and Mrs. Gayle Wachuku.

I am indebted to my good friends, Dr. Boniface I. Obichere and Dr. Uga Onwuka, whose companionship contributed toward making my Oxford days a very happy time. Finally, without the understanding, encouragement, and support of my wife, Patricia, it would have been impossible to write this book. My deepest gratitude is to her.

Contents

LIST OF ABBREVIATIONS

B.D.	*British Documents on the Origins of the War, 1898–1914*
B. Mus. Add. Mss.	British Museum, Additional Manuscripts
B.S.A.C.	British South Africa Company
C.A.B.	*Cabinet Papers*
C.H.B.E.	*Cambridge History of the British Empire*
C.O.	Colonial Office Correspondence, Public Record Office, London
C.O.C.P.	Colonial Office Confidential Print
D.N.B.	*Dictionary of National Biography*
E.A.P.	East Africa Protectorate
E.H.R.	*English Historical Review*
F.O.	Foreign Office Correspondence, Public Record Office, London
F.O.C.P.	Foreign Office Confidential Print
G.D.D.	*German Diplomatic Documents, 1871–1914*
Hansard	*Hansard's Parliamentary Debates*
I.B.E.A.C.	Imperial British East Africa Company
J.A.H.	*Journal of African History*
J.C.P.	Joseph Chamberlain Papers
N.U.	National Union
Parl. Pap.	*Parliamentary Papers*
P.M.G.	*Pall Mall Gazette*
P.R.O.	Public Record Office, London
Q.V.L.	*Letters of Queen Victoria*
R.N.C.	Royal Niger Company
S.P.	Private Papers of Robert, Third Marquess of Salisbury
U.J.	*Uganda Journal*
W.O.	War Office Correspondence, Public Record Office, London

PART I

The Victorians and the Politics of Empire

Chapter I

Salisbury and Victorian Expansion

Men are the stuff of which history is made. Therefore, any historical explanation which separates the historical actor from the act, the man from the politician, is bound to be sterile, without life, without color, without substance, and consequently without meaning. There is a natural correlation between the private and the public life of a historical actor, between his feelings and his actions. A study of the essential characteristics of such a figure helps a historian to comprehend and explain why a statesman handled great historical movements or made important historical decisions in the way that he did.

In this chapter we will attempt, difficult as it is, to show the historical significance of Salisbury's personal characteristics in one of the great movements in modern world history: the European partition and conquest of Africa. We shall also examine his diplomatic methods and his concept of pacific imperialism which are apt to be misunderstood.

The Essential Salisbury

The Earl of Clarendon once said to a friend: "Salisbury is an enigma to me, and I wish you could tell me what he really is."[1] This remark, made in the early seventies, could easily, with justification, be made today without receiving any satisfactory explanation. Herein lies the fascination in the study of Salisbury. For over half a century all sorts of writers have attempted, in varying degrees, to find out what kind of man he really was.[2] The picture still remains confused. Salisbury's deliberate impersonality has successfully defied all attempts to penetrate the statesman and get at the man. He still fascinates; he refuses to come alive in print.

Lady Gwendolen Cecil has left us an authoritative account of her father's early years. The picture is that of a gloomy and frustrated childhood with repercussions which manifested themselves in later life. His experience at school, which he had described as "an existence among devils"; his loss of his mother before he was ten; and the experience of living with an elder brother, a confirmed invalid, who "died, practically of old age, before he was fifty"—all these could hardly fail to affect the susceptibilities of a child, himself born two months premature, and whose own life was already marred by ill health. The surprising thing about Salisbury is not that he failed to match the charisma of leaders such as Disraeli, Gladstone, or Chamberlain; it is that he lived to be prime minister longer than any other holder of that office in the nineteenth century since Liverpool; it is also the discovery by the sixties that he would have been a remarkable man in any sphere of activity other than politics. No child psychiatrist could have predicted that the bad-tempered, moody, nervous, retiring, shy, studious, and uncompanionable boy would grow up to be a successful leader of men, and an admirable and imposing figure in international politics.

The explanation lies in his powerful intelligence and strength of character. It was his favorite thesis that character is the most essential element in a man's equipment for political life. He was too modest to boast of this possession in himself.[3] But right from his Eton days he had shown in no unmistakable terms that he resented being bullied into doing things against his will. And as a young man he had gone ahead and married a girl of his choice despite family objections. He did not hide the fact that, rather than be dictated to by others, he would prefer to make ends meet by writing for the periodicals.[4] It is absurd that such a man could be described as "the prisoner of . . . Chamberlain and of the unscrupulous imperialists, the prisoner even of . . . Rhodes."[5] Throughout his life Salisbury uncompromisingly guarded against any interference with his independence both in private and public life. Salisbury, it has truly been said, was "not a man to be guided by others."[6] Nor did he attempt to undermine the independence of his Cabinet colleagues. His maxim was: "Never jog a man's elbow when he is holding the reins."[7]

This adherence to native independence was equally observed in his family life.[8] It was nevertheless a happy family life from which, undoubtedly, he derived much of his strength as a political leader. Even a fleeting glimpse of the life of the Cecils at Hatfield would be incomplete without any mention of Lady Salisbury. In the observant eyes of a young girl, Blanche Dugdale, on a visit to Hatfield, Lady Salisbury appeared as "a big woman, (who) moved ponderously with immense dignity. Her hair was grey and rippled from the parting in the middle of her broad forehead; her face was florid; her mouth was large and firm, widening often into laughter."[9] Affectionate, charming, understanding, and intelligent, she also embodied other characteristics lacking in Salisbury's make-up. She was openly masterful and "liked a crowd for its own sake."[10] She even used to frequent a Working Man's Club in the East End of London.[11] Unlike her husband, she was always unpunctual; and Salisbury used to say that he had read all the Church Fathers while waiting for her.[12] But it was largely due to her that the distinguished parties at Hatfield House owed their success. She was reputed to have said that she had never met anyone who could bore her.[13] But her husband, "without looking bored . . . never seemed really happy."[14] Lady Salisbury did not care much for social rank and once confided in a friend that she would have been much happier if her husband was "only a farmer."[15] But both shared alike the unflinching aversion to the suffrage cause, and an almost unquestioning acceptance of the Christian faith.[16] And where they differed in their endowments they tended to be complementary to each other. Nevertheless, Lady Salisbury exercised some influence over her husband. "With the possible exception of his [Salisbury's] wife," writes Lady Gwendolen, "I am unable to fix upon any individual whose character or opinion left any trace upon his own."[17] With her death in 1899, Salisbury's participation in politics, already greatly minimized by ill health, declined substantially; and Lady Gwendolen practically became everything for him and for the family at large.[18]

Salisbury's dislike of publicity was another trait in his character traceable to the frustrations of his youth. The fear of physical insecurity he had felt as a boy developed, in later life, into a fear of the crowd and a terror of the press. Contemporaries knew little of him and therefore misinterpreted him. "Lord Salisbury is one of the most fascinating figures in our public life," writes one of his biographers. "Perhaps it is that we know so little of him. The average man knew more of . . . Gladstone, and knows more of . . . Rosebery, than some of his friends know of . . . Salisbury."[19] He still appears as a quaint, curious figure who, "like St. Paul," in the words of Percy Colson, "was born out of due time."[20] This trait hardly made him a general favorite. He was highly respected certainly, and sometimes admired, but never loved. It was doubtful if he had any real friends. Unlike Chamberlain, and so many others, he never projected himself as the beacon light of the new imperialism. And yet he played a greater part than any other in reshaping the map of Africa. Under Salisbury's rule the following territories were added to the British Empire:

	Square Miles	Population
Central Africa Protectorate	38,000	850,000
East Africa Protectorate	1,000,000	2,500,000
Nigeria	500,000	35,000,000

Orange River Colony	48,326	210,000
New Guinea	88,410	350,000
Rhodesia	750,000	600,000
Socotra Island	1,382	10,000
Transvaal	119,139	1,094,000
Upper Burma	83,473	3,000,000
Wei-Hai-Wei	20	350,000
Zanzibar and Pemba	1,020	250,000
Total	2,678,156	44,420,000[21]

In most of the controversial issues of his day, he attached himself to no faction, and in some instances he kept his opinions to himself. It is easy to see this ostensible indifference as exhibiting a lack of interest. It would be mistaken to hold such a view, for he watched every event with great interest and had decided opinions, independently arrived at, after an examination of the available evidence. He was always willing to modify these views on the basis of new evidence made known to him, or on the sheer force of the opposing argument. The fact, however, was that his views on imperial and foreign affairs were, on the whole, far better informed than those of his colleagues and his judgments so invariably sound and wise that it would have been difficult to reject them. But to the public he did not always appear to be firmly in control of external affairs. He never stamped his individuality on the public consciousness. He was not a man to be talked about and known. At once reserved, proud, shy, and self-restrained, he evoked no public enthusiasm. His reputation as a political force has suffered in consequence.[22] A contemporary journal observed after his death:

> Lord Salisbury's habitual self-suppression had made it specially difficult to trace his influence upon his party and upon public affairs. And yet a year has scarcely passed before we begin to see it more clearly and vividly than at any time during his working life.[23]

Another contemporary presented the same point more vividly:

> The Lord of Hatfield, sitting aloof from the turmoil of parties, serene and massive, leaving the House of Commons to jangle, and the platforms to reverberate, while he swayed the balance of Britain's fate with firm, unerring hand, he was an impressive figure; perhaps the most impressive in Europe since Bismarck. But he had never become interesting, as Mr. Gladstone was, and Lord Beaconsfield, or Mr. Chamberlain is, as Lord Rosebery might be if he chose . . . .

His last illness, his death, attracted singularly little attention even in these journalistic days. The newspapers paid their
perfunctory "tributes"; the public remained, I fear, indifferent.
. . . They held a service in honour of Lord Salisbury on the last
day of last month, and it passed almost unnoticed. There was no
crowding, no throng of eager sightseers, outside Westminster
Abbey; a few policemen were dotted about the precincts, but
they were scarcely needed. Indifferently, the passers-by on foot,
or on the roofs of omnibuses, turned their heads as the solemn
note of the bell crossed the rattle of Victoria Street, and now and
again some faint strain of Schubert or Chopin was wafted
through the windows of the great Minster. But men and women
went by upon their own occasions, casual, inattentive, not paus-
ing to remember that here was a solemn ceremony in memory
of one who had been a Prince among his peers, who had sat in
council with Emperors and Kings, who had swayed the destinies
of a quarter of the human race, and had gone to his rest after
being three times Prime Minister of England. *Sic transit gloria.*[24]

This lyrical and almost pathetic prose tells, in a nutshell, the story
of Salisbury. To a large extent, the lack of feeling on the part of the
public was of his own creation. He would have been shocked if
they had reacted otherwise. He sought no popularity; he even went
to great pains to avoid it.[25] Salisbury detested "restless egotisms"
which, he said, sometimes made politics a "cursed profession."[26]

This attitude made some contemporaries regard him as haughty,
pigheaded, cynical, an aristocrat who looked down on the common
man. Salisbury, on the contrary, was also humble, humane, and modest. These latter characteristics were dismissed as either an aristocratic aloofness or a curious pusillanimity in one outwardly so strong.
But he was genuine enough; and his behavior was unforced. Sometimes his firm and unbending attitude baffled friends and foes alike;
sometimes his propensity to compromise and his innocent modesty
and delicious simplicity made him appear admirable. He was said
to have concluded some observations he had made on a memorandum by Nathaniel Curzon with the following words: "I have no positive claims to authorship, but by eliminating your most interesting
paragraphs I shall always feel I have had a negative share in a great
work."[27] And on resigning the premiership in July 1902, he wrote to
Devonshire: ". . . In taking my official leave of you, I desire to thank
you most warmly for your kindness and forebearance which during
the last seven years have enabled us to carry through a difficult ex-
periment with very fair success."[28] Coupled with this modesty and
humility was his humanity and benevolence. But he never projected
himself as a philanthropic do-gooder or an ardent humanitarian. In

fact, he was one of those who clearly saw through the more hypocritical aspects of some Victorian philanthropists. On the slavery issue, however, he tended to allow political expediency to obscure moral considerations.[29]

Mr. John Morley once remarked that Salisbury hardly made a speech "which does not contain at least one blazing indiscretion." This negative aspect of Salisbury's character has been explained away as "provocative candour."[30] But these indiscretions, of which there were many examples,[31] did indeed shock the more conventional of his contemporaries, and he suffered in reputation as a result. "The phrase would become quotable apart from its context," observes Lady Gwendolen, "and indeed would sometimes survive for years to be applied to a wholly different set of circumstances."[32] Provocative candor or not, Salisbury's "rash and rancorous tongue" was a grave blot in his career. In his younger days political mudslinging was his forte; in later life—when with the disappearance of Bismarck and Gladstone he had become Europe's leading statesman —he tried, not entirely successfully, to put a check on his indiscretions. His tongue still wagged—sometimes thoughtlessly cruel, sometimes needlessly severe. He was a phrase-maker in politics, and like all phrase-makers his phrases were not necessarily evidence of his policy. More caution and discretion in quoting these expressions are recommended.

In general outlook Salisbury was essentially English. He had a feeling of innate superiority to foreigners which, curiously enough, did not deter them from admiring him. This feeling, as we shall see later, formed the basis of his concept of pacific imperialism. He had a profound belief in the natural ability of the Englishman, given equal chances, to get the better of the foreigner. He had a genuine affection for England. "He is," wrote Stead, "John Bull through and through, who is very glad he was not born a Russian, or Prussian."[33] He never understood the French. When Waddington[34] was recalled from London, he wrote: "I am very sorry for the loss of Waddington. It was a luxury to have a French minister who worked on principles intelligible to an English mind."[35] On another occasion he wrote: "The French are sore and sulky with us—I cannot make out why."[36] Nor did he understand the Germans. "It is puzzling to me," he confided in Ambassador Malet, "to know why Prince Bismarck ever thinks us worth conciliating. None of the battles he may have to fight will be fought within striking distance of the sea—and it is only on the sea that we can be of any use at all."[37] He regarded the Germans as dreamers, unpractical, sentimental, and incapable of unity.[38] "The conduct of the German Emperor," he minuted in 1895, "is very mysterious and difficult to explain. There is a danger of his going completely off his head."[39] The Italians presented to him an irresistible object for cynical remarks. "The great trouble of the hour seems to be Signor Crispi;"[40] "The Italians will never lose anything for want of asking;"[41] "*Ecce iterum Crispimus*"[42]—these were typical of his sneering remarks.

He once described a letter from Victor Morrier[43] relating to Portugal's behavior during the boundary delimitations with Rhodes as demonstrating

> both a striking and amusing illustration of the different national characteristics of the English and the Portuguese . . . the quiet taciturn energy and resource of the one race, and the boastful noisy fecklessness of the other. Rhodes does not hold here the language which is attributed to him in the Colony. He is not contending for more than the "plateau" and admits that the Portuguese have a right to Matikessi. These Portuguese are the most unsatisfactory people to negotiate with I have any experience of. When they are pressed in argument, instead of arguing back again, they throw themselves on their backs and scream. . . . The difficult point to bring home to them is that it is of no use for them to claim rule over African territory unless they can colonize it. If they cannot provide settlers of their own blood, we can of ours: and we shall do so, whether we—that is Great Britain—desire it or not. And a country once inhabited by men of English or Dutch race, the Portuguese had better allow us to govern it; for it is quite certain that *they* will not be able to do so.[44]

Surely, an anti-imperialist would not have reacted to the Portuguese in this vein. Nor did the Irish or the Scots escape his sneer. The Irish, he said, were as incapable as the Hottentots of governing themselves; and of the Scots, Lady Frances Balfour relates what he said:

> Think of Salisbury, saying with an apology to me, that there is a great likeness between the Scots and the Jews: Both began by being turbulent and ill to govern, both accepted a formal and austere religion; and both have become commercial. From whom but his Lordship would I stand such things.[45]

Understandably, he left the Welsh alone, his first ancestor having originated from there.[46]

This snobbish attitude was not generally displayed in his diplomatic practice;[47] but it would not be unfair to say that, in many respects, he demonstrated a fine example of big power diplomacy, and he always maintained the "Big Brother" attitude toward the Colonies. This was another aspect of his diplomacy that is not generally recognized. In 1889, during the discussions on the Mixed Tribunals in Egypt, France, aided by Greece, attempted to use the larger Egyptian question to blackmail England. Only the antics of Greece infuriated him. "I do not see why we should submit to be tormented by Greece," he wrote. "Could they not be subjected to a very restrictive interpretation which would deprive them of their virus? Pray turn this over in your mind."[48] In another letter he described the Greeks as "the pests of Europe," who were always around whenever the situation was critical and ripe for blackmail. "I have no European reason for suggesting that favor should be shown to them."[49]

The Italians fared no better. They were "exceedingly tiresome with their misplaced and suicidal African ambitions; and I have no wish that these aspirations should be gratified at the cost of any solid sacrifices on our part." He dismissed them as a "restless and unreasonable" people who were beginning to bore everyone. Diplomatically, the value of an Anglo-Italian alliance was questionable. In itself it was not worth much; but it was necessary to maintain the good will of Germany which was essential to England if France and Russia were to be kept in check. He therefore refused to rate the Italian alliance as "high as some other objects of political desire." It was desirable, but not worth the payment of a great price "even in African square miles. We are negotiating on these African matters with somewhat greater ease now that we have agreed with Germany and France."[50] In dealing with Portugal he not only dismissed its claims as having archeological foundations, but was obliged to get what he wanted by issuing an ultimatum to the Portuguese government. When Portugal capitulated, he replied, on being congratulated on his achievement: "Poor Portugal! We have come to some sort of an arrangement which I trust will reasonably suit the British South Africa (Coy) without upsetting the Braganza dynasty. But people are not reasonable, either at Lisbon or Cape Town."[51] And thus died Portugal's grand "idea of a band across Africa"[52] from east to west.

His attitude to these smaller and weaker nations can of course be attributed to the fact that European peace depended on maintaining good relations with the big three.[53] After all neither Italy, Greece, Portugal, Spain, nor Belgium was more troublesome to England than France, Germany, or Russia. It must, however, be noted that the First World War was sparked off by an event in an obscure Balkan village.

Salisbury was by no means an aggressive minister in external relations. By the early sixties he had already set out his blueprint in foreign affairs. "Moderation," he said, "was not cowardice. We fervently desire peace; but we desire it in the only way in which it can be had. Peace without honor is not only a disgrace, but, except as a temporary respite, it is a chimera."[54] Further, he wrote:

> Courtesy of language, a willingness to concede, a reluctance to take offence, if they are impartially extended to all, will always, even when they are carried to excess, command respect and admiration. . . . It is only when the two qualities of heroism and meekness are cunningly combined that they earn unmitigated contempt.[55]

To the principles set out in the above excerpts must be added his disinclination to discuss hypothetical contingencies. As soon as he took office in 1895, he wrote an interesting minute on the pending African negotiations:

> As to the African questions I have some doubt of the policy of discussing disagreeable contingencies which are purely hypothetical. It reminds me of the two anxious couples [*sic*], who broke off their intended marriage, because they could not agree as to the second name of their [future] third son.[56]

In the same month he reminded Dufferin that, in diplomacy, it was "one of the beatitudes of the *possidentes* . . . that it is to their interest to hold their tongues."[57]

Salisbury regarded his diplomatic methods as more important than his aims.[58] He was a hard worker. His hours were mapped out daily from 8 a.m. to 1 or 2 a.m. He had no time for social life.[59] He worked on the principle that foreign relations could not be treated in isolation; but he also paid much attention to local factors in taking imperial decisions. He prepared his ground thoroughly beforehand and on the basis that a diplomat must have two alternative solutions to a single problem. He revered facts, treaties, and undoubted rights, and preferred practical conclusions to the dead reckoning of logic. He knew what he wanted and to what extent he would go to get it. Unlike the Jingoes, he could easily see the foreigner's point of view and drop his claims on the basis of the facts. The accusation of "graceful concessions" was continually made against him by the "Little Englanders," which was odd considering their philosophy. At one breath they sneered at his pusillanimity, and at another, they manufactured some Cobdenite instincts in him.[60] But he saw his attitude toward the African problem differently. "It is not that we did not exert to the utmost every right that we now possess," he explained, "but that, under the guidance of our mentors and tutors in the past, we had yielded up the territory which now, in vain, we desire to possess."[61] The point to note, however, is that the phrase, "graceful concessions," does not deserve the importance attached to it. It is a felicitous, but meaningless, phrase.

Salisbury's relations with his officials abroad as well as with his permanent officials deserve some comment. He did not initiate the practice of inviting ambassadors to express their candid opinions on important issues through the medium of the "private letter." He was perhaps the best exponent of this practice, and he used it to effect. These private letters must not be regarded as self-sufficient in themselves. They must be used in conjunction with the strictly official documents, to which they are complementary. They are, however, indispensable to the study of the essential Salisbury. They reveal his humor, wit, simplicity, and modesty; they lend weight to his deserved reputation as a writer; they show him as at once cautious, firm, and tactful; and above all, they expose his immense knowledge of affairs and of diplomacy. Unfortunately, toward the close of his last ministry the volume of these letters, still substantial, declined appreciably. Both Salisbury and his proconsuls had become well acquainted with their respective duties. The broad lines of policy had already been mapped out, and the occasions for asking and giving directions had diminished. Moreover, Salisbury's health was failing and he no longer paid the closest attention to details. His long experience had also taught him that "writing to Ambassadors generally does harm."[62] Nevertheless, he tended to write more to those ambassadors whose judgments he valued most. In the 1870s he used to consult Lord Lyons on all sorts of questions and offered him, in the beginning of his second ministry, the foreign secretaryship. Lyons turned down the offer because of ill health and also on account of his lack of parliamentary experience. But he still retained, except in name, the "position of a Vice-Foreign Secretary."[63] With the possible exception of Cromer, no ambassador was accorded this prestigious position in the nineties; but then, the old hands, Malet, Dufferin, and Morrier, had gone; and the younger men, Currie, Monson, Lascelles, and Rumbolt, though brilliant and experienced diplomats, were completely overshadowed by Salisbury. Of these, he tended to suspect the soundness of Monson's judgment. Generally, however, he maintained an excellent relationship with these ambassadors. He treated them with courtesy and understanding, and they respected and admired their chief. Cromer particularly, though instinctively a Liberal, gave the impression that he would rather serve under Salisbury than under Kimberley or Rosebery. On the whole, only a minor diplomat, himself a strong Liberal of the intellectual kind, Cecil Spring-Rice expressed his dislike of what he considered to be the new image of Salisbury. "I distinctly dislike," he wrote, "the brutal tone of the English papers and the would-be jauntiness of . . . Salisbury. Is an English Lord really the type of courtesy?"[64] He was here protesting against Salisbury's Sudan policy. He did not hide his detestation of many aspects of Salisbury's imperial policy. He particularly opposed the reconquest of the Sudan because it would be difficult diplomatically, and wrote contemptuously of the justification for the advance on Dongola.[65]

Another person who did not agree with all of Salisbury's policies or his method of applying them was Curzon, his Under Secretary for Foreign Affairs. The two men contrasted vividly in age and temperament. Salisbury had offered him the job specifically for his knowledge of Eastern affairs.[66] In the beginning he was poorly briefed on the policies he was obliged to defend in the Commons. The result was that, in his attempt to impress, Curzon was prone to overstate his case, and consequently gave the impression of being too clever by half. And in some cases, he was obliged to defend policies with which he did not necessarily agree. The truth was that Curzon tended to see eye to eye with Chamberlain rather than with his chief. But he respected him immensely. Nevertheless, he grew increasingly impatient of Salisbury's cautious diplomacy, and it was even rumored in London circles that Curzon was afraid that Chamberlain might use this as an opportunity to oust Salisbury from the Foreign Office and install himself.[67] This was a curious development for Salisbury never felt more secure in his office than now; admittedly, a couple of unfavorable by-election results may have worried party workers. But Salisbury could still leave Balfour in charge of the Foreign Office and spend long holidays abroad without fear of a palace revolt. Moreover, contemporaries tended to overrate the influence of Chamberlain. Among most Tories he was thoroughly disliked; and it was generally believed that one reason for Balfour's popularity among them was that "Arthur . . . keeps Joe out of the leadership."[68] Indeed in this race for the succession Chamberlain was running a poor third behind Balfour and Hicks-Beach.[69] Lady Frances perhaps provides the explanation:

> He is a Birmingham Radical, hampered by what he said when he was . . . not a Unionist. This brought him into contact with other influences, and he has now shaken hands with a Duke, which did him more good than he likes to acknowledge. Don't think me spiteful! I own his speaking gifts, but he belongs not to the true leaven.[70]

Chamberlain's ambition or the Curzonian clique was therefore of little consequence to Salisbury. And after Curzon had left the Foreign Office to become the viceroy of India, he was to confess, indirectly, that he had been unfair, and even rash, in his assessment of Salisbury's diplomacy. He could now realize, he wrote, "how premature first judgments are apt to be; what rewards there are for prudence and courtesy and consideration; and how wonderfully perseverance is justified of her children."[71]

Salisbury's dominance over his permanent officials in the later nineties was complete. In July 1896 Anderson died, and neither Hill nor Bertie carried much weight. Sanderson had little knowledge of African affairs. In the Colonial Office, too, the old guard had gone, and Chamberlain, like Salisbury, was complete boss of his department. It is amazing to discover how much imperial decisions were influenced by these two politicians rather than by the old-fashioned officials. "Those who had the privilege of knowing Lord Salisbury well," Midleton has noted, "quickly fell under his spell"; but he obtained their submission purely by a deep knowledge of his subjects, and the ability to put this knowledge across in a lucid and logical way, devoid of cant and of pomposity, but practical, balanced, and fair. He never adopted a chilly and unsmiling visage—a Hicks-Beachite method of handling officials—to achieve his ends. When St. John Brodrick succeeded Curzon as Salisbury's assistant, he was warned that his chief "is very difficult to move, but he comes down like a bag of bricks when he does move." This was a correct assessment of Salisbury; but the officials of the Foreign Office nevertheless worshipped him. Contrary to popular belief, Brodrick testifies to the fact that Salisbury perused each document before coming to a decision. His comments, always made in red ink, contain as few words as possible. They are often humorous and direct to the point. And as Brodrick also admits, they were seldom faulty.[72]

After Salisbury's retirement from the Foreign Office in 1900, he assigned the under-secretaryship to his son in order to be kept in touch with developments. Even then he used to go occasionally to the Foreign Office "to push Lansdowne off," as he put it, "he is always getting stuck."[73]

Another paradox in Salisbury's personality was his attitude to British institutions. His deep and sincere attachment to most of these, especially the monarchy, was undoubted. Sometimes, however, he gave the impression of treating some of them with irreverence. His dislike of the House of Commons was apparent; he never stopped railing at the working of the Treasury; he spoke of Parliament as a stumbling block in the sphere of diplomacy; but he attempted no changes. He loved poking jokes at the bishops, and shocked those who had expected more reverence from him.[74]

His attitude to the British Constitution was Whiggish. He appeared to have entertained little respect for the English parliamentary system. He often complained that it worked badly; that its administrative machine was utterly cumbrous and tiresome; that, under it, no ministry could be expected to keep British armaments genuinely efficient. Where one would have expected some changes—this being the case—Salisbury indulged in the gloomy satisfaction that it was much better to have such a machine than to have none at all. "We must work with the instruments we have" and make the best of it, was his motto. He was irritated by the party system which he considered irrational in substance and logically indefensible. Yet, he accepted it, arguing that the cabinet system would be unworkable without it. A contemporary journal observed after his death: "You can only expect moderate achievement from a person of this conviction. You could only do imperfect work, with imperfect tools."[75]

Salisbury and the Concept of Pacific Imperialism
This then was the man who was to participate more than any other person in reshaping the map of Africa. Initially, as we saw, he had no individual opinions on Africa. But when he became Foreign Secretary in 1878, the whole business of imperial policy was brought forcibly before him. This was the era of the so-called imperial indifference which has been questioned in a brilliant study.[76] This was also the so-called period of the informal empire. Indeed, the term "informal empire," a historian's invention,[77] does not properly explain, at any rate, Salisbury's own conception of imperial ventures at this time. Nor does it explain the conception of Disraeli. The two Tory leaders had similarly broad views on the empire. Disraeli wanted the empire preserved, and increased if possible, and accused the Liberals of "letting down the Empire." Salisbury endorsed such a view and dismissed the Liberals as people "who disdained Empire, who objected to Colonies, and who grumbled about even the possession of India."[78] The policy of the Conservative party, he claimed in 1878, was "to pick up the broken thread of England's old Imperial traditions."[79] And yet Disraeli has been regarded as the apostle of British imperialism while Salisbury is not! At this period Salisbury did not go on the stump advocating the imperial mission of the race. But in private he made his views clear. He was not concerned with laying a strategy for Africa, but with future expansion wherever it might be. His knowledge of imperial issues was still grossly inadequate. He advocated neither a forward, nor a consolidationist, policy; not even an informal empire as we know the term. In a private letter to Sir Richard Temple he laid down his general strategy of expansion:

All the way from the Aegean and Mediterranean seas to the Indus there is a vast region in which the existing forces of Govt. are slowly perishing. It is not the case of bad laws or a temporary feebleness or rapacity of rule. The vital forces of the body politic are dying out. The expense of Govt. is incessantly increasing; taxes are pushed to their utmost limit: trade is wasting away: depopulation is setting in: and all the distinctions which separate these peoples from mere nomad tribes threaten to disappear. *They are conscious of it themselves and are on the look out for some Govt. more living than their own, which shall rescue them in time.* [My italics.] Few who are acquainted with the East think that England can safely look on till the process of decay has eaten out all the powers of resistance. The domination of Russia on those countries might not enable or incline her to march on India; but it would not the less make our hold of India more difficult and condemn us to a more costly and more repressive Govt. in that country. The remedy which many are at first sight inclined for is partial or complete occupation—either of Mesopotamia or of Persia or of Afghanistan. It would be an extreme remedy—pressing heavily on our Exchequer, and with a weight almost overwhelming on our recruiting machinery. *There is an intermediate course between military occupation and simple laissez faire. It is a process of which there are already some examples: but for which there is at present no expression. I will call it the pacific invasion of England.* [My italics.] It has been largely practised in Egypt, with excellent effect; it is going on, more slowly, in China and Japan. The principle of it is that when you bring the English in contact with inferior races, they will rule, whatever the ostensible ground of their presence. As merchants, as railway makers, as engineers, as travellers, later as employees like Gordon, or McKillogs, or as ministers like Rivers Wilson, they assert the English domination, not by any political privilege or military power, but right of the strongest mind.

The taking of Cyprus, and the acquisition of a right to reform Asia Minor and Mesopotamia, will I hope give opportunity for this pacific invasion. If it is effective, it will furnish the best of bulwarks against Russian advance. Cannot something of the same kind be done in Afghanistan? *Once obtain the unrestricted right of access, and in a few years you will govern without ever drawing a sword.* [My italics.][80]

A few weeks earlier he had instructed Northcote to promote "that pacific invasion of Englishmen, which is our principal reliance for the purpose of getting power over the country."[81] Obviously Salisbury was writing with his experience at the India Office behind him.

But this concept of pacific imperialism equally applied to any future advance in Africa as far as he was concerned. He saw the same appalling decay of indigenous governments and subsequent developments show that, given a free hand, and granted such a collapse, this was the policy he would have preferred to pursue in Africa; and indeed, did pursue for awhile in Egypt. He wrote to Lyons:

> I told Goschen that we were very anxious to work with the French; and that we intend to take no violent means of placing ourselves in a position which would make them subordinate. But I told him I nevertheless, had faith in the English influence in Egypt drawing ahead: a result which in my belief depended not on any formal acts, but on the natural superiority which a good Englishman in such a position was pretty sure to show.[82]

These few excerpts may shock those who believe that Salisbury exhibited no racial arrogance; his constant hammering on the "natural superiority" of the English vis à vis other races can only be interpreted as racial arrogance. What is of interest in Salisbury's concept, however, is that it was a subtle way of expressing what Mary Kingsley and the *Spectator* were openly to express later on "that it is the business of England . . . to take over and rule the inferior races of mankind";[83] or what Kipling was to popularize as the "white man's burden" of governing people incapable of governing themselves. Salisbury, of course, could argue that such a domination would be imposed upon England by the decay of these nations. But that was precisely the same point made by the *Spectator*, Kingsley, or Kipling. What Salisbury had objected to was the brandishing of this idea as if to hit somebody on the head with it, or to seize forcibly a territory simply because it was believed to be in decay, or because it would look well if painted red on the map.

This concept of pacific expansion was reflected in Salisbury's attitude to the conquest of Africa up to the 1880s. In West Africa he seriously reprimanded Governor Rowe, who had offended against his canon of expansion by annexing Katanu.[84] In East Africa he refused to involve his government with Mackinnon's request for a concession on the mainland.[85]

So long as England had a free hand in the colonization of Africa, Salisbury would gladly have depended on the "pacific invasion of Englishmen" to achieve his ends. But that was asking too much in a rapidly changing world. Indeed, he was to confess later on that events in Africa had developed with "startling rapidity." "When I left the Foreign Office in 1880," he added, "nobody thought of Africa. When I returned to it in 1885, the nations of Europe were almost quarrelling with each other about the various portions of it which they could obtain."[86] It was this upsurge of European interest in Africa, arising partly out of local factors in Africa itself, that first punctured the whole concept of pacific expansion. It led Gladstone's second ministry, to revert to the strategy of using private enterprise —the Chartered Company administration—as a means of cheaply acquiring an empire.[87] This was a return to a device already unpopular since the time of Adam Smith. Adam Smith had opposed the adoption of this method in the eighteenth century on the grounds that it was undesirable to turn merchants into Sovereigns, and that such concessions conferred negligible responsibility to the British Crown. Now the Liberals, ill disposed to the adoption of a forward policy in Africa, felt that this was a better method than mere scuttle in the face of European competition. And where it was impossible to resort to this means of imperial advance, the Liberals declared the territory concerned a protectorate.

When Salisbury returned to the Foreign Office in 1887 he found the Liberal device very handy and very useful. Indeed, it was a substantial modification of his earlier concept, but like the Liberals, he realized that it was a safer method than plunging his government head-long into territorial conflicts in Africa with other powers. In fact the position of English politics made such a policy impossible had he desired it. He lacked a safe majority; and he was plagued by the "Home Rule" dispute. "All the politics of the moment," he confessed, "are summarised in the one world 'Ireland'."[88] To the queen he wrote: "Torn in two by a controversy which almost threatens her existence [England] cannot . . . interfere with any decisive action abroad."[89] "When we are thinking about Ireland which is very commonly the case," Dilke also has written, "we are apt to forget all else, and both our relations with foreign powers and those with our dependencies drop into the background."[90] On the whole, it is fair to say that the period 1872–92 is not a fair one to select in judging Salisbury's attitude to the European conquest of Africa. It was not until 1895 that he was in a position to attempt a forward policy without fear of domestic complications. His excessive caution in dealing with the European powers, or in assuming direct responsibilities in Africa and elsewhere is therefore understandable. That he showed no anxiety at direct annexation in this period, or even in the earlier period, is no evidence that he was unwilling to control Africa. Indeed, as early as 1887 he was advocating that "a claim of sovereignty in Africa can only be maintained by real occupation of the territory claimed"[91]—a view which he reinforced in 1894:

It is not safe in these days to establish your title to large territory . . . and then to leave it there without any effort to assert
your title in a more practical and more effective fashion. The
whole doctrine of paper annexation is in a very fluid and uncertain condition . . . I believe that, in order to make your claims
over these vast regions a genuine one, and one which the public
opinion of Europe will respect . . . you ought to show that you
are gradually assimilating it, gradually making good your possession of it . . . .[92]

In fact his attitude toward the partition problems of the eighties
show that he was immensely interested in the whole operation, and
was determined that his country should take second place to none
in Africa. But he also realized that circumstances had changed and
that England was no longer the sole master of the entire continent.
"It was impossible," he admitted, "that England should have the
right to lock up the whole of Africa and say that nobody should be
there except herself."[93] And in defending the Heligoland Treaty in
the House of Lords on July 10, 1890, he reaffirmed, more or less, his
concept of pacific expansion, and showed why it had been found
necessary to modify it:

Up to ten years ago we remained masters of Africa, practically,
or the greater part of it, without being put to the inconvenience
of protectorates or anything of that sort, by the simple fact that
we were masters of the sea and that we have had considerable
experience in dealing with native races. So much was the case
that we left enormous stretches of Coast to the native rulers in
the full confidence that they would go on under native rulers
and in the hope that they would gradually acquire their own
proper civilization without any interference on our part.
     Then, suddenly, we found out that that position, however
convenient, had no foundation whatever in international law.
We had no rights over all these vast stretches of Coast, both on
the West and East coasts of Africa. We had no power of preventing any other nation from coming in and seizing a portion
of them.[94]

It must be noted that should any of these countries be in a state
of decay, Salisbury would have had no qualms about taking over
through what he had called "the pacific invasion of Englishmen."
     By the time Salisbury was voted out of office in 1892, he had
acquired immense and intimate knowledge of African affairs. The
center of interest in imperial affairs had shifted from Asia to Africa.
And through patient and practical management and astute diplo-

macy, he had laid the foundation for a positive policy for Africa which was to receive energetic application in his last ministry. More importantly, he had managed to do so without coming to blows with any other power. But even after 1895 he still emphasized the need for pacific imperialism if the circumstances permitted that course.[95] Any assessment of Salisbury's attitudes to imperial expansion generally, and to Africa particularly, in order not to be sterile, must take his concept of pacific expansion into consideration. It was far from being a policy of scuttle.

Chapter II

Commerce and Empire: The Decline of the "Great Victorian Boom," 1872–1902

Introduction

Historically economic motives have always loomed large in processes of empire building. Every student of African history concedes the primacy of economic interests in the rise of the great empires during Africa's golden age. The historical explanations of their decline and fall have always had a strong economic orientation, but the correlation between economics and the rise of empires is not a phenomenon peculiar to African history: it is a general historical phenomenon. Since the beginning of history, Africa has faced an assortment of foreign conquerors all initially driven by stories of its enormous wealth—real or imaginary—to invade the continent. Whether similar impulses drove the European conquerors of Africa in the nineteenth century has ever since been a subject of great historical debate.

Hobson and Lenin may be said to have raised this debate to the level of an academic discourse when they implied in their books[1] that the European conquest of Africa had primarily economic roots. This view, prima facie, is neither original nor profound. It was a belief generally held by many contemporaries. It must be noted too that the authors did not totally exclude noneconomic, or even non-pecuniary, factors in their analyses but they attached little importance to them. However, by linking imperialism with monopoly capitalism Hobson and Lenin initiated a major debate in European history. It is significant that the Hobson-Leninist thesis was not seriously challenged until communism became a serious threat to the capitalist system of the West. The numerous attacks on Hobson and Lenin are therefore more concerned with capitalism than with imperialism as such. Nor are these attacks designed to offer a historical explanation of the motives that lay behind European adventures in Africa during the era of conquest. Indeed for both Hobson and

Lenin as well as for their opponents, Africa has been only incidental to the debate, the tenor of which has developed into a sort of family quarrel watched by the exponents of the new African history with studied aloofness. This is not surprising because the theory of capitalist or economic imperialism, as far as Africa is concerned, has an air of historical unreality about it. Indeed, the historical interpretations of the European conquest and partition of Africa have been confounded by rhetoric and meaningless theorizing. Epigrams, wisecracks, felicitous phrases, and incrusted generalizations—apparently meant to attain quotability but of little value to our understanding of this major historical movement in Africa—have issued from the pens of scholars of varying persuasions. Others resort to statistical tables adroitly employed and balance sheets of imperialism boldly and prematurely drawn to demonstrate how profitless the African adventure was for the adventurers.

The European partition of Africa is of great significance for African historical development; its consequences still live with us and will continue to do so for generations to come. For these reasons a few more observations on the historiography of European expansion in Africa will not be out of place here. It is not our intention, however, to analyze or survey the tremendous amount of literature on the theories of modern imperialism.[2] These observations are only intended to form the background against which the argument of this chapter will, hopefully, become comprehensible.

First, the assumption of the theoreticians of imperialism that the motives behind the European conquest of Africa can be discovered in the nineteenth century is invalid. It neglects the many centuries of Afro-European relations prior to this century. These relationships were rooted in trade—predominantly the slave trade—the economic orientation of which no one doubts. They also fail to realize that the slave trade and its suppression marked the first stage of the conquest. Attempts to replace the slave trade with legitimate commerce ushered in a new era of relationships between Africans and Europeans. Problems arising out of this development led to the second stage of the conquest.[3] How then can a historian arrive at a historically valid theory of imperialism by limiting his field of operation to the nineteenth century?

Second, the argument that statistical evidence drawn from European trade departments of the nineteenth century shows that Africa yielded miserable dividends to European businessmen and others who cared to invest there is not altogether true. If one bought shares on the Stock Exchange in anticipation of a great dividend and instead lost money in the transaction or only showed marginal profit, is this an argument against one's initial pecuniary motive in the venture? Again, the other argument which states that since only a few European entrepreneurs cared to invest in African ventures, Hobson's economic thesis fails in Africa also ignores at least one historical and economic fact. No entrepreneur worthy of the name invests without security. The irony is that while seeking to bring stability to Africa for the purpose of trade, the Europeans often destabilized it. We must also reject the assumption—now that quantitative historiography is attracting some attention—that statistics can provide a historian with answers to historical problems rather than enable him, at best, to frame the right questions. Moreover, trade and investment statistics relating to Africa in the nineteenth century are meagre, incomplete, distorted, and often worthless. Worse still, they contain only declared values. Sir George Goldie, for example, deliberately destroyed his papers and thus made it impossible for historians to determine the extent of the wealth he amassed in Nigeria.

Third, if Africa was economically worthless, why then did the European powers persevere in partitioning and conquering it? In an attempt to answer this simple but realistic question the theoreticians of imperialism indulge us in more rhetoric about national prestige, European diplomacy, the inherent attraction of imperialism for the masses, the humanitarian and civilizing mission of the European race, the strategic importance of Egypt in the maintenance of the important sea route to the East. In other words, Africa was partitioned without the Africans!

As the strategic thesis seems to hold sway at the present moment and relates more to Britain than to other European powers, let us pursue it a little further. Basically it asserts that Africa was economically worthless; that the leading European partitioners with the possible exception of Leopold II and the later Francesco Crispi were not imperialistically minded; that if they had had their choice they would have preferred to maintain informal influence in Africa. But this was not to be. They stumbled into Africa not because of European considerations but because of crucial changes in the African polities themselves. And once they stumbled in, they could not scramble out. The most crucial of these changes was the collapse of the Khedival regime in Egypt and the rise of a new white power structure in South Africa. Once Britain occupied Egypt in 1882 it found itself in a sort of bondage. Thus began the scramble for Africa. Egypt then is the peg on which the partition of Africa hangs. As far as Britain was concerned Africa was no more than "a gigantic footnote to the great Indian empire" where Britain was doing good business. Indeed, we are assured, there were no fortunes to be made in

Africa (the fact that Cecil Rhodes became a millionaire within a few years and before he was thirty-two years old is an irritating fact that is best ignored) and that the imperialist powers found little value in Africa.[4]

This famous thesis assumes that there is an iron law of expansion which leads historical actors by the nose. It seems to echo the Hegelian thesis that history leads the wise man and drags the fool. By implication too the theory asserts that European statesmen of the nineteenth century were fools. This is a more serious way of reasserting Seeley's thesis that Britain acquired its empire in a state of absentmindedness. But supposing the strategic thesis can be sustained —which is historically improbable—it implies at least that British expansion in the Indian subcontinent had strong economic roots. If we conceded this point, then at least in relation to India, the Hobson-Lenin thesis is vindicated. And unless again we accept the existence of an iron law of expansion, then we must conclude that the economic incentives in the East must have been of such tremendous magnitude as to compel European powers to help themselves to other peoples' belongings, ride roughshod over the laws of nations and contemptuously infringe their rights[5] by haphazardly sharing-out a whole continent among themselves without reference to the owners. This is difficult to believe. The European statesmen of the nineteenth century were far from being fools.

From the above observations, it is clear that the current theories of imperialism are vulnerable because they are historically indefensible. This chapter proposes no general theory of imperialism; instead it examines the extent to which contemporaries in Britain, and Salisbury in particular, linked the expansion into Africa with commerce; and it also attempts to relate the state of the British economy in the period under survey to the attitudes of contemporaries toward imperial expansion abroad, thereby reaffirming our initial assertion that economic considerations have always loomed large in imperial expansions, at any rate, in Africa.

New British Markets and Foreign Competition

"You cannot get them to talk of politics so long as they are well employed," wrote William Matthews in 1883.[6] Economic factors, social conditions, and politics are delicately connected. The historian who discusses the one in isolation of the others does so at his peril. To dismiss economic motivations as an unimportant factor in imperial expansion is as delusive as to argue that these motivations alone were the only justification for imperialism.[7] The most surprising thing about the theory of economic imperialism or of any of the current theories, is its failure to take into consideration what the participants said, or implied, motivated their actions. What the opponents of economic imperialism are doing, in effect, is to use present-day knowledge in interpreting what happened in the past and under different circumstances. The reverse should be the case. Instead of posing the question: Was Africa worth having?, we should ask: Did contemporaries believe that it was worth having? And if so, why?

"New markets! New markets!", wrote Frederick Greenwood, "is the constant cry of our captains of industry and merchant princes, and it is well that to them the ear of Government should willingly incline. It ought to do so, and it does."[8] By new markets he meant primarily those regions yet unacquired by any European power, for example, western China, Tibet, and tropical Africa.[9] The argument was that the acquisition of these markets—which implied the control of the countries themselves—would nullify the effects of hostile tariffs by creating an open door to world trade, and to British trade in particular, thereby helping to cure its economic ills. This argument was given more weight by the industrial unrest and unemployment which occurred in the early nineties.[10] In 1891 Salisbury advocated African expansion as indispensable to British prosperity, employment, and world power.[11] The British Chamber of Commerce declared: "there is practically no middle course for this country, between a reversal of free-trade policy to which it is pledged, on the one hand, and a prudent but continuous territorial expansion for the creation of new markets."[12] On subsequent occasions Salisbury, Rosebery, and Chamberlain endorsed this view. In 1895 Salisbury warned that "at a period when the other outlets for the commercial energies of our countrymen were being gradually closed by the enormous growth of protectionist doctrines amongst other States it was our business in all these new countries to smooth the path of British enterprise and to facilitate the application of British capital."[13]

In an important speech at Bradford, in the following May, he dwelt once more on the same theme. He spoke of "the dreary period of general depression and difficulty and distress through which we have passed for the last few years"; and he blamed it on hostile tariffs. To avoid repetition of such depression, he implored his audience "to make our way not only in the civilized, but in the uncivilized, markets of the world." This was the method, he said, their ancestors had adopted when Napoleon, by his Milan Declaration, had closed the outlets of British industry, and had triumphed in the end against the despot.

It was that, one after another, you opened the less civilized portions of the world to your industry, and in proportion as Europe was closed to you, America and Africa and Asia were opened to you. But let us not forget the lessons which that experience taught us. Many men have dreamt that it would be a pleasant thing, so to speak, to close the capital account of the Empire and to add no further to its responsibilities. Many men have thought we have expanded far enough. "Let us draw the line," they say; "let us set up the temple of the god Terminus, and let us never go beyond it." But that is not the condition which fortune or the evolution of the world's causes has imposed upon the development of our prosperity. (Cheers.) If we mean to hold our own against the efforts of the civilized Powers of the world to strangle our commerce by their prohibitive finance we must be prepared to take the requisite measures to open new markets for ourselves among the half-civilized nations of the globe, *and we must not be afraid if that effort, which is vital to our industries, should bring with it new responsibilities of empire and Government.* [My italics.] (Cheers.) I feel that, in the present state of things in Africa and in the East, that consideration is not out of place. It is a consideration which ought never to be absent from the minds of the great captains of industry in towns such as this, where the forces of industry are centred upon what case we take—whether there is an adequate popular power behind in order to support those who wish to go on is the path which has won for England its spendid empire and its commercial supremacy, or in the path of these who wish to close the account and say that the growth of England has closed evermore. It will depend on you and on all who are interested in the trade of England, and I entreat you not to think it is a mere question of sentiment whether we should accept the openings which fortune gives to us in other lands. It is a question that involves our prosperity and our commercial existence to the last extent, and it is a question upon which the deciding voice of the commercial and industrial classes of this country will have to pronounce, whether our prosperity is to go on, as in the past, increasing, or whether from this moment it is to decline.[14]

Chamberlain might as well had made this speech. Why then is Salisbury regarded as apathetic toward imperial ventures while Chamberlain is not?

When Salisbury returned to power a few months afterwards South African Chartered shares shot up from £1 to £8.[15] From now on Chamberlain, ably supported by *The Times* and the great majority of the British press, as well as the Chambers of Commerce, became, as it were, the official spokesman for the need for new markets. But Salisbury had already made the points which Chamberlain was now to popularize; and with an effective and loquacious aide like the secretary of state for the Colonies, the prime minister was satisfied to stay in the background. In November 1896 Chamberlain asserted that "commerce is the greatest of all political interests. . . . All the great offices of State are occupied with commercial affairs."[16]

The Times, too, published an article entitled: "The Commercial Value of Africa." It showed that the immediate commercial value of tropical Africa was not startling, but admitted that given suitable conditions necessary for commercial development, the situation would drastically change. The same was true of India which, under British guidance, was now more valuable commercially than the whole of Africa. It concluded:

> The fact is that up to within the past few years Africa has hardly been needed by the rest of the world except as a slave market. But her turn has come, and the need for her co-operation in the general economy of the world will become greater and greater as population increases, as industry expands, as commerce develops, as States grow ambitious, as civilization spreads. It is a discreditable anomaly that at this advanced stage in the progress of the race nearly a whole continent should still be given over to savagery. . . . We now take only what is most easily reached. . . .[17]

In September *The Times* emphasized the dangers of foreign competition and renewed Salisbury's earlier call. "Some countries in which we once had a monopoly of the supply," it lamented, "have been learning of late to manufacture for themselves, and have become more or less independent of us. In others, the strain is caused by the competition of foreign traders, who contrive to draw to themselves no small share of business which we have been in the habit of considering our own."[18] A year later, it wondered whether British merchants ever bothered to read the Blue Books published for their benefit. "If the supremacy of British commerce is to be preserved," it warned, "our traders must bestir themselves betimes."[19] Indeed, *The Times* proudly acknowledged that British imperialism was economic.[20] So also did an economist, Miss Farraday.[21] The *Pall Mall Gazette* affirmed that Britain desired Africa primarily for its trading needs, and even felt a tinge of pride in saying so. It wrote:

> Nor have we gone to the equatorial regions from religious or humanitarian motives. Missionaries and philanthropists, indeed, complain sometimes that their work is hampered by Downing Street regulations. Still less have we sought out the African in order to endow him with the vices (and virtues) of western civ-

ilization. The fact is that when what has been done through pure love of adventure and the pride of power has been eliminated, the dominating force which has taken us to Equatorial Africa is the desire for trade. We are in these tropical countries for our own advantage, and only incidentally for the good of the African. Nor is there in this anything immoral *per se,* though first to last, from the Guinea Coast Slave trade to gin and gunpowder, we have done our share to demoralize the native. This has been the result rather than the intention of our trade, and what we have now to do is so to rearrange our methods that while trade is further developed the African shall be protected from evils to which he has hitherto been exposed . . . . It reaffirmed its faith in the "gospel of trade."[22]

Writing many years afterwards Lugard more or less endorsed these views. He argued that the trade of British tropical Africa was "more than double that of India per head of population, and more than a quarter of its total volume, and is equal per head to that of Japan."[23] Chamberlain was said to have been interested in Nigeria "because it produced palm oil."[24] And in 1898 Benjamin Kidd published a series of articles in which he produced statistics—the exact source of which he did not indicate—to advertise the growing importance of tropical commerce. He argued "that our own trade with the tropics is already a very large proportion of our total commerce." He showed that, taking British trade with *all* her Colonies and Dependencies, that trade with her tropical empire considerably exceeded her trade with her nontropical Colonies and Dependencies, including Canada, the Cape, Natal, New Zealand, and Australia, Queensland excepted. Again, taking the English-speaking world as a whole, but excluding their trade within their own frontiers, their trade with the tropics accounted for 38 percent of their total trade with the rest of the world. Also the United States trade with the tropics accounted for 65 percent of her total trade with the rest of the world. And the combined United Kingdom and United States trade with the tropics averaged 44 percent of their total trade with the rest of the world outside English-speaking countries. Kidd asked his readers to heed the Frenchman who said: "Colonization is for France a question of life and death—either France must become a great African Power or she will be in a century or two but a secondary European Power; she will count in the world scarcely more than Greece or Rumania counts in Europe."[25] And Kidd himself prophesied that the struggle for tropical trade would be "the permanent underlying fact in the foreign relations of the Western nations in the twentieth century" because of their dependence on tropical products and the mutual profitability of trade.[26]

The Decline of Britain's Commercial Supremacy

Were these fears justified? Indeed they were; but contemporaries tended to exaggerate the imminence of Britain's economic collapse. Between 1846 and 1872 British trade "increased greatly while that of other countries, comparatively speaking, remained at best stationary."[27] And from 1860 to about 1872 Britain had perhaps the fastest economic rate of growth in the world.[28] After 1875 the rate considerably slowed down, and the trend continued to about 1914.[29] By the mid-eighties the situation had become one of considerable concern to the government; and led to a series of official enquiries.[30] In 1895 farmers from all over the country were driven by the continuing agricultural depression to urge Salisbury to resort to protection; but he refused to comply.[31] There was also a gradual price decline which set in about 1873 and lasted to about 1894. From then to the end of the century there was gradual improvement.[32] But of greater consequence was the rising competition of other powers and their adoption of protective tariffs injurious to England's foreign trade, which constituted "one of the most powerful influences on the state of the British economy."[33] The rate of growth of English exports after 1875 declined considerably until the close of the century, when its performance began to be "comparable to that of the mid-Victorian years."[34] The result was that the comfortable commerical supremacy which England had maintained up to about 1872 began gradually to be reversed. It was not that the country was stagnating as such; but that she was gradually being equalled, and in certain aspects surpassed, by the United States, Germany, and to a negligible extent, France. But, to take some concrete examples: In 1881 British coal-miners numbered 382,000 and exported £8 million worth of coal; in 1901 the number had increased to 644,000, and coal exports had soared to £38 million. This sounds impressive until it is compared with America's performance, which by 1900, had outstripped England.[35] And the impact of America's emergence as a large-scale world exporter of manufactures caused alarm in England.[36] In the important iron and steel industry, England had, by 1900, been pushed from first to third position behind Germany and the United States. In 1871 England produced just over 6½ million tons of pig iron; Germany and the United States produced 1½ million each. In 1902 England increased its production by only 2 million to 8½ million; Germany stood at par with it, while the United States, which had already overtaken it in 1886, now produced over 17 million tons.[37] Perhaps an overall picture of British, American, German, and French total exports and imports from 1854 to 1902 will make the picture clearer. The following official charts are succinct and self-explanatory.[38] The figures cited are exclusive of bullion and specie.

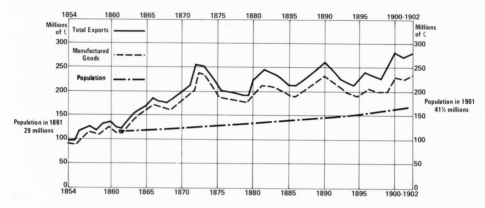

Fig. 1. United Kingdom—total value of the exports of British produce and the value of the exports of manufactured and partly manufactured goods for a series of years

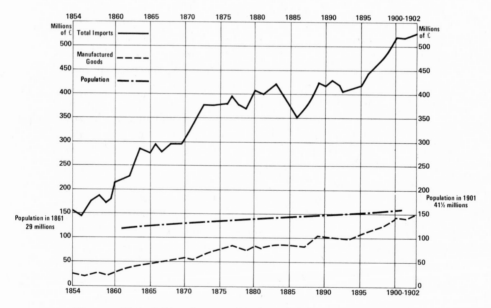

Fig. 2. United Kingdom—total value of the imports (including reexports) and the value of the imports of manufactured and partly manufactured goods for a series of years

Figs. 1–8 adapted and reprinted from "Memorandum on British Trade and Industry, 1903" (cd. 1761). N.B. The population line is drawn to a scale four times that of the imports and exports.

Fig. 3.   United States of America—total value of the exports and the value of the exports of manufactured goods for a series of years

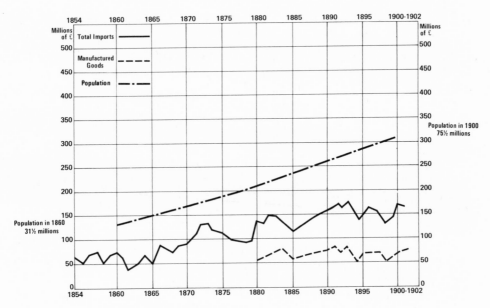

Fig. 4.   United States of America—total value of the imports and the value of the imports of manufactured goods for a series of years

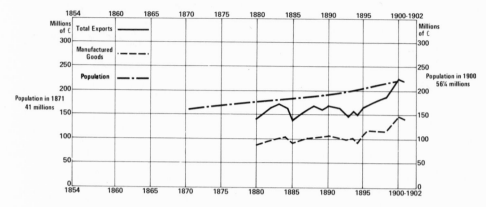

Fig. 5. Germany—total value of the exports and the value of the
exports of manufactured goods for a series of years

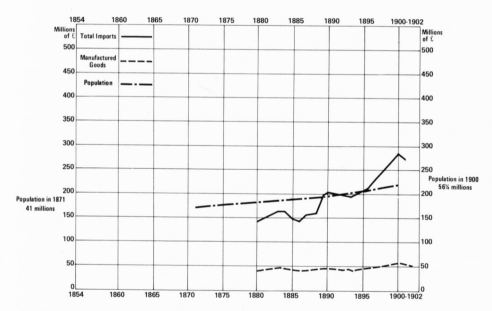

Fig. 6. Germany—total value of the imports and the value of the
imports of manufactured goods for a series of years

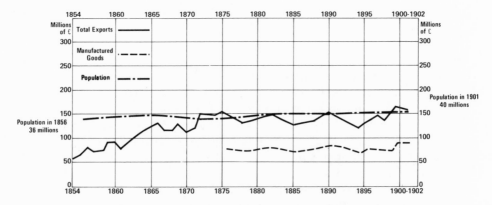

Fig. 7. France—total value of the exports and the value of the exports of manufactured goods for a series of years

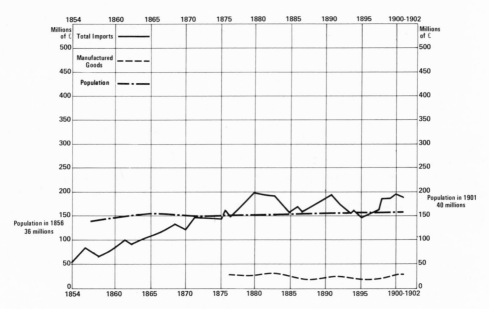

Fig. 8. France—total value of the imports and the value of the imports of manufactured goods for a series of years

Certain points, however, need to be emphasized. The charts demonstrate that, while America, Germany, and France maintained some sort of reasonable equilibrium between exports and imports, British imports far outstripped its exports. In other words, Britain was living beyond its means and had a balance of payments crisis especially between 1890 and 1902. Around 1872 Britain earned just over £250 million from its total exports; its imports amounted to just over £350 million. By 1895 its total exports fell to just over £200 million, while its imports stood at just over £400 million, i.e., almost double the exports. The period 1890–95 was a particularly bad one for British trade. Exports took a disastrous dive, while imports doubled exports. This gave rise to the cry for new markets. Between 1895 and 1902 there was a steady recovery with exports reaching an all-time high or around £275 million in 1900; but this was vitiated by a phenomenal rise in imports to around £525 million in 1900. Again, the period 1895–1900 coincided with the extension and consolidation of Britain's imperial hold in Africa.

Evidently, those who cried for new markets had every reason to be alarmed. It can, of course, be argued that since the cry for new markets only became loud in the 1890s when Africa had practically been partitioned, it was a mere rationalization after the event. It must be pointed out however that those in authority were not unaware of Britain's economic difficulties in the 1880s. That this consideration may have driven them to participate in the greatest international shareout in world history cannot be ruled out. Rosebery's summary of the partition as pegging out claims for futurity explains a great deal about this. Moreover, the fact that the rationalization itself should take a strong economic orientation is in itself significant. Indeed Africa may have been partitioned in the 1880s, but this was only on paper. The real partition took place in the 1890s with effective occupation. A more interesting question, however, is whether these unprotected markets, after acquisition, fulfilled the expectations held out for them. This is open to debate. Some contemporaries thought they did; others dissented. But no one disagreed that British commerce was not flourishing. Optimists, like Kidd, placed a high store on tropical commerce. Lord Masham was convinced that trade followed the flag;[39] as also was *The Times*, though in regard to Africa, it believed that the fruits of the annexations belonged to the future.[40] Writing in 1904, Maxse was emboldened to ask:

> What would be the attitude of the discredited apostle [Cobden] were he with us today? He would be compelled by facts to recognise, little Englander though he was, that the Empire and

the Empire alone had saved this island from industrial collapse by taking in ever-increasing quantities the goods rejected elsewhere. Possibly Cobden might be sufficiently sagacious to pocket his political prejudices in the interests of his economic faith, and turn his remarkable energies to the development of the Colonial market. . . .

Our problem, in a word, is to recreate the Empire which Chatham founded and which Cobden failed to lose.[41]

Was Maxse's optimism founded? In 1872 British exports to its possessions amounted to £60 million; in 1902 they soared to £109 million. Its export trade with all Europe was £108 million in 1872; in 1902 it was £96½ million. With the United States it was £40,700,000 in 1872 and £27,800,000 in 1902. "Thus the decrease of 11½ millions in our European trade," wrote Marston, "and of 13 millions in our trade with the United States, had been wiped out by an increase of 49 millions with British Possession." In other words, it means that "in 1902 we sent as great a value of goods to our Colonies as we did to Germany, Holland, the United States, South America, Mexico, France, Russia, China, Turkey, and Persia combined."[42] Board of Trade statistics point to a similar conclusion as follows:[43]

	Principal Protected Countries and Colonies	*All Other Countries and Colonies*	*Total of All Countries and Colonies*
Exports of All Articles of Br. Produce	*Percent*	*Percent*	*Percent*
1850	56	44	100
1860	51	49	100
1870	53	47	100
1880	49	51	100
1890	46	54	100
1900	45	55	100
1902	42	58	100
Exports of Manufactured and Partly Manufactured Articles			
1850	57	43	100
1860	50	50	100

1870	50	50	100
1880	47	53	100
1890	44	56	100
1900	47	58	100
1902	38	62	100

They show clearly a reversal of British export trends between protected and unprotected markets in the years 1850–1902. In 1850 protected countries got 56 percent of British exports, the others got 44 percent; in 1902 it was 42 to 58 percent. Treated separately, manufactured articles showed even a more marked trend in reverse. The proportion in 1850 was: protected 57, others 43; and in 1902: protected 38; others 62. The report comments:

> The change has been a continuous one, but it operated most rapidly during the first decade (1850–1860), and during the last few years (1890–1902). No doubt some allowance should be made for the expansion of the British Empire which took place during those two periods, e.g., the consolidation of the Indian Empire in the fifties, and the extension of British dominions and protectorates in Africa in recent years. But after allowing for this there can be no doubt as to the effect of continental and American tariffs in checking our export trade, especially in manufactured articles, with the groups of "protected countries" during the last two decades.[44]

Of course the free traders held other views. Lord Farrer, a staunch Gladstonian, questioned the concept that trade followed the flag. "It is not necessary to extend our Empire in order to maintain our trade," he wrote, "and that extension of Empire is not necessarily followed by increase of trade. Each separate extension must be judged on its own merits." He produced figures to prove his case.[45] Nobody would question Farrer's contention. But he did not reject the argument that trade did follow the flag in some instances. Masham's rebuttal of Farrer was not based on what the latter said, but on his statistics. "I know well from long experience that Lord Farrer's figures are never to be trusted," he replied, "it is not that the figures themselves are incorrect, but they are put in such a way that the reasoning founded upon them is entirely misleading and delusive."[46] Hobson, another strong Gladstonian, went further to put forward the argument, now popular, that British trade with foreign countries was by far greater than her trade with the empire; and he rejected the "open door" concept since, in practice, it involved "the policy of forcing doors open and forcibly keeping them open."[47] But Hobson, too, had missed the point. In the period under survey he could not rebut the contention that Britain's imperial trade had increased faster than that with foreign countries. He also failed to take into consideration the simple fact that the trade of the African tropics, for example, was still largely undeveloped and that Britain only took what could be easily taken.

It is clear that by 1895 most people of note believed that Britain's economic situation was not flourishing. There was a feeling that it must expand its commerce in unprotected markets or perish. "Our natural inheritance," wrote Kidd, "is the trade of the world." He advocated the maintenance of a navy stronger than those of the other nations put together to protect this trade against competition.[48] Campbell-Bannerman pointed out "that 12 million of our people are underfed, and on the verge of hunger."[49] The Cobden club admitted that "our oversea trade has increased less rapidly than our population."[50] Others longed for the return of "the great Victorian boom," and "the good years"; but as a shrewd observer had recently remarked, millions still lived "below the poverty line" during those so-called years of prosperity.[51] If, then, all shades of opinion wanted the extension of British commerce, how could this be achieved? In this they disagreed. Imperialists saw the salvation in territorial expansion. Little Englanders rejected this course but produced no tangible alternative especially as free trade had not exactly solved Britain's commercial problems. Few, however, advocated protection, except, of course, the advocates of an imperial *zollverein*.

Salisbury, as usual, held to no rigid line. He urged his countrymen to use their individual and corporate ability and sagacity to beat down foreign competition. Where these proved inefficacious, he was prepared to annex.[52] We find him in 1897 once more emphasizing the novelty of the second empire and advising caution as the best guarantee of "a tremendous imperial destiny."[53]

He had not much respect for economic theory. But he always described himself as a free trader and dismissed lightly the protectionism of his university days. Yet he often bantered what he called the Holy Doctrine of Free Trade, which, he said, had no claim to infallible orthodoxy. "I am afraid," he once said, "that the utterances of political economy nowadays are only too apt to be 'Gladstonized'."[54] In 1865 he repudiated the view that free trade was the cause of English prosperity in the 1840s. He put it down to the gigantic gold discoveries in California and Australia.[55] He could always produce hypothetical illustration to prove that free trade had not helped England to secure open markets abroad. But he never repudiated the doctrine. During the last months of his life, he was alarmed at Chamberlain's attitude to this question. Yet he talked glibly of Foreign Office retaliation, and has, consequently, been described as a Foreign Office retaliationist.[56] Indeed, during the backwash of the fair trade agitation in 1885 he toyed with the idea of protection and was roughly handled by F. A. Channing.[57]

Chapter III

Changing Attitudes toward British Expansion, 1888-1900

A study of British public opinion before 1888 reveals little public enthusiasm for imperial adventures in Africa. This is not to suggest that the British public was uninterested in assuming imperial responsibilities in that continent. If public reaction to the new imperialism of the 1890s is any guide, there is no doubt that imperialism held an inherent attraction for them. During the paper partition of Africa in the 1880s the masses appeared unconcerned precisely because they did not comprehend what was going on. Few could read and write; and few still could afford to consult the highbrow newspapers and journals which appealed only to the upper and middle classes. The government, too, deliberately gave African affairs a low profile largely because of the political instability of the mid-eighties caused by the Home Rule imbroglio.

In studying Britain's changing attitudes to African expansion, the Reform Bill of 1884 must merit consideration. This bill added an impressive number of voters to the electoral register. The result of this development was that politicians were forced by circumstances to appeal to the masses. The days of the rotten boroughs were over. And though superficially it appeared that the proud patricians were still living securely in their ivory tower, it was clear that their best days were gone. For Salisbury that was a frightening thought. That was why he regarded the new House of Commons with undisguised contempt, sneered at the new journalism, and opposed democracy. The truth however is that toward the close of the century he could no longer ignore these new forces. On the contrary, he turned them to the advantage of the Conservative party.

Salisbury, along with other politicians, businessmen, newspapermen, popular historians, and novelists helped to teach the masses the values of an African empire and found them very receptive to the idea. This was possible because the Education Act of 1870 had increased the reading public by the 1890s. Had the new electorate, the new democracy, and the popular press opposed imperial adventures in Africa, Britain could not have afforded to play a dominant role in the conquest of Africa. The irony of the situation is that Britons quickly lost their head and Salisbury found himself in an embarrassing position. We watch him struggling to the end of the century to keep the new forces in harness. Thus, the erroneous impression has been created that Salisbury cared little for African colonization.

We said earlier that there is little evidence of any general public enthusiasm for the empire before the late eighties. It must be pointed out however that the Conservative party had all along identified itself with the imperial idea. Its main concern was to prevent the disintegration of the empire. The Home Rule issue was seen as a first step toward disintegration, and the Liberal party a willing instrument in this direction. These fears were expressed in Salisbury's article, "Disintegration," in which he bitterly attacked the Liberal party's attitude toward the empire.[1] A few years later he accused Gladstone of grasping "the sceptre of empire as if it burned his fingers:"[2] and he asserted that Gladstone's advocacy of Home Rule had "awakened the slumbering genius of Imperialism."[3] Indeed, his contention was that if Ireland went, the rest of the empire would, sooner or later, follow its lead.[4] He saw it as his duty and that of his party to prevent such an occurrence. The Primrose League was therefore formed around 1883 partly as a rallying call for the maintenance of the empire,[5] and by 1899 its membership had risen to some 15,000,000.[6] Other events which, according to Salisbury, helped to awaken imperial consciousness were the Majuba Hill disaster and the death of Gordon.[7]

In June, 1883 the Lancashire Union of Conservatives and Constitutional Associations had sent a manifesto to Salisbury deploring the Liberal government's policy in India, Africa, and Ireland.[8] This was followed by two resolutions from the Wandsworth and Putney Workingmen's Conservative Association deploring the same government's policy relating to the Suez Canal and the territories adjoining it. They demanded that English interests be protected.[9] In 1884 several resolutions from all over the country were passed criticizing the Liberal government's imperial policy. Salisbury expressed his sympathy with all these resolutions and associated himself with their views.[10] On South Africa, he assured the lord mayor of London that "some day or other that that terrible blunder [Majuba Hill] will have to be repaired."[11] But when he was actually in office he lamented that "in their heart of hearts members of Parliament have made up their minds to abandon South Africa if ever it threatens to cost any considerable expense again."[12] This is odd since, with the mineral revolution, South Africa had acquired added importance to the British.

So long as Africa was not a major issue in the spectrum of the public's conception of the empire, Salisbury could safely promote his "pacific invasion of Englishmen" in that continent for all that it was worth. But to a people imperially conscious by the last decade of the nineteenth century, such a policy was a nonstarter. Moreover, by granting a charter to the North Borneo Company, and by proclaiming protectorates over some part of New Guinea, Bechuanaland, and the Niger District, Gladstone had staked his country's interest in tropical expansion. This, confessed William Harcourt, was a curious demonstration of anti-imperialistic principles.[13] In 1886 a charter was granted to the Royal Niger Company for the purposes of trading and administering the Niger Districts in the name of the British crown. Salisbury did not retard this action. In 1888 he granted a royal charter to the imperial British East Africa Company, and in 1889 to the British South Africa Company. And he spoke with satisfaction of "three great associations . . . formed for the purpose of pushing forward the civilization of Africa."[14] This was far from being an anti-imperialistic sentiment. Indeed by participating in the Berlin Conference of 1884–85, Britain had committed itself to imperial expansion in Africa. That commitment Salisbury honored during his years of office. And he did so without making much noise about it. It was not however until about 1888 that Salisbury himself was knowledgeable enough in African matters to turn his attention in that direction. "So shrewd, sensible, acquainted with African questions and conditions," wrote Johnston after his interviews with Salisbury, "and retentive of memory." "I left his room a little awed, but secretly much elated," he continued. "It was a great step in advance to meet a secretary of state who, as far as Africa was concerned, knew what he was talking about."[15] He also noted Chamberlain's comparative ignorance of African matters.[16] He even claimed that Salisbury instructed him to write an article putting "the whole African question lucidly before the public."[17] Oliver has argued that this article, though retaining Johnston's individuality, is "the clearest surviving exposition of Salisbury's African policy."[18] But Johnston's main thesis was the Cape to Cairo dream to which Salisbury did not subscribe.

Public interest in Africa was slow and gradual. Salisbury did not strive to do anything in advance of public opinion. He could not afford to do so. It was the battle over the retention of Uganda that proved conclusively that attitudes were changing and that governments could count on the support of the public in imperial ventures in Africa. By the close of the century public interest in Africa amounted almost to a revolution.[19] The imperial idea became a household phrase. Spender wrote:

> All through this time one heard the strains of the big brass band playing the new imperial tunes. Chamberlain was its conductor, and there were many sorts of instruments in it. Kipling played incomparable solos, and after him Henly. The newspapers crashed their accompaniments. The themes were both commercial and patriotic. To carry the flag into new worlds . . . was supposed to be an end in itself; but trade, we were assured, would follow the flag, and the whole world was a potential market.[20]

And another contemporary wrote:

> I am informed by those in the talking profession that there is no topic more popular upon a political platform at the present day than the expansion of the British empire and the increase of British trade, more especially in regard to Africa. Upon the one side of politics "our civilising mission" and "provision for posterity" form our theme; upon the other we declaim against "insane expenditure," "land hunger" and the rest.[21]

"For a time," wrote Victor Berard, "it was quite a moot point whether imperialism exercised any real influence over the English heart and mind. Today there is no doubt; imperialism is all-triumphant."[22] Beatrice Webb noted in her diary (January 25, 1897): "Back to London, Imperialism is in the air—all classes drunk with sightseeing and hysterical 'loyalty'. . . ."[23] What brought about this change?

The New Electorate, the New Democracy, and the Popular Press
"A hypothetical historian," wrote Kennedy Jones, who wished to study the "Decline and Fall of the British Empire," should begin in 1870, the year of the first important Education Act.[24] By the late eighties the children who benefited from this Act had constituted a totally different problem quite alien to the early or mid-century—the problem of a working-class elite or semi-elite, whose tastes, habits, and political ideals, differed from those of their seniors and socially and financially betters. Some of them were to constitute the new electorate and became an important factor in the new democracy. Some even rose to be the so-called lower-middle class, who believed they could succeed in the world provided they had the taste for high adventure and great enterprise. This was the group whose imaginations were deliberately stirred by Rudyard Kipling, Joseph Conrad, Louis Stevenson, W. E. Henly, Rider Haggard, G. A. Henty, Conan

Doyle, John Buchan, and some lesser writers. Their theme was the love for adventure, either as a destitute sailor in the China or South Seas, or as the indefatigable white man in the tropics battling against immense odds and emerging victorious in the end. They glorified the British empire and the British race, emphasizing "the white man's burden." Africa was romanticized especially by Haggard, and the imaginations of the young empire builders of later years were fired. Numerous political orators, popular historians, and scientists enthusiastically sold the imperial idea to a gullible public. The man-in-the-street, too, wrote David Thomson in a perceptive passage,

> came into his own as the century ended—the product of industrialism-plus-democracy which the twentieth century was to rechristen "the common man." If his entry into his political and cultural inheritance was heralded by an outburst of rancorous patriotism and a cult of brutal impatience with all resistance to British rule overseas, that was but over-compensation for the utterly unromantic conditions in which his civilization forced him to live. . . . The 'nineties felt "naughty" mainly because they made a convention of unconventionality.[25]

The educated of this generation, unlike their elders, cared little for Dickens and Thackeray, for Tennyson and Browning, for politics Disraelian or Gladstonian style. They worried little about Huxley or Darwin—if they ever heard of them—and if they did they were ready to stand Darwin on his head as purely and simply the exponent of the superiority of certain races over some others, with its tintinabulation of survival of the fittest. The educated public, therefore, read with enthusiasm the defense of the British empire by such eminent historians as W. E. H. Lecky, J. R. Seeley, and J. A. Froude as a mission divinely ordained. Even Carlyle scorned those who advocated the equality of men, and refused to believe that "Quashee Niger" was equal to Socrates or Shakespeare. Yet this same Carlyle popularized the notion of mission in imperialism.[26] They were the new imperialists, the jingoes, who "were living almost consciously in the end of a great age, deliberately fin de siècle."[27] They revelled in the martial headlines of the *Daily Mail* and the *Pall Mall Gazette*, and would go all the way with Chamberlain in his Act of Vigor to defy whomever it might be. They were at once Victorian and un-Victorian—people whose influence had been greatly enhanced by the Franchise Extension and Redistribution Acts of 1884 and 1885.[28]

Of course the rising tide of imperialism ought not to be seen solely in class terms, for it pervaded all sections of the community and cut across party lines. "Nothing is more remarkable," wrote a bemused contemporary "than the complete change that has come over Englishmen with reference to the extension of the Empire."[29] Among the upper and middle classes were to be found many excessively patriotic individuals who fervently believed in the existence of an English destiny; and who saw themselves as God's chosen people to right the wrongs of the world and rule over the "lesser breeds without the law."[30] There were also the young noblemen who, according to Lord Grey, were inspired by "the jolly, reckless spirit of adventure, which aims at making a million in half an hour and then clearing home to Piccadilly."[31] On the whole, it was a confidently reckless age—a recklessness which reflected in the actions of the imperial proconsuls, and typified by the ebulition of Carter in Yorubaland and the unmagnanimity of Moore at Benin.[32] John Kirk complained:

> . . . we are now tapping a lower grade of officers for these high posts. When first our African Empire began we were fortunate in having the choice of good men for the highest posts, but behind them came a low class unfit for high positions, and these are the men now getting power into their hands. Some of these second rates were waifs of society, good enough to act under orders but not the men to uphold the dignity of the Empire.[33]

To direct imperial affairs under these circumstances was an immense and uncomfortable task. But the saving grace was that on imperial questions, at the time, the gulf between the government and the public was negligible. There was, therefore, no organized pressure to force the government to undertake any drastic action abroad. Occasionally, however, the public reacted decisively if they felt that their interests had not been protected.[34] Consequently, by 1895 Salisbury was no longer directing the affairs of a nation whose gospel was Cobdenism, and to whom Bright was an oracle: A shrewd historian noted:

> The members of the London Stock Exchange or the Manchester Cotton Exchange, who acclaimed Rhodes and Jameson in the 'nineties, were the sons of men who in the 'sixties had acclaimed Bright. A new pride in Britain's conquests went with a new sense of Britain's trade needs. The latter gave the deeper impulse; even Lord Salisbury, who was no expansionist by instinct, countenanced (in 1890) the argument that "trade follows the flag."[35]

Though few questioned the free trade doctrine, the arguments for new markets had an irresistible and practical appeal.

Times had changed; and individuals too. The General election of 1895 perhaps demonstrated the phenomenon of the times. It may not be too much to claim that imperial issues turned the tide in favor of the Unionist party. The Unionists campaigned on the ticket of the "consolidation and extension of the empire."[36] Liberal leaders campaigned on various issues, but carefully avoided dragging in the empire.[37] And the Liberal party was soundly thrashed in the elections.

The completeness of the Unionist victory baffled party leaders who had not expected a landslide.[38] Harcourt, Morley, and many prominent Liberals were defeated. "Heavens! What a smash! Alas, poor Morley! I confess I was sorry for Harcourt but I shed no tears over the philosopher in politics," wrote Chamberlain. "There has been nothing like it since the defeat of the little Englanders after the Crimean War."[39] This epitomized the general reaction. Naturally, various reasons for the defeat were adduced for many months afterwards. Topping the list was the view that it was a revolt against little Englandism.[40] Chamberlain telegraphed to Glasgow: "Rejoice that Glasgow is joining Birmingham in defence of the Empire."[41] He was not alone in this belief. The significance of the view, however, does not lie in its veracity, but on the fact that it was held by many contemporaries. It was argued that foreign affairs do not win elections; the decisive factors were often local. But everyone sought in vain for any decisive local factors. As one Liberal put it:

> A like phenomenon is seen in the country. Manchester agrees with London, and Bradford and Newcastle are in harmony with Manchester and Liverpool; and if Bristol, Edinburgh, and Glasgow are divided, the voice of Birmingham is, as all expected it would be, singularly loud and determined.[42]

Indeed, when all due allowance is made for all other factors, the question of the empire, uncharacteristic as it may have been, was, in the opinion of most contemporaries, the most important influence in the elections. "The result of the last election," wrote the *P.M.G.*, "shows that England approves of honourable alliances framed to resist attacks upon Imperial Unity."[43] And the *Daily News* complained: "In the narrow, ignorant, and parochial minds of politicians who are always boasting and swaggering and blustering about the Empire, foreign affairs have little or no place."[44] No one would have written in this vein a decade earlier.

The desertion of the Liberals on the imperial issue by their most influential supporters, especially in the Lords, started some considerable time before 1895. At the close of 1894 Salisbury had addressed himself to this phenomenon and had come to the conclusion that "the most marked and sudden secession was due to their unexpected tam-

pering with the integrity of the Empire."[45] And as the century closed
the party, lamented Gladstone, was gradually being deserted by the
mercantile, industrial, and professional talent, as well as other men
of wealth and influence.[46] "Candidates must have been difficult to
find," writes Maccoby, "and money could hardly have been plentiful
in the Central party funds."[47] That this lack was reflected in the results of the elections is undeniable; but it by no means explains the
unanimity of trends throughout the whole country, or the defeat of
such stalwart little Englanders as Harcourt and Morley. Indeed, a
survey sponsored by the *Quarterly Review* came to the conclusion
that imperialism and not "local or exceptional causes" was responsible for Salisbury's victory.[48] Admittedly, this was a partisan survey;
but its conclusions seem to be logical and based on facts. The Liberals themselves conceded that the appeal of new markets had robbed
them of victory.[49] But there were other reasons besides: the decline
of the Liberal party organization or even of liberalism as an effete
creed; the personalities of Salisbury and Rosebery, of Chamberlain
and Harcourt—all these were contributory factors. But what stands
out clearly is the view that the election result was a massive revolt
against mid-century Manchesterism. Clearly, "the classes admitted
to power under household suffrage" were not committed to Cobdenism, Morelyism, or Harcourtism. Free Trade and nonintervention
had not improved their lot. They were prepared to try something
else. Socialism was still an ideal with potentialities not many understood. "Mr. Keir Hardie is ridiculed; Mr. John Burns is preferred,"
wrote one reporter. "The Newcastle Programme, I was informed by
one man 'we don't care a d . . n for,' "[50] and Fabianism was intellectual and vague.

　　Although the General Election of 1895 appears somehow freak-
ish, it is nonetheless significant. It is often argued that despite the
huge margin of 152 seats, the two parties were almost evenly balanced.[51] This assessment ignores certain fundamental facts. Of Liberal seats in the 1892 Parliament, the Unionists gained 110; the former gained 20. Unionist votes increased by 128,053; Liberal votes
declined by 93,006. One hundred and twenty-four Unionist seats
were uncontested as against 52 uncontested opposition seats, 42 of
which were Irish constituencies. Again, London, with a population
by far greater than that of Ireland, "has little more than half its
parliamentary representation."[52] The inevitable conclusion, therefore, is that when the necessary adjustments are made, it will be
found that the two parties were by no means equal in the country.

　　The election is also of interest for the conversion of Scotland to
the Unionist cause,[53]—a conversion which became revolutionary after

the general election of 1900.[54] The Unionists maintained their ground in Ireland; but many Welshmen who had abandoned their faith in 1895[55] repented by 1900.[56] Scotland waited till 1906 to return to its true allegiance. In 1895, however, the *Observer* could boast that "the Glaswegians are great colonizers and have always been sound on Imperial questions."[57]

This somewhat detailed analysis of the 1895 election is necessary; in a democracy, it is at their peril that governments lose sight of the trend of public opinion. If the electors could revolt against Liberalism in 1895, there was no reason to suppose that they could not treat the Unionists in like manner in 1902.[58] Increasingly, people were taking more interest in imperial affairs, and as a contemporary put it, "the tendencies and aptitudes of the United Kingdom, on the Imperial side, have been subjected to very varied and searching tests since the popularization of the electorate."[59] "A majority," Balfour once said, "is not an inanimate machine, and those who use it must be prepared to humour it."[60] "During the Queen's reign every Minister who, after a year's tenure of office, or more, has dissolved Parliament," Salisbury also remarked, "has been turned out within a year by the Parliament he has summoned. There is no exception to the rule."[61] Once more Salisbury has demonstrated his concern for public opinion.

Perhaps the greatest importance of this election to our study is that for the first time in his career Salisbury was in a position of real power. His ascendancy over his contemporaries, British and European, was generally acclaimed.[62] The Unionist starred imperial questions and won overwhelmingly. Every indication pointed to a growing interest in the empire. The British people, indeed, had proved very teachable in these matters.[63] And imperial affairs were quietly relegating foreign affairs proper to second place. Indeed, the position in which Salisbury found himself in 1895 was a very unhealthy one in a democracy. Not since the days of the Glorious Revolution had any statesman found himself in a position just short of dictatorial. The strength of the conservatives in the Commons was unassailable; in the Lords they controlled four fifths of the seats. They boasted of "riches, rank, broad acres of land and ancient lineage." Besides these privileges they possessed, as one Liberal conceded, "an almost embarrassing wealth of talent and capacity."[64] Contemporaries realized the situation full well and were asking themselves, "How, then, is Lord Salisbury likely to use that power? . . . What will Lord Salisbury do?"[65]

The continuing disintegration of the Liberal party which was making party divisions rather tenuous, and the almost unanimous advocacy of the press for a forward policy, made these speculations even more pertinent, especially in imperial policy. Though he was concerned about the deplorable state of the Liberals,[66] the main difficulty revolved on how to treat a jingo press. While he was not the sort of man to lose his head in the face of popular acclaim, he realized, as a good politician should, that it would be suicidal to turn the press against him. It is of course usual for some to brush off the influence of the press in politics. There was the story of "an ardent Yorkshire politican, groaning under what he regarded as the unjust aspersions of his critics," who cried: "What is the Press? It is nobbut an oligarchy that calls itself a 'we'."[67] And yet he was very much worried. But at a period when the press was the only organ of *mass* information, few would doubt its influence. This was particularly so when the Education Act of 1870 had within a generation increased the reading public by millions who then, having "been taught reading require something to read."[68] This created a new problem for the journalists and press barons who had hitherto not written for the unprivileged section of the community.[69] It also created a new problem for the politicians who were unused to dealing with a massive articulate or semi-articulate public who were thirsting for information.[70] In order to meet their needs, popular journalism, about which volumes have been written, was born. Soon, the press became the established "information market"[71] from which individuals gathered their facts rather than from books.[72] *The Times*, the *P.M.G.*, the *Daily Mail*, the *Evening News*, and so forth were deployed to sell the imperial idea to an enthusiastic public. The plan worked admirably:

> We discovered at once [wrote Kennedy Jones] an abounding desire for knowledge on all matters affecting the Empire. We realized that one of the greatest forces, almost untapped, at the disposal of the Press was the depth and volume of public interest in Imperial questions. . . . The British beyond question are an imperial race . . .
>
> I have always found the British public deeply interested in Imperial affairs.

Soon, too, the press and universal education became identified with democracy. When Chamberlain in 1896 initiated his "new diplomacy" by publishing his exchanges with Kruger during the Jameson raid controversy, he was, by implication, giving sanction to this idea. When Salisbury in 1898 took the journalists into his confidence during the Fashoda affair,[73] or when he took the unusual step of publishing the Fashoda papers, he was acknowledging the influence of the press and the new democracy. Indeed, Salisbury went further to emphasize his new trend of thought when, during the Khaki Election, he issued his own address "to the electors of the United Kingdom."[74] This must have been a humiliating experience for the proud patrician. Salisbury may have scorned the press; the *Daily Mail* may have been "written by office boys for office boys"; he could no longer afford to ignore them.[75] More and more, politicians and parties curried the favor of the press; and identified themselves with them.[76] Spender, as the editor of the *Westminster Gazette*, was "an unofficial member of the Liberal Cabinet"; when J. L. Garvin edited the *P.M.G.*, he was "a dreaded influence in Tory circles," and ruled "by terror"; and St. Leo Strachey of the *Spectator* was the "watch-dog of Tory traditions."[77] So was the *Standard*. "The press," indeed, had become "the nervous system of the modern body-politic";[78] and it had also become an important factor "in the formation and guidance of public opinion."[79] Provincial politicians began increasingly to use the provincial press to debate their opposing views on some major national issues. How the public used this mass of information is difficult to determine. However, it is indisputable that politicians and diplomatists began seriously to take notice of the press.[80] "The power of the press," wrote Lord Bryce toward the end of his life, "seems the greatest danger ahead of democracy."[81] It was indeed a very serious danger insofar as politicians could do nothing about it,[82] especially if the newspapers misused their powers.

Another important point to note was the desertion of the Liberals by the press at this time. Spender lamented that "the Liberals had nearly all the largest circulations against them."[83] This was no exaggeration. In sum, then, the great majority of the press was in support of the general lines of Salisbury's imperial policy. So was the country. But there were some individuals who would have been happier if he had shown a stronger and more positive attitude. However, that was not his way, and the result was that the jingoism of the press, as well as of some of the masses, made his diplomatic work much more difficult. In the eighties he conducted his diplomacy quietly and almost single handedly with little interference from outside. Now, that was not to be. "Our newspapers," he complained, "do us an infinity of harm with Germany and Russia";[84] and if one may add, with France as well.

To understand Salisbury's reaction to this phenomenon, one must, first of all, understand his attitude to democracy and public opinion generally. One must also realize that this was the period, when, according to the Duke of Bedford, "home affairs have been somewhat overshadowed by the exciting turn which events have

taken abroad," and when there were "no longer politicians of any influence in this country" who did not profess some sort of imperialism.[85]

Salisbury, as the opponent of democracy, is well known; but
Salisbury as the great minister of the democracy which he had opposed is an interesting subject for study. What interests us particularly is how his pathological fear of democracy influenced his attitude to the empire. First, it made him against Irish independence;
and he curiously explained away the Jameson raid as demonstrating
the results of an extreme case of Home Rule. Second, he saw democracy as the greatest danger to an expanding empire and desired a
tighter central control. Hence he was not enthusiastic about colonial
self-government. In the eighties, however, he was to confess that, as
a result of the striking manifestation of the reality and sentiment of
Greater Britain, his misgivings had been "entirely without foundation and mistaken."[86] But there is no evidence to suggest that he
shifted his ground as a result. And third, having failed to keep
Britain an aristocracy—believing sincerely that that was the only way
to save the state from certain peril—it was characteristic of the man
that he strove to keep the new forces of democracy in harness, at any
rate, in the imperial sphere. As *The Times* put it:

> He measured them, gauged, to some extent, their nature and
> their force, checked their extremes, appreciated something of
> their worth and their capacity, and held them more or less in his
> hand. He was able to look at them somewhat as a coachman
> looks at his horses; he harnessed them, and managed to keep
> them in the straight road.

Herein lies the key to the understanding of Salisbury's attitude to
the new imperialism. While he did not believe in democracy in principle, he had a profound belief in the empire. What he achieved at
the close of the century when the ghost of imperialism was abroad
in the land, was not to denounce the ghost which he had helped to
bring to life, but to prevent it from getting out of hand. He worked
quietly, in the background, to achieve this aim. Consequently, he is
not generally associated with British fin de siècle imperialism. It
would have been out of character had he behaved like Chamberlain
or Rosebery, Rhodes or Ellis Ashmead-Bartlett. But all of them were
pursuing the same ends, with Salisbury acting as the controlling influence.[87]

The resignation with which Salisbury accepted democracy manifested itself in his growing susceptibility to public opinion. In 1889
Salisbury confessed to Herbert Bismarck: "We live no longer, alas,

in Pitt's times; the aristocracy governed then and we were able to form an active policy. . . . Now democracy is on top, and with it the personal and party system, which reduces every British Government to absolute dependence on the *aura popularis*. . . ."[88]

Indeed, his celebrated indifference to public opinion has been exaggerated. His monumental indifference to his audience may be explained away as being compatible with his retiring nature. True, he certainly was suspicious, and even afraid, of popular movements and refused to give the impression that he was modeling his policies on them. However, his response to what he called the "great inarticulate" of his fellow countrymen was instinctive. He understood their feelings and their prejudices. He tried hard to appreciate them. Sometimes he sought for, and welcomed, information from anyone or from a group of people. He consulted the newspapers, British and foreign;[89] he listened to party agents and organizers in the constituencies, particularly to "Skipper" Middleton, the chief Conservative party agent and Akers-Douglas, his chief whip toward the end of his career; he listened to local politicians with whom he came in contact during his speaking tours throughout the country. No one could possibly say what use he made of the information so collected. But it is reasonable to assume that if he was indifferent to public opinion, he would not have concerned himself with this method of gathering information—a method described as "the scientific ethos applied in politics." "It was one of . . . Salisbury's paradoxes," wrote G. M. Young, "that only uncontentious legislation should be brought before Parliament: if it were contentious, then public opinion was not ripe for it."[90]

Lord Cecil of Chelmwood claimed that Salisbury paid little attention to public opinion in external affairs.[91] Nevertheless, it has been demonstrated that in dealing with the Anglo-Portuguese boundary question (1889–90) he attached great importance to the religious opinion mobilized in support of the British claims.[92] There are many examples from Salisbury's private correspondence to show that, in most of the external difficulties with which he had to deal, he reckoned with public opinion.[93] Sometimes he appeared to be anxious to have a clear indication of the general drift of opinion on specific issues;[94] sometimes he complained of the unpredictability of English opinion which "passes with great rapidity out of a condition of apparent languor and indifference into a condition of violent excitement which carried every party and Government with it . . . it is never safe to trust the apparent apathy of the English people."[95] On another occasion he declared: "When the opinion of your countrymen has declared itself and you see that their convictions—their firm, deliberate, sustained convictions—are in favor of any course, I do not for a moment deny that it is your business to yield."[96] Occasionally, however, he chastised English opinion for its greediness: "It is a very remarkable peculiarity of the public in this country that people always desire to eat their cake and have it."[97]

Shades of Opinion in Parliament

In a study of the 1895–1900 Parliament certain facts emerge: the decline of the Irish factor as a political force; the disunity and dwindling influence of the Liberal opposition; the decline of Cobdenism; the imperialism of most members; and the dominance of the Unionists in both Houses.

Though the Irish nationalists just about held their ground in the general election, the Nationalist party was a shadow of its former self. This situation cannot be accounted for solely because of the Unionist majority. Parnell's fall had caused a serious rift among its members. Instead of presenting a united front, they grouped themselves as the Separatists or Healyites, and the Redmondites; while Justin McCarthy's dwindling supporters hardly took any active part in politics. In Ireland, the situation was even more acute. The issue centered between the Clerical and Anti-Clerical parties, and their antagonism reached its peak during the 1895 Elections. The priests even disagreed among themselves; the Parnellites had not successfully formed any worthwhile amalgalm "with the old rump of Fenianism"; the Irish-Americans had largely cut off supplies to their kin at home, thus diminishing their influence in the Irish struggle; and the dominating political influence of the clergy increasingly came under fire. The impecunious state of the Irish parties—as they must now be called—made it difficult for them to take part in debates at Westminster in large numbers. Their continuous absence, it was reckoned, put Salisbury's permanent majority at 200 instead of 152. This is of interest in our study. "The Irish Nationalists," rejoiced *The Times*, "can no longer claim to make and unmake Ministers."[98]

The situation had more serious repercussions. "Home Rule, then, is dead," reflected one Journal. "What of life remains in the 'Liberal' party?"[99]

Nor did the situation escape Salisbury's sneer:

> Look at the case of Ireland. The flash with which the genius of Parnell illuminated the gloomy history of Irish disaffection has entirely disappeared, worn out. Irish agitation has perished by its congenital disease. If Richard Strongbow could come to earth now he would say, 'Why, things are exactly as they were when I was there. The Irish were quarrelling so then that I had no

difficulty in conquering them, and they are quarrelling so now that they will be unable to shake off the influence and power of England.[100]

So the Irish too were part of the Englishman's burden of governing those incapable of governing themselves. "Irish difficulties" mused an Irish cynic, "England's opportunity."[101] But characteristically, Salisbury did not see it that way. Having failed to subdue Ireland by a few "years of resolute government," he decided to "kill Home Rule by kindness." The attempt also failed. Irish opposition to British imperialism was irreconcilable; yet the Irish did not fit into the traditional pattern of Little Englanders. They were merely protecting their own interests. In any case their best days were over, even before the Unionists came to power. "The commonplace in English politics upon which nearly everybody at present agrees," wrote Professor Mahaffy, "is that *Home Rule is dead.* You seldom hear it mentioned in political circles in any other connections. One Party proclaims it aloud, the other *sotto voce.*"[102] Nevertheless the Irish parties were determined to oppose any adventures in Africa.

The Liberal peers fared even worse than the Irish contingent in this Parliament. They numbered only thirty, and only a few of them participated in debates on imperial policy. Those who participated displayed little trace of little Englandism. Rosebery agreed with Salisbury's imperial policy and said so himself on several occasions. Kimberley[103] was too nice a man to be idealistic. Like Salisbury, he tended to judge every issue on its merit. And like Campbell-Bannerman, he was neither a "pro-Boer," nor belonged to the war party. In July 1895, for instance, Kimberley "had proposed to force the Dardanelles [but] Harcourt had stopped him. If the *Daily Chronicle* only knew!", Dilke noted in his "Memoirs."[104] Ripon, too, showed little opposition to government policy until the Boer War unsettled his equanimity.[105] Indeed, there was precious little difference between the attitudes to imperial expansion of Salisbury, Rosebery, Kimberley, Ripon, and Bannerman, except that Salisbury was leading a party officially committed to expansion, while the others belonged to a party in disarray over this very issue.

Another interesting thing to note about the Lords in this period was that the mass of them "had been drawn from the purest Liberal sources by the most trusted Liberals," but since Palmerston's death, had defected to the Tories almost en masse because of disagreements over such issues as the maintenance of the empire, property, and the established churches.[106] Salisbury's dominance over the House of Lords was complete. He had no compere.

In the earlier days the picture was slightly different. Then, he had the reputation of being "industrious, pugnacious, vigorous, and eloquent."[107] Later on, one critic wrote: "He is downright dictatorial, and truth to say, he treats his peers with something akin to contempt."[108] But in the eighties Salisbury used to cross swords with Earl Granville, and people wondered which of them was the better debater.[109] Now, the situation had changed. The Liberals seemed to have had no fire left in them, and Salisbury adopted the more congenial role of the father-figure, with Rosebery as the admiring son in external affairs.

In the Commons, opinions were better crystalized. Here it would be easier to speak of the big Englander and the little Englander. But the division still cut across party lines. Broadly speaking, however, the Unionists were known, and wished themselves to be known, as the party of empire; while the Liberals were supposed to be anti-imperialist.

The Big Englanders

The big Englanders, or the forward school of opinion were those who, generally speaking, believed in imperial expansion wherever possible. They were those ideologically opposed to Cobden and the Manchester School. Among them may be found the Jingoes (economic and philanthropic pressure groups, Radical and Tory Imperialists); the Moderate Forwards; and the Liberal imperialists.

Jingoism was no more than "the conventional label for a boastful and aggressive patriotism," applied rather indiscriminately by politicians to their opponents as a term of abuse. In general, advocates of expansion called themselves Imperialists, while their opponents dismissed them as Jingoes.[110] And the opponents of expansion called themselves Anti-Imperialists, while their opponents dismissed them as little Englanders. In reality jingoism and little Englandism, at their most extreme, were only representative of a tiny minority on either side. At the one extreme was Ashmead-Bartlett,[111] and at the other, Henry Labouchere, both of whom the House of Commons never took seriously.[112] But jingoism, as a broad political terminology, comprised a lot of influential politicians throughout the country. They were characterized, and often admired, by their forceful language, and their obsession with the maintenance of national honor and prestige. They would fight rather than knuckle down to threats; they would make no concessions without receiving an adequate exchange. They did not deliberately look for trouble, but were prepared to meet force with force. They believed in the effective de-

fense of the empire; they would be quite prepared to execute Palmerston's *Civis Romanus* policy without bother. All in all, fin de siècle
jingoism was a revolt against mid-century Manchesterism. Or as
Gladstone put it: its major characteristic was "no longer war fever,
but earth hunger."[113] It had its beginnings in the formation of the
Primrose League[114]—a league which has been described as "a scandal
to hard-headed positivism" which "cut clean across class lines."[115]
Jingo imperialism was commercial, excessively patriotic, sentimental,
and sometimes religious. They strongly believed that imperial expansion, especially in the neutral markets of the world, would restore
Britain to her former commercial preeminence. Indeed, it is difficult
to draw a clear distinction between the various types of jingoes. But
the missionary or philanthropic jingo was most concerned with his
propagation of Christianity and civilization, though he tended to be
happier if his pet tribe was under British rule, even if it had to be
subdued by force. Toward the end of the century, however, the influence of the humanitarians was on the wane. "It seems to me,"
wrote one M. P., "that the 'Times' attaches too much importance to
such communications (re. Slavery), as the Anti-Slavery Society is for
all practical purposes moribund, and its finances last year were allowed to drift into a hopeless state of confusion."[116] The mercantile
jingo reacted as the missionary jingo especially as he feared foreign
prohibitive tariffs. In west Africa particularly the "mercantile interests" were "very powerful."[117] The political jingo used the arguments
of the other two to advance his cause. He also impressed a gullible
public with talk of England's great imperial destiny and world
power. And like Rhodes would proclaim with absolute frankness:

> I might remark that the world is limited in size and that if you
> loze [sic] a piece of it by delay the chances are you will not get
> it back again . . . a piece of country[118] getting on the size of
> France is worth not lozing [sic].[119]

The military jingo justified annexations for strategic reasons—detect-
ing keys, real or imaginary, all over the world. These various groups
had powerful support in the country, among the captains of industry,
in the press, at court, in the empire at large, and even among the civil
servants.

The Moderate Forwards—undoubtedly the most numerous of
any particular group—represented by Salisbury, Goschen, Balfour,
Devonshire, Kimberley, Hicks-Beach, Ripon, Bannerman, and so
many other influential politicians of the day, believed in the empire
in principle, but advocated "sober," "sane," or "commonsense" im-

perialism.[120] They disliked the jingoes as much as they disliked the little Englanders.[121] To the jingo Salisbury showed no mercy; to the little Englander he gave cold comfort. In domestic, foreign, and imperial issues, Salisbury's characteristic caution was apparent. Sometimes he unsettles any fixed views we may have about him; occasionally, some enthusiastic little Englanders tended to deduce from his speeches traces of their creed and lavished praises on him.[122] But, in reality, the only thing he had in common with them was moderation in handling foreign difficulties; yet, this very group were loudest in accusing him of "graceful concessions." Salisbury's attitude to the empire and the new imperialism still baffles open-minded historians. Perhaps a few selections from his speeches may settle this point. He once described his attitude in the following words: "We are trustees for the British Empire." According to him such a principle should govern all government activities. Again, on imperial expansion he said:

> Therefore it is that we are all anxious above all things to conserve and to strengthen the Empire because it is to the trade that is carried on within the Empire that we look for the vital force of the commerce of this country.

And as early as 1870 when few showed any outward manifestations of interest in the empire, he not only supported Disraeli's imperial policy, but added:

> Where the English rule and English influence enter, peace and order revive, prosperity and wealth increase; and therefore it is that the prospect of English rule is welcomed by men of every race and every creed. Have we a right to throw away, to conceal in a corner, such an influence as this?

Compare these excerpts with his speeches cited elsewhere in this work, and one would agree with the contemporary who remarked of Salisbury:

> As a matter of fact he has not been against Colonial expansion *per se*, but only against the Palmerstonian policy of "fighting everybody and taking everything," which is calculated to incite foreign passions against us and to impose upon us responsibilities out of all proportion to our resources.[123]

In other words, one must not confuse means with ends. And to those who interpreted Salisbury's expansionist policy as no more than a concession to Chamberlain and the jingoes, *The Times* explained:

This curious error, which continental Conservatives and Moderates in different countries appear to share with the most bitter Radicals, is scarcely consistent with any knowledge of the series of brilliant and impressive speeches in which the late Prime Minister has, during the past quarter of a century, striven to develop the Imperial ideal.

"In Egypt and in the Sudan," *The Times* wrote, "in South Africa and in most of our other African possessions he has secured our rights for all time."[124] But in securing these rights he never employed the style of the jingoes. He detested imperial hooliganism, or indeed, hooliganism of any sort. "I am an utter unbeliever," he once said, "that anything that is violent will have permanent results."[125] Indeed his subtle defense of Britain's imperial interests led a disappointed Labouchere to declare in the Commons: "Lord Salisbury . . . [is] a jingo, but there [is] method in his madness."[126]

Perhaps the best explanation of Liberal Imperialism is that it was that kind of imperialism which believed in the maintenance and extension of the empire as a phenomenon of the times. In other words, the Liberal imperialist found it compatible to be a Liberal at home and imperialist abroad. Unlike the Tory imperialist, he would gradually train the dependencies to govern themselves. Unlike the little Englander, he was a neo-Palmerstonian: "a Palmerston—with nerves." But strictly speaking, he was not a jingo. He paid lip service to Home Rule and was not a dogmatic free trader. He would neither abolish it nor support an imperial *zollverein*, nor did he support imperial federation.[127] In general, he supported Salisbury's imperial policy but would have preferred him to have shown the positive attitude of Chamberlain. He was essentially a Liberal and had too much positiveness in his character to have been a Moderate Forward. Led by Rosebery, Fowler, Asquith, Grey, and Haldane, and popularly called the "Balliol Set," they were young, intelligent, influential; and on great imperial issues could muster nearly as much, and sometimes more, support than the Gladstonians.[128] Given the usually small attendance of the Irish contingent, they raised Salisbury's majority on such occasions permanently to around two hundred and fifty. Like the jingoes or little Englanders, they were a curious amalgalm of individuals joined together only by their belief in the integrity of the empire and in the establishment of claims for futurity.

Indeed, Morley's dismissal of Liberal imperialism as a "Chamberlain wine with a Rosebery label" had some element of truth in it. Campbell-Bannerman, for example, never seriously opposed the creed.[129] Nevertheless, imperialism made cooperation among Liberals impossible especially as they tended to see their disagreements in personal terms.[130]

The Consolidationists

Strickly speaking every politician toward the close of the century was, in a certain sense, a consolidationist. Not even the neo-Cobdenites advocated the dismemberment of the empire; not even the jingoes wanted unlimited expansion, whatever their opponents may have said. The difficulty was of course that, sometimes, to consolidate, it was found necessary to expand. It would have been a silly policy, for instance, to consolidate British hold on the West African coast while allowing the interior to pass into other hands. In the 1880s, when the possession of spheres of influence was more or less an admissible formula, such a policy might have made some sense. But by the 1890s when effective occupation and treaty rights took precedence over paper annexations, consolidationism, as a strategy of imperial expansion, lost its force. Yet, later expansionists could justifiably claim that they were in reality consolidationists since they were only making good claims already broadly established. The characteristic of the earlier consolidationists was that they feared the dangers of unlimited expansion.[131] They only differed from the Moderate Forwards in that the latter were aware that occasionally expansion and consolidation went hand in hand. By the nineties, however, the Consolidationists had been absorbed by them.

The Little Englanders or "Faddists"

"We are not quite sure that any British statesman ever deserved the name of 'little Englander,' convenient as the expression may be for the purposes of electioneering controversy," wrote the *Edinburgh Review;* "but we are certain that it was never applicable to the Liberal party as a whole, nor indeed to any of the great men who have led it." Indeed, at this period, "almost all British politicians, Conservatives, Fabians, and Liberals, proudly acknowledged themselves as 'imperialists.'"[132] Bannerman captured the spirit of the times when he observed: "We hear a good deal in these days about a thing called 'imperialism,' and everybody is contending with everybody else as to the best form of imperialism to profess." Gladstone was a Gladstonian—a free trader—and not a little Englander. He often talked Manchester and occasionally acted jingo. In that respect, the *Review* was right, and so was Bannerman. In a way, the anti-imperialists of the nineties were not little Englanders; neo-Cobdenites would perhaps be a better description. They did not preach the abandonment of the empire, but behaved rather like the consolidationists of the eighties. They were, however, the nearest thing to the mid-century Radicals[133]—people dismissed by Salisbury as "sentimental Radicals" and indeed "the truest Radicals" with "no clear and definite object to attain."[134] Led by Morley, Harcourt, Ellis, Labouchere, and Dilke, they constituted, even within the ranks of the Liberal party, a declining but vociferous minority. Sincere, passionate, idealistic, humanitarian, they lacked political genius, and were hopelessly inarticulate. They hated wars, restless egotisms, and pecuniary greed; they protested vehemently against "stock-jobbing Imperialism," farcical philanthropy, and fanaticism of any sort. And because Salisbury hated these things too, they, Harcourt excepted, erroneously believed that he was one of them and blamed his expansionist policy on Chamberlain, in whom they saw the embodiment of all their hates. But certainly they hated Chamberlain most because, by joining the Tories, he had stabbed his friends in the back, and had "sold his old true self to the devil." They were jealous of his successes; and since it was generally admitted that the public would go all the way with the colonial secretary, they did their best to discredit him politically. They saw the court, the aristocracy, and the military services as preaching expansion in order to enable them to bestow aristocratic patronage and practice nepotism, or as a means of affording some sort of outdoor relief for the upper classes. The money lavished on imperial expansion, they argued, could be put to better use at home. They were free traders and noninterventionists, first and last, and rallied round Gladstone. The political death of their leader after 1894 meant also a further dwindling of their influence.[135] The division lists of the period testify to this fact. By hanging on to "the carcases of dead politics," as Salisbury put it, they helped, unintentionally, to popularize imperialism, and to kill the old England to which Morley claimed he belonged. Little England, indeed, had proved to be "the euthanasia of the old England."

In England it was not unusual to regard them as cranks, faddists, lovers of foreigners, and advanced Radicals, who posed a threat to the empire, property, and the establishment. Even the newly enfranchised working classes voted Tory more than the little Englanders did; and were it not for the Celtic fringes wherein their leaders sought refuge, their political importance would have slumped more disastrously than it did. Indeed, by 1900 they were believed by some to comprise one-fifth of the Liberal party; and their stand on the empire was believed to be the cause of their decline.[136] Yet some of them—especially Dilke—were honest, unselfish, even patriotic—people whose niche was hardly politics, but without whom the House of Commons would have been unbearably dull. The outbreak of the

Boer War, though it sharpened the divisions in the Liberal ranks, did give the anti-imperialists a new lease of life.

The Monarchy and the Court

Any discussion of domestic factors affecting imperial expansion which excludes the monarchy and court is bound to be incomplete. After all, it was around the monarchy that the concept of empire centered. Until the seventies, however, Queen Victoria hardly identified herself with the empire. Nor did she participate in politics generally. After 1871, it is generally believed, her personal popularity and influence rapidly grew. She came out of her self-imposed seclusion and began to take an increasing interest in the affairs of state, to the chagrin of Radicals like Dilke and Chamberlain.[137] She upheld the external policies of Disraeli and Salisbury, and was a bitter opponent of that of Gladstone. In 1886 a great Colonial Exhibition—the so-called "Colinderies"—was held in London. It was a great success. Enthusiatically supported by the public, it yielded a profit of £30,000. The Colinderies's success and the Imperial Federation League's propaganda culminated in the holding of the first Colonial Conference in 1887 in London, which also coincided with the Queen's Golden Jubilee. These events identified the queen with the new imperialism, and according to Newton, signalled the "victory of imperialism over the public mind"—thus dashing the hopes for the Manchester School.[138] And she became in her life time, the legendary great white queen, not because she was the Queen of England, nor because she had vast connections in Europe, but because she was the head of a world-wide empire. She did not consciously seek to be a legend; but the situation must have been satisfying to her feminine sensibilities, and her conception of the honor and power of Britain. Hence she would see her empire extended rather than diminished. In 1890 she was unhappy about the Heligoland Exchange; in 1892 she wrote to Rosebery: ". . . the public at large will think we are going to pursue a policy of giving up everything and lowering our position . . . the difficulties are great doubtless in Uganda, but the dangers of abandoning it are greater." She was not a jingo in the accepted sense of the word; yet she admired Rhodes. On imperial disputes she upheld what one of her biographers has called "the doctrine of territorial compensation," that is, "that imperialist annexations by one Power justified similar annexations by other Powers." She believed it was England's mission to spread civilization and Christianity. Yet, curiously enough, she was lukewarm toward the missionaries. Like Salisbury, she preached caution in dealing with other powers over territorial disputes; above all, she advocated fair play: "It is I think important that the world at large should not have the impression," she wrote, "that we will not let anyone but ourselves have anything, while, at the same time we must secure our rights and influence." Occasionally, however, she would appear bellicose, but on reflection, would revert to her basic caution and moderation.[139] This was precisely because she had "the utmost horror of war, on the simple but sufficient ground that you cannot have war without a great many people being killed." Certainly she was a forward;[140] but, following the classifications used in this book she would come under the category of a Moderate Forward.

Like Salisbury, again, her main interest was external affairs. She insisted on being fully informed on imperial, foreign, and military matters. She was "the mother of Europe, and her influence was felt in most European countries"; her long experience of foreign relations proved to be of immense advantage in later years. During these years Salisbury was her friend and adviser. He treated her with deference, and came to rely on her assessment of foreign politics, and utilized the exceptional position she occupied in Europe.[141] Her influence in home politics was equally enormous, and she often interfered in ministerial appointments, and did not hide her antipathy to the little Englanders. She disliked Gladstone and expressed her uneasiness about entrusting her empire to an "old, wild, and incomprehensible man of 82½ [Gladstone]."[142]

If contemporary accounts were true, the court, as distinguished from the queen herself, must have been furiously jingo. The Prince of Wales was described as "a strong conservative, and a still stronger jingo . . . and wanting to take everything everywhere in the world." "Of course," wrote Harcourt from Balmoral, "the tone of the whole entourage here is of the most vehement Jingoism." The Royal Dukes, too, favored the assumption of imperial responsibilities.[143] In October, 1895 Salisbury directed that the Prince of Wales should be allowed to peruse all collections of telegrams received by, and sent from, the Foreign Office.[144] What influence, if any, he wielded as a result is not easy to determine. The monarchy and court may not have directly influenced imperial decisions, but certainly they wielded a great and indirect influence through their important connections in the City, in commerce and industry, in the military and naval services, in politics, and indeed, in the country at large.

To sum up: It seems to be a sacred cannon of British historiography that external affairs never had any decisive influence in domestic politics. By implication this means that domestic factors were never decisive in formulating external policy. The naivety inherent in this doctrine is the assumption that domestic and external affairs are separable. They are not nor should they be. It is not surprising, therefore, that imperial historians have not considered the examination of the interrelations between the two arms of government policy a worthwhile exercise. We have attempted to show in this chapter how Salisbury's handling of imperial expansion was influenced by the changing attitudes of Britons toward the assumption of imperial responsibilities.[145]

We argued that Salisbury would have been content to have adhered to his concept of pacific expansion had not other factors, international and domestic, combined to make such a course impossible. Once he became aware of this situation, he quickly adapted himself to the new course of things.[146] He was not opposed to the growing interest of his countrymen in Africa; on the contrary, he had helped to create the atmosphere for this interest. But what he did—and this was his great achievement—was to stabilize the new forces of imperialism and to prevent them from getting out of hand. Imperialism may have inherently appealed to the masses but the public was not responsible for the conquest of Africa. It merely accepted and encouraged, rather than initiated, the conquest. Salisbury was able to stabilize the new forces because of his great personal gifts, and because of his unassailable parliamentary and political position toward the close of the century. In the remaining two parts of this study we watch Salisbury's imperial diplomacy at work in strategic areas of Africa as well as the African and European reactions to it.

PART II

West Africa, 1865–1900

Chapter IV

The Struggle for the Niger, 1865–84

The River Niger is one of the great waterways of Africa and of the world. Along its banks have grown, over the centuries, some of the great civilizations that have today become a source of pride to black peoples all over the world. With its major tributary, the Benue, the Niger straddles West Africa like a gigantic letter "Y" from south to west and from south to east. The history of the Niger and the Benue is, in large measure, the history of West Africa. The struggle for the Niger, therefore, in the second half of the nineteenth century is a major movement in West African history. It is, in short, a study of the imperialism of conquest in West Africa.

It would be unhistorical to argue that the European powers had a calculated policy to conquer and administer the Niger states. On the contrary, Europe's energetic "quest for the course and termination of the River Niger" between 1788 and 1830 was motivated by geographical and commercial considerations. When, in 1830, the Lander brothers, Richard and John, proved to the outside world, if not necessarily to the West Africans, that the great Niger flowed into the Atlantic through the Bight of Biafra from the Fouta Jallon highlands, the event was greeted "as the greatest geographical discovery that has been made since that of New Holland."[1] But soon the geographical importance of this knowledge gave way, in the eyes of capitalist Europe, to its commercial implications. This is important, for the imperialism of conquest in West Africa is, in essence, the imperialism of commercial enterprises. Political domination was the inevitable consequence of the former.

The year 1830 has, therefore, been properly described as "the year of destiny" in West African history.[2] It marks an important stage in the European conquest of Africa. The discovery of the Lander brothers itself emphasized Europe's technological power, a power made possible by the industrial revolution which, ironically, was partly financed by the slave trade carried on predominantly in the Niger states.[3]

From 1830 to the end of the century the eyes of capitalist Europe were focused on the Niger and its hinterland. Britain, France, and Germany saw the river as a great highway of commerce which inevitably became a highway of the imperialism of conquest. Salisbury's very important role in the conquest of West Africa has never been emphasized. After considering the relevant background information, this part of the book will focus on this point.

The Aftermath of the 1865 Declaration

It has often been argued that between 1865 and 1895, Britain pursued a policy of indifference, and sometimes of scuttle, in West Africa. And yet it was precisely during this period that large chunks of the choicest territories in this part of Africa were added to the British Empire. The resolve shown after 1895 then, is significant only because of Britain's determination, even at the risk of war, to make good claims already broadly established. Many factors, as we shall see, were responsible for this forward policy. Official indecision before 1895 is not tantamount to a policy of scuttle. It can only be explained in terms of the complicated strategy of Victorian expansion.

Two main principles governed British policy toward West Africa between 1807 and 1865: namely, the suppression of the slave trade, and its replacement with "legitimate commerce,"[4] which was to be controlled by British entrepreneurs. The question then is whether Britain had a West African policy after 1865. Salisbury believed that there was a fixed policy up to 1895. This policy was characterized by control through commerical enterprise and informal influence.[5] The weakness of this explanation is that Salisbury failed to take into account European and African challenges which had driven Britain to shift its West African policy considerably. Far from pursuing a fixed policy Britain was, up till 1884, pursuing a policy of drift, responding here and there to African, French, and German initiatives.

The year 1865, however, was epoch-making in West African history. In that year, a select committee of the House of Commons recommended a partial withdrawal from this region and retrenchment in governmental expenditure. Much has already been made of this ambiguous report as influencing British attitude toward imperial expansion in West Africa for the next thirty years.[6] There is some truth in this. The report, however, was primarily concerned with retrenchment. On this issue, there was no division of opinion. But the incidental question of territorial withdrawal was regarded with reservation, not only by some members of the Committee, but also by the Foreign and Colonial Offices.[7]

This is hardly surprising, since the Committee's findings reflected more the Cobdenite views of Adderly[8] and Stanley[9] and their supporters than those of the witnesses it examined.[10] The Committee was not only hopelessly out of step with events in the west coast but was also openly prejudiced. In consequence, its positive influence lasted only a few years before it was overtaken by "the logic of facts."[11] Soon Foreign Office officials became convinced of the impossibility of standing by its tenets for, four months after the committee had reported, Lord John Russell made it plain that the protection of British traders would not be limited to the coast but should be extended to "the Oil Rivers . . . where a very valuable and increasing trade is carried on. . . . "[12] This view was later to be upheld by the earl of Clarendon who added 'that it would be impolitic to withdraw all protection and support from this trade at a time when it appears to be satisfactorily increasing and developing itself into a valuable commerce. . . ."[13] Nor was Lord Kimberley, the colonial secretary, disposed to discourage Governor Glover's attempts to open interior roads in the Lagos hinterland. On the contrary, he gave direction that "such a wise policy" should be approved: "I shall learn with much satisfaction," he wrote, "that he has succeeded in establishing a secure communication with the interior free from the interference of the Egbas."[14] But Kimberley, like the others before him, was not yet ready for any ambitious policy of expansion. The administrator of Lagos was further instructed to limit his activities to cultivating "friendly relations" with the Yoruba, to gradually "feel our way to direct intercourse" with the interior, "and not attempt to force on such intercourse by coercive measures."[15]

The report fared no better at the hands of the members of the new House of Commons which met in May, 1874. The Commons passed a motion, without a division (May, 1874): "That this House is of opinion that . . . it would not now be desirable to withdraw from the administration of affairs on the Gold Coast."[16] It must be borne in mind that the resolution approving the Committee of Inquiry which gave rise to the 1865 report was prompted by events in the Gold Coast and was carried with reference to them.

Consequently Carnarvon, now colonial secretary, initiated a policy in West Africa which has been described as a "New Course."[17] It was, in essence, a cautious repudiation of Adderley and Stanley. In March, 1874, A. W. L. Hemming produced a memorandum critical of the 1865 resolutions relating to imperial expansion:

> . . . with regard to the Resolutions deprecating any new acquisition of territory, it may be a question whether they were not violated in principle by the transfer of the Dutch Settlements in 1872, though on the other hand, it might, perhaps fairly be contended that this measure was one of those which were "necessary for the more efficient and economical administration of the Settlements we already possess."
>
> The fact is that the Resolutions were altogether vague and inconclusive, and while they declared it impossible for the country to withdraw from any of its engagements on the West Coast of Africa, they at the same time fettered the hands of H. M.'s Govt., and hampered its action in pursuing a firm and distinct policy towards the natives.[18]

The dilemma of the government was real enough. Nevertheless, a gradual and cautious, if haphazard and opportunistic, expansion was carried on in various forms, either by direct military intervention with a consolidationist aim in view, as in the Ashanti War of 1873, or by means of informal influence as practiced in the Oil Rivers, until the menace of other European Powers, coupled with the expansionist ambitions of certain African potentates, created a situation which demanded a positive policy on the part of Britain.[19] But before then the 1865 Resolutions, as a statement of official policy—which, in fact, they were not—had become a dead letter. They had been broken many times even before the Berlin Act of 1885 finally ended them. Had this policy been observed, Salisbury himself later said, "no addition whatever would have been made to the strip of territory then possessed by Great Britain upon the West African Coast."[20]

On the question of retrenchment too, the Report was never obeyed. Expenditure, instead of declining, did, in fact, increase.[21]

Did the resolutions therefore not have any influence on the future attitude of government toward West Africa? It would be wrong to hold such a view. For one thing, they gave rise to official indecision; for another, their influence was purely psychological. At a time when the country was faced by so many global questions of varying importance, it seemed natural that less attention should be paid to a region from which the House of Commons had recommended retrenchment. Any attempt to pursue a forward policy before the time was ripe was considered likely to lead to serious trouble. Parliament would either refuse to vote the money for such a policy, or the Treasury, which was Gladstonian in its methods almost to the end of the century, would simply refuse to recommend such an expenditure to Parliament. With its hands so fettered, the imperial government, for a long time, did not attempt to compete with the expensive military operations of France in the west of the Niger.[22] Instead, it opted for the safer "policy of advance by commercial enterprise."[23] Any effective military expeditions aimed at French encroachments could easily have been mounted from bases in the Colonies of the Gambia and Sierra Leone. But the revenues of these Colonies barely sufficed for their administrative expenditure; and any such policy would have placed an unbearable strain on their already fragile economies as Parliament could not be expected to sanction the use of British resources. The Asante expedition of 1873 was the exception to this pacific policy. Generally, however, it was thought safe to pursue a policy of drift so long as no major national interest was at stake. This policy was hardly as negative as it has been made to appear, for within its limits, Britain did make some substantial progress, while, at the same time, guarding the stability of the older colonies.

Attitudes change very slowly; and old views die hard. This was the point made by Salisbury in a speech in 1898:

> But you cannot so easily get rid of the *errors* [my italics] of the past. . . .
> When you have announced a policy of that kind of course the Departments of the Government and the representatives of the Crown in various parts of the world accomodate their course and their proceedings to that which has been laid down by the highest authority, and you cannot return from that error except after the lapse of a very considerable time. . . .[24]

By 1895 a new generation of men had grown up in the departments of Government and among the representatives of the Crown abroad, as well as among the ranks of the members of Parliament—uncommitted individuals who had no difficulty in shaking off what were considered errors of the past, and were ready to judge problems on their own merits.

This was also true of public opinion generally. Before the 1890s British public opinion could, at best, be described as not hostile to West African questions. Those interested in external affairs were, no doubt, aware that the slave trade in that region had been virtually suppressed, thanks, they were assured, to the philanthropic mission of their race; equally, they had learned that West Africa was unfit for European settlement: but as this knowledge could hardly have had any direct effect on their private lives, it would be surprising if they had shown any unusual interest in West Africa. The majority of the population were ignorant of these affairs. They were more interested in their social problems than in any schemes of expansion. The public may have relished small frontier campaigns; they may have even rejoiced over the smashing of this or that potentate; but the evidence tends to demonstrate that the majority had not the slightest idea of what the campaigns or little wars were all about. The public, therefore, offered no guidance to governments, especially in West African matters. When Clarendon wrote that "There is no care in this country for our African possessions (meaning West Africa). I believe that an announcement of intention to get rid of them would be popular,"[25] he was perhaps speaking the truth. But he was unsure of the foundation of his belief and was therefore compelled to do nothing about it. Such an announcement could likely have produced exactly the opposite effect. That underrated student of British opinion, Salisbury, looking back on this situation nearly thirty years later, was to remark: "It is one of the difficulties which the Foreign Office labors under that it has to represent the somewhat violent change from one policy to another."[26]

There was another reason why British governments held back from a vigorous interference in West African affairs. It was due to the understandable satisfaction resulting from their belief that, because they were in possession of most of the west coast their position was unchallengeable, and that given time, all opposition would fade away.[27] This optimism was also evidenced in the public's general attitude toward the empire. Well aware of the vast extent and might of this empire, the general public was disposed to dismiss as unthinkable any question of a war with a major European power for the sake of further territorial expansion: "why should there be war. We have enough, and to spare, of the earth's surface," was the way a contemporary described the reaction. Some were prepared "to help Germany, as one of the Teutonic family, to help herself to other peoples' belongings"; and, while others admitted that France's petulance over Egypt, West Africa, Siam, and Newfoundland was exasperating, they nevertheless believed that war with France or with any other nation was "unthinkable."[28] Later, when it became apparent that both France and Germany were challenging, not without success, England's imperial predominance all over the world as well as her economic superiority, this feeling of satisfaction was to be displaced by a kind of chauvinism which some Liberals found unbearable, but were disposed to regard as a temporary deviation from the national ethos.

It may perhaps be worthwhile, at this stage, to make a few observations on the reasons often given as to why British governments
held back from a forward policy in West Africa. First, there was the
unhealthiness of the climate. Certainly this was a factor. But it must
not be stretched too far. For one reason or another, contemporaries
were prone to exaggeration on this point.[29] In any case, this does
not explain the comparative resolve shown in some other tropical
climates. Second, it has been stated that there was no economic incentive to justify such a policy.[30] This, indeed, is surprising because
the argument totally ignores contemporary opinion.[31] Modern
scholars are prone to worship statistics and make comparisons.
There is perhaps nothing wrong in this; but nineteenth-century
trade statistics should not be taken on their face value for these figures are deceptive and untrustworthy and must be used with reserve.
They were calculated on *declared* values, and as has been pointed
out, "customs declarations are notoriously liable to be affected by
prevailing rates of duty."[32] Moreover, there has been a tendency to
compare—disadvantageously—African trade returns and investments generally with those of other European countries, or of the
United States of America, or even of India. But the conditions were
hardly similar. Such statistics, extracted from regions already ru-
ined and depopulated by the slave trade, and whose hinterlands
were as yet unexploited, and whose politics were in a constant flux,
are bound to be misleading. Very few businesses could afford to invest their money under such circumstances.[33] To trade with freedom
and advantage it was found necessary to govern. The politicians
concerned, without thinking that West Africa was an Eldorado,
knew this. Distinction, therefore, must be made between the existing economic reality and the anticipated economic reality. There
is scant evidence of any serious economic depression in West Africa, which Robinson and Gallagher claimed existed—except perhaps in the Gambia—in the 1880s.[34]

During the period when there was mounting parliamentary
criticism of these West African settlements, Palmerston still urged
the desirability of protecting their commerce, even if it meant the
use of "the Cudgels of a Police or the Sabres and Carbines of a Gen-
damerie." Admitting that "trade ought not to be enforced by Cannon Balls," he nevertheless was convinced that no successful commerical enterprise could be carried on without security, and that
that security was often unattainable without the employment of
physical force. Moreover, he went on:

It is not easy to put a limit upon the Resources which Africa
affords for advantageous commerce with England. Cotton,

Palm Oil, Groundnuts, Coffee, Ivory may be obtained in immense quantities, and of course in exchange for the Productions of British Industry. The advantages to be derived from a great Increase of our Trade with Africa, would infinitely counterbalance the small expenditure necessary for protecting that Trade in its infancy.[35]

Again, after 1895 the main reason for advocating a forward policy in West Africa was the great importance of its commerce, and because of rivalry for limited assets. Even before 1895 numerous British trading companies were operating vigorously throughout West Africa and, by the end of the century, had ruthlessly displaced the famed West African middle men. At the same time British traders, consular officials, and missionaries were systematically undermining the social, political, and economic structures of many West African polities.

Third, it has been argued that "the Foreign Office went on yielding to European rivals on the west, the better to defend the strategic interest on the Nile."[36] The vulnerability of this thesis has already been exposed by two important articles published a few years ago,[37] and should not detain us here.

One fact, however, remains indisputable. Between 1865 and 1895, the British government's attitude toward West Africa, in comparison to the resolve shown elsewhere, was indecisive and opportunistic. This was not because they considered the climate fatal, nor due to the lack of economic incentive, nor because the official mind was disposed to sacrifice the West African Empire for supremacy in the Nile Valley. It was primarily because of the uncertain reaction of public opinion, and because of the mistaken conviction that Britain's position on the west coast was strong enough, and therefore could effectively withstand foreign competition without any undue exertion on the part of the imperial Government. Before 1895, it had already become obvious to them that the position was changing to their disadvantage and that France had emerged as a major threat.[38]

European Challenge

Had other European powers not entered the race for the commercial penetration of the Niger states in the 1870s and 1880s, a race which was to develop into a scramble, Britain would have adhered to its policy of advance through commercial enterprise and informal paramountcy. Salisbury, particularly, would have continued his policy of pacific conquest until challenged, as inevitably he would have been, and indeed was, by West African potentates. The gradual extension of European trading activities into the hinterland after the 1860s was bound to start some trouble sooner or later. The French were moving steadily deeper and deeper into the valley of the Senegal and were planning to construct a railway between Senegal and the Upper Niger, and between Senegal and Algeria. The aim of this policy appears to have been to divert most of the Niger hinterland trade toward the areas of their influence thus placing British trading posts in a vulnerable position. This overt intrusion into what Britain rather arrogantly considered its natural preserve demanded some counteracting response.

Since 1830 Britain had established a commercial empire over the Niger Delta states, thanks to the discovery of the Niger and the efforts of the Royal Navy to stamp out the slave trade. By 1864 twenty-one British firms were operating in these states. By 1885 this commercial empire had become a political one and had been extended to include the Niger hinterland. The volume and value of the Niger trade during the period of informal hegemony was greater than that of the formal British colonies in West Africa—the Gold Coast, Sierra Leone, and Gambia. While legally the French could not—nor had they any desire to—challenge British suzerainty in these formal colonies, their action appeared to be directed against Britain's informal empire in the Niger states. But these were the areas where Britain was doing very good business. By 1878 four major British firms and numerous smaller ones and individual entrepreneurs were trading in the valley of the Niger. Fourteen steamers plied the river to the numerous British trading posts. They could now navigate the Niger upward to six hundred miles from the coast. At the same time the commercial war which had been raging since the 1850s between British traders, between them and the African middle men, and between the African middle men themselves, for the control of this trade, was becoming unbearable. Now the French and, later, the Germans appeared on the scene and began an unexpectedly purposive West African adventure.[39]

The French challenge to the British position in West Africa was mounted from Senegal. This was largely due to the energetic efforts of Louis Faidherbe, governor of Senegal (1854–61; 1863–65). Faidherbe, far from considering Senegal as important in itself, actually saw it as providing a springboard for the occupation of the Niger. The creation of a French Niger empire was his goal. Commercial expansion was only a prelude to the acquisition of such an empire. It was largely through his efforts that France secured complete control of the Senegal. With his departure in 1865 the idea of a French Niger empire was temporarily shelved. His successor,

Pinet-Laprade (1865–69), lacked Faidherbe's enthusiasm for empire and was content to pursue a cautious policy. This was also true of Colonel Valiere, Laprade's successor, who was especially ordered to extend French trade and not French political hegemony. The result of this policy was that neither Faidherbe's French colonial empire of the Niger nor even French commercial expansion made any substantial headway before 1876,[40] a vindication of Palmerston's and Faidherbe's axiom that commercial supremacy was impossible without political control.

The defeat of France by Prussia in 1871 and the loss of Alsace-Lorraine, however, helped to revive French enthusiasm for an African empire. The creation of the Commission for Scientific and Literary Voyages and Missions (1874) in the Ministry of Public Instruction emphasized this new attitude. It also marks the beginning of a new era of French exploration in Africa, and underscores the new ebulition of French public opinion with regard to imperial expansion. Hitherto France had not boasted of great African explorers; the big names had been predominantly British. It is significant, therefore, that in 1874 the French government sent out Pierre Savorgnan, a naturalized French citizen of Italian ancestry, on a mission to Ogooue. His great exploits (1875–79) were to become a model for subsequent French explorers.

This new attitude coincided with the governorship of Colonel Louis Briere de l'Isle (1876–81) in Senegal. It was this man who was to revive Faidherbe's Niger policy. He at once instructed his political adviser, Captain C. Boilève, to renew the policy of treaty making with Africans. This energetic policy culminated in the French occupation of Matacong, claimed by Britain, on March 14, 1877. This event marked the first serious French challenge to British influence in West Africa. But the French did not push their luck too far. On the contrary, desirous of avoiding a colonial conflict with the greatest sea power in the world, the French government discouraged any further expansion of its Senegalese colony in the direction of the Niger. This policy decision notwithstanding, Briere despatched Captain J. S. Gallieni, who had succeeded Boilève, to reestablish contact with the Tuculor empire now ruled by the eldest son of Al-Hajj 'Umar called Ahmadou. Gallieni's expedition led to the treaty of alliance signed at Nango (1881). He was not reprimanded by his government.

In spite of this treaty, however, Borgnis-Desbordes, head of the Haut Fleuve district from 1880 to 1883, was given permission by the French government to capture Bamako and surround Mourgoula where Emir Abdullah, a friend of France, was king. The occupation of Mourgoula was accomplished in 1882 without resistance. Between 1883 and 1885 Borgnis and his successor, A. Combes, extended French influence in western Sudan. It must be noted that Abdullah of Mourgoula, Mountaga of Nioro, and the other petty rulers of the states now being occupied by France were subjects of Ahmadou with whom the French had signed the accord of Nango. This was the normal strategy of the imperialism of conquest. Treaties were useful so long as they served the interests of the colonizers. The struggle between the great Samory Toure and the Sarakole marabout, Mahmadou Lamine, gave the French an opportunity to play the honest broker and, by 1885, Commandant H. Frey had extended French influence further east.[41]

By the early 1880s the French appeared to be threatening British influence even in the Lower Niger. In January, 1883 a French protectorate was proclaimed over Porto Novo. With the premiership of Jules Ferry which began in March, 1883, French expansion in West Africa became more aggressive. Cootenoo, Aghwey, Great Popo, and Little Popo were annexed. This was the beginning of the colony of Dahomey. These annexations closed the corridor between the British colonies of Lagos and the Gold Coast.

The Ministry of the Marine also was determined to support French traders on the Lower Niger in their conflict with British traders. Frequent naval visits to the Niger were being urged by French imperialists; and in 1883 a French military expedition managed to sign a treaty of protection with King Pass-All of Malimba. King Bell, who claimed to be Pass-All's overlord, warned the French that his country had a similar treaty with Britain, but he was ignored. The attempt, however, of the same expedition to renew the French commercial treaty of 1841 with Bonny was rejected by the king of Bonny.

This was not all. In August, 1883 the French entered the Niger Delta—traditionally Britain's preserve—once more and tried unsuccessfully to conclude a treaty which would have placed Brass, Britain's long-time enemy, under French suzerainty. The leader of the French expedition, Mattei, nevertheless, proceeded to Ibi on the Benue, secured a treaty, and hoisted his country's flag. Mattei also challenged the British in Nupe and dreamed of joining forces with Desbordes on the Upper Niger.

French traders, apparently spurred on by these activities, began a more spirited challenge. They operated twenty-five stations on the Niger, about as many as Goldie's National African Company. On the Benue the French had four stations and were trading farther upstream than the N.A.C. This was a development which began with the visit of Compte de Semelle to the Lower Niger in 1878. The visit marked the beginning of French intervention in this area. Its achievement was a promise given by Umoru, ruler of Nupe since the death of Masaba in 1873, of free French trading activities in his kingdom. Semelle also acquired land for his future trading stations; and on returning to France, formed the Compaignie Française de L'Afrique Equatoriale for the purpose. Although the British fore-stalled Semelle's plans, he had managed to set up stations at Aboh, Onitsha, and Eggar on the Niger as well as at Lobo on the Benue. Goldie's N.A.C. was, at the same time, trading in these areas. On Semelle's death the French War Ministry now entrusted the direction of his Niger operations to Commandant Mattei who quickly broke Goldie's monopoly in the Lower Niger and Nupe. French floating stations in the Lower Niger were reckoned at seventeen in 1882 and soon increased to twenty-five.

These developments caused alarm at the Foreign Office especially as it was well known that French merchants exercised much influence on their government's West African policy. Moreover, Britain considered France protectionist in its economic policy.[42] British reaction to the French challenge was dictated primarily by this consideration.

It was not only with the French that Britain had to contend. German entry into the struggle for the Niger caught everyone off guard. Surprisingly, a lot of work has been done on German enterprise in Africa;[43] it is surprising because German colonialism was short-lived, even if momentous, and Germany's African possessions inconsequential in comparison to those of Britain and France. The explanation probably lies in the German impact on Europe as a result of the two world wars, and in the career of Bismarck with his reputed aversion for colonial ventures. After the German victory over France in 1871, Bismarck was said to have boasted that Germany was a satiated power, that his map of Africa lay in Europe. He was, therefore, quite willing to spur "the steed of French ambition cascading in the sands of the Sahara" where he hoped they would find things "heavy going." Why then did Bismarck authorize a spirited German acquisition of African colonies in the early eighties?

A logical explanation for this volte face would be that Bismarck was driven to do what everyone else was doing; that Germany would lose nothing by participating in a free-for-all booty. But historians are not always logical animals. Various considerations therefore have been introduced to explain away Bismarck's action. First, it is believed that Bismarck acted merely because he saw colonization as a useful weapon against the Radical party during the elections of 1884. In other words, he was pandering to German public opinion.[44] Second, diplomatic historians argue that his action was determined by considerations of European policy. The leading exponent of this theory, A. J. Taylor, is convinced that German expansionism was anti-British in origin especially when Bismarck failed to forge a Franco-German entente; while others find the solution in the British occupation of Egypt in 1882.[45] Third, a proposition, now largely discredited, but not necessarily demolished, asserts that Bismarck's anticolonial posture was mere hot air; that his plans to make Germany into an African power were prepared long before 1884; and that he acted when the opportunity was ripe.[46] Fourth, a recent contribution to this debate repeats the well-worn view that no European nation—with the possible exception of Belgium and Portugal—cared for African colonies. At best they wanted protectorates, failing either informal influence or control through chartered company administration. This, it is submitted, was true of Bismarck. And as for his earlier antiexpansionist attitude, "a complex of economic and political considerations" forced him "to reconsider his position."[47]

Here again, Turner, like all the others, is merely begging the question. The motives behind Bismarck's imperialist venture, however, is not our primary concern. But it must be pointed out that all the prevailing arguments are circumstantial. We may never know why Bismarck acted in the way that he did. It is a pity that he was out of power during the Heligoland negotiations. Had he been in charge, we might have been in a better position to put the pieces together. What is a historical fact is that Germany intervened decisively against Britain in the scramble for Africa and added a new dimension to the imperialism of conquest. In West Africa this intervention complicated the struggle for the Niger and forced Britain to reconsider its West African policy.

Germany was not a newcomer to the Niger states in 1884. Since the 1830s German merchants from the Hanseatic ports had been carrying on a thriving business in Liberia, Togoland, Dahomey, Lagos, Cameroons, and Gabon. In Togoland a German evangelical mission from Bremen was gradually establishing its position. Commerce and Christianity went hand in hand, and between 1871 and 1883 exports from West Africa to Hamburg increased by 183 percent; while Hamburg's exports to West Africa increased by 560 percent. By 1883 German warships had also started making occasional visits to West Africa. In all these ventures Bismarck never showed any unwillingness to support German traders when under pressure.

This was particularly true of his dealings with merchants from the Hanseatic ports who were being induced to enter the *zollverein*. In June, 1883 Bismarck had made it clear to the French that he was prepared to support actively German merchants who were being bullied by Britain and France on the west coast. He not only ordered the warship *Sophie* to pay a visit to the Popos in Dahomey but appointed the famous explorer, Gustav Nachtigal, as an imperial commissioner charged with the responsibility of surveying the possibility of entering into treaty obligations with the chiefs. Indeed the German estimates for 1885–86 had provided for a resident consul in West Africa; and the Senate of Bremen had demanded a "trade-colony."[48]

If European powers were perplexed by Bismarck's actions in 1884 it was simply because they had accepted his public statements at their face value and had not bothered to anticipate the logic of his actions. The eventual annexation of South West Africa clearly emerged as a source of irritation to the Cape Colony. In West Africa, Nachtigal's mission was a challenge to British influence, especially as Bismarck had sounded Ferry's opinion with regard to Franco-German colonial cooperation. Declaring colonial policy as the protection of our fellow-country-men—a phrase calculated for domestic consumption—Bismarck ordered, in July, 1884, the annexation of Togoland, Cameroons, and Southwest Africa. Nachtigal accomplished his mission with unbelievable speed. The paper occupation of both Togoland and Cameroons was achieved in less than ten days!

The occupation of Togoland is particularly important for it marked Germany's first African colony. Ironically too, it was to breed ill feeling between Germany and France. Although it was of minimal significance to British influence, it forestalled any plans Britain may have had of claiming that area. In the delimitation accord of December, 1885, German Togoland included Porto Seguro and Little Popo, formerly under French influence. The occupation of the Cameroons caused more alarm in Britain largely because of events leading to it. The most important result of these annexations was that Germany had strong enough cards to play, as an African power, at the Berlin Conference.

British Reaction
British response to the European challenge was slow in coming but gradually became more purposive. Baffled initially—rather naively —by a challenge to the status quo, the British rose to the occasion in two ways: commercial competition and shrewd diplomatic negotiations.

Based on their four West African colonies the British had been moving gradually but steadily toward the hinterland. This does not suggest a policy of scuttle. Whatever the private opinions of some individual ministers may have been, the fact remained that there was no intention to carry out the 1865 recommendation. In the Lower Niger and Delta states particularly—the richest prize among the West African states—Britain was determined not to have a rival power. Shackled, however, by the decision of 1865, but not prepared to disavow it openly, governments were averse to a forward policy. This attitude remained valid as long as the numerous British traders had a free hand—unencumbered by African potentates and foreign powers—to carry out their enterprises. It is not surprising then that the consulate at Lokoja was closed down in 1869. The French challenge was still something in the future; the kingdom of Nupe was not hostile. In its place Britain looked to Nupe to provide the necessary protection for its traders.

The power of Nupe was substantial. Its Etsu (Emir) was a powerful monarch ruling a centralized state, possessing a standing army, and all the paraphernalia of a strong government. Given such a system, and granted the friendship of Nupe, British naval protection was considered unnecessary.

In June, 1871 the Foreign Office despatched W. H. Simpson to secure formal Nupe protection of British traders whose commerce in this area was prospering. Masaba, the Nupe king, fell for the bait because he reckoned on using the backing of these traders to consolidate his shaky throne. Masaba had been a friend of Dr. Baikie, the formulator of quinine (1854), and the first British consul at Lokaja. The policy of the British government pleased him particularly because, as he confessed to Baikie, he "could never sleep with gunboats in the river." Moreover he nursed ambitions of being the unqualified middleman controlling the trade of the western Sudan and Europe. Such a position would enable him to found a substantial Nupe empire; and since such an empire would serve the function of developing British trade in the Niger and Benue basins—which it did for awhile—Britain was prepared to pander to Masaba's dreams and a treaty was signed.[49] Britain however had other ideas of this sort of relationship, which would save money and unnecessary trouble; it would serve as a check against any French expansion from the Senegal to the Niger.

Southward, where Britain had allowed its traders to spread British influence to the hinterland, things were getting out of hand. It was not that the dazzling reward which they sought was not there, but that there were too many competitors for it. This, at least, was part of George Goldie's (George Goldie Taubman's) diagnosis of the situation when he arrived in the Niger Delta in 1877. Moreover these squabbling traders had taken no steps to deal with the growing French threat since 1874. Despite this threat Goldie knew that in reality, except for the British, there was no European presence between the Lower Niger and the frontiers of Tunisia and Algeria. He appeared more worried by the threats posed to British commercial hegemony by the trading states of the Niger Delta. He proceeded therefore, between 1877 and 1879, to secure the amalgamation of the rival British companies. He called the new company the United Africa Company. Lord Aberdare, formerly a government cabinet minister, was its chairman. This was a wise policy, politically motivated. Among the aims of this company were to end the excess competition which was throttling trade, to thwart French ambitions on the Lower Niger, and to supplant the monopoly of the African traders with that of the company. Goldie, the driving force behind these aims, was no humanitarian. An atheist, "who had fled England to escape from the sound of church bells," he was to become an imperialist par excellence, and partly realized in West Africa, his childhood dream "to color the map red."[50]

In June, 1882 Goldie reorganized the U.A.C. and renamed it the National Africa Company. His avowed aim, through a royal charter, was to acquire political power over the Niger states. But to do this he had first to eliminate the French challenge which had begun to cause alarm at the Foreign Office. Goldie at once entered into negotiations with the French commercial companies which were trying to break his monopoly. His aim was to absorb them into his own company. The negotiations lasted for six months and failed owing to "the patriotic scrupples [sic] of the French Directors." Goldie then threw down the gauntlet. A "severe competition" followed, and after fifteen months the uncompetitive French firms were forced to request "fresh interviews which resulted in the National Africa Company buying both of the French companies on most satisfactory terms."[51] Thus died French commercial ambitions on the Lower Niger.

Goldie's interest in Nigeria was first commercial, and then political. He recognized that the second was a sine qua non for the first. He knew that British position was unchallengeable in the Delta. That was why he directed his efforts to the hinterland. Here he began a policy of collecting treaties with African leaders by which they ceded their territories to the N.A.C. He employed twenty gunboats with which he bombarded recalcitrant African rulers. Goldie was ruthless and unscrupulous in his dealings. He tolerated no obstacles—African or European—to stand between him and his dreams of a Nigerian empire. By 1884 he had collected thirty-seven dubious treaties of protection,[52] and by 1886 the number had risen to 237.[53] Goldie therefore presented the British government with an interesting decision to make.

Goldie also secured British interests against the Germans. True, the German firms in Guinea did not pose any serious threat to British commercial dominance. But in Northern Nigeria, the Germans nearly pulled off a surprise paper annexation similar to their earlier exploit in the Cameroons. It was Joseph Thomson, the N.A.C. representative, who checkmated them in 1885.[54]

Goldie had performed an invaluable job for Britain. Salisbury, and later Earl Granville, the liberal foreign secretary, though they offered him no open support, were nevertheless unprepared to discourage him from carrying the burdens of empire in Nigeria. Indeed he suited their purpose. Goldie, too, would have had little success were he not convinced that the metropolitan power would eventually come to his rescue. Even if ministers were unwilling to do so—which was most improbable—public opinion would have forced their hands. It is, therefore, wrong to argue that Goldie was acting purely independently. On the contrary, through diplomatic initative and consular activities, British governments wanted to maintain British paramountcy. And at the Berlin conference Goldie's and the consular treaties proved invaluable for claiming the Niger.

On the diplomatic front, British reaction was shrewd, quiet, and determined. Contrary to popular belief, Salisbury, who was British foreign secretary from 1878 to 1880, did not ignore the French challenge. If he moved slowly and cautiously, looking over his shoulders, it was because of the factors we have already discussed. The entry of France in the Lower Niger, if unchallenged, would dislocate the status quo. This development thus placed the imperialism of conquest in a broader perspective. The aims of traders might be primarily local but a good diplomat and politician must take other factors into account. Advance by commercial enterprise would, without imperial backing, yield doubtful dividends; pacific conquest had proved a nonstarter and illogical as, indeed, it was bound to be. A new strategy had to be devised, and it was. Britain now had to reckon with the existence of other powers, and, through quiet diplomacy, to carve out for itself as much of West Africa as it could for future use. On no account, however, would the states of the Lower Niger be sacrificed.

As far back as 1868, England and France were engaged in frontier difficulties on the West African coast before they were in contact in the hinterland. Negotiations were opened in 1870 to settle these differences on the basis of mutual concession of territories. The outbreak of the Franco-Prussian war halted these negotiations. They were resumed in 1876. It was then definitely proposed that the Gambia should be ceded to France in exchange for the posts she held "between the Rio Pongoas and the Gabon." Parliament and various mercantile bodies in Britain united in opposition to end what would have been an intelligible and comprehensive settlement.[55] Britain had no intention of fobbing off Gambia to France without a substantial quid pro quo. The aim of Britain's offer was to divert the French away from the Lower Niger. Moreover the outcry over small Gambia served notice to succeeding British administrations that the British people would not tolerate any tampering with the integrity of the empire.

In 1878, Salisbury, hitherto secretary of state for India, for the first time was brought into direct contact with affairs in West Africa of which he knew little. Suspecting the undependability of British opinion, he found it necessary to pursue a cautious policy aimed at preventing a head-on collision with any major power, especially France. He expressed to Lord Lyons, British Ambassador to France, his anxiety "to work with the French everywhere."[56] But this was the period when Britain's "prancing proconsuls" were beginning to display an aggressive spirit in the slave coast and around Porto Novo. Governor Glover's policy of expanding the Lagos protectorate aimed at incorporating, under his sphere of authority, the Yoruba empire of Oyo which had disintegrated since Kakanfo Afonja's successful rebellion. His plan entailed expansion not only toward the hinterland of Lagos but also westward along the coast to Porto Novo. The governor of the Gold Coast was also planning to expand eastward to Porto Novo. Both governors had their eyes on the customs revenues from the ports of Dahomey. A successful execution of this policy would have linked together the British colonies of Lagos and the Gold Coast.

By July, 1876, Commodore W. Hyde Hewett, with the approval of the British cabinet, had blockaded Dahomey as a punishment for the "diabolical practices" of King Gelele. This action had greatly alarmed French agents at Whydah especially when it became clear that Hewett's blockade was meant to extend from the Gold Coast to Lagos. The combined opposition of Gelele and the French led to the lifting of the blockade. The French nevertheless remained suspicious of British aims, and shortly afterwards they claimed Kotonou. Governor Rowe gave notice of Britain's intention to collect customs duties in the Scarcies. France responded by claiming Matacong.[57]

Now it was Britain's turn to be apprehensive. Lord Lyons interpreted the French actions as "checkmating our policy on the African coast" so as to "force us to reopen negotiations for an exchange of territory."[58] Apparently in retaliation for French moves an enthusiastic Governor called Ussher—and not Governor Rowe as Salisbury thought—without orders from home, annexed Ketenou (Katanu). And Salisbury's diplomatic plan was in ruins. He wrote angrily to Lyons:

> Governor Rowe [*sic*] has had no better occupation for his spare time than to annex some place, with an unrememberable name, near Dahomey on the Lagoon.
> Really these proconsuls are insupportable. I believe it is a reply to the annexation on the part of the French of some other place on the coast: the object of both powers being, in promotion of commerce to acquire the means of blockading Dahomey by Customs Duties.
> I have implored the Colonial Office to recall Governor Rowe, but if the French should raise the question (they will probably tell you the name which I have forgotten) the best way of treating it will be to throw out the idea of coming to some arrangement as to infliction of penalties on the king of Dahomey, whenever his impulsive nature shall require it.[59]

I have quoted this famous passage in full so as to present its significance in perspective. It has often been used to show Salisbury's lack of interest in West Africa.[60] Ussher (not Rowe) was asked to be recalled not because he annexed a territory "with an unrememberable name," but because he acted without instructions. In fact he was not even recalled but only censored for "unauthorized and dangerous exercise of power." It was one of Salisbury's beliefs that only those elected by the people had the right to make decisions—especially those decisions likely to lead to explosive situations.[61] If proconsuls were allowed to act like Ussher, he feared that a dangerous situation might arise; and he was not sure how the public might react, especially with respect to serious diplomatic complications which "produce resentment on the part of that Power with whom, more than any other, it is the interest of this country to live on terms of friendship."[62] It must nevertheless be noted that Salisbury had no intention of withdrawing unilaterally from the occupied territory without first establishing the legitimacy of the French claims.

That, in fact, was the object of the next letter to Lyons. The British ambassador was instructed to find out "what is really the temperature of the French Foreign Office on the subject." If they possessed any fair claim to the territory, Salisbury was prepared to evacuate just as the French had done over Matacong. But although he objected to the policy of retaining a hold over Dahomey, he warned that

> hauling down our flag and handing back territories to a native Power is apt to be mistaken in these parts. I should therefore be loth to accede to the present French demands unless in your opinion a serious irritation was likely to be the result of our refraining from doing so. It must be remembered that they began the grabbing by taking *Kotonu*, and therefore a more equitable way of settling the matter will be to adjust all these West African questions at once—Matacong-Scarcies-Kotonu—and Katanu; and this, subject to any opinion you are led to form, is the policy I should propose to follow.[63]

Here is a typical justification of that shrewd remark: "Refusals to annex are no proof of reluctance to control."[64]

About a month later Salisbury hinted at the desirability of settling "our African difficulties which required an early and general adjustment" as well as the Newfoundland question.[65] Salisbury valued Lord Lyon's opinions. While the ambassador wished that "the Proconsul (Ussher) had been sacrificed to the Manes of the King of Dahomey's Grandfather before he added a new difficulty to our relations with the French navy department," he nevertheless acquiesced in the policy sketched out by the foreign secretary. He only regretted that the "House of Commons is so intractable about the Gambia."[66] Further investigations were to show that the fuss engendered by Ussher's presumption was out of proportion to its expected consequences. M. Waddington, French Foreign Minister, occupied with French internal politics, showed no irritation over Ketenou. In fact, the exact demands of the French were not known. Nor was there any suggestion that the British should evacuate, at any rate for the present.[67] In fact, the proposal for a general settlement of these West African problems was temporarily abandoned.

Until public opinion began to show some interest in West Africa—largely due to Chamberlain and the French—Salisbury was disposed to pursue a vague and opportunistic policy. Occasionally, however, he displayed some degree of firmness, as when, during the Anglo-French negotiations on the Newfoundland fisheries question, he instructed Lytton, now British ambassador in Paris, to give no ground to Ribot. He feared that the French foreign minister would

> try to Bargain for some African equivalent—evacuation of Egypt, Tripoli, Something in Tunis—or even the Gambia. But

I would not allow him for a moment to believe that such propositions will be listened to. We at least cannot go on with a policy of Exchange; and he must understand that this negotiation must be confined wholly to Newfoundland. . . .[68]

Coming from a man whose West African policy since 1882 was supposed to consist in yielding ground to the French in order to safeguard Britain's position in Egypt,[69] this quotation is important. It adds more weight to the view that the repercussions of Britain's occupation of Egypt have been stretched unnecessarily far.

By 1880 the two major African issues with which Salisbury was confronted occurred in Egypt and West Africa. In neither case did he pursue a forward policy; nor did he pursue a policy of scuttle. On the contrary, he was determined to maintain the status quo. In West Africa, particularily, this policy suited him because here the status quo favored his country. Moreover since the Paris Congress of 1878 he had been cultivating cordial relations with France. The French, on their part, were anxious to reciprocate this friendship, but events in West Africa were drawing the two countries apart.

The Gladstone ministry of 1880–85 did not substantially reverse its predecessor's reaction to the European challenge. With regard to African problems, up to this period, British governments had spoken in the same idiom. Convinced of the superiority of their resources in the Niger over the French, they had bristled with confidence in dealing with any threat. When Kimberley, Gladstone's colonial secretary, was warned of the French plan to connect the markets of Hausaland and those of Senegal, he reacted with confident complacency: "We shall get to the Hausa country via Lagos long before the French,"[70] This was hardly an antiimperialistic sentiment. Were he opposed to the scheme of British entanglements in West Africa, his natural response would have been: "To hell with the markets of Hausa country." And yet, "Gladstone's second administration," we are assured "was totally devoid of imperial ambitions in West Africa."[71] The fact remains, however, that this administration did not abandon Gambia despite V. S. Couldsbury's depressing account of his expeditions there between January 22 and April 21, 1881. Couldsbury had undertaken this expedition to forestall further French expansion in the western Sudan but was himself forestalled by the French, aided by natural disasters.[72] Sierra Leone was not sacrificed; and this ministry took practical steps, as we shall see, to secure British paramountcy on the Lower Niger. This was, in part, what Harcourt meant when he ridiculed the so-called antiimperialistic posture of this government.

Far from pursuing a policy of disengagement in West Africa, Granville reopened the 1876 negotiations which were abandoned due to the opposition of British public opinion. He must have realized that for any future negotiation to be fruitful it must produce results acceptable to the public. In 1881, therefore, commissioners were once more appointed to settle Anglo-French differences. This resulted in the convention of 1882 which, as far as demarcation was concerned, was limited in its objectives. It merely settled questions in regard to the drainage area of certain rivers in Sierra Leone by mutual concessions. But it also gave Britain complete control of the Scarcies, and France that of the Mellicourie, rivers. This time, however, the Convention was not ratified due to the hesitation of the French chambers. The respective governments nevertheless observed its stipulations.[73]

As a result of purposive French activities in the Niger and Congo region, Britain was also driven to act to maintain its permanent position in West Africa. Brazza's famous expedition to the Congo had resulted in the acquisition of treaty rights with the African kings. These treaties were ratified by the French chamber and this was the beginning of the French colony of Brazzaville. The French initiative not only undercut King Leopold of Belgium's expectations in the Congo but also drove the Portuguese out of the Congo altogether. Portugal appealed to Britain for support. Britain laid down rigid conditions for this support, among which were, first, British rights to levy duties on the trade of the Congo; second, the appointment of an international commission to supervise the navigation of the Congo; third, a demand that Portugal compensate Britain elsewhere; and, as one official put it, the British scratched their heads "to think of all the things we can ever want from Portugal in Africa."[74] This stiff attitude drove the Portuguese to revive the old idea of a Franco-Portuguese partnership in Africa in which the French were naturally interested. Nothing, however, came out of this idea. Nor did the Anglo-French Portuguese Treaty of February 26, 1884, by which Britain guaranteed "to prevent either France, or an international syndicate directed by France, from occupying the mouth of the Congo" count for much. At the Berlin Conference of 1884–85, it was Belgium and France, and not Portugal, whose rights on the Congo were, one would be tempted to think by the hand of Providence, internationally recognized. Driven from this very important region of Africa which it had desolated for centuries, Portugal was forced to retain Angola which it had been attempting to colonize since the eighteenth century.[75] For our immediate purposes, however, what is important is the fact that a much vaunted antiimperialistic British administration, "unimpressed by the dingy annals of the west coast,"[76] had proved to be such a tough bargainer in, and utterly Machiavellian in its approach to, West African questions.

In the Lower Niger the British government was also toughening its imperialistic posture. By April, 1883 the idea of British protectorates in this region was circulating in the Foreign Office.[77] In the same year an African Department of the Foreign Office was created and placed under the competent direction of H. P. Anderson. Between 1883 and 1896 Anderson remained the undisputed boss of this department[78] and was largely responsible, together with Salisbury, for mapping out the strategy of the imperialism of conquest. Anderson's first important memorandum on the West African question suggested the British acquisition of the Oil Rivers before dealing with the French.[79] By the close of 1883, the cabinet had endorsed Anderson's strategy. Hewett was dispatched to the Niger and Cameroons to secure treaties of protection with the African rulers.[80] The aims of this mission included also the smashing of the Niger middle men and the keeping out of the French from the Lower Niger. It was not, however, until May 1884 that all the necessary documents were prepared.[81]

But how serious was the French threat in the Lower Niger by 1884? Indeed not serious at all. They never seriously intended to displace the British in this area. The odds were immensely against such a policy. By 1884 Goldie had bought out the French companies and was in a formidable position. British gunboats had blasted Idah and Aboh in October, 1883 simply because they were suspected of being friendly with the French. This display of gunboat diplomacy demonstrated to the French where power actually lay. Even before the Hewett mission became a reality, the French were aware—even if the British were not—that their future on the Niger was doomed. The new French policy on the Niger was to use whatever influence it possessed "to bargain for political neutrality of the river and equal rights for trade." But the Foreign Office would only entertain this policy "at the price of sacrificing substantial French interests elsewhere in Africa."[82] This is interesting for even after the British occupation of Egypt it was the French, not the British, who regarded their Niger possessions as expendable. France knew it could not afford the luxury of risking Britain's disfavor. M. Courcel, French Ambassador to Berlin, bluntly told the German Foreign Minister in 1884 that "not even the support of Germany and her allies could protect us against all the difficulties which England might create in all parts of the world if she were moved by feelings of real hostility towards us."[83] In short France was not prepared to make things difficult for Britain anywhere for fear of severe retaliation. Indeed France had already conceded the Lower Niger to Britain by 1884.

If the odds favored Britain in the Niger, they were to be against her in the Cameroons. The story of how Nachtigal, the German commissioner for West Africa, beat "too late Hewett" to the race for the Cameroons is well known. What is curious has been the attempt to see the indecision which led to the loss of the Cameroons as demonstrating British lack of interest in the acquisition of African colonies. If Britain placed a low priority on the Cameroons, it had every reason to do so. No one anticipated that the Germans would grab it in 1884. The Hewett mission was intended to forestall a possible French challenge and promote British trade. The Cameroons was under informal British consular power. It was neither particularly rich nor significantly strategic. There is no reason therefore why this country should be selected to test the degree of British interest in African territories. And in any case it was generally regarded as forming part of the British sphere of interest. What is significant was that the German action proved conclusively to the British government that the days of informal hegemony were gone. A "legal" title to a territory—however dubious—coupled with "effective occupation"—however tenuous—alone conferred international respect.

Britain learned its lesson the hard way. The loss of the Cameroons caused it to open a new phase in its West African policy. Between July 14 and the end of August, 1884, Hewett had collected numerous treaties of protection in the Delta and Lower Niger.[84] Goldie, as we saw, had also secured similar treaties in his areas of operation. At the Berlin West African Conference which followed soon afterwards, British delegates had little difficulty in persuading the powers to recognize British ascendancy in the Delta and Lower Niger states. By 1885 then, the first phase of the struggle for the Niger had gone in Britain's favor. It had claimed, and got, the important portions of West Africa while France and Germany were left with the remnants.

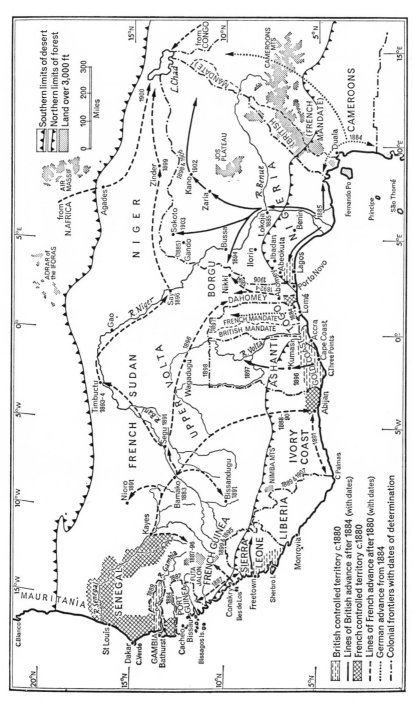

The European Advance into West Africa

Reprinted from *The History of West Africa*, by J. D. Fage, by permission of Cambridge University Press. © 1969 Cambridge University Press.

Chapter V

The Struggle for the Niger, 1885–97

The Berlin West African Conference is a landmark in world history. Its major significance, however, is apt to be overlooked. In her detailed study of this conference,[1] Crowe has competently demonstrated that it did not partition Africa,[2] nor was it noteworthy in international law. Far from ensuring free trade in the basins of the Congo and the Niger, the aftermath of the conference ushered in an era of strict trade monopolies. Far from internationalizing the center of Africa, it Belgianized it. The conference was vague as to the slave trade as well as to the lofty humanitarian idealism which was said to have animated it. And the much vaunted resolutions concerning effective occupation were "as empty as Pandora's box."[3]

This important study also asserts that the conference, although anti-British in origin, was "a diplomatic triumph" for Britain because it resulted in the breakdown—for good—of the Franco-German entente—the entente which was, in large measure, responsible for summoning the conference in the first place.[4] Egypt was hardly mentioned at the conference and Crowe's study does not support the view that Germany used the occupation of Egypt to blackmail Britain. On the contrary, it casts doubt on the diplomatic genius of Bismarck since the great chancellor in the end upheld the reverse of his earlier intentions.[5] Equally importantly, it was an Anglo-French combination which weakened the doctrine of effective occupation. Germany, being new in the field of African colonization, argued strongly for effective occupation while Britain and France, both as old hands in the business and as the first and second colonial powers respectively, stood to lose by its strict application.[6] It is, therefore, incorrect to interpret British and French earlier inclination to exercise "authority" rather than "jurisdiction" as evidence of disinterestedness in colonial acquisitions. Germany, nevertheless, achieved something significant at Berlin. As a result of its aggressive intervention in Africa, it killed the Anglo-French "Monroe doctrine" for Africa. Given the force of European nationalism in this period and the interplay of European power politics, the doctrine had no chance of permanence. It is to Salisbury's credit that he grasped this point clearly and decided to share control. Unfortunately, many historians have failed to grasp this point as clearly and consequently have tended to play down, even to the point of cynicism, Salisbury's great contribution to the European conquest of Africa.

Important as it is, Crowe's study is an exercise in European diplomatic history and has little to say about the implication of the Berlin Conference for African history. This raises two questions: Should a history of the Berlin Conference ignore its African dimension? Should an attempt to analyze this dimension be dismissed as moralizing which is outside the competence of the historian? For the African historian these questions are naive, irrelevant, and hypocritical. We are dealing with a conference concerned with the future of Africa, not of Europe, and yet Africa only appears incidentally in our analyses! The Berlin Conference is the culmination of Europe's desire—since the beginning of European expansion in the seventeenth century—to impose by force, if need be, its collective will over those of the non-European world, to export its culture and civilization, and above all, to exploit the resources of the world. Africa happened to provide the best classic example of this ambition. The Christian church did not question the ethical basis of the conference. Both during and after the conference, no one was outraged in Britain. Parliament did not consider it necessary to debate the issue. Similar reactions also occurred in other European countries. What should have been exposed as an overt and contemptuous act of international brigandage was instead glorified as "the white man's burden." This brings me to the second question. Should a historian pass judgment on the ethics of empire? The prevailing conviction, in relation to Africa, is negative. But this is odd since European history itself is replete with moral paradigms. Even the belief in the white man's burden is a moral or ethical judgment. The very nature of the historical discipline makes a moral position, a point of view, inescapable.

West African Response to the European Conquest
After the conference, European nations, armed with a new code of conduct called the Berlin Act, proceeded to partition and conquer the African continent. How did West African states respond to this challenge?

The problem of African resistance to European imperialism has become an important theme of African history only in the last couple of years.[7] The myth that European soldiers marched through most of African states, never seriously hindered, has been exploded. There is however a danger that this myth may be replaced by another: that of tremendous African military resistance. A further myth which has been exploded is the view that resistance was a futile, gallant anachronism while collaboration was a sophisticated, rewarding exercise.[8] It is now clear that nearly all African states collaborated when they had to and fought only in the last resort. Recent collaboration and resistance studies however lack a theoretical model and for very practical reasons concern themselves with centralized states.

African collaboration and resistance followed the classic game theory employed by the mathematical sciences. The nonzero-sum game is the classic collaboration theme. Here there is a basis for collaboration because of the mutual advantages to be derived from such an indulgence. The zero-sum game is the classic resistance theme. Here the basis for collaboration is lacking because of a clash or a conflict of interests. In either case, however, each party is struggling to maximize its advantages and minimize its disadvantages. But collaboration often led to conflict and conflict might result in collaboration. The question then arises whether it is correct, as is the practice, to categorize some African states as resisters and others as collaborators. Such a categorization is valid provided the time factor is clearly delineated. In other words, it can be stated that state A collaborated between, say, 1840 and 1884 and resisted between 1885 and 1900; or that state B resisted between 1840 and 1884 and collaborated between 1885 and 1900. But it would be wrong to categorize A as a collaborator and B as a resister. It must also be pointed out that collaboration did not necessarily involve a willingness to surrender sovereignty to an invading European power. It was more often seen as a way of ensuring the preservation of that sovereignty.

Nowhere in the nineteenth century was this game theory more pertinent than in the European confrontation with West African states. During the era of informal influence in West Africa[9] the game theory worked beautifully. The slave trading states resisted abolition; the weak states needed European protection against their stronger neighbors. The structural instability of most of these states made it difficult for the metropolitan powers to maintain their territorial integrity in the face of the European impact since some of their components, themselves earlier victims of African imperialism, readily collaborated with Europeans for the purpose of regaining their independence. States which failed to observe the antislavery treaties were shelled by European gunboats although the Europeans constantly failed to observe their treaty obligations when it suited their interests not to do so. The result in such cases was that the collaboration model broke down and gave way to military resistance. Increasing interference by European consuls in the affairs of African states entangled them in domestic politics and before they knew what was going on they found themselves the potent power in such states. The establishment of commercial enterprises and the scrambling of the missionaries for African souls aided the erosion of the authority of the African rulers. A power vacuum was thus created; and to fill this vacuum so as to protect trade and safeguard the missionaries, it became necessary to annex. By 1885 most of the states which had come into contact with Europeans had already been so undermined that a military conquest did not present an insurmountable obstacle. In the period before 1885 military resistance was the exception rather than the rule; in the period after 1885 the reverse was the case.

The military union called the Asante empire provided a unique exception to this general hypothesis. Asante resisted the imposition of British rule throughout the nineteenth century. Between 1823 and 1900, the Asante fought eight engagements with the British, losing six of them and winning two. Six of these engagements and the two Asante victories occurred between 1823 and 1874. It was the Asante-British War of 1873–74 that finally broke Asante power. The wars of 1896 and 1900 were not wars strictly speaking but punitive expeditions.[10] By an imperial order-in-council of September 26, 1901, Asante was annexed to the British crown. The order declared unequivocably that the country had been "conquered by Her Majesty's forces." Another order-in-council of the same date annexed the Northern Territories of the Gold Coast.[11] The Fante, Asante's cousins to the South, provided an instance of the numerous cases in West Africa where collaboration turned to resistance, and where the need for collaboration in the first place was dictated by fear of annexation by a stronger and more aggressive neighbor. By 1867 the Fante, realizing the futility of collaboration, made a bold bid to free themselves from Britain. British reaction was swift and decisive. King Aggrey of Cape Coast was exiled to Sierra Leone for leading this resistance. By 1874 the Fante confederation, formed in 1868, was dissolved and annexed together with the rest of southern Ghana to the British empire.

The establishment of a settler colony at Free Town between 1787 and 1807 meant that sooner or later the colony must expand northward if it was to survive. For over a century, however, Britain pursued a cautious policy of expansion, gradually restricting the authority of the hinterland chiefs without controlling their affairs. But in 1896, as a result of spirited French activities in the hinterland, Britain declared a protectorate over what is today called Sierra Leone. And since Sierra Leone was to bear the expense of its administration Governor Cardew (1894–1900) found it necessary to impose a Hut Tax. Now to tax an African was to spell out to him clearly his loss of sovereignty. The resistance of Chief Bai Bureh of Kasseh should be understood against the background of the declaration of the protectorate and the Hut Tax. Bureh, a renowned warrior, achieved what few African states achieved in the nineteenth century: he united the chiefdoms of Temne against the British. Bureh's resistance was well disciplined and organized and, despite the smallness of his forces, provided the British occupation of Sierra Leone with a tough opposition. He was eventually beaten and exiled.[12] Bureh's resistance, or what Cardew called the Hut War, was another instance of the futility of collaboration and peaceful coexistence.

In the western Sudan Afro-French relations also demonstrated the futility of collaboration. The celebrated resistance of the great Samory Toure was resorted to after Samory had humiliated himself in a vain attempt to avoid a conflict. By 1885 it had become clear to him that collaboration with the French was doomed to fail because France now wished to be master of the western Sudan. By 1888 he had reorganized his army and adopted the European model of infantry warfare. When the expected confrontation took place he waged a total war. He mobilized the masses, adopted guerrilla tactics, and pursued a scorched earth policy. He was captured in 1898 and exiled to Gabon where he died in 1900.[13] In Senegal, the *damel* of Cayor, Lat-Dior, fought against the French for three years. He, too, had started off collaborating with the French and was acclaimed as a "modernizer." But then when Faidherbe attempted to replace him with a puppet he had resisted him. And when the successors of Faidherbe offered him generous terms, he once more collaborated with them. But finally when it became clear that collaboration was eroding his sovereignty he fought to the death in 1886.[14] The short-lived Sarakole empire of Mahmadou Lamine was founded in Senegambia as the result of the movement to rid the Sarakole of French and Tukolor imperialism. In the beginning Lamine had extended the hand of friendship to the French while, at the same time, he was consolidating his empire at French and Tukolor expense. He started his operations against the French when they were fighting against Samory and Senegambia was denuded of troops. Ahmadu, ruler of the Tukolor empire, engaged in suppressing the rebellion in Kaarta since 1884, was not strong enough to challenge Lamine. The French were forced to stop temporarily their operations against Samory in order to deal with Lamine. The Tukolor, though they were resisting French expansion, decided to ally with the French to remove the Sarakole threat. The allies attacked Lamine in March, 1886, but it was not until December, 1887, that he was defeated at the battle of Toubakouta. Lamine managed to escape from this battle but was later found dead in mysterious circumstances. The death of Lamine ended his empire and ensured French supremacy.[15]

Formal Franco-Tukolor alliance began, as we saw in the previous chapter, with the accord of Nango. This was the culmination of the policy initiated by the *Jihad* leader, Al-Hajj 'Umar, founder of the Tukolor empire, in 1848. He had promised the French free movement in his empire in return for a monopoly over the purchase of French arms. Nothing came of this proposal because the French feared that a well-armed 'Umar would pose a dangerous threat to the French coastal settlements. 'Umar died in 1864 but his policy of exchanging guns for trade remained unchanged. The accord of 1881, however, was short-lived. In their bid to establish a Sudanese empire, the French violated Tukolor territorial integrity by seizing Kitar (1881) and Bamako (1883) as well as other petty states tributary to the Tukolor. And yet because of fear of the Sarakole, the Tukolor did not break the alliance. The other reason for this moderate policy was because the Tukolor empire was experiencing internal strains at this period. Aware of these problems, and convinced that the Tukolor ruler, Ahmadu, eldest son of 'Umar, was in no position to pose a serious threat to them later on, the French signed another treaty with him in May, 1887. At the same time, the French commander Lieutenant Colonel Gallieni, used his secret agents to instigate more dissensions within the empire. Gallieni's successor, Major Louis Archinard, had no use for Ahmadu's cooperation, and in February, 1889 he seized the isolated Tukolor fortress at Koundian. The defenders gave a good account of themselves but the fort still fell. In 1890 Archinard captured the Tukolor capital of Segu after stiff resistance. It was only after the loss of Segu that Ahmadu decided on general resistance against the French. At the battle of Youri (January 3, 1891) the Tukolor army was annihilated, some 3,000 of them dead or captured. Ahmadu fled to Masina. He came back in 1892, reentered Segu, and resumed his resistance. After a series of defeats he fled once more from his country and took refuge in the Sokoto empire, his mother's homeland, and died there in 1898. Before his first flight the French had set up Agiubu as a loyal collaborator and Tukolor resistance came to an end.[16]

Events in the kingdom of Dahomey followed a similar pattern. Up to the 1870s Franco-Dahomean relations were based on trade and were not hostile. Indeed, Dahomeans had looked upon the French as simple traders and sailors who could not fight. By the 1880s the situation had changed. The French demanded Cotonou and the Fon, Glele, refused to cede it. In 1883 Porto Novo was granted French protection and Cotonou and Ouidah were being squeezed. In 1888 Porto Novo, encouraged by France, seceded from Dahomey, and in 1889 France demanded the surrender of Cotonou once more. Rather than yield to this humiliation, and realizing that he could not expel the French, King Glele poisoned himself (1889) while a French mission was still visiting his court. Glele, convinced that "he who makes the powder must win the battle" had done everything, including suicide, to avoid a fight with the French. His son and successor, Behanzin, reversed his father's policy. He had inherited a kingdom weakened by dissensions and in which the monarchy was, at best, the most powerful, among other powerful subjects. This weakness did not deter Behanzin from putting up a creditable resistance before he was captured and exiled to the West Indies in 1892. In 1894 the French colony of Dahomey, larger than the kingdom of Dahomey, was founded. Although the kingdom came to an end in 1892 the legal fiction of the existence of the Fon dynasty continued but was buried for good in 1900.[17]

The British invasion of the sovereignty of the states of southern Nigeria which began with the appointment of John Beecroft in 1849 as British consul to the Bights of Bini and Biafra, with his headquarters at Fernando Po, had led to the bombardment of Lagos in 1851. The landing of British troops from the sea was gallantly contested but eventually Britain got the upper hand, deposed Oba Kosoko, and replaced him with his uncle, Akitoye, who became their puppet. Military occupation, however, proved difficult because the British consul had no military force at his disposal and had to rely on the new Oba to enforce law and order[18] although British naval power could be counted upon to quell any resistance. In 1861 Britain decided to end this state of affairs by formally annexing Lagos as a British colony. The treaty of annexation was signed only on the threat of naval action. Lagos formed the genesis of the British colony of Nigeria. It was from Lagos that Britain launched the conquest of Yorubaland. The expansion of the colony was gradual and was encouraged by British missionaries, traders, and administrators. By 1890 it had expanded northward to Badagry and eastward to Itsekiriland. Up to 1890 we have little evidence of sustained opposition to this expansion. It was the Ijebu who provided the only serious challenge to British expansion. In general, however, British agents did not risk a confrontation when they lacked a military advantage. On the contrary, they employed diplomacy, intrigue, and subversion to achieve their goals. In 1892 Governor Gilbert Carter felt himself in a strong military position and provoked the Anglo-Ijebu war. At the battle of the Temogi (May 19, 1892) the Ijebu army fought gallantly but the maxim gun—a revolutionary invention in 1890 and not yet employed in a war in Europe—prevailed. The Ijebu surrendered and organized no further resistance. The road to Ibadan blocked by the Ijebu was reopened. No other serious resistance was encountered from Yoruba country most of which was annexed to the Lagos protectorate in 1893.[19]

In the Niger Delta the British were exercising considerable influence by 1885. The commercial rivalry which had been going on among the "palm oil ruffians" and the Delta middlemen between 1807 and 1856 had developed into a commercial war between 1856 and 1886. This had led to British interference in the internal affairs of the Delta states and greater involvement in local politics—a development covered up adroitly by the British as stopping the slave trade. It was Consul Hewett, for example, who supervised the appointment on July 12, 1884, of Nana Olomu—the uncrowned king of the Itsekiri—as the governor of Bini River. Nana therefore had started his relations with the British as a collaborator. The commercial rivalry between him and the European firms, however, and the support given by the British government to these firms, caused the breach with Nana. Although Nana had accepted British protection, it must be noted that, following King Jaja's example, he had carefully excluded the free trade clause. The British agents also cultivated collaborators among Nana's enemies. The breach reached a head in 1890 when Nana was deposed as governor, but he still fought to retain his power. The British, however, soon found an excuse to attack Itsekiriland and destroy what was left of Nana's power. The Ebrohimi expedition of 1894 ended with the destruction of the town and the flight of Nana. On October 30, 1894, the former governor appeared in Lagos, gave himself up, was tried, and found guilty of disregarding his treaty obligations, making war on Britain, disturbing the peace, and monopoly of trade. He was deported to Accra.[20]

In 1872 the independent kingdom of Opobo, ruled by Jaja, was recognized by the British consul. This was the climax of Jaja's rise to eminence, from a slave to a king. By the 1880s he had become the greatest king in the Niger Delta. The Bonny kingdom from which he split was weakened by internal dissensions, and the monarchy was a shadow of its former self. King George Pepple had long been a British puppet. The fact that the great Jaja needed Brit-

agents did not risk a confrontation when they lacked a military advantage. On the contrary, they employed diplomacy, intrigue, and subversion to achieve their goals. In 1892 Governor Gilbert Carter felt himself in a strong military position and provoked the Anglo-Ijebu war. At the battle of the Temogi (May 19, 1892) the Ijebu army fought gallantly but the maxim gun—a revolutionary invention in 1890 and not yet employed in a war in Europe—prevailed. The Ijebu surrendered and organized no further resistance. The road to Ibadan blocked by the Ijebu was reopened. No other serious resistance was encountered from Yoruba country most of which was annexed to the Lagos protectorate in 1893.[19]

In the Niger Delta the British were exercising considerable influence by 1885. The commercial rivalry which had been going on among the "palm oil ruffians" and the Delta middlemen between 1807 and 1856 had developed into a commercial war between 1856 and 1886. This had led to British interference in the internal affairs of the Delta states and greater involvement in local politics—a development covered up adroitly by the British as stopping the slave trade. It was Consul Hewett, for example, who supervised the appointment on July 12, 1884, of Nana Olomu—the uncrowned king of the Itsekiri—as the governor of Bini River. Nana therefore had started his relations with the British as a collaborator. The commercial rivalry between him and the European firms, however, and the support given by the British government to these firms, caused the breach with Nana. Although Nana had accepted British protection, it must be noted that, following King Jaja's example, he had carefully excluded the free trade clause. The British agents also cultivated collaborators among Nana's enemies. The breach reached a head in 1890 when Nana was deposed as governor, but he still fought to retain his power. The British, however, soon found an excuse to attack Itsekiriland and destroy what was left of Nana's power. The Ebrohimi expedition of 1894 ended with the destruction of the town and the flight of Nana. On October 30, 1894, the former governor appeared in Lagos, gave himself up, was tried, and found guilty of disregarding his treaty obligations, making war on Britain, disturbing the peace, and monopoly of trade. He was deported to Accra.[20]

In 1872 the independent kingdom of Opobo, ruled by Jaja, was recognized by the British consul. This was the climax of Jaja's rise to eminence, from a slave to a king. By the 1880s he had become the greatest king in the Niger Delta. The Bonny kingdom from which he split was weakened by internal dissensions, and the monarchy was a shadow of its former self. King George Pepple had long been a British puppet. The fact that the great Jaja needed Brit-

Events in the kingdom of Dahomey followed a similar pattern. Up to the 1870s Franco-Dahomean relations were based on trade and were not hostile. Indeed, Dahomeans had looked upon the French as simple traders and sailors who could not fight. By the 1880s the situation had changed. The French demanded Cotonou and the Fon, Glele, refused to cede it. In 1883 Porto Novo was granted French protection and Cotonou and Ouidah were being squeezed. In 1888 Porto Novo, encouraged by France, seceded from Dahomey, and in 1889 France demanded the surrender of Cotonou once more. Rather than yield to this humiliation, and realizing that he could not expel the French, King Glele poisoned himself (1889) while a French mission was still visiting his court. Glele, convinced that "he who makes the powder must win the battle" had done everything, including suicide, to avoid a fight with the French. His son and successor, Behanzin, reversed his father's policy. He had inherited a kingdom weakened by dissensions and in which the monarchy was, at best, the most powerful, among other powerful subjects. This weakness did not deter Behanzin from putting up a creditable resistance before he was captured and exiled to the West Indies in 1892. In 1894 the French colony of Dahomey, larger than the kingdom of Dahomey, was founded. Although the kingdom came to an end in 1892 the legal fiction of the existence of the Fon dynasty continued but was buried for good in 1900.[17]

The British invasion of the sovereignty of the states of southern Nigeria which began with the appointment of John Beecroft in 1849 as British consul to the Bights of Bini and Biafra, with his headquarters at Fernando Po, had led to the bombardment of Lagos in 1851. The landing of British troops from the sea was gallantly contested but eventually Britain got the upper hand, deposed Oba Kosoko, and replaced him with his uncle, Akitoye, who became their puppet. Military occupation, however, proved difficult because the British consul had no military force at his disposal and had to rely on the new Oba to enforce law and order[18] although British naval power could be counted upon to quell any resistance. In 1861 Britain decided to end this state of affairs by formally annexing Lagos as a British colony. The treaty of annexation was signed only on the threat of naval action. Lagos formed the genesis of the British colony of Nigeria. It was from Lagos that Britain launched the conquest of Yorubaland. The expansion of the colony was gradual and was encouraged by British missionaries, traders, and administrators. By 1890 it had expanded northward to Badagry and eastward to Itsekiriland. Up to 1890 we have little evidence of sustained opposition to this expansion. It was the Ijebu who provided the only serious challenge to British expansion. In general, however, British armies properly drilled and trained to deal with contingencies. The European powers were aware of these weaknesses. And it is against the background of this knowledge that the imperialism of conquest should become comprehensible.

Salisbury and the Diplomatic Defense of the Niger, 1885–92
By 1882 British position was entrenched in the Gold Coast (Asante power having been broken in 1874), in Sierra Leone, Lagos, and Gambia. We saw that by 1884 Britain had won the struggle for the Lower Niger, a victory confirmed at the Berlin Conference. France, too, as a result of the energetic exploits of its explorers had established a strong position in the Upper Niger, a fact recognized also at the same conference. It is therefore misleading to assert that by 1884 Britain had been "routed elsewhere along the coast" and "was at last beginning to defend the British sphere in the Delta."[31] Another fiction is one perpetuated by the Foreign Office. The extension of British territory just prior to and during the Berlin Conference was undertaken, as Flint has correctly pointed out, "under the curious fiction that no additions were being made to the British empire. Expansion was carried out by the Foreign Office, using consular officials, under the theory that the establishment of protectorates was essentially diplomatic work."[32] Thus has arisen the argument that Britain had no territorial ambition in West Africa until propelled to develop such an appetite by the "repercussions" of the Egyptian occupation; and that, later on, Salisbury was willing to sacrifice these territories for the grand imperial strategy of maintaining British supremacy in the Nile valley.[33] The evidence on which this bold thesis is based is not only circumstantial but runs counter to the historical developments we have been discussing. If any overriding motive can be assigned to British strategy, it is the protection of trade.[34] But in order to protect this trade it was found necessary to annex when it became clear that local authority had broken down as a result of the European impact or that African rulers posed a greater danger to this trade than any European power. Even after 1885, whatever interpretations historians may wish to place on the subtleties—or vanities—of the official mind, the hard evidence remains that before or after 1882 Britain yielded no territory it *effectively occupied* in West Africa to any other power; and, at the end of the day, it won the richest territorial prize—in terms of quality if not necessarily quantity—in West Africa. This underscores the essentially economic dimension of British activities in the west. There was no better exponent of qualitative rather than quantitative expansion than the third Marquis of Salisbury.

It is against the background of the foregoing that we ought to comprehend Salisbury's diplomatic defense of the Niger. He had no wish to rule the whole of West Africa. Nor did he believe that that would be a practical or worthwhile undertaking. He had no intention of yielding what his country possessed—not claimed—without an adequate quid pro quo. Equally he refused to yield valuable territories to his opponents, the title to which they could not prove except in return for an equally valuable exchange. There is nothing restrictive or antiimperialistic per se in this policy as is usually assumed.

As soon as the Berlin Conference was over Britain and Germany began discussions to define the boundaries between the "Oil Rivers" and the German Cameroons. In June, 1885 an Anglo-German Treaty accomplished this purpose and reached a commercial agreement.[35] For Britain this was a notice that it would brook no interference in the Oil Rivers. The treaty was followed up immediately by the proclamation of the Niger Districts protectorate to comprise "the territories on the line of coast between the British protectorate of Lagos and the right or western bank of the Rio del Rey" as well as the "territories on both banks of the Niger, from its confluence with the River Benue at Lokoja to the sea, as well as the territories on both banks of the River Benue, from the confluence up to and including Ibi."[36] This declaration was appropriately notified to the other powers. In the same month Gladstone's government fell over the Irish question and Salisbury became prime minister for the first time. It was he who arranged to grant a royal charter to Goldie's company although his government fell before the charter was officially issued on July 12, 1886. Within the same year Salisbury was back in power with a slim majority. And faced with big problems at home and abroad he was compelled to move cautiously. Arguing that the interests of the company and that of Britain were inseparable he hoped that Goldie would do all in his power to extend British authority in the Sokoto caliphate and the Niger Bend which the French were threatening.

In July, 1886, Sir Percy Anderson, head of the African division of the Foreign Office, wrote a memorandum in which he summarized the position in West Africa and gave reasons why British governments had held back from a vigorous interference in its affairs. It was, he argued, due to the understandable satisfaction that, because they were in possession of most of the west coast, their position was unchallengeable, and that given time, all opposition would peter out. He went on:

> Great Britain has an open question with France on the western frontier of Lagos, but we have not been pressing it, as we are in possession of most of the disputed points and have ground for hoping that France, if left alone, may retire from a position into which she has been pushed by speculators whose venture is not prospering.

The Germans he considered to be no problem. After all, they had not made a good job of their own protectorates. Their Cameroon settlement had proved a failure, and even within it, Britain still held Victoria (Ambas Bay). The French might be pushing with great energy from Senegal to the Upper Niger, and had acquired an immense region north of the Congo, but they "have not as yet utilized it." The British, on the other hand, "have added to their old possessions the protectorate of the whole coast from Lagos to the Cameroon Settlement, as well as that of the Lower Niger and part of the Benue." In addition, he went on, Goldie would soon have the responsibility to administer the Niger and Benue territories. His "company has a large capital, is well managed, and is confident of successful trade. It has at present no foreign rivals." The Oil Rivers Coast was already under consular superintendence. And as soon as the R.N.C. began its administration, he would propose a general reorganization of the entire consular system on the west coast with the aim in view of reducing expenditure.[37] Here we have a very clear picture of the working of the official mind which studies in this area have consistently neglected to note. It made no mention of Egypt and gave no indication that Britain was willingly to yield its possessions to others. Nor was there any question of concentrating British priorities in East Africa as against the west.

One of the aims of granting a charter to the R.N.C. was to use it to extend British authority where it did not exist. The difficulties of the company which made the accomplishment of this goal impossible at this time have been studied in detail.[38] To these must be added African opposition which barred its expansion northward. As early as 1887, it had become clear to Salisbury that diplomatic action was necessary if further territories were to be added to what Britain already possessed. Such an addition was necessary as otherwise the Lower Niger and Britain's other possessions in West Africa would be stifled by a "trans-Saharan" French empire. To achieve this aim the French had decided on the "total conquest" of the Sudan.[39] Baffled by the acquisitive propensity of the magpie which the French were displaying everywhere at a time when the country was faced with many enemies, Salisbury wrote to Ambassador

Lyons: "The French are inexplicable. . . . It is very difficult to prevent oneself from wishing for another Franco-German war to put a stop to this incessant vexation."[40] As no such war was in the offing, he had to do something to restore the British initiative. He proposed a comprehensive settlement of Anglo-French difficulties in West Africa,[41] a proposal accepted by the French after several discussions.[42] The negotiations were to follow the lines which Salisbury had suggested in 1879.[43] The result was the Agreement of August 10, 1889, which delimited Anglo-French boundaries in Senegambia, on the Gold Coast, and on the Slave Coast, including Lagos. It was based on a mutual concession of territories. The agreement also provided for the appointment of special commissioners to trace on-the-spot boundaries which had only received general definition.[44]

In 1890 another important step was taken toward settling these differences. The French government, worried by the progress of the two countries on the Lower and Upper Niger, "suggested that a point should be agreed on beyond which neither should pass."[45] This gave rise to the famous Say-Barruwa Agreement of August 5, 1890 (the second article of the declaration of 1890). It also provided a basis for further territorial arrangements to the west and south of the Middle and Upper Niger.[46] This agreement was a diplomatic triumph for Salisbury. As he understood it he not only saved the important Sokoto caliphate—where Goldie had no serious foothold—for the R.N.C. and therefore for Britain but, as he also admitted, the French got in return "what agriculturists would call light land."[47] And yet Salisbury is said to have made generous concessions to France in West Africa in order to protect the Nile Valley! Another Agreement of June 26, 1891 placed Kouranko under British protection. Thus, the closing up of the interior around Sierra Leone was completed.[48] On April 1, 1891 Salisbury appointed Major Macdonald as the Consul-General and Commissioner for the Niger Coast Protectorate. He was to be aided by six vice-consuls and was instructed "to pave the way for placing the Territories over which Her Majesty's protection is and may be extended, directly under British rule."

Thus before he left office in 1892, Salisbury had both on paper and on the ground annexed large areas of West Africa. The Liberals, who returned to power in August, 1892 followed the general lines of his policy. In 1892, commissioners were appointed in obedience to the declarations of 1889 and 1890.[49] They agreed in principle that, west of the Niger, the boundary between their respective spheres should stretch "from Say to the north-west angle of the Neutral Zone" and run from there to Bontuku (a French possession). This was no definite agreement; it was a friendly understanding.[50] On July 12, 1893, the commissioners signed an agreement at Paris which fixed Anglo-French boundaries on the Gold Coast.[51] Earlier, on April 14, 1893, an agreement had been signed at Berlin which fixed Anglo-German boundaries on the west coast of Africa.[52] Another Berlin Agreement (November 15, 1893) settled boundary differences between the two countries in Africa generally. This agreement confirmed the earlier settlement of April 14.[53]

Another effort was made in 1894 to settle Anglo-French difficulties. Difference of opinion as to the possession of Nikki made agreement impossible.[54] But at the beginning of 1896 an arrangement was reached with France relating to differences in Tunis, Siam, and west of the Lower Niger. The success of this arrangement led to the belief that attitudes on both sides were no longer as stiff as they had been and that the situation, therefore, was favorable for proposing that the suspended "Niger Negotiations should resume its meetings."[55]

The Howard-Larrony Negotiations, February to May, 1896

France accepted this view,[56] and fresh commissioners were appointed.[57] They were required "to act under the original stipulations."[58] Salisbury instructed Dufferin in general terms. Howard should try "to secure an equitable settlement" which would give to both countries "such access to the markets of the interior as will enable them to pursue their legitimate development without hindrance." He reminded the ambassador that already directly, and sometimes indirectly, through the medium of the Niger Company, Britain had made various treaties with Bona, Mamprussi, Sansane-Mungo, Gambaga, Mossi, Borgu, Gwandu, and Gurma. There was a belief that these treaties were prior to those concluded by France in those regions. These treaties were to be compared with those of the French, and then it would "be seen what either side is ready to concede."[59]

The commission held its first meeting on February 8, 1896. Howard ruled out any discussions respecting the navigation of the Niger. It was therefore agreed that the discussions should commence at the point where Hanotaux and Phipps had left off in 1894 "and in accordance with the bases which were agreed upon then."[60] The implication here was for an agreement to be possible, the 1890 line should be recognized. Unfortunately, Larrony was ignorant of what passed between Hanotaux and Phipps. The meeting broke up to consult with Berthelot, the Foreign Minister.[61]

The next meeting, on February 14, was devoted to the Say-Barruwa Agreement. Larrony, armed with better information, agreed to continue the Hanotaux-Phipps "Pour Parlers" of 1894, but contended that those discussions were merely a "Premiere avant Projet" for future talks. They did not, therefore, constitute the substance of an arrangement. He went further to offer the French interpretation of the 1890 Declaration, arguing that it forbade Britain to advance northward, and France to advance southward, over the line, but that France was at liberty to acquire any territory not belonging to Sokoto to the south; that Monteil had made treaties in the Say-Argungu-Gomba triangle involving territories independent of Sokoto; that France had rights over Yola (where a British post was in existence); that France was free to conclude a treaty with Bornu as no other power had done so, and as it was not part of Sokoto; and that the governments should examine their respective titles in the above mentioned regions. Howard rejected the French interpretation.[62]

Anderson described the French claims as "monstrous." He was loth to pay them "for surrendering" what they could not gain by arguments. In the last analysis, he was prepared to submit to international arbitration, and even suggested that Baron Lambermont, an international lawyer of repute, would be ideal for the task. If France rejected this solution, he suggested a resort to a little blackmail: to publish the Mizon correspondence to show the world that that officer violated the engagements undertaken by his government. As to the west of the Niger, Britain could put forward its treaty rights with Gourma and Sanssane-Mungo, since the only way of meeting "the exaggerated French pretensions" would be "by advancing our pretensions a good deal beyond what we are prepared to accept."[63] Salisbury minuted:

> Yes. Make two despatches as to the Say line. Point out that if our agreements are not to be interpreted according to the plain meaning of their words, any further agreement on the subject would be useless as it would be impossible for us to foresee what the second agreement might be held to mean. But I want the document if any—in which this strange pretension is recorded.[64]

After reading the document, Salisbury drafted a long letter (in his own handwriting) to Dufferin. It is a masterly argument for the British case as well as for the part he played in the 1890 Declaration, which was negotiated between himself and Waddington, who had since then died. The second article of the second part of that convention says:

The Government of Her Brittanic Majesty recognizes the sphere of influence of France to the south of her Mediterranean possessions up to a line from Say on the Niger to Barruwa on Lake Chad drawn in such a manner as to comprise in the sphere of action of the Niger Company all that fairly belongs to the Kingdom of Sokoto.[65]

Salisbury simply interpreted this to mean that France possessed the territory north of the line, and Britain that south of it. He explained that he and Waddington met alone on several occasions before they came to this conclusion, and that if the provision meant something other than that explicitly stated, "it never would have been signed by me." In the House of Lords, in 1890, he had explained this meaning of the convention to their Lordships; and Waddington, who had read the speech, did not protest at this interpretation. On the contrary, he had written to Salisbury commenting on another portion of the speech.[66] The "strange" French interpretation was therefore new to him, and "I have read it with a surprise to which I find it difficult to give full expression." He therefore declared the question not negotiable by the Commission.[67]

Dufferin communicated the substance of this letter to Berthelot, who professed ignorance of the question. He did, however, produce an ingenious interpretation of his own which left the British ambassador dumbfounded. Accepting that the line ran from Say to Barruwa through the territory of Sokoto, he argued that "its subsequent direction was left vague." On the one hand, if the line curved toward the north, why should it not, on the other, "be drawn in a corresponding curve along the southern borders of Bornu, provided only it reascended ultimately to Barruwa." "I had great difficulty," wrote Dufferin, "in realising that such an extraordinary contention should have occurred to the mind of his Excellency, and I hardly knew in what terms to continue the discussion."[68] Certainly, it did not occur to Berthelot that, if two powers agreed to draw such a line, ex hypothesi, unless a clause provided for the contrary, it should be a straight line. Perhaps Dufferin was right when he said that Berthelot "is almost paralysed by the work of his new and unaccustomed Office." Moreover, his health was bad; he had lately suffered a domestic affliction; and, more importantly, knowing little of the question, but aware that the Colonial Group in the Chamber of Deputies attached great importance to it, he was inclined "to screen himself behind his Commissioners, who themselves probably take their orders from the French Colonial Office," which also made Hanotaux its "mouthpiece" rather "than a free agent."[69]

Three further meetings with Berthelot produced no results. He maintained frankly that he knew nothing of the question and suggested, irrespective of what Salisbury had said, that it should be left to the Commissioners. But he refused to abandon his theory of the meandering line. As neither side was disposed to give way, it was decided to let the matter rest for the time being.[70] Salisbury wrote sarcastically to Dufferin:

> It is a pity that Berthelot's ingenious theory of the coiled boundary should not be preserved for the benefit of the future negotiators and students. It is to be noted that Berthelot entirely accepts my contention that all one side of the line is British—all the other side French: only his notions of a line are eccentric. This is a valuable admission and should not be neglected.[71]

It must be noted that the law officers were not quite in agreement with Salisbury's interpretation. They pronounced that the line gave Britain territories "only as far as [they lie] East of the Niger," and not to the west of it. "We do not," they concluded, "think that the effect of the 1890 Declaration taken as a whole is to recognize British influence as paramount in the district between the Middle Niger and a line drawn southward from Say."[72]

Attention was now turned to the examination of treaties and to possible territorial exchanges. In December, 1895, Lord Selborne, the Under Secretary of State for the Colonies, had suggested to Chamberlain the probability that France might, in return for the cession to it of Dominica, waive its claims in Newfoundland and cede to England Dahomey and its hinterland. This information was passed on to Salisbury[73] who favored the idea, but expressed his ignorance of the value of Dominica. However, he accepted Chamberlain's suggestion that the admiralty should be consulted as to the strategic value of this island. He only feared that "the Admiralty, according to my long experience, might say with Mephistopheles: *'Ich bin der Geist der stets verneint'*." Again, Germany was then negotiating with France about the countries west of the Lower Niger, and he feared that France might sell to England what it had already sold to Germany. He added in a footnote: "It is curious that very much the bargain you now propose was suggested to me by the late Lord Derby some four or five years ago."[74] Goschen confirmed that Dominica had no strategic value, and that although it possessed good soil and good climate, it did not pay its way commercially. It could therefore be dispensed with. If France accepted this arrangement, Chamberlain proposed that Britain would demand, in addition, a free hand in the New Hebrides "which is a probable ground for contention in the future." Britain would also, in turn, cede these territories to Germany in return for a free hand in the neutral zone. She would also demand an adjustment of Togoland's western boundary, as well as an abandonment by Germany of any claims to Samoa since "the Australian Colonies are very eager on this latter point." He ended rather meekly: "I am encouraged by your letter to place these suggestions fully before you."[75] Salisbury put forward this plan to Courcel, who was staying at Hatfield. The French ambassador turned it down on the plea that there was a strong sentimental feeling in France for those territories.[76]

Between February 8 and May 22, the commission held twenty-one meetings. The first two of these were devoted to the discussion of the Say-Barruwa question; the remainder to the discussion of their respective treaties west of the Niger and north of the ninth parallel. They are, undoubtedly, the more boring part of the proceedings, and only their important aspects will be discussed here.

As soon as the commission got down to business, the French government was subjected to mounting pressure from certain sections of their community. The French African Society passed a resolution calling on their government to defend energetically French interests, and to check the encroachments of the Niger Company on the Niger and the Benue. This resolution was supported by the Society of Political and Commercial Economy and several Chambers of Commerce.[77] The *Figaro* urged "the capital importance to France of maintaining a port on the Benue and her interests at Yola."[78] In England, the Venezuela boundary dispute, the Jameson invasion, and the advance to Dongola, temporarily over-shadowed West African questions. There was, therefore, no comparative pressure. But it was well appreciated in London that if essential English interests were bartered away without a substantial quid pro quo, the government would be in some trouble.

This was the setting as the commissioners went about their rigorous but thankless task. Larrony spent the early meetings picking holes in the British treaties.[79] He did a very good job of this although some of his criticisms were utterly naive. For example, one reason for rejecting the Fergusson treaties was because they were made by a black man.[80] There were, however, some reasonable objections to them. First, they had, he argued, the character of "simple commercial arrangements"; and, second, they were not signed by the chiefs, and crosses were put in the spaces reserved for signatures. As to the Niger Company's treaties, he had few good words to say. He made no comment on the 1885 treaty with Boussa, but objected strongly to that of 1890 because, while the 1885 treaty was concluded with a king, that of 1890 was made with an Emir;

neither the Emir nor the king of Boussa had any sovereignty over the whole of Borgu; and, finally, the treaty had not been followed up by effective occupation. The Lugard Treaties fared no better: he asserted that Lugard had not treated with the king; and he pointed out some irregularities in the treaties themselves. Howard refused to accept the French criticisms, but reserved reply.[81]

At the next meeting Howard contested the validity of almost all the French treaties.[82] From the start, therefore, the commission was doomed to failure as neither side was prepared to concede any points. But Anderson was disposed to keep them talking and to exercise patience. "All this is only preliminary work,"[83] and "Still debating treaties,"[84] are his familiar minutes during this stage of the negotiations. Occasionally, he reassured the impatient Colonial Office: "The Commissioners are making a very good fight."[85] "They have got their case up very well."[86]

But by March, Courcel's patience was running out. He plainly told Sanderson that the Commissioners were making no progress, an opinion which Anderson rejected.[87] The French ambassador also admitted that Berthelot was personally ignorant of the Niger question. However, he explained that the French aims were twofold: first, "to obtain for France a connection between the hinterlands of Dahomey and her possessions on the Upper Niger"—including Nikki; and second, to get a port on the navigable portion of the Lower Niger, "that is to say, an establishment on the right bank at Boussa and a port at some place lower down, below the cataracts." He also revealed that France would recognize British claims to Bornu and Adamawa if she were allowed to advance freely through Baghirmi on the east side of Lake Chad to the north. In addition, he demanded "free passage for their caravans by way of Bornu and Sokoto."[88] Courcel called again on Sanderson (March 13) and consented to the commission's continuing its work.[89] In an interview with Salisbury, the ambassador put forward the same demands he made on Sanderson. But this time, "he treated as a mere formality [?] any French pretensions to the east of the River [Niger]."[90] In fact, these demands were already known to the Foreign Office.[91] Berthelot himself did not care for Bornu. "If only the Colonial Party would leave him alone," Dufferin had written, "I do not think he is very excited over these African questions, though he complained that the Niger Company impeded and bullied French traders."[92]

But the Colonial Office would not hear of a French territorial access to the Niger.[93] This was Chamberlain's first direct interference since the negotiations were restarted. He was in good company for Anderson was on his side:

This proposal is one which we ought not to accept. The port is not wanted for communication with the Upper Niger from which the broken water would separate it, but for the purpose of ousting Great Britain from the exclusive control of the Lower Niger. . . .[94]

Salisbury had reservations but did not object:

I agree as to the port, but the caravan might be met by a promise to open particular roads under special regulations.

I have a strong feeling that the monopoly of the Niger cannot be permanently held.[95]

After some discussions with Courcel and Colonel Everett (who was on a visit to London from Paris and who had replaced Hemming at the commission), Anderson came round to the Salisbury point of view. He was convinced that the only impediment to an agreement was the question of "a port below the Boussa Falls . . . I should not squeeze them too hard about the monopoly of the Niger."[96]

Howard was instructed to break the deadlock. At the meeting of April 27, he offered to give up the town of Nikki and a considerable part of its dependencies; north of Borgu, he conceded Gourma, Liptako, Yagha, and Guelajo—all of which Britain claimed belonged to Gando; and east of the Niger, he offered to cede part of the Say-Gomba-Argungu triangle.[97] Privately Larrony was pleased with the concessions but decided to await instructions from Hanotaux, who had replaced Berthelot on the fall of the Bourgeois Ministry. These offers were made in return for the French relinquishing their demand for a port on the Niger.[98] It turned out, however, that the authority to make these concessions was given in a private letter by Anderson, the draft of which had mysteriously disappeared.[99] In other words, Salisbury was not aware of it. He observed:

The papers raise no recollection in my mind of having been asked to authorize so large a concession as that of the line to E[ast] of the Dahomey line.

The working of the two Offices [i.e., the F.O. and the C.O.] has made confusion. The Permanent Officials in each Office imagined a consent has been given by the S. of S. of the other S.[100]

The documents do not reveal any confusion. It is likely that Anderson had acted solely on his own initiative, forgetting momentarily, that Salisbury, and not Kimberley, was the foreign secretary. But no harm was done. Hanotaux not only rejected these concessions, but also asked for more. The bemused Howard adjourned discussions for consultations.[101]

Anderson was furious. "Hanotaux must mean to break off negotiations," he minuted to Salisbury.[102] Salisbury rejected Hanotaux's counterproposal, which, if accepted, would have strangled both the Lagos Colony and the Niger districts. He advised:

> We clearly cannot accept these suggestions or any of them. But if—as seems probable—he [Hanotaux] wants a noisy breach with us for some Parliamentary purpose, we are merely playing into his own hands by laying down such a general doctrine as Howard purposes.[103] The arguments against this proposal should be fully stated: but we had better avoid any general counterprinciple.[104]

In a long letter to Dufferin Salisbury sketched out a short history of the origins of the Niger negotiations. He expressed his "surprise" at Hanotaux's counterproposal because of its apparent greediness. It "is an entirely new departure," he told the ambassador, which "renders the past work of the Commissioners inoperative and leaves no ground open for future discussions by them. It substitutes absolute surrender by one party for an amicable arrangement between the two Powers." Dufferin should, therefore, instruct Howard to reject officially the French demands.[105]

When the commissioners reassembled on May 22, Larrony slightly modified Hanotaux's proposals. This was flatly turned down, and the negotiators adjourned once more for consultations.[106] "Wait next French move," was Salisbury's reaction.[107] And as the French made no move, the Howard-Larrony negotiations ended without achieving much.

"Le Silence"
Dufferin sincerely believed that the break up of negotiations was a calculated move on the part of Hanotaux. In their weekly meetings the French minister had resolutely refused to transact any business. Hanotaux's first task as soon as he took office, Dufferin ruefully reported to Salisbury, was "to level in the dust the elaborate edifice which Howard and his colleagues had been painfully constructing in West Africa. Nor did this piece of vandalism surprise me."[108] Apparently, Hanotaux had thrown overboard his own maxim: *"Le Silence est la mort de la paix."* And how right that maxim was! For had the uneasy silence which existed for the next fifteen months continued longer, the impending storm created by the zig-zag territorial occupations by the two powers would have been disastrous for West Africa and for the powers themselves.

While negotiations progressed Chamberlain had remained unusually quiet. But in July he expressed his approval of the stand taken by Salisbury, adding that Britain should spare no efforts, now that negotiations were at an end, "to strengthen our position in the countries to the north of Ashanti and the Gold Coast." He urged that Mossi, Gurunshi, Bona, and Lobi should be secured to Britain.[109] Everett shared this view but feared that France would never give up its claims to Mossi and Bona.[110] So did Howard. Nevertheless, Hill[111] urged that Bona should be occupied by a detachment of the Gold Coast Constabulary, which should also "visit Wa"; that the Niger Company should be asked to occupy all the places they held west of the Niger; and that an English officer should pay a visit to the king of Mossi.[112] Salisbury's only fear was the suspicion that the Treasury might oppose the expenditure involved.[113] But soon afterwards he approved the occupation of Gambaga by the Gold Coast Constabulary. The proposal was Everett's which was supported by Governor Maxwell.[114] Maxwell was also willing to send an armed escort on "a peaceful mission" to Bona, Wa, and Mossi, the cost to be defrayed by the Gold Coast Colony.[115] Salisbury approved,[116] and Sanderson observed: "I concur in all these proposals. The French and Germans will not like it; but they have no valid ground for protesting."[117]

In August, Howard had assured Salisbury that Hanotaux would insist on an access to the navigable Niger and had strongly advised against it. To consolidate British claims, he had not only urged the desirability of a more active policy west of the Niger, but also had suggested that Britain should undertake the defense of the Niger Districts administered by Goldie.[118] Everett, who equally shared this view, believed that, in addition to Boussa, both Kishi and Kiama should be occupied since these territories would give the French a preliminary step to obtaining a foothold on the right bank of the Niger. Their occupation by Britain would, therefore, effectively block the French advance and "greatly strengthen our position." And if Goldie refused to play, then Lagos should be ordered to do so.[119]

While these suggestions were being examined, a report appeared in the French press that Lieutenant Voulet had occupied Wagadugu, the capital of Mossi.[120] This raised an interesting problem. If Britain abandoned Mossi, it would have lost its trump card since it had been decided that that territory was to be offered to France in return for the extension of the British "frontier westward to the Komoe and Dokhosie rivers."[121]

The Gold Coast authorities had no knowledge of this reported occupation.[122] They were consequently asked to confirm its authenticity as the French government had issued no official statement.[123]

Meanwhile, Hanotaux, worried by Goldie's warlike preparation, wished to know its objective.[124] (Goldie's real objective was to smash the ruler of Nupe—considered as a sort of overlord of Illorin—and consolidate his position. It was believed that by suppressing Nupe, the power of Illorin would be destroyed. This would fulfill the demands made on him by the C.O.) But Courcel, who was expected to "be less able to ask subsidiary questions," was merely told that the object of the expedition was to restore order to Illorin whose ruler had become a nuisance to the Lagos Colony.[125]

Toward the close of 1896, the Niger question, indeed, became very disturbing to Hanotaux. He was particularly worried by the activities of the Niger Company. Under pressure from his Colonial Ministry and the Chamber of Deputies in regard to "British encroachments and pretensions," he came back to his old maxim that the best way to avoid an explosion was by talking.[126] The Foreign office was also thinking along the same lines.[127] But what would be the acceptable basis for a resumption of negotiations? Everett wrote privately to Hill: "I discovered what I think might constitute a very satisfactory quid pro quo for, at least, the triangle of territory which lies south of the 9th parallel in Hanotaux's second proposal." This involved the sacrificing of a "bit of Lagos for the Gaman country." He was convinced that France would jump at the idea. Daffina, Yatenga, Borgu, and Leaba would also be conceded to it, if, in return, Britain got Bona, Lobi, Mossi, and "the 14th parallel of latitude from the Niger to Lake Chad." But the only problem would be the question of the port on the Niger especially as Goldie had warned on several occasions that "if ever the French get a port on the Niger, I will sell up the whole business and clear out." The alternative, therefore, would be to take over the administration of the company's territories. Then, the French could be given access to the Niger in the vicinity of Fort Arenberg in order to satisfy their amour propre. Everett was convinced that if his proposals were accepted there would be a "possibility of doing good business and probably finish the whole thing off in a month, or six weeks at the outside." If, on the other hand, negotiations were delayed much longer, he feared that the French would before long be in occupation of the territories the government had held out for concessions.[128] Neither the Foreign Office nor the Colonial Office was sanguine as to these suggestions.[129]

Hanotaux was simply informed that both his proposal of May 8 and its modified form of May 22 were not even a basis for discussion. With regard to the Say-Barruwa line, too, Salisbury remained immovable. Then came this important paragraph:

The progressive nature of British and French sovereignty or protectorates over the waters of the Niger . . . clearly recognized in the 30th and 31st Articles of the Berlin Act and H. M. Govt. consider that, pending the report of the Commissioners, neither Power is precluded from extending its influence over territories within the scope of the Commission's labours, where no previous treaties have been concluded by the other and from which it is not debarred by mutual agreement between the Governments of the two countries. It is the duty of the Commissioners to examine and determine, subject to the approval of their Governments all questions arising out of such action. . . .[130]

It is strange that Salisbury should have adopted such a line, knowing full well as he did, that France was more active than Britain in the territories under dispute. But as Hill explained:

We thought it well to put in the paragraph about the common right of extension, because on the one hand France has advanced and will not withdraw, and, on the other, we are on the point of occupying Bona and against which they may probably protest. The words seem to forestall such objections and not to weaken our case.

Colonel Everett is not sanguine that M. Hanotaux will accept our line. If he declines a resumption of work on our terms we must be content to hold our own where we are.[131]

In March, 1897 the French occupied Boussa and installed a resident there.[132] This was a strong measure on the part of the French government especially as it was followed by a disinclination to resume talking. It may be, as Hill pointed out, that Hanotaux's intention of delaying the resumption of negotiations was "to confront us with a *fait accompli*."[133] Goldie was therefore instructed to occupy all unoccupied positions in Boussa below the rapids, taking care to avoid a collision.[134] But Lord Scarborough replied that, as the company held Liaba and Bojibo with their troops, there were no other places which could be occupied with advantage.[135] Britain simply protested to France.[136] But Hanotaux refused to answer.[137]

In the same month the French occupation of Wagadugu was confirmed.[138] It would appear that in this game of "common right of extension," enunciated by Salisbury, the French were winning. But there was this reservation, namely, that they deliberately ignored British treaties (sometimes with justice),[139] and sometimes on the ground that Britain was not in effective occupation of the territories claimed by it.[140]

The whole situation appeared to be confused. While Hanotaux argued that the French occupation of Boussa was justified;[141] Courcel blamed it on the officer on the spot who "misunderstood or exceeded his instruction."[142]

In March, Salisbury had suggested a limited or selective international arbitration to settle the Niger question. But this had been turned down by Courcel because it would involve a lengthy process, when what was needed was a speedy settlement.[143]

But how could any settlement be reached, let alone a speedy one, without a resumption of negotiations? Having occupied Mossi, Gurma, and Boussa, Hanotaux, with his hand strengthened, was prepared to resume negotiations.[144] But the Foreign Office insisted on making a formal protest about Boussa before complying.[145] This was duly done[146] to the annoyance of Hanotaux who grumbled that Britain could not have chosen a more inopportune moment to express its differences with France as this would be seen in Constantinople as showing a lack of cohesion between the two countries should they threaten a joint action against the Sultan. This, of course, implied that the Sultan's dread of this action would be impaired.[147] The prospects of a resumption of negotiations thus faded away.

With Salisbury's permission Chamberlain had interviewed Goldie on May 27 about the possibility of a common action between the Niger Company, Lagos, and the Gold Coast to protect themselves against French aggression. Goldie had absolutely refused to discuss the question and consequently no definite understanding was reached.[148] As there was growing danger that the French might occupy Sokoto, Goldie's action was incomprehensible. True, he relied on his treaties to prevent any French encroachments, but he was not unaware that France contested the validity of these treaties, or that it was categorically stated that wherever the French flag once flew, there it must remain. Maybe, as Chamberlain complained, he was deliberately making it impossible for England to secure an equitable settlement with France.[149]

The weakness of the English position lay in the fact that the government was not prepared to go to war over the disputed territories. Hill observed with exasperation:

> It is not the fault of the Foreign Office that the Colonies have been too careless or too poor to raise more troops and occupy more hinterland sooner. We have done all we can by diplomatic methods.
>
> Our weakness lies in the fact that, happily, we do not want to fight for the coveted territories. . . .[150]

The French have regular troops in Mossi, Gurunshi, and Gurma, with white officers: the Colonial Office do not like his [Captain Steward's] remark that we are too late and that the French are in occupation almost everywhere, but I fear it is true.[151]

Goldie was formally asked to state his position.[152] He boasted of his "1,000 *thoroughly* trained coloured troops, with ample artillery, machine guns and military stores." But he would only be prepared to drive the French out of Boussa as soon as the dry season began, if his company's frontiers would be guaranteed against attack from the Niger Coast Protectorate, and if Britain would prevent reinforcements being sent to Dahomey. He utterly disdained the idea of ceding the French a port on the Niger; and he warned that it was the duty of the imperial government to protect his company against foreign invasion.[153] "I fancy," observed Hill, "Sir George now wants to force the hand of the govt."[154]

The remaining three months before the last stage of the Niger Commission began were crucial ones. There appeared to be a total lack of communication between Paris and London. There was instead a resort to the chess board policy of occupying points all around each other's posts. The danger of war, which neither claimed to want, drew nearer. Wiser counsels were needed, but none seemed available. Salisbury, irritated by what he called the "incomprehensible" attitude of the French, was not of the yielding disposition. But he was anxious for negotiations to be restarted if only the result might be to cool down the temperature of feelings on both sides. The Colonial Office was not of the same mood. They wanted to occupy more territories which would give Britain a stronger hand when negotiations were resumed. They therefore defended the British occupation of Bontuku not only as a reprisal against the French occupation of Dagarti but also as a defensive measure against Samory's *sofas* whom the French were unable to keep in order.[155] Salisbury was so furious with the French that he did not object: "Captain Mitchell need not be withdrawn except on military grounds."[156] Hill protested vigorously against what amounted to a tit-for-tat policy, which might in the end put England in the wrong and complicate further the existing situation. If, he asked, England had no intention of fighting France over the disputed areas, what guarantee had it that France would not adopt a contrary policy if its territorial rights were violated? Bontuku was accepted to be French; the British forces must therefore withdraw as soon as a French force arrived. "I see no harm—tho' it leads to a *reductio ad absurdum*," he wrote, "in what one may call the 'chess board policy' of occupying points all round French posts in disputed territory, so long as we are strong enough in men and supplies to do so."[157] He was therefore opposed to this line of action because of his belief in the military inferiority of Britain in those parts. But Salisbury overruled him: "The French have become so continuously aggressive that some definite action is necessary."[158] Sanderson backed Hill hinting, however, that "the whole thing depends on how far we are disposed to go."[159] Salisbury was adamant: "I am afraid it is impossible to sit still and watch the French occupying all we claim,"[160] he retorted. Monson, who supported the Hill-Sanderson line approached Salisbury with more subtlety. He wrote to his chief:

> As it has been decided that we shall adopt energetic action in Nigeria I can only express the hope that the measures set on foot will be supported by unmistakingly adequate preparations which will make the French understand that we are in red [*sic*] earnest in asserting our rights.

He urged, at the same time, that Britain must endeavor to act within the limits of international law.[161]

Oddly enough, the French could not comprehend the reason for the strong feeling in England about these West African matters.[162] Salisbury, therefore, set down the reasons why. "France," he said, "now claims as hers by occupation nearly all territories under discussion." Did not Courcel himself, he asked, on the advice of his government, "fell to the ground" the principle of effective occupation advocated by Britain at the Berlin Conference? Since then the system of spheres of influence had been successfully applied. In the present state of Africa, a reversion to effective occupation would result in political chaos especially if the existing chess board policy were continued. Moreover, the French only applied this system to Britain and not to themselves. Salisbury summed up the attitude and intentions of his government:

> In the opinion of H. M. Govt. the intention of the Powers assembled at the Conference of Berlin and Brussels and their efforts for the welfare of the African races can only be fulfilled if the Powers territorially interested in that continent agree to work in separate spheres for the common end, arranging those spheres by mutual concession. A contrary policy, involving as it must, rival military expeditions, can only ruin commerce and create confusion and distrust among the natives, which, however anxious the governments may be to localise the complications which must ensue, they may find it impossible to avoid their reacting on the higher interests of European policy.[163]

This dispatch nicknamed by F.O. officials as "The Famous no. 259" was carefully supervised and corrected by Salisbury before it was sent out. It is, in fact, a great document, details of which space has not permitted me to give. It is honest in its intentions, brilliant in its style; it makes clear Salisbury's attitude toward West Africa. It had to wait for Queen Victoria's approval and was therefore dispatched on September 7. It had attached to it a list of British treaties.

The passage thus quoted characterizes the authentic Salisbury. But Hanotaux was not impressed. He was more interested in scoring diplomatic successes at frequent intervals than in questions of international legality.[164] Proposals for the renewal of discussions had been made to him on January 14, April 15, and July 13, but he had delayed reply until September 5. Equally, for many months, he gave no answers to communications sent to him on the West African question.[165] And meanwhile, the French continued to "violate" what the British considered to be their territories and to erect tariff walls wherever they were in occupation.[166] This brought numerous protests from British Chambers of Commerce which grew in pressure when negotiations were restarted.[167]

It is not surprising, therefore, that Salisbury proposed a departmental conference to review the situation and submit proposals. This conference included representatives of the Foreign and Colonial Offices as well as Colonel Everett and Goldie.[168]

Earlier Chamberlain had refused to resume negotiations as long as the French held Boussa.[169] But now he jumped at the idea of this conference, and at once drew up a scheme for a West African force, to which the Director of Military Intelligence, Sir John Ardagh, added some observations regarding its composition. Ardagh also advised that Goldie should use his company's forces to hem in the French at Boussa with the object of driving them out before the new force was raised. Chamberlain was prepared to advance money, if necessary, to Goldie, not for the purpose of attacking the French at Boussa, but simply to starve them out. He was, however, required to retaliate if attacked.[170] Hill feared a possible collision: "It seems to me to go beyond the chess board policy, but it might be discussed at the conference. . . ."[171] Salisbury simply replied: "We had better work up our Blue Book case as fully as possible."[172] At a preliminary meeting of this departmental conference on September 2, the West African Frontier Force was set up. The Chamberlain-Ardagh proposals were also adopted.[173] But a further conference with Goldie at the Foreign Office showed that it was impracticable to starve out the French at Boussa. In fact, after reconsidering the earlier decision, Salisbury had arrived independently at the same conclusion. The reason was mainly due to the physical structure of the surrounding country. But it was further feared that the operation, instead of starving out the French, might end up by starving out the king of Boussa and his people.[174]

Monson, too, feared that this "policy of militant energy" would be very much resented in France. It might result in some continental combination against England. Nevertheless, as the regions in dispute had been adjudged to be worth the employment of such measures, he warned that the force under contemplation should be strong enough to do its job effectively and thoroughly "in the face of rivals so active, enterprising, and perhaps I should add unscrupulous."[175] Monson was well aware that the root idea of the projected force was, by effectively occupying more territory, to secure for Britain a commanding diplomatic position when negotiations were resumed. The French, on their part, recognized this a long time ago and had assiduously been working toward that end. Hanotaux's constant remark that these African questions were unimportant should therefore not be taken seriously. As Monson put it to Salisbury:

> I do not think he [Hanotaux] would have the courage to utter this opinion in public. But I imagine that H.M.G., however disinclined they may be to depreciate the prospective value of Nigerian expansion, are not less desirous than M. Hanotaux professes himself to be, of preventing its becoming the cause of international danger.[176]

Salisbury did not share Monson's fears of the activities of the Colonial party and of international combinations against England; but he was impressed by his urgency.[177]

Meanwhile Goldie was talking "very big about what the Company could do if they were given a free hand." But he had refused to take any action until his future was clarified. He even suggested the seizure of a portion of the French Ivory Coast,[178] which brought out the remark—"He is hardly sane"—from Salisbury.[179] Nevertheless, he was asked to occupy Kiama and Nikki if the French were not in occupation. If the French were there, he was to occupy adjacent villages. He was assured that all his expenses would be refunded to him.[180] At the same time, Salisbury issued the following instruction to Governor McCallum:

> In case of absolute necessity you are authorized to resort to force to prevent violation of British territory. But great caution is necessary, and you should be sure that the case is perfectly clear and that you have distinctly superior force.[181]

He was also to occupy Okuta, notwithstanding the probable resumption of talks, since the French had sent an expedition to occupy Nikki.[182] But already McCallum had complicated the situation by intercepting French dispatches from Dahomey passing through Saki and arresting the messengers.[183] Foreign Office officials were alarmed at such an action in time of peace.[184] But Salisbury approved the governor's action because, he said, the dispatches were seized "at Saki which the French had occupied in defiance of International Law. They have no grounds of complaint."[185] He referred the matter to the law officers and reminded them that the Anglo-French position at Saki was certainly not in a state of war, "but neither was it peace." He went on to defend the governor's actions:

> These actions have a bellicose tendency; but if they are warlike in their character, it is to the category of unilateral war they belong. They were more in the nature of reprisals, or pacific blockades. General Ballet was making war on us, but we were not making war on him.

He therefore refused to listen to the objection that because England and France were not at war, "we have no business to seize the French despatches."[186] Nevertheless, the law officers pronounced against him;[187] the messengers were released; and as the French took no action a dangerous situation was avoided. To prevent similar occurrences which might lead to disastrous results, the need to reconvene the suspended Niger negotiations had since become very urgent.[188]

Chapter VI

The Struggle for the Niger, 1897–1900

So far, the cabinet and Chamberlain had meekly accepted Salisbury's leadership in the West African negotiations. This is contrary to the widely held view that Salisbury cared little about West African matters. Chamberlain, particularly, had been bogged down in parliamentary work as well as in the Jubilee arrangements and had had no time to study the numerous papers. But it will be noticed that Salisbury had not, as yet, conceded any major points. On the contrary, the degree of his firmness had been remarkable.

Chamberlain Intervenes
In September, 1897, Chamberlain, on holiday, and with more time on his hands, revitalized his 1895 enthusiasm about West Africa. A few months before he left for Interlaken he had hinted to Salisbury his displeasure at making any more concessions to France except for an adequate quid pro quo.[1] He plainly accused the foreign secretary of "graceful concessions" in Siam, Madagascar, and feared, most likely, in Tunis. "What is the result?," he asked:

> We . . . have thrown away all our cards and they keep theirs in their hands. . . .
> I firmly believe that if we do not show them that we will not be trifled with we shall finally be driven into war, with the disadvantage of having already surrendered much that is valuable.[2]

This was the accusation generally leveled at Salisbury by the London press and even by those members of Parliament who were supposed to be antiimperialists. Apparently Chamberlain shared this view. But it was proved to him—as it could not have been proved to outside critics—that, like the rest, he was ignorant of the intricacies of the various negotiations. In a word, Salisbury denied having gracefully conceded anything.[3] His exposé completely revealed the baselessness of Chamberlain's lugubrious vaticinations. The colonial secretary replied with an unaccustomed modesty:

> I feel ashamed to have given you so much trouble although I am very glad to have the information you gave me.
>
> I am sure that there is a general belief—which I ignorantly shared—that we have made important concessions to France without receiving anything in return. Your letter makes the case clear and I regret that you are not able to publish your despatch.[4]

As if to soothe the wounded vanity of his colleague, Salisbury offered to take charge of the Colonial Office while Chamberlain was away, remarking rather humorously: "I think it will be well to sum up our grievances against the French if only to prevent them from forgetting that matters have come to something like a deadlock at Constantinople."[5]

This preliminary is important for it set the tone of the Salisbury-Chamberlain relationship in the following months.

Chamberlain did not favor the proposed resumption of negotiations, but was prepared to leave the matter in the hands of the prime minister. He wrote to Selborne:

> The fact is that the question which is of the most serious importance and might if badly treated involve a European war must be decided ultimately by the Foreign Office, which knows better than we do the nature of our relations with France, and by the Prime Minister who is responsible in a peculiar sense for all questions of peace or war. Accordingly I should in any case yield to Lord Salisbury's wishes, although I desire that before deciding he may have before him my reasons for differing from the course he proposes.[6]

What was Salisbury's proposal? It was not a policy statement. He merely expressed his intention of accepting Hanotaux's strong request that talks should be renewed.[7] He also feared, among other things, the imminent danger of an act by an English or French frontier officer making war inevitable. In fact, he was so earnest about this that he instructed Selborne to secure the immediate agreement of both the Treasury and the War Office to the speedy connection of the extreme frontier of the Lagos hinterland with a military telegraph. "I shall be easier when that is done," he confided to his son-in-law.[8] He also complained to Sanderson: "I want to begin the negotiations in real earnest: but I cannot get an answer from Chamberlain."[9]

But Chamberlain saw no definite reason to resume talks. Even if the French resolved to "be nasty," as Monson feared they might be, he was prepared, "at all risks," not to sacrifice the West African empire, and would resist all attempts to bully or defraud his country. The only way to get anything out of the French was to convince them "from the first, that they had tried our patience too far and that they must give way or take the consequences."[10] Here lies the essential difference between Chamberlain and Salisbury. It is not a question of ends, but rather a question of methods. While the former favored the positive approach of a Palmerston, the latter favored the more traditional method of patient but firm negotiation. But in fairness to Chamberlain, he did suggest a meeting of the Principals—between Salisbury and Courcel in London, or between Courcel and Chamberlain himself in Paris, or any similar combination—instead of a meeting of delegates, because, as Courcel himself had admitted to him at a dinner at the French embassy, "delegates have no power to give way; it is only the Principals who can arrange such a matter." He admitted that a discussion by the Principals would take time, but would serve some purposes: it would allow the West African Force time to become effective; "the Russian fever may abate"; and a possible change in the French ministry might eliminate M. Lebon. An alternative to this suggestion would be arbitration. He concluded: "I think I have now placed you in full possession of my views. After Lord Salisbury has seen them I am perfectly content to accept and support any decision at which he may arrive."[11]

Salisbury's amiable reply reveals no serious differences between him and the colonial secretary, except that he believed that, in diplomacy, talking was better than silence:

> Selborne has shown me your letter touching the Niger negotiations. I look upon the questions at issue much from the same point as you do, but I do not go so far as to say that they furnish a ground for declining to negotiate. . . ."[12]

He knew that it would be humiliating to order any government to withdraw from positions held without negotiations. And as the French had shown a strong resolution to stay at Boussa, the ministers concerned might lose their jobs if they were bullied out of the place. This might be dangerous for international relations. Everything therefore should depend on the strength of the British case because

> If it is weak or too subtle for the average British mind we shall not be sustained here in pushing it to the extremity or even the limits of war. . . .

I do not understand how Messrs Everett and Antrobus could have told you that our case is a very strong one. I have always regarded it as a case common in diplomacy, where we have claimed a good deal more than we can establish a sound claim for, in order to furnish material for an exchange which will enable the French to recede from untenable positions without discredit. I agree that the Boussa case is *really* strong; and that we ought to put it in the forefront. But beyond this our argument is shady.

He went on to show the "fragile character" of the British claims. He was convinced that even if the French claims were no better than Britain's "we should have no justification for war in the eyes of the British public." But as negotiations were due to begin in about ten days he advised that Hausas and gunboats should be collected as soon as possible to occupy the uncontested territories and so save them from the French. Nevertheless, he insisted on the old system of a commission as against a meeting of Plenipotentiaries, which, although it had many attractions, had been found wanting by precedent.[13]

Again, Chamberlain expressed his wish to be ruled by Salisbury and to "keep out of it altogether."[14] He did not keep out for long, for about a week later, he was hinting to Selborne that he was prepared to defend British interests in West Africa "even at the cost of war."[15] He also insisted on the retention of Bontuku—a French post occupied by Britain in the nature of a reprisal—but was forced once more to yield to the force of Salisbury's argument against such a course.[16]

Privately, Monson was accusing the Colonial Office of inactivity in past years. He saw the situation in West Africa as "the struggle of the last century in India transferred to Africa, with all the chances in favour of the French."[17] Sanderson sent a copy of this letter to the Colonial Office who commented: "So we did but we could not move the F.O."[18] But Salisbury explained: "Cabinets and Parliament were still partly under the Manchester heresy. The C.O. officials I believe did all they could to struggle against forces too strong for them."[19]

Toward the end of September Chamberlain confirmed officially his willingness to resume negotiations.[20] In pursuance of Salisbury's advice two gunboats were dispatched to the Niger. Other military preparations were also set on foot. But Salisbury was against precipitating a war, and made it plain that Goldie "must relinquish all control of any forces he lends to us. He is very masterful and not a little cranky." His strategy was neither to fight the French nor to yield anything to them. But he suggested a defensive alliance with Samory which would make the French position untenable.[21] There was mounting excitement in Paris. But Hanotaux's attitude was described as "markedly friendly and conciliatory."[22] The French press was in no such mood. The *Temps,* a semiofficial organ, accused England of bluffing and warned that France would never succumb to intimidation.[23]

On October 16 Salisbury convened another meeting at the Foreign Office. The purpose of this meeting was to work out a strategy for the British commissioners. They must retain for Britain Sokoto and its dependencies; and to be able to do this they were required to secure, as far up as possible, both banks of the Niger. No further concessions were to be made for, as the French were now so anxious to resume talking, the onus must be on them to make proposals. In regard to trade, equality of treatment was to be given to France. The commissioners were to insist on the hinterland and priority of treaties doctrines as the principles of the negotiations; effective occupation should be rejected. Mossi and Gurunshi were to be bartered, if necessary, for the Lagos hinterland. Gurma was also to be conceded in the last resort. If agreement was impossible on these lines, Britain was determined to continue its operations, irrespective of the expense, making sure to avoid a collision. Salisbury threw out Chamberlain's suggestion that a joint commission on the spot could be set up to settle disputed treaties, because, presumably, he considered British claims "shady."[24]

But already Monson, convinced of Hanotaux's conciliatory disposition, had got Salisbury's permission to propose to the French minister that the main points in dispute might be profitably discussed between Monson and himself directly. The members of the commission might be used as a sort of subcommittee to work out points of detail. Hanotaux was delighted at the proposal and a meeting was fixed for October 20.[25] This proposal was similar to one suggested by Chamberlain which Salisbury had earlier rejected. Salisbury did not really share Monson's optimism, but allowed him to try his luck if only "to convince impartial students of the controversy that you are right." He was instructed in accordance with the decisions arrived at during the meeting of October 16. The only addition was that Salisbury was now willing to accept the effective occupation doctrine if the French insisted on it, provided "they must be held to it strictly." His change of attitude was based on the understanding that the French did not actually effectively occupy their territories north of the ninth parallel. In that case, Britain would be at liberty to occupy them especially as the projected frontier force should give it a useful advantage. He rejected the probable objection that such occupation might lead to war with France because "neither nation is disposed to face the vast cost and risk of war for the sake of a malarious African desert."[26] He admitted that there would be much "grumbling, and much menace; (and) a period of alienation"; but it would go no farther than that especially as Britain would soon hold all the cards. The French, therefore,

> cannot afford to let the quarrel go on indefinitely. . . . Though, therefore, we enter the campaign late, and have to pay the penalty of some months of neglect—due to having trusted too much to the Niger Company—I think we have certain essential advantages which the French have not, and which will give us a fair arrangement at the end, and if we are careful neither to yield, nor to come into collision. Any collision, of which *we* were guilty would be a mistake, because it would enable the French to range on their side the undoubted aversion of this country for war.

He nevertheless insisted that the Anderson concessions of April, 1896 were "an excessive complaisance" and should "be regarded as having lapsed, and will not be repeated."[27]

Hanotaux and Monson met on October 21.[28] The meeting ended in disorder. The former, having lost his temper on several occasions, put himself at a diplomatic disadvantage and Monson was obliged to adjourn the discussion sine die.[29] The French minister was convinced from the start that the dispatch of arms to West Africa, coupled with the tone of the English press, suggested strongly that the British government was bent on provoking a conflict.[30] They agreed, however, to recall the commissioners to continue their discussions at an informal level[31] (the informal nature of the talks was strongly insisted on by Hanotaux[32]). To create a better atmosphere for future negotiations Britain decided to withdraw from Bontuku, provided the French would undertake not to allow Samory to use it as a base of operations against British territories. If the French allowed this to happen after evacuation, Britain reserved the right to claim compensations for any damages done to British interests.[33] It was further agreed that armed marches across each other's territories should be prohibited.[34]

The Gosselin-Le Comte Negotiations: October, 1897–June, 1898
The commissioners[35] resumed work on October 29 after a lapse of nearly eighteen months. Hanotaux insisted that discussions would

be informal and unofficial—binding on neither government—and that no information should be leaked to the press. Contrary to instructions, Gosselin offered to deflect the Phipps-Hanotaux line so as to give Nikki to France, as a result of which Le Comte offered to give up French claims south of the 1890 line, provided they got access to the Niger. Gosselin only promised commercial facility. France also renounced all claims to the Say-Gomba-Argungu triangle, but insisted that wherever the French flag had once flown, there it must remain.[36]

The immediate offer of Nikki astonished both Salisbury and Chamberlain. Gosselin was firmly instructed to barter Nikki—and only in the last resort—for a valuable quid pro quo. He was therefore forbidden to volunteer any more offers in regard to Gurma, Gurunshi, and Mossi except in the last resort and for a valuable exchange.[37]

At the next meeting the French claimed a right on the Benue River—which they had earlier abandoned—as part of the Senegal hinterland; they equally claimed large areas in the hinterland of the Gold Coast on account of the large amount of blood and treasure they had expended in that region, against which, they argued, Britain could only show the fragile Fergusson treaties.[38] To give Salisbury time to consider these new developments Everett, who was slightly indisposed, was instructed not to recover before the next session. Accordingly, he suffered a convenient "relapse"![39]

Curiously enough—considering that the French had slightly shifted their position of May, 1896—Chamberlain was dissatisfied at the way things were going. He insisted that Hanotaux must change his attitude or there would be no more "transaction." He must abandon his notion about the flag; he must withdraw from Boussa; and the French "must choose another principle on which to stand." If they chose "effective occupation," he advised that negotiations should be suspended for six months to give each country sufficient time to occupy as much of West Africa as possible. If the French rejected this proposal as dangerous, then they would have no alternative but to accept either the hinterland or priority of treaties doctrines. But he was willing to give up claims to Mossi and Gurma in return for a customs agreement.[40]

Earlier, at a conversation between Hanotaux and Gosselin, during which both bandied about the likely reaction of the public opinion of their respective countries as a result of any surrenders by either party, Hanotaux made three important proposals necessary for any agreement. The first concerned the means of communication. By this he meant what he called "facilities at certain points."

This was another way of putting forward his demand for a *chinde* on the Niger. The second was the question of tariffs. This was to be organized in the nature of the Congo Agreement. And the third dealt with the question of territorial compensation. Here, he was vague as to what the likely concessions ought to be. But the idea of the proposals was that they should be discussed in detail by the commission.[41]

In Paris the talks were following no organized pattern. Binger, having failed to make out a case for the extent of the Senegal hinterland, resorted to the well-worn tactics of dismissing all the disputed territories as worthless. To Gosselin's retort that, if such were the case, the territories should be abandoned to England, he could only reply that he did not have a free hand to do so.[42]

By this time it had become apparent that the commission was getting nowhere.[43] To break the deadlock, Everett had produced his notorious "Summary" (at any rate from the Colonial Office point of view), in which he exposed the uselessness of the Niger Company's claimed rights over Borgu, Gurma, and the territory stretching to the south of Say between Gurma and the Niger. In Nikki, he also argued that the British claims could not be established.[44] These arguments impressed Monson and Gosselin. Their reaction boiled down to the simple fact that Britain must make some concessions if anything was to be achieved.[45] Monson was particularly furious with both the Colonial Office and the Niger Company. He complained to Bertie:

> The C.O. ought to have got up their case better. . . . Verily they have been like the Scriptural party who mocked the assistance of Balaam. . . . They (the R.N.C.) seem to me to be a disingenious lot, and to have grossly misled H.M.G. both as to their rights, and their measures of defending them. Goldie talked of being able to sweep the French out of Boussa if left to himself, and I believe they would simply eat him up.
>
> If we break off negotiations the French will be in Gando before we can get near the place, and they mean to do it.[46]

In a long private letter to Salisbury, he further expressed his disappointment at finding that the British case was not as strong as he had been led to believe, and strongly rejected any suggestion of general arbitration.[47]

Chamberlain rejected outright Everett's conclusion and was shocked at "the sudden change" in Monson's attitude. He went to considerable length to disprove Everett's contentions,[48] and asked Salisbury "to delay the negotiations for a few days until we can exhaust the subject of Colonel Everett's memorandum."[49] After a close study of the question, Salisbury backed Chamberlain, arguing mainly that Everett's "Summary" related only to the Niger territories and did not "throw doubt upon the validity of the British claims to any of the places which it is essential to secure."[50]

Monson had earlier reminded Salisbury that no progress was being made over the negotiations.[51] This had driven the foreign secretary to summarize once more the usual British case and his attitude to the whole question and thus tossed the ball into the French court.[52] This, in a way, was a very adroit move for it was to British interests to spin out the negotiations as long as possible.[53] The summary rejection of Everett's "Summary" was therefore doubly understandable. Moreover, Salisbury was not in sympathy with Monson's uncompromising attitude. He wrote to Chamberlain:

> I deplore the line Monson's views have taken. There is something fatal in the air of Paris. Everett goes in the same direction and Phipps in the former Commission was just as bad.[54]

On his own initiative Monson summoned the commission to meet on November 26, but instructed Gosselin to make no mention of the limited arbitration which London was prepared to propose and adhere to in the last resort, because, in his opinion, such a proposal would lead to a provisional suspension of the conference—a fear shared also by Gosselin and Everett.[55] This move, in a way, paid off. Le Comte, unexpectedly, abandoned French claims east of the Niger if they could get satisfaction west of it; but he also requested a port on the Niger. The French commissioner's attitude was "most conciliatory," and "at times, apologetic." When they alluded to a port on the Niger, they "approached us more in the character of petitioners begging for an indulgence which they hoped, if possible, to obtain."[56] This submissive attitude was due, Monson claimed, to the strong resolution now shown by Britain in West African matters; to the Parisian press which no longer regarded Britain as bluffing; and to the fact that the prospects of obtaining a continental coalition against England had faded away.[57] He also wrote to Sanderson, oozing satisfaction if not complacency, at the way things were going, and adding rather boastfully: "I have of course not carried out my instructions, and for this I am solely responsible. I hope to be forgiven."[58] "I am inclined to think that a solution is in sight," Salisbury himself wrote delightedly. "The gist of the matter is the access to the Niger. If that can be arranged I don't think there will be any insuperable difficulty about territory."[59]

At once Salisbury produced a long memorandum in which he

made out a strong case for giving the French a *chinde* or enclave on the Niger, and a right of way from there to Dahomey's northern boundary—a right which they would be asked to use in the form of an easement.[60] He was firmly supported by Hill.[61] But Chamberlain and Bertie were strongly opposed to the idea.[62] Chamberlain argued that such an enclave would lead to complications in the future; that it would not be tolerated by public opinion; and that it would be unanimously opposed by all "the Parties in Britain." He went on:

> In any transaction the sacrifice made by both sides should be similar in character. Doubtful claims may be exchanged for doubtful claims, and rights for rights; but the French only propose to abandon doubtful claims in exchange for the surrender by us of undoubted rights. . . . They assume the position of a man who after stealing my purse should then ask for my watch in consideration of a promise that he will not strip me of my clothes.[63]

The question of the *chinde* was temporarily shelved, but not abandoned.[64]

Like the 1896 discussions, a considerable part of the Gosselin– Le Comte negotiations was devoted to the examination of treaties and to the rights of the two countries in the Gold Coast hinterland and the territories west and east of the Niger.[65] The commissioner's enquiries went into such minute details that it was feared that the proceedings were "becoming a little undignified."[66] Witnesses were examined and cross-examined; the same claims, as in 1896, were advanced by both sides over and over again; and each party rejected the validity of the other's treaties. Only minor concessions in terms of territories were made by either side. Rightly or wrongly, Salisbury left the discussions entirely in the hands of the British delegates, intervening only in matters of details.[67] It suited his calculations to prolong the discussions as long as possible so as to give him time to bargain from a position of strength.[68] But Gosselin, after a careful examination of the issues involved, was forced to report home "the indubitable strength of the case against us." He urged Salisbury to make concessions to France if he wished agreement to be reached.[69]

To Chamberlain such a statement was heresy. He accused Monson, Gosselin, and Everett of blatant pro-French bias. He taunted them for their "implied menace of war" with "a combination of hostile nations," and sneered at what he believed was Colonel Everett's tame acceptance of Colonel Monteil's authority. However, only if France accepted the establishment of an identic tariff system in West Africa would he agree to any territorial concessions. But, if, as was likely, Hanotaux turned down this proposal, and if all compromise failed, he was prepared to submit the entire question to arbitration, since loss by arbitration did not involve loss of honor "whereas the Commissioners' proposals do."[70]

Salisbury never seriously supported general arbitration because he was convinced that the British case was weak; but he favored the identic tariff proposal. At once he informed Hanotaux in the sense urged by Chamberlain, observing that "Our object is . . . not territory, but facility for trade."[71] Gosselin made the same proposal to Le Comte, who declared that he had no authority to commit his government.[72] But surprisingly, Hanotaux accepted the fiscal proposal. He only feared the opposition of Meline on the economic, and that of Lebon on the territorial, questions. He, however, hoped to get his way; and Monson was convinced of his determination to do so.[73] Yet, at the meeting of February 24, 1898, the fiscal engagement turned out to be the main obstacle in British proposals.[74] Why was this? It happened that, as expected, Meline and his cabinet unanimously opposed the measure, but to an extent that Hanotaux had not anticipated.[75] The French fears, too, were genuine. They were not merely inspired by an antagonism against England but by the existing economic reality. It was France's intention to protect the foreign trade of her colonies against the commercial might of England. France was mainly an agricultural country and the chamber was strongly protectionist.[76] The French cabinet, therefore, did not fail to realize the absolute inefficacy of their efforts, in such a system, against a superior competition from England. Hanotaux did not win over his colleagues until March.[77] If the French finally gave way, it was after a tough battle, during which they realized that there was no other reasonable course open to them. They did, however, get in return a territorial makeweight in Mossi—a concession, which was all Britain was prepared to make, and even so, with much difficulty.[78]

Another important issue of the negotiations was the French demand for a territorial access to the navigable Niger. The question which was temporarily shelved in December due to the opposition of Chamberlain and the cabinet, was soon reopened by Hanotaux who insisted that no agreement was possible without it.[79] The cabinet did not object to a French access to the Niger in principle. What they rejected was the French possessing any territories on the banks of the Niger. As Salisbury put it to Bertie:

I do not think that the Cabinet, as at present disposed, will give any territorial possession to France on the banks of the navigable Niger. But I think a general negative statement to that effect is going further than is necessary to carry out the view of the Cabinet.

Our line should be to offer access to the Niger in the former [?] and under the conditions mentioned in the Colonial Office letter to us. But we ought not to recognize the possibility of the territorial solution until it is proposed by France. If so proposed, it would, according to the present view of the Cabinet, be rejected. But that concrete rejection would not preclude us from accepting later if we saw cause for doing so a proposal practically of the same kind. But if we lay down an abstract negative now it would interpose an almost insuperable obstacle if the course of events should make us wish to revert to this solution.[80]

Salisbury therefore yielded to the weight of opinion in the cabinet but managed to leave the option open to modify the position if it became necessary. He made it plain to Hanotaux that what he desired would not only be "incompatible with the position secured to Great Britain at the Berlin Conference" but would also cause a disharmony in the working of the two governments in the areas concerned, thus defeating the objects of the negotiations. He proposed, instead, an arrangement resembling the Franco-German agreement in Togoland which would allow escorted French invalids to pass through British territories to the Niger; and a lease of land to them "at a convenient point on the Niger subject to British jurisdiction," provided France accepted the identic tariff proposal and the Say-Barruwa Agreement as interpreted by Salisbury.[81]

This was a far cry from what the French desired. By a *chinde* they meant, first, a lease to them of a piece of land for wharves and warehouses near the mouth of the Niger and a strip of territory about twenty miles wide, stretching from Nikki to the navigable Niger "on which France would have no sovereign rights and across which British trade should pass freely to or from the north." Both leases were required for 99 years. Gosselin regarded this proposal as inadmissible; Hill considered it worth examining further, but nevertheless instructed Gosselin to reject it. Second, France wanted the lease of a port for 99 years with right to transport merchandise free of duty, to any section of the French possessions from any point on the right, or west, bank of the Niger at about 9 degrees north and vice versa. Gosselin accepted this as a basis for discussion.[82] But

Hanotaux followed up these proposals by producing a sketch which he called a *"Projet de Convention."*[83] This was nothing more than a comprehensive restatement of French views already rejected by Britain. In fact, Hanotaux's tactic was to use, as Chamberlain quickly pointed out, "the maximum concessions of Britain as a stepping-stone for more demands while making no concessions themselves."[84] But the French minister insisted that his proposals were made as an evidence of *"sentiments conciliants."*[85] Monson, however, turned them down and advised that the Foreign Office should prepare a counter-project.[86] Gosselin and Everett, too, rejected them and accused Hanotaux of a "breach of faith."[87] To Chamberlain they were "most discouraging." He warned that they would constitute a *barriere infranchisable* to further negotiations. He also rejected Monson's suggestion of a counter-project because, in his opinion, "we have debarred ourselves from any power to put forward a maximum of our demands by already producing an irreducible minimum."[88]

By this time Salisbury was on the continent recovering his failing health. Balfour was left in charge of the Foreign Office. His brief career at this post was distinguished by no serious departures from his uncle's attitude to the negotiations. He at once refused to accept Hanotaux's *esquisse* as even a basis for discussion.[89] But he persuaded Chamberlain that it might be worthwhile to prepare a counter-project in the manner advised by Monson.[90] This project, like Hanotaux's, was a summary of all British proposals to date. The only thing new was the official granting to the French of an entrepot at the mouth of the Niger, including the lease of territory demanded by them, as well as modified transit regulations for the navigation of the Niger.[91] Privately, Balfour did not expect that all his proposals would be accepted. He was willing to modify some of them if serious objections should be raised.[92] But at the meeting of April 29, Le Comte accepted "in their entirety" British territorial proposals west of the Niger, provided Britain reconsidered the question of the possession of Bona and Lobi, restrict the area of French territories where the fiscal proposal would operate, limiting its duration to thirty years; and allow unarmed French troops to pass through British territory by way of the Niger.[93] But Salisbury, now back at the Foreign Office, insisted that Mossi must be included in the fiscal arrangement because Britain "also have public opinion to satisfy" especially as Mossi was "essential to the commercial interests of the Gold Coast." He only unwillingly allowed unarmed French troops to pass through British territory—and "would certainly not agree to it unless Bona and Lobi were recognized as British"—on condition that they applied separately to Her Majesty's government for permission to allow the troops to pass on each occasion.[94] As to the French access to the Niger, he saw "no objections on ground of general principle," but observed: "Whether there are any real practical objections to the proposed arrangement is a matter on which the opinion of C.O. is important, as they will have to carry out the arrangements."[95]

The "Fate of Negotiations Hangs on Illo"

From this time onwards the main issues appeared to have been settled and Hanotaux was anxious to sign the convention not only because he was expected to be out of office, but also because Lebon was expected to lose his seat. He feared the possibility of the existing French cabinet resigning en masse on the meeting of the new chamber. It was therefore impossible to forecast how a new French cabinet would react.[96] But Monson "found it materially impossible to go as fast as he (Hanotaux) wished."[97] The ambassador, therefore, had good reason for confidently reporting that the "French seem disposed to give way all round."[98] But not quite. The question of the interpretation of the 1890 line, of the nature of the transit regulations for the navigation of the Niger, and of the ownership of Bona, Lobi, and Illo still impeded any agreement.[99] The first two issues were quickly resolved; the 1890 line being decided in Britain's favor, although France obtained the northern and eastern shores of Lake Chad.[100]

Hanotaux introduced the question of Illo late in the day. But Salisbury, fearing that "public opinion in regard to this matter . . . is equally strong in this country" refused to concede Illo as well as Bona and Lobi.[101] Hanotaux was adamant, and Monson wrote feverishly from Paris: the "fate of negotiations hangs on Illo."[102]

Unfortunately, Chamberlain had taken a strong line over these territories. He was, however, persuaded to abandon Bona and Lobi. But he demanded, in return, territorial concessions in the Volta region; in Sierra Leone (Simitia to be given to Britain); that the radius from Sokoto be extended to the fourteenth parallel; and that the trade regulations as proposed by Britain be accepted by the French. Britain was in occupation of Bona and had made treaties with the chiefs. But as Bertie pointed out: "Bona and Lobi may be worth little or nothing. It is not now a question of their intrinsic value. . . . The points seem to be: Have we gone so far in our demand for them for the govt. to lose credit here; to lose face with the natives generally; to give to France and other Powers the impression that we can always be squeezed. . . . Bona and Lobi are on all fours with Nikki."[103] Chamberlain refused to "give up Illo on any pretext."[104] He stressed that, left to himself, he would surrender none of these territories,[105] and that rather than make any more concessions, he would run the risk of breaking up the negotiations.[106] In fact, he went so far as to summarize all the demands to be made on the French in totally undiplomatic language.[107] "If we send the C.O. letter to the Commissioners as an instruction," noted Hill, "it is an ultimatum."[108] Salisbury advised that any instructions must contain the substance of Chamberlain's views, "but in language consistent with a continuation of negotiations."[109] On the morning of May 29 the revised draft by Salisbury was sent to Birmingham by the 10 a.m. train before dispatching it to Paris. But Bertie raised the question as to what would happen if Chamberlain rejected the draft and wished "to leave no loophole as to Illo," which the draft appeared not to have done. Salisbury regarded the question as irrelevant. "I do not understand my language to have left any loophole about Illo," he observed, "but I merely adopted a more seemly form of expression for Blue Book use after the rupture. I think if Mr. C. alters it I should see it again."[110] Here again is a perfect example of the difference between Salisbury and Chamberlain—both wanting the same things but going their different ways about them. Chamberlain made no alterations and the dispatch was sent.[111]

Hill had argued unsuccessfully that, by giving up Illo, Britain would only "lose some 15 miles of river," but would retain far more than she wanted in 1895, when she was prepared to make large concessions to Germany north of Gomba. "If it is thought we were too liberal then," he added, "it is at least the fact that the intention was based on careful thought and study by Sir P. Anderson, a recognized expert." He summed up his attitude:

> It is unnecessary for me to dwell on the higher political aspects of the negotiations or on the Parliamentary questions, both British and French, which are involved. They will be sufficiently present to H. M. Govt. My object is to point out that from a purely material point of view we shall, without holding out for the Bona and Illo pieces of territory now under discussion, get territory equal to what we were prepared to accept in 1896, that we shall add fiscal advantages, and shall settle the Say-Barruwa controversy. If we retain our control of the Niger Navigation, can we ever hope for more from postponements with a continuation of the Chess board policy?[112]

Salisbury, realizing that Illo, in itself an unimportant place, was likely to ruin any hope of agreement in this eleventh hour when every other point had been virtually settled, decided to take up the matter privately with Chamberlain:

> I think we have come to a critical point in the West African negotiations and must consider our further course carefully. As I understand it, if they get Illo, we get Bona, and the Niger arrangements in essentials according to our latest demands. I cannot find that we have any claim to Illo by treaty *eo nomine*; and it lies only ten miles to the East of the 1896 line which we formally accepted. It is not a place on which much stress has been laid in the negotiations so that the concession of it would involve no "climbing down." It is, indeed, on a "trade route"; but the doctrine of the immutability of the trade routes has been, I think, a little over done. Our object in pushing into this country is to bring the commerce down the Niger and a railway between Gando and Jebba cannot lie in the very far future after the country is settled. The cession of Illo, does not therefore seem to be an important cession. . . .
>
> [Lugard had shown that] we cannot take any measures for meeting the French concentration at Illo, without finding ourselves at war with Gando and Sokoto. It will be a war in which we shall be very far removed from our base, and in which we shall have to meet the two most powerful principalities of those regions. We know so little about those countries that we cannot discern what sort of difficulty it will be that this contingency will open to us—but it may be very grave and its cost will certainly buy out the value of Illo a hundred times over. I say nothing about the quarrel with the French for that is familiar ground.
>
> I therefore should very confidently counsel the abandonment of Illo on the assumption, of course, that we receive in return the rest of our latest conditions. The division of yesterday in the French Chamber seems to me to lend considerable urgency to this view.[113]

Chamberlain was not impressed by the Foreign Office arguments.[114] Salisbury therefore hinted that he would bring the matter before the cabinet as soon as Devonshire returned from Ireland where he had been on a visit. He did, nevertheless, try to overwhelm the colonial secretary with what perhaps is the most interesting argument throughout the negotiations. Repeating that he was "wholly unconvinced of the value of Illo," and that Britain had no real claim to it, he tried to placate his colleague by conceding that he would nevertheless prefer to give up Bona instead of Illo "because our title to Bona seems to me positively bad." He went on:

> It will be a pity if we break off negotiations for it will add to our difficulties in the Nile Valley. But unless we have very bad luck, the rupture ought not to lead to war with France so long as troops are kept to the present level. But if we are to send British or Indian troops, in the hope of fighting another Plassey with Lugard as our Clive, and Sokoto as our Bengal, the prospect becomes much more serious. Our Clive will be in no danger of being astonished at his own moderation. There is no loot to get except in Goldie's dreams.
>
> If you wish to come to terms it would be prudent to do so before we take Khartoum. We shall get nothing out of the French Assembly after that event.[115]

But Chamberlain was far from being overwhelmed. He merely repeated that he would only give up Bona, not Illo, and added rather amiably:

> In this difficult business I desire to meet you by giving up everything that does not appear to me essential to our honour and our interests.
>
> Illo is, in my opinion, one of the exceptions—Bona is not.[116]

As Britain, in the end, retained Illo, it is fair to assume that the cabinet overruled Salisbury's objections. Why the cabinet and Chamberlain should have felt so strongly about Illo—a relatively unimportant place—is not exactly clear. The controversy over Illo was the only notable victory—if it could be called such—gained by Chamberlain over Salisbury in the entire Niger imbroglio. It must be admitted, however, that the foreign secretary was not intent on giving up Illo on ground of general policy; in other words, it was not a policy victory. He merely wished to concede it—especially as it was not a place of major importance, and as Britain had no serious claims to it—to avoid the break-up of the negotiations which were practically concluded. What would have been the position if Hanotaux, in his anxiety to sign the Protocol, had not let everyone off the hook by being content to make do with Bona,[117] is not the business of the historian to speculate about.

The settlement of Illo ended the partition of West Africa. The commissioners spent the rest of their meetings putting the final touches to the draft agreement. On June 14, 1898, the Niger Convention was signed at Paris[118] and Hanotaux was "gratified" at the outcome.[119]

While negotiations progressed in Paris, the opposition in England and their press, as well as the Parisian press, were spreading the rumor that there was a struggle for the control of policy between Salisbury and Chamberlain. They went so far as to assert that the cabinet was divided into two factions—with Salisbury at the head of the peace faction, who were disposed to make unlimited concessions to France; and Chamberlain at the head of the war party, who were itching to go to war with France over West Africa rather than make any concessions.[120] As the reader will have realized these views must not be taken too seriously. In the first place, there is no evidence of a *struggle* between the prime minister and his colonial secretary. Undoubtedly, they disagreed as to what to concede and what not to concede, and as to the best method of handling the diplomacy of the negotiations. But again and again, Chamberlain, as has been shown, yielded to the force of the better argument. There were no threatened resignations, no recriminations, nobody was denounced openly or secretly; and, on the whole, their differences were resolved with remarkable amiability. True, Salisbury did make a private jest that Chamberlain "hated giving anything away"; but the latter explained that he only objected to giving away something for nothing.[121] True, Salisbury confided in Queen Victoria that "Chamberlain is a little too warlike, and hardly sees the other side of the question."[122] He even went so far as to speak of the attitude of the Kaiser and that of Chamberlain in one breath. "The one object of the German Emperor," he wrote to Balfour, "has been to get us into a war with France. I never can make up my mind whether this is part of Chamberlain's objects or not."[123] There is no doubt that the colonial secretary gave the impression of being more belligerent and more rumbuctious than any of his colleagues. Such characteristics are not unusual in a person of his temperament. He may have blown hot and cold over French pretensions; he may have spoken privately and publicly of the need for firmness; but he was no more ready to go to war with France than Salisbury was. Nor was Hanotaux. When the West African difficulties had reached a feverish pitch in March, 1898, with rumor of war in the air, and Wilkinson had written to him: "If there is a war, you have to run it,"[124] there is no evidence to suggest that Chamberlain jumped at the idea. During the South African imbroglio, it was Chamberlain, not Salisbury, who got cold feet as the dateline approached. The details of the Niger negotiations give the lie to those who believed and still believe, that Salisbury was Chamberlain's poodle. As one peruses the documents, one is again and again drawn to the belief that the two ministers differed only as to means, not ends. This difference was largely due to their widely opposite personalities. There was no struggle for control of policy.

It is much more difficult to assess the attitudes of the rest of the cabinet because of lack of concrete evidence. Minutes of cabinet discussions were not kept at this time. But the views of certain ministers on specific issues, outside their own departments, may be gleaned from their private correspondence (always scattered and scanty in this direction), from their diaries and autobiographies (not always reliable), and from the foreign secretary's reports to the monarch of cabinet meetings (which are sketchy and do not appear to have been regular), or occasionally from the *Queen's Journal*. But it can be confidently said that there was no division into a war party and a peace party. The ministers who received copies of important documents were Balfour, Devonshire, Hicks-Beach, Goschen, and Lansdowne. (Queen Victoria and the Prince of Wales also received copies.) One gets the general impression, however, that there was a remarkable unanimity as to general policy.[125] Occasionally, as on the question of the French access to the Niger, or on the retention of Illo, the cabinet took a firmer line than Salisbury; in most cases, they deferred to his better judgment;[126] always, they considered the West African question as ugly, and of immense importance, which required delicate handling.[127] There was a general belief that the French were painstakingly nasty. That was why the occasional blusterings of Chamberlain, though viewed with concern, were treated with understanding. Usually, Balfour was a Salisbury man; Devonshire and Lansdowne appeared to have refrained from interfering in the affairs of departments outside their own, unless called upon to do so; Goschen and Beach occasionally spoke out on specific issues. Usually, Goschen offered his support: "The Niger looks ugly. I am hastening on the gunboats, but the strike delays us";[128] or, "the despatch of the gunboats to the Niger will be known soon," and adding, "I wonder what the French will say. Our counter-occupations have at least had this result—that Hanotaux answers the despatches."[129] When Chamberlain refused to resume negotiations in the autumn of 1897, Goschen, while supporting the Salisbury line that talks should be started, nevertheless, showed an understanding of Chamberlain's point of view, and mildly chastised Salisbury for saying that he was "yoked with Chamberlain":

> I am, of course, extremely anxious about the Niger, as strong as you are about the necessity of holding our own against the local French encroachments, and quite prepared to follow you

in all you may think necessary. But you used a phrase in your last letter, that in this business you were yoked with Chamberlain, and I gather from a despatch of Monson that it is . . . Chamberlain who wishes to abstain from further negotiations with the French. If there should be any difference of opinion on this vital issue between Chamberlain and you, I venture to think you should summon a Cabinet. . . .

I fancy Chamberlain is not so averse to a war, as others may be. He is sick of the French antagonisms in so many quarters, and no wonder.

However, he considered that the moment was not opportune to "quarrel with the French who had lost their heads, because of the growing Russian ebullition."[130]

Hicks-Beach, too, intervened about this time over the projected frontier force. He argued, rather unsuccessfully, that since negotiations were to be resumed the force would be unnecessary, because "when raised, they will want something to do and may therefore, in spite of ourselves, get us into trouble . . . with Sokoto, or other powerful states, even some remote from the coast." He therefore suggested "a reciprocal agreement with Hanotaux that neither side shall occupy any fresh points pending the negotiation."[131] But the Foreign Office, unlike Hicks-Beach, were convinced that Hanotaux would observe no such agreement. There was a belief that "the French will derive undue advantage from promises on both sides which are unnecessarily large—for we shall keep them, while they will not."[132] However, Hicks-Beach warned that "a forward policy in too many places at once had been disastrous for England before and would likely be so again." "What is going to happen in Nigeria and the Gold Coast Hinterland?," he asked. "I really don't know: but Chamberlain will try to do a good deal if you don't stop him."[133] A little hard on Chamberlain, perhaps; but Hicks-Beach never really cared for Chamberlain's methods. One point is fairly clear: there was no Chamberlain faction, even among the Liberal Unionists, in Salisbury's inner cabinet.

One interesting development, however, of the West African question was the changed attitudes of the organs of public opinion and the growing influence of the Chambers of Commerce. As early as 1895, Lugard wrote of the Chambers of Commerce: "It is interesting to note how within the last few years the Chambers of Commerce of England and Scotland have spoken with one voice in favour of expansion."[134] It could fairly be said that, on the whole, they urged the government to pursue a firmer policy. Parliament, which a generation earlier had advocated a policy of scuttle, was now in favor of a forward policy in West Africa. So also were the press and the Chambers of Commerce. Their influence on Salisbury's attitude may be difficult to assess, but equally naive to reject. A shrewd parliamentarian summed up the situation when he said that what Salis-bury was frightened to do ten years ago, he could

> afford to do now because his position is stronger. To protect British trade, and, above all, the British Empire, this great majority was sent to sit on this side of the House. It must be worthy of its traditions, or it will fall.[135]

These organs, too, gave a mixed reception to the 1898 Convention. The expansionists, led by the *Daily Mail,* saw it as another sellout to the French. They believed that only Chamberlain prevented a disastrous agreement from the British point of view. To the moderates the agreement represented the best that was possible under the circumstances. The Chambers of Commerce were prepared to overlook everything else because of the fiscal provision which they considered to be to their advantage. The most astonishing reaction came from the liberal press. The *Westminster Gazette* saw the Convention as only "A Crumb of Comfort";[136] to the *Daily Chronicle,* it "is the latest addition to the list of our 'graceful concessions'";[137] the *Daily News* was convinced that Salisbury made "very large concessions" to France, and added: "but for a wonder Lord Salisbury has obtained something in return," namely, "the open door in West Africa."[138] And these were the organs held up as the opponents of expansion![139] In Paris, too, the press denounced the agreement as disastrous for French interests, and Delcasse, who succeeded Hanotaux as foreign minister, feared that the Chamber would strongly oppose ratification.[140]

The public on both sides were, of course, ignorant of the details of the negotiations. But it was agreed not to publish the records because it would be "a hazardous proceeding."[141] With our better knowledge nowadays, it is easier to see that Britain did considerably better than France.[142] Salisbury conceded nothing that his country could establish an indisputable claim for; on top of that, there was the fiscal clause. Not without justification, he considered the convention "a good job"—a sentiment shared by Queen Victoria.[143] Salisbury's satisfaction is understandable. Toward the last stage of the negotiations, he discovered, after seriously studying the papers, that a good deal of the British claims were "shady" because she had claimed more territories than she could establish strong claims for. Gradually, he began to shift his ground. He knew that when the chips were down, he would not be justified, in the eyes of the British public, to go to war with France over what he considered shady claims, some of which were unimportant in themselves. He realized, as also did *The Times*, that

> had we placed less absolute reliance upon the goodness of that title [i.e., at the back of the Gold Coast Hinterland where Salisbury was supposed to have made concessions], and exerted ourselves in time to establish effective occupation of the regions we claimed, we should have been able to vindicate our rights without serious controversy.[144]

That Britain failed to occupy effectively the territories she claimed, or even to conclude unequivocal treaties of protection, was hardly the fault of France. What Salisbury's critics had done was to confuse claims with legal rights.

This being the case, it is difficult to see how the thesis can be upheld that Salisbury consistently yielded territories to France on the West Coast in return for supremacy in the Nile Valley.[145] There is no concrete evidence of such an arrangement. Whenever Hanotaux had vaguely raised the question of a comprehensive settlement of all Anglo-French difficulties all over the world, Salisbury had resolutely refused to follow it up; always, he had tossed the ball into Hanotaux's court and had asked him to make definite proposals which never came.[146] Nowhere in his dispatches did Salisbury mention the Nile Valley as influencing developments in West Africa. He studiously refrained from bringing up the Egyptian question to complicate an already complicated position. He knew that no amount of territorial concessions, at this time, would reconcile France to Britain's occupation of Egypt. If Britain made unwarranted concessions to France in West Africa—a theory to which I do not subscribe—it was not because of a determination to maintain her undoubtedly superior interests in the Nile Valley. Perhaps, Monson deserves the last say. As soon as the convention was signed, he wrote to his chief:

> I hope you are satisfied with the result of the Niger Negotiations. I never expected that they would end so well, until I began to see that the French government had become really anxious to settle the matter. After all we have secured much better terms than the French originally dreamed they would be compelled to concede to us; and considering the disadvantages under which the negotiations started I think that the British public ought to be grateful to them.[147]

The behavior of the French in the following twelve months does not exactly suggest the activities of those who had secured important concessions. Despite the signing of the convention they consistently violated British territorial rights and several protests were addressed to the French government.[148] It was not until June 13, 1899 that the convention was ratified by the French Chambers after much difficulty.[149] Thus, the thorny question of the Niger was at last settled. And Salisbury was vindicated: he obtained, in the end, more than he could have got by provoking a fight in a time of many international crises. For some years to come, European boundaries were readjusted in West Africa. But these were of minor importance.

PART III

East and Central Africa, 1884–1900

Chapter VII

Zanzibar: Save Me from My Friends

The Omani eviction of the Portuguese from the East African coast and the defeat of Napoleon at Waterloo had given Britain command of the Indian Ocean. Thus began the era of Omani-British alliance which eventually resulted in the loss of Omani independence and the dismemberment of the Omani empire. In the beginning the British had assumed that the Omani exercised considerable sovereignty in the interior of East Africa. In reality, however, major efforts by the Arabs to penetrate the East African interior were made only during the reign of Sultan Sayyid Said (1806–56), and of his successors Sayyid Majid and Sayyid Barghash. Omani imperialism was basically economic rather then evangelical or political. Arabs were encouraged to trade in the interior, and financial backing, in the form of credits, were offered to them. These traders founded settlements in the Unyamwezi town of Tabora and the Ha town of Ujiji on Lake Tanzania. Their commercial influence also extended to parts of Kenya (outside of Mombasa and other coastal towns), Uganda, Central Africa, and the Congo. The degree of Omani control over these traders is not clear. Nor did their accepted political control over the coastal towns go unchallenged. And yet the well-known saying: "When they pipe in Zanzibar, people dance on the shores of the great lakes," had an element of truth in it, for the Arab traders—especially slave traders—played a significant role in undermining the political equilibriums with which they came into contact. The Arab commercial empire in East Africa was at its zenith during the second half of the nineteenth century; Zanzibar was its base, and it was from the Zanzibar base that the British conquest of East Africa was accomplished.

Prelude to Conquest
The crisis of the Omani empire started with British efforts to suppress the slave trade in the sultan's dominions. In 1822, Britain had used its influence, buttressed by its command of the Indian Ocean,

to secure the Moresby Treaty which made "illegal," throughout Said's dominions, the "sale of slaves to subjects of Christian powers." It also limited slave traffic to ports in his Oman and African dependencies. Said had signed this treaty primarily to stop British interference during the ensuing conflict with the Mazaria of Mombasa. The so-called "Owen Protectorate" of Mombasa (1824) strained the alliance; but in 1826 Britain renounced the protectorate.[1] Thus a major obstacle to Said's liquidation of the Mazaria was removed. This was achieved in 1837. In 1840 Said transferred his capital from Oman to Zanzibar. The first country to have formal diplomatic relations with him was the United States of America (1836). Britain (1840) and France (1844) followed the American lead. The curious thing about these relationships was that Zanzibar was not allowed to open up consulates in the other countries. Nevertheless Zanzibar became the first state in tropical Africa to be accorded that degree of European recognition, although it was clear the British were there to enforce the Moresby treaty and promote their trade.

European friendship did the sultans more harm than good. It tightened the noose around their necks and around the slave trade; it got them caught in the spider's web of European diplomacy and imperial aims. There was no one to save them from their European friends. The Africans hated the Arabs more than they did the Europeans. In 1845 the Hammerton Treaty further restricted the slave trade to the sultan's East African territories. Neither the sultan's Arab subjects nor the French had any intention of obeying this treaty. Forced, therefore, by internal instability and French menace, Said began to lean more and more toward British protection.[2] It is not surprising that in 1861 Britain could intervene effectively in the succession dispute which erupted as a result of the death of Said in 1856. The late sultan's dominions were divided between his sons Thuwain and Majid. Thuwain got Muscat and Oman; Majid became Sultan of Zanzibar and its dependencies. And, as part of the settlement, "the independence of Zanzibar" was proclaimed.[3] By the joint declaration of March 13, 1862, Britain and France recognized this independence and ratified the Canning Award of 1861.[4]

Despite the 1862 declaration Majid's hold on his dominions was unstable; his soldiers were unreliable, and when he was attacked by some Arab slave traders from the north he could not defend himself and decided to buy them off with money.[5] From that day the writing was on the wall. Britain had formed an alliance of friendship and commerce with a strong African state and within half a century had reduced it to impotence without firing a shot. For Majid the

British alliance had not been remunerative. Britain could not even save him from his subjects. He therefore became opposed to further restrictions of the slave trade. Worried by his increasing dependence on Britain, in 1859 Majid had signed a treaty of amity and commerce with the Hanseatic Republics in the hope, probably, that they might provide a counterweight to British power. By 1870 German trade with Zanzibar was second only to that of Britain.[6] However, as long as the sultan's power remained weak, and the slave trade continued, the Hanseatic alliance would not be strong enough to save Majid from British interference. On the contrary, it was instrumental in Bismarck's interest in Zanzibar which, in turn, led to the partition of the Omani empire. Majid's death in 1870 without an heir worsened the political situation. Barghash, his half-brother and great rival, who had led the succession dispute in the 1850s, and had been exiled but later recalled, was now to be set up as sultan of Zanzibar by H. A. Churchill, British Consul. It was agreed, as part of the deal, that Barghash would observe all the antislave trade declarations.[7] Thus a succession war was avoided and the impact of British influence further confirmed.

Natural disasters also weakened the sultanate. In 1870 an outbreak of cholera was reported and some 200 persons were estimated to have died daily; the value of slaves consequently dropped to below a dollar per head.[8] On April 15, 1872, a hurricane attacked Zanzibar and destroyed the sultan's fleet anchored in the harbor as well as approximately two-thirds of the clove and coconut trees[9] —in short the mainstay of the island's economy. Without his fleet and considerably impoverished, Barghash's already weak position became more tenuous; the need, among Arabs, for the continuation of the slave trade and for slaves to plant new cloves became stronger. Faced with strong Arab opposition to the suppression of the slave trade, afraid of losing his throne since he was militarily and economically weak, Barghash was compelled to disavow all the understandings he had made with Churchill prior to his accession to power. It was not until June, 1873 that he was forced by John Kirk (then British Consul-General) under threat of a British bombardment from the sea to accede to the recommendations of Sir Bartle Frere's parliamentary committee which had visited Zanzibar in January. Kirk's gunboat diplomacy resulted in the Treaty of June 5, 1873, by which the slave trade was abolished throughout the sultan's dominions.[10]

That Barghash was forced to sign this treaty in the face of Arab opposition is further proof that the 1862 independence declaration was not taken seriously by the British. Subsequent developments will lend more weight to this view. Barghash paid a state visit to England in 1875; but this was another diplomatic exercise for as soon as he returned home, he was induced to form a strong and efficient army to enforce the antislave trade declarations. This army was to be commanded by a British officer, Lieutenant William Lloyd Mathews. From then onwards it became no secret that Britain was the de facto power in Zanzibar.

Salisbury and the Partition of the Omani Empire, 1885–90

Until 1884 British influence in Zanzibar had not been seriously challenged by any other European power and seemed assured. Britain, too, having undermined the power and prestige of the sultans, had no clear idea of what to do with the sultanate and its dependencies. As Salisbury put it: "Keeping every other nation out on the bare chance that some day or other our traders will pluck up heart to go in is a poor policy."[11] It was Salisbury who restored the British initiative in Zanzibar but the push to partition the Omani empire came from Germany. During the Berlin Conference it was rumored that Bismarck was planning to declare a protectorate over Zanzibar, a rumor which Berlin roundly discounted.[12] Britain, nevertheless, was aware that the German threat to its position as well as to that of Barghash was a reality but Gladstone had enough on his plate to bother about Zanzibar. He even opposed the proposed annexation of "the Kilimanjoro district,"[13] but in deference to the Colonial Office argument that the British position in Zanzibar should be maintained, and the German intrusion checked, at least "from an Indian point of view,"[14] he authorized a strong protest to be sent to Germany. Earl Granville, Foreign Secretary, stated in this dispatch that East Africa was understood to be "beyond the sphere of German political interest." On the other hand, "For the greater part of the present century the sultans of Muscat and Zanzibar have been under the direct influence of the United Kingdom and of the Government of India." Germany was asked to recognize the sultan's independence.[15] Bismarck grasped at once the hypocrisy of this dispatch. If Zanzibar was independent, he retorted, then Germany had a right to make a treaty with it. This being the case, the question of endangering British interests was absurd. Granville had no answer to the Bismarckian logic.[16] Once more it had become clear that informal influence was not enough to keep others out.

In the meantime Germany's energetic explorers led by Karl Peters rushed to East Africa to secure as many "treaties" as possible from the African rulers. In a matter of weeks they had secured numerous and dubious treaties and faced their government with a fait accompli. Bismarck opposed their proceedings publicly but never-theless used the treaties to his advantage. For example, on February 20, 1885, Usagara, Ungulu, Ukami, and Unzina were formerly placed under German sovereignty; a part of the Kilimanjaro district and Witu were also acquired by Germany. Sultan Barghash's pro-tests at these high-handed mutilations of his dominions only served to cause "considerable irritation" in Germany.[17] German gunboats were dispatched to Zanzibar "to bring the sultan to a more correct bearing."[18] Salisbury, who succeeded Granville in June and was ignorant of the affairs in Zanzibar, advised caution while he studied the question. But he was too politically weak at home to adopt a strong stand abroad. Moreover the Suez crisis and the Khartoum humiliation had complicated the diplomatic situation. He therefore advised Barghash to recant, under protest, for complaining about German seizure of his territories. Barghash had no choice but to comply. He offered the Germans favorable terms of trade and al-lowed them practical domination of the port of Dar-es-Salaam. The German colony of Tanganyika was in the making. This capitulation meant, indeed, as Coupland has rightly pointed out, that "Bismarck . . . had openly and directly challenged the championship of the Sul-tan's rights which Britain had maintained for half a century."[19]

But it meant much more than that. It had demonstrated that in-formal paramountcy had no validity in the law of nations; it had exposed the hollowness of the Anglo-Zanzibar alliance. When the Liberals returned to power, the earl of Rosebery suggested the ap-pointment of an Anglo-German commission "to investigate what are the just limits of the Sultan's dominions."[20] It was left to Salisbury, however, to renew the Rosebery initiative and negotiate the delim-itation treaty of 1886.[21]

While negotiations were in progress Salisbury suspected Bis-marck of double-dealing.[22] He noted that the Chancellor was "itch-ing to confiscate the coast as well as the interior. This is, I think, an unwise display of swagger. The coast cannot be of the slightest use to Germans or to any other Europeans." Although he was not in a position to take a tough line, he nevertheless made it plain that "The only issue to the discussion which would be intolerable to us would be the possession of one or two free ports by the Ger-mans, and the rest of the coast in the hands of Zanzibar, and a heavy tariff. This would of course make the Germans the monopo-lists of the Big Lakes market."[23] This is interesting. Salisbury's in-terest in Zanzibar, it seems, in terms of the broader imperial strat-egy, was to prevent the Germans from monopolizing the markets of the hinterland. He therefore was "quite ready to let him [Bismarck] have any portion of the Spanish dominions he may take a fancy to" if he would loosen his squeeze on Zanzibar and continue "his good offices" in Egypt.[24]

Bismarck's squeeze on Zanzibar was indeed becoming scandalous. The supposedly antiimperialist Chancellor openly meddled in Barghash's private family affairs in pursuance of imperial aims. He authorized the use of Madame Emily Ruete, the sultan's exiled sister, now conveniently married to a German, for provoking a German attack on Zanzibar. Madame Ruete, now also "a German subject" was sent to Zanzibar "in the protection of the (German) navy" to "make her claims" for an equitable share of the family inheritance.[25] According to Muslim law, however, Ruete was a nonperson. As Barghash put it: Ruete had "disgraced the family and done acts punishable by death, and, having since abandoned the Mohammedan religion, she was dead at law."[26] In short anyone could kill her without fear of punishment. Bismarck gambled on this happening or on the sultan being sufficiently angry with his sister upon her arrival in Zanzibar to strangle her. If this happened, Bismarck would order the bombardment of Zanzibar as retribution for the killing of a German subject. Alternatively, he would attempt to stir up a popular revolution in Zanzibar.[27] Britain discovered this plot and prevented what would have been one of the worst scandals of nineteenth century European imperial history. Barghash still refused to have anything to do with Madame Ruete but consented to pay Bismarck an agreed sum of money "to use as he thought fit." Bismarck accepted the money![28]

Salisbury did not wish to strain Anglo-German relations. He needed Bismarck's "good offices" in the other diplomatic problems facing Britain.[29] And since Bismarck had embarrassed himself over the Madame Ruete affair, and had made no territorial gains, Salisbury was disposed to let sleeping dogs lie. But more importantly, he did not wish to run the risk of imperiling the negotiations. It was not until June 9, 1886, that the unanimous report was signed by the British and German negotiators. By this time the Liberals had come back to power. Within the same month Gladstone was defeated over Home Rule for Ireland and Salisbury was back to power as prime minister with Lord Iddesleigh as his foreign secretary. By October both governments ratified the agreement, and the Delimitation Treaty was signed on November 1.[30]

This treaty is significant. It placed Zanzibar and most of its dependencies within the sphere of influence of Britain. It assured German political influence in East Africa, thereby breaking the British monopoly. The supposedly independent sultan of Zanzibar was informed, but was allowed no voice, in regard to the partition of his empire. By the terms of this treaty all that was left of the empire were the islands of Zanzibar, Pemba, Mafia, Lamu, and the coastal strip just over 1608 kilometers long, running southward from the Tana River to Ruvuma. The rest passed over to the British and Germans, the latter gaining control of those dependencies in the Tanganyika littoral. Barghash's protests to London and Berlin were contemptuously treated. His request to be given six months to consider the treaty was not granted. "No extension can be given," was the telegraphic reply from London. "We have done our best in Your Highness's behalf. Our friendly advice is that you should accept at once. Your interests would be endangered by delay."[31] Berlin replied in the same tone and on December 7 Barghash was forced to sign the treaty. It has been contended that the agreement of 1886 "favoured Germany because Britain wanted German friendship at that moment more than Germany wanted British."[32] But it must be added that the German gain did not lie in the extent and quality of the territories acquired but only in the fact that Britain no longer exercised a monopoly of political interest in the Omani empire. Moreover, the German show of great enterprise and energy from 1884 onwards and the comparative British inactivity were bound to be reflected in the treaty. Looked at from the German point of view, it is fair to say that the Germans obtained what they deserved and not that the treaty favored Germany.

For Barghash one tragedy followed another. In December a Somali was alleged to have killed a German called Juhlke at Kismayu. No motive for the murder was given. The alleged culprit was "tried" and expectedly found guilty. He was sentenced to life imprisonment. But the German government demanded that the Somali be executed at the site of his alleged crime; a demand to which Barghash yielded only "under threat of naval action."[33] Salisbury merely expressed astonishment at what he described as Bismarck's "strange proceedings" in East Africa.[34] In February, 1887, Portugal, which had been ignored by the powers during the 1885–86 delimitation meetings, decided to grab by force part of what was left of Barghash's empire. The Portuguese governor general of Mozambique "presented an ultimatum requiring the Sultan to recognize the Rovuma as the Portuguese frontier within twenty-four hours." Barghash ignored the ultimatum and Portugal bombarded the villages of Mninjani and Tungi for five days before landing soldiers to burn what remained of them. Barghash once more capitulated[35] and his friends did not come to his aid. It was no surprise that when Holmwood, British Consul-General in Zanzibar, saw him in March, 1887 he was "on the verge of distraction and for the time quite unequal to facing his difficulties."[36] In February, 1888 Salisbury wrote of him: "It would be awkward in one sense if the Sultan were to take this moment for dying—though the difficulty with France would be counter-balanced by the circumstance that Germany is for the moment muzzled."[37] Barghash refused to do Salisbury any more favors by staying alive. On March 27, 1888, he died, a heart-broken man, at the early age of 51. On the same day, the British commander of his troops, Mathews, promptly installed the dead sultan's brother, Sayyid Khalifa, in his place as another British puppet.

With the death of Barghash the conquest of East Africa proceeded with amazing rapidity. On September 3 Salisbury granted a royal charter to William Mackinnon's Imperial British East Africa Company (henceforth I.B.E.A.C.) to operate in the British sphere of influence. Earlier on April 28, the German East Africa Company had been formed to operate in the German sphere. And in November the German protectorate of Witu was announced. But Karl Peters's push toward the mainland encountered strong Arab and Swahili resistance. Soon the company found itself in trouble when the Swahili chief, Abushiri bin Salim, an opponent of the sultan, led a popular revolt against the invaders and Bwana Heri of the Zigua people. The revolt was so serious that it was rumored Bismarck might pull out of East Africa altogether. Salisbury minuted: "Very good news. If the Germans go we shall have plenty of leisure to deal with the natives."[38] This is authentic Salisbury. It was the European challenge to British position in Africa which had forced him to modify his strategy of the imperialism of conquest. Reluctance to speed the pace of conquest has erroneously been interpreted as opposition to imperial expansion.

Bismarck, however, had no intention of abandoning East Africa. On the contrary, he promptly dispatched a German gunboat to crush the revolt and rescue the company. Salisbury became apprehensive of this show of force and ordered British warships to enforce a joint blockade with Germany. He argued that he wished to make sure that the Germans behaved with "such moderation as suits our ideas"; and to prevent a possible German bombardment of Zanzibar should the sultan be drawn into the quarrel. But the Germans, apparently taken in by this gesture, expressed anxiety that Salisbury might endanger his position in Britain by going too far to meet German wishes in Zanzibar. This would be tragic since they preferred him in office to Gladstone.[39] Portugal and Italy also joined the blockade. And a local incident had assumed international dimensions. Abushiri was eventually hunted down and hanged in

December, 1889. A Swahili poet later wrote of him: "He was brave as a lion and intolerant of oppression; where there was trouble, he would be in it."[40]

Meanwhile it had become apparent that the 1886 Treaty did not fix the "spheres of influence" of the two countries to the westward. Thus the rivalry between the two companies widened. But the I.B.E.A.C. seemed to have had a built-in advantage. It was favored by the sultan; it was given full judicial and political power over the mainland territory between Kipini and Umba for half a century; and it also levied customs duties in this territory but paid the sultan some compensation. By 1888 the company claimed to be exercising political authority over some two hundred miles of territory from the coast toward the hinterland. To the north it disputed with Italy the sultan's ports of Kismayu, Merca, Mogadishu and Warsheik. These ports were surrendered to Italy which undertook to transfer them to Britain—and did so—in a subsequent arrangement. The I.B.E.A.C. also occupied Pate and Manda islands by the end of 1889. The proceedings of both companies created suspicion. The Germans suspected Mackinnon of attempting to join hands with Cecil Rhodes in Central Africa, thereby forcing them out of Tanganyika; Mackinnon suspected Karl Peters of attempting to dislodge the British from Uganda. Mackinnon also continued the attrition of the sultan's territories. He saw to it that Lamu, claimed by Germany, was given back to the sultan, who was promptly compelled to surrender it to Britain.

Within Zanzibar itself the Arabs had not meekly accepted their humiliation. Their numerous intrigues and German subversion, implicit and overt, were making Britain's position intolerable. "You have to govern an imbecile Sultan," Salisbury had warned Gerald Portal, "and make him like the operation" in the face of "encouragements to revolt against you."[41] It was not an easy task. Salisbury therefore decided to remove once and for all the German menace before dealing with his "natives." Mackinnon had not been much use to him. So he suggested a comprehensive arrangement of Anglo-German differences in East Africa. The result was the Agreement of 1890 by which Germany abandoned the Witu Protectorate and recognized British supremacy in Zanzibar and Pemba. France also agreed to forget the 1862 Declaration in return for a French protectorate over Madagascar.[42] Salisbury had sealed off Zanzibar from German imterference because, as he put it, "The English and Indian interests are both too strong" to meddle with it.[43] And yet when he had earlier been warned that the Germans "are deliberately working to ruin the sultan, to drive out the British Indian traders, and to

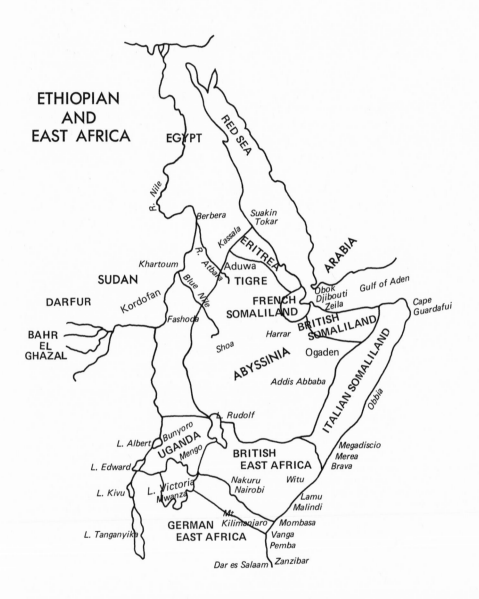

ETHIOPIAN
AND
EAST AFRICA

EGYPT

RED SEA

R. Nile

Berbera

Suakin
Tokar

Kassala

ERITREA

Khartoum

R. Atbara

Aduwa

TIGRE

ARABIA

SUDAN

Blue Nile

DARFUR

Kordofan

Fashoda

FRENCH
SOMALILAND

Obok
Djibouti
Zeila

Gulf of Aden

Cape
Guardafui

BAHR
EL
GHAZAL

Shoa

Harrar

BRITISH
SOMALILAND

Addis Abbaba

ABYSSINIA

Ogaden

ITALIAN SOMALILAND

Obbia

L. Rudolf

Bunyoro

L. Albert

UGANDA

Mengo

BRITISH
EAST AFRICA

Megadiscio
Merea
Brava

L. Edward

L. Kivu

L. Victoria

Mwanza

Nakuru
Nairobi

Witu

Lamu
Malindi

L. Tanganyika

GERMAN
EAST AFRICA

Mt
Kilimanjaro

Mombasa

Vanga

Pemba

Dar es Salaam

Zanzibar

produce anarchy with a view to some gigantic robbery" he had replied, perhaps for the benefit of future historians: "I doubt this view
very much. There is not enough to rob." It can, of course, be argued
that "the English and Indian interests" were strategic, not economic.
This would be incorrect because Salisbury had earlier pointed out
that the East African "coast cannot be of the slightest use to Germans or to any other European power" and that he was protecting
the Great Lakes' markets. There has been a regrettable tendency on
the part of some historians to accept ministerial minutes uncriti-
cally.

Having settled with Germany, Salisbury lost no time in dealing
with the sultan. Euan Smith was asked to persuade the sultan to
issue the famous decree of August 1, 1890, by which it was promul-
gated that after that date, all sale, exchange, purchase, or inheritance of slaves, were prohibited. But clause two of the same decree
stipulated as follows: "We declare that, subject to the conditions
stated below, all slaves lawfully possessed on this date by our subjects shall remain with their owners as at present. Their status shall
remain unchanged."[44] In November, 1890, Zanzibar was formally
proclaimed a British protectorate.[45] Thus Britain's de facto power
in Zanzibar had become a legal fact. The ten-mile strip stretching
from Vanga to the Juba was not included in the proclamation. Afterwards this area became known as the Kenya protectorate, and
the hinterland between Mombasa and the Rift Valley became the
East Africa protectorate and was administered from Zanzibar. With
some adjustments these two protectorates became the Kenya colony
in the twentieth century.

Salisbury and Slavery: Festina Lente

The Zanzibar protectorate was proclaimed despite suggestions to
hand over the territory to the Colonial Office. Salisbury disliked Colonial Office methods of administration and was determined to govern the new territory in his own way. He wrote to Euan Smith, its
first administrator:

> I am very anxious to do everything as peaceably as possible
> on the East African coast for several reasons—and notably be-
> cause it is the best chance of upholding the Sultan's revenue.
> If there was any great shakeout or disturbance, it would stop
> trade for a time, and when *trade resumed*, it would seek the
> direct route through the ports on the African coast, to or from
> the interior markets, instead of going round by the island. But
> the present [illegible] trade enjoyed by the island may last for
> a long time, if complete tranquility prevails.[46]

Here is an interesting economic argument for going forward slowly, which is not only sound, but must also be borne in mind in assessing Salisbury's imperialism of conquest. Euan Smith did not disappoint him for he was not the type of person to attempt bold innovations. By 1891, Euan Smith's health had failed and Salisbury appointed Gerald Portal to succeed him. He commissioned the new man to "make the Protectorate a reality," but at the same time advised him to "conceal the iron hand in a liberal allowance of velvet."[47]

Portal showed great energy and ability in getting things done. In a temperature of about 100 degrees Fahrenheit, he was "working an average of about thirteen or fourteen" hours a day "without moving from my table."[48] Spurred on by his enthusiasm, he began to press the sultan too far in the direction of reforms. But Salisbury, while recognizing his good intentions, was obliged to apply the brakes. He wrote to Portal:

> We have a character to maintain among Mahommedan races. It would be bad for us if they believed that our preponderance was dangerous to their material interests, and especially the material interests of the most powerful persons among them. Such a reputation might do us no serious harm in Zanzibar, where almost everything is within the range of our guns, and yet it might produce very inconvenient results upon the mainland of Africa and even in India.[49]

Salisbury had remarkable ability for anticipating the repercussions of a particular policy in one part of the empire on the others. When, therefore, Portal further advised the total abolition of the sultanate, he was lectured on how a similar policy had driven Indian princes into mutiny about a generation earlier. Moreover, Salisbury did not think that, for legal and other reasons, it would be "an unmixed blessing if Zanzibar became British territory." It would mean the end of the "semipatriarchal government" invented by Portal himself, and the governing of the territory "according to the strictest rules of the Colonial Office" which "would probably result in an early and permanent deficit in your Budget."[50] So Zanzibar had to be governed according to the more benevolent rules of the Foreign Office!

Under Rosebery and Kimberley no arrangements were made to reverse the course adopted by Salisbury. But by March, 1895, the Liberal government, pressured by the humanitarians and the Tory opposition, had pledged themselves to abolish the legal status of slavery in the islands of Zanzibar and Pemba, but were unable to redeem this pledge before they were voted out of office in June.

However, in August, Arthur Balfour renewed the pledge on behalf of the Unionists.[51] On December 7, Bishop Tucker, who was in England, had an interview with Salisbury on the question during which he put up a good case for abolition. Salisbury sympathized with him but pointed out the practical difficulties. He, however, asked the bishop to talk to Curzon, the person charged with piloting the government's case through the House of Commons. During the interview with Curzon, Hardinge, also in England, was present. Curzon refused to commit the government to any course of action. But he assured the bishop "that all that you have said shall have the fullest consideration." Satisfied, Tucker returned to Africa a happy man.[52] Consequently, in March, 1896, Balfour's pledge was reinforced by Curzon. Curzon also stated that Hardinge, due to be in England on leave in the following summer, would be given instructions to abolish the legal status of slavery in the islands and inaugurate a new system on his return to his post. But due to the illness of his *locum tenens*, Hardinge was forced to return suddenly to Zanzibar before his leave expired without the instructions. It was therefore decided to telegraph them to him.[53] Sir John Kirk was a little unfair to the Foreign Office when he complained to Lugard: "As to Slavery at Zanzibar nothing has been done. They are too busy shooting the Swahile [?] of the mainland to trouble about the islands. . . ."[54] On April 22, 1896, Kirk further commented: "The F.O. have done nothing. The truth is that Anderson and every official (except Hill) hates meddling with the Slave Trade."[55]

Between 1895 and 1900, the slavery question was the central point in Salisbury's dealings with Zanzibar. In December, 1895, he had produced an interesting memorandum on the subject. In it he showed his essential conservatism and caution. The abolition of the legal status of slavery in Zanzibar, he argued, was not yet politically sound. The measure was being "taken purely in deference to British feeling, and will probably be injurious to the industry of the islands," in which case, "the British Treasury is bound to give very substantial assistance in order to carry this measure through."[56] This is, of course, a valuable admission of the influence of public opinion on this question. He further added that the Treasury must "make it perfectly clear to all lawful possessors that they will not be deprived, without adequate compensation, of the property which has been guaranteed to them," because the Arabs would be embittered by an arbitrary proclamation. He summed up his views:

We are holding in East Africa a vast extent of territory with an infinitismal force. The result of the defeat of the Italians in

Abyssinia will be known over the whole continent; and if, as is very likely, it is followed by movement of the Khalifa, some effervescence of feeling among the Arabs within our own Protectorate on the mainland will not be an entirely improbable contingency. It is always to be remembered that excessive parsimony in compensating the Dutch owners of slaves at the Cape in 1834 was the cause of their trekking, and of the ultimate foundation of that Boer Republic which is so infinitely troublesome to us now. . . .

I should recommend that we should not attempt in London to solve the question as to what slaves are and what slaves are not lawfully possessed.

He also recommended the use of the existing tribunal, or if possible, the creation of a new one, to determine this. The tribunal must possess local knowledge and perform its work on the spot.[57] Chamberlain also produced a counter memorandum in which he questioned the wisdom of granting compensation to slave owners.[58] This important document reveals two things particularly. One is that Salisbury approached the slavery question from a purely political and practical angle rather than from purely moral and humanitarian considerations. The other is his dependence on the opinions of the man on the spot whom he happened to trust.

In January, 1896, Salisbury asked Hardinge for his personal opinions on the antislavery legislation. His views, treated sympathetically by the premier, received considerable opposition in the cabinet as well as in Parliament. Hardinge urged that the antislavery legislation should be postponed because its promulgation would ruin Arab landowners since freed slaves would simply refuse to work for wages. This, he argued, would lead, with serious consequences, to unfavorable Arab and Mohammedan reaction to Britain's position in Zanzibar. He advised that the Arabs should first be taught how to work for wages before the slaves would be gradually freed.[59] In February, Curzon argued that the legal status of slavery could easily be abolished in the islands because there were bluejackets and warships in the harbor—all ready to enforce such a decree. But in the mainland, the situation was different. Here, British control was slight, and such a decree would largely be a dead letter. He urged that the main interest in the mainland was "to consolidate the administration of the Protectorate and to commence the Uganda railway, and we need not manufacture difficulties for ourselves." Moreover, no one had pledged Parliament that slavery in the mainland would be abolished; and the "fanatics" had always concentrated their efforts on the islands. The mainland, therefore, "can afford to wait." He also urged that abolition in the islands should be postponed "for one or two years as a possible solution to the compensation difficulty," which should only arise if the sultan's revenues suffered materially from diminution in the production of cloves. In such a case, the British government should give a grant-in-aid to Zanzibar.[60]

Curzon's memorandum was followed by yet another one by Anderson, who, apparently drawing from the arguments pressed by Hardinge, on Rosebery, Kimberley, and Salisbury, stressed the certainty of Arab rebellion as a result of any arbitrary legislation.[61] It must be noted that the Foreign Office originally toyed with the idea of extending the sultan's direct authority either as far as to the confines of Uganda "or at least over the coast strip from the Umba to the Juba, including Witu." This idea was killed by Anderson, who convinced Rosebery that it would be better to buy off the sultan at an annual stipend of £17,000, and that what was soon to become the East Africa Protectorate should be administered by Her Majesty's Political Agent in Zanzibar. Hardinge himself admitted that he stressed his preference for the earlier proposal "for it recalled the method under which my old chief Lord Cromer had governed Egypt, and it had the advantage, in my eyes, of conciliating the Arabs and Mahommedans generally, the most civilized native element in East Africa." He was, however, overruled by Rosebery. The sultan, who had schemed to obtain this extension of his authority, and consequently, of his prestige, was very disappointed, and his faith in the good will of Her Majesty's Government, according to Hardinge, was severely shaken. From then onwards he started recruiting a personal bodyguard.[62] Earlier, Hardinge had reported to Rosebery that the Arabs were talking of "dying in defence of their religion, their rights and those of their children," against the Christians who wished to deprive them forcibly of their slaves.[63]

The Arab aristocracy numbered only between five thousand and six thousand out of a total population of just over two hundred thousand. There was also "a trading class of British Indians; [and] a middle and lower class native trading and artisan elements." At the bottom of the ladder were the slaves, estimated at one hundred and forty thousand. The aristocracy owned most of the slaves; they constituted the monied class; and they provided the petty official hierachy, such as the *cadis, walis,* judges, and so forth. It was the Foreign Office argument that Britain could not afford to dispense with their loyalty. And as they were essential to the country's prosperity, it was argued that their ruin, by abolition without compensation, would spell bankruptcy for the state. They could even, as a result, be driven into the German mainland, where it was understood that an effort engineered by the German authorities was being made to establish a rival Arab sultanate in exile under the refugee pretender to the Zanzibari throne, Sayyid Barghash. It was therefore British policy to convince the aristocracy that they had nothing to fear and that they would not be harshly treated by the Foreign Office. The aristocracy were not the only ones that merited consideration. The small shop-keepers and the artisan class also owned slaves; and these slaves often appeared to be their only property. The bulk of the Arab forces—military and police—were also slave owners. These lower classes, too, must be assured that it was not the government's intention to make them suffer. This was considered very necessary as the sultan's bodyguard alone consisted of a thousand men, a good deal of whom were slaves, but who apparently liked their jobs. Already, the growing insolence of these soldiers, even to British officials, had forced the Foreign Office to instruct Hardinge to reduce their number. Anderson, consequently, urged that, because of these considerations, the promulgation decree should be preceded by precautionary measures, and suggested the withdrawal of British warships from Delagoa Bay to Zanzibar.[64] This was perhaps going too far. But the situation was considered as serious as that. And seen in this way, the Foreign Office attitude to the abolition question becomes quite intelligible. In any case, Zanzibar was a protected state ruled by Britain through an Arab sultan, with an administrative staff consisting mainly of Arabs, all with vested interests. But in fairness to the Zanzibar government, they were quite prepared to pay the compensation to the slave owners—including themselves of course—from their own Treasury. Anderson, too, believed that this compensation should be paid "as a matter of policy and justice," and abolition to be carried out "without delay," because it would "be the best course to let the Arabs feel the effects at once."[65] When Anderson died a few months later, Kirk, who had never liked him, wrote delightedly to Lugard: "Anderson's death *may* simplify the slave question."[66]

It is quite clear from the above arguments that Foreign Office officials were all in agreement with Salisbury's views in essentials. But another point is also clear; they all, Salisbury included, tended to model their views, more or less, on Hardinge's. This cannot be said of the rest of the cabinet.

Meanwhile the Arabs had rebelled as a result of the revocation of the Charter of the Imperial British East African Company, which they felt was a prelude to having their country taken over completely. By July, 1896, the rebellion was brought under control. But no sooner was this victory achieved than Sultan Sayyid Hamed bin Thwain died suddenly. That was on August 25, and rumors began circulating that he had been poisoned.[67] On the same day, Bishop Tucker arrived in Zanzibar, and has left us an account of what followed.[68] Sayyid Hamoud had been set up by Rennell Rodd in 1893, after an attempt by Khaled to seize the throne on the death of Sayyid Ali bin Said had been foiled. From that date onwards, Khaled became persona non grata to the British government. So, in June, 1896, Hardinge had recommended to Salisbury that Sayyid Hamoud—a man believed to be better disposed to British control than his rival, Khaled—should be next in line to succeed his cousin Thwain.[69] The death of Thwain in August presented Khaled with an opportunity to try a second coup d'etat. Apparently, he had been planning for this, for he was supported by about eight hundred men of the late sultan's bodyguard as well as some disgruntled elements in Zanzibar, mostly from lower classes. The palace was occupied within hours of the reported death. With Salisbury's permission, Basil Cave, the Acting Consul-General, bombarded the palace on August 27. He was aided by Admiral Rawson, who entered the harbor with the East Africa squadron during the crisis. Khaled was decisively beaten and escaped to the German territory in the mainland. Meanwhile, Hamoud had stayed at home awaiting developments. After the flight of Khaled he was formally installed as sultan on certain conditions. First, the Consul-General was to be in command of the armed forces in Zanzibar; and second, no state property should be alienated without the consul's approval.[70] The sultan, owing his throne to the protecting power, was thus to be reduced to a docile servant of the British crown. The Arabs, too, as Cave quickly pointed out to Salisbury, had "received a lesson" which they would always remember, and which would cause them to be reasonable whenever it was decided to abolish slavery in the islands.[71]

In England, the press and some members of Parliament clamored for the total abolition of the sultanate and the transference of the territory to the Colonial Office.[72] This implied, of course, the summary abolition of slavery without compensation to the owners. But Salisbury took no notice. Among the press, however, there were those like the *P.M.G.*, who preached gradualism in tackling this problem.[73] But they were in a minority. The difficulty involved in any summary abolition was, in any case, increased by the fact that the late sultan possessed very many slaves which had illegally passed to his successor and cousin, apparently without any protest from Hardinge.[74] This was an illegal procedure because the law explicitly stated that inheritance of slaves could only pass from father to son. Kirk bitterly criticized Salisbury for appointing another sultan on the advice of Hardinge, "Against all I can urge," and was furious that Hardinge "even insists that the new man must have all the State slaves given him because he holds no law applies to the State or the Ruler. It is wrecking the whole thing."[75] The British government was therefore faced with the absurd position of illegally allowing the sultan to keep the slaves while making preparations to pay him compensation for them when the antislave legislation was passed. In fact, Curzon had argued very strongly that Sayyid Hamoud should not be allowed to inherit these slaves.[76] But Bertie, using all the Salisbury-Hardinge arguments against driving the sultans too far, had rejected this suggestion.[77] And Salisbury had backed him up strongly.

> It appears to me that our prospects of emancipation will not in any case affect the Sultan's slaves. We propose that the status of slavery shall not be recognized in any Court.
>
> But I do not imagine that if the slaves refuse to obey him, they would now be brought before any court. They will be dealt with by other methods—which will not have lost their efficacy.[78]

Hicks-Beach was unimpressed by the Foreign Office attitude. He did not hide his wish to annex Zanzibar formally, following France's precedent at Madagascar, "and get rid of the dummy government." He also urged a considerable cut in the new sultan's revenue—allowing him "no more than enough for his housekeeping and his harem"; an entire abolition of his troops and guards, which would be temporarily replaced by an Indian regiment, but "ultimately by a native force in our pay." He went on:

> We should take his land, free his slaves on it, and either sell, or work it for the benefit of the government.
>
> I should think the "saving," as they say at the Treasury would well pay for the charge. If not, of course we could increase the grant. But surely it would be a great advantage to deprive our dummy or his family of all means of intriguing and mischief in future; and would be a step towards the easy abolition of the whole thing at the vacancy.
>
> I merely send the above for what it may be worth. Please *don't* trouble to answer.[79]

The last paragraph shows how much free hand the cabinet allowed Salisbury in these East African questions. It will be noted that Hicks-Beach's views were precisely those urged by Portal nearly five years before. But, nevertheless, Salisbury did reply. He lectured the chancellor, as he had done Portal, on the wider implications and repercussions of the actions they contemplated. But while admitting "that there is another side to the question, which I certainly had not sufficiently considered," Hicks-Beach reminded the prime minister that "my ideas are those of the Colonial Office" and that the British fleet could easily dominate the islands and annex the country without bloodshed.[80] Evidently, the chancellor was unconvinced by Salisbury's argument: but he chose not to pursue the question further. Kirk also "urged the Foreign Office to have no more Sultans, to make this the turning point and on taking the power in their own hand to abolish the status of Slavery at the same time."[81]

The full force of the Foreign Office arguments and proposals were flung at the cabinet on December 29, 1896, in a powerfully argued memorandum by Curzon.[82] It is a restatement and a reinforcement of the arguments we have been examining. It is of course difficult to say how every individual member of the cabinet received a measure which, in fact, constituted a precedent by paying compensation for the simple abolition of the legal status of slavery, and not slavery itself, since no minutes existed. But there are some important indications. A few days after the cabinet had met, Chamberlain produced a counter memorandum in which he made it clear that he was strongly opposed to compensation. He also warned that such a policy would force the Anti-Slavery Society to arouse public feeling against the government. He failed to see that the British government had any moral obligations to slave owners. And he reminded his colleagues that Britain ruled Zanzibar by right of conquest, and that it had always been Britain's policy to abolish slavery under its flag.[83] Another indication came from Goschen. "On the slavery question," he wrote to Salisbury a few days later, "I am much struck by the force of Chamberlain's argument against compensation. On the papers circulated, I should vote with him. . . ."[84] Hicks-Beach, too, argued strongly against compensation.[85] And in March, 1897 he told Salisbury, "I have no confidence whatever in the decision of the native tribunals on the question of compensation."[86] So, apparently did Balfour,[87] although he spoke up for compensation in Parliament.[88]

One point, however, is certain: the cabinet in general agreed that the legal status of slavery should be abolished in the islands as soon as possible. The difficulty arose over compensation; but this was soon settled in favor of the Foreign Office view with no objections from any cabinet member. Once more Salisbury had demonstrated that in East Africa, he was determined to run things his own way.

On April 5, 1897, the legal status of slavery was abolished in the islands of Zanzibar Pemba.[89] The mainland was left untouched. The difference between the legal status of slavery and slavery itself is very important. If the latter had been abolished the result would have been that the islands' 140,000 slaves, out of a total population of 220,000, were ipso facto, free at a blow. This was not done largely due to the economic and social effects of such a course of action.[90] But the legislation as decreed only meant that every slave was by law free to claim his or her freedom before a court established for that purpose. He had only to identify himself before this court and sign papers which registered the fact. The implication of this decree was that slave labor, as was usual in British colonies, was not outlawed as a criminal offense. Curiously enough, the Anti-Slavery Society and other missionary societies had not pressed that it should be outlawed. It was in Parliament that such an advocacy was strong, but unsuccessful.[91] The implication of the decree goes farther than a mere deviation from the established procedure. A slave, desiring his freedom, must go before Arab *walis*—themselves, a slave-owning class—who presided over the district courts. If his application was rejected, he could appeal to the sultan. But there is reason to suppose that there was collusion between the sultan and these *walis* as to how to handle such an eventuality. Certainly a collusion existed between some slaves and their masters. Hardinge himself wrote to Kirk about "Collusion between native and slave master detected in order to get compensation," to the delight of the latter who commented: "He does not like this as it verifies what I said he laughed at. So he is to have the poor devil flogged 100 lashes at the corner of the street!! Is he mad? He finds there will be a charge now estimated at £4,000 per year as compensation, so say in 5 years £20,000. He asked for £300,000!! This shows the utterly reckless way he works. . . ."[92] Moreover, many slaves were unable to read the decree which was published in Arabic and posted in public places. These *walis*, too, were entrusted with the oral dissemination of the news. The appointment of two European slavery commissioners to supervise, but not to execute, the functioning of the decree was hardly a good enough safeguard against underhand dealings. On top of it all, a slave owner received financial compensation for each slave who became free. The law, therefore, could do nothing for a slave who, through ignorance or necessity, refused to be free. According to Kirk, Indians were God-sent agents to make the slaves aware of the decree. He wrote: "Hardinge dislikes the Indians (who are my friends) and does love the Arabs whom I distrust as an agency for good. Now these Indians have been paying 20 coppers a day for labor. Of this the laborer being a slave has to render 10 coppers when he goes home to his master. Now the Indian tells the laborer 'You are free, why give 10 coppers to your old master?' "[93] And although open cruelty was forbidden, nothing was said about private cruelty. There is little doubt that some slaves had a rough time at the hands of their masters while the machinery of the law went about its leisurely way.

The decree had other anomalies which exasperated Bishop Tucker and his sympathizers. It must be remembered that Mombasa and the coastal districts within the ten-mile limit were part of the sultanate of Zanzibar, and that events there affected the missionary activities in the east coast especially as fugitive slaves frequently sought sanctuary in the missions.[94] The decree did not affect these areas and some fugitive slaves were forced to return to their masters. In fact, the law did not tackle the fugitive slave question with any clarity of purpose until June 24, 1897, when Attorney General Webster enunciated his famous law which reads as follows:

> The Attorney General has laid down that a British subject anywhere, in whatever service or employment he may happen to be engaged, if he takes part in restoring to his master or otherwise depriving any person of his liberty, on the sole ground that he is a fugitive slave, is breaking the British law and exposing himself to penalties. I have to inform you [Hardinge] for your personal guidance, that you should conform your conduct to the law thus laid down.[95]

Tucker was delighted; but Hardinge was furious. Salisbury wrote consolingly, but resignedly, to his pro-consul:

> The doctrine laid down by the Attorney General in debate was unexpected and to many of us quite new. Some learned barristers say that it is not good law. But having been publicly laid down by the present Attorney General and confirmed by his predecessor, it would not be decorous and indeed scarcely safe for any officer of the Crown to disregard.[96]

Webster's directive, indeed, was not openly disregarded, but somehow twisted by the authorities. In Pemba, for instance, where it was reported that, for many months, the slaves were not made aware of the existence of the decree,[97] the vagrancy law in it continued to be interpreted to suit the slave owners. It was interpreted to mean that a slave must obtain an alternative employment before his freedom was granted to him. If he failed to do this and ran off, he was liable to be prosecuted for vagrancy. It was not until November 1899 that the Anti-Slavery Society forced this interpretation to be abandoned.[98]

The decree, too, did not affect concubines. This meant that former slave girls could, overnight, be promoted to the title of concubines while leaving their position unchanged. It is not surprising therefore that Tucker dismissed the antislavery legislation as "truly a disappointing outcome to the struggle of years."[99] And in September, 1897, he sounded another battle cry when he exposed these anomalies in a letter to *The Times*.[100] But despite all efforts not many slaves had been freed by 1900.[101]

Why was Salisbury so sympathetic to the slave owners? Was it not odd that the man who seemed to be pleading for the Uganda railway primarily on the effect it would have on the stoppage of the slave trade, and who was talking glibly of the "civilizing, Christianizing" mission of the race, was at the same time, championing the cause of slavery in Zanzibar and Pemba? Thus put, the question is perhaps an unfair one. In the first place, there was a difference between the slave trade and slavery as practiced in the above islands. Moreover, slavery here had become a way of life which had grown through centuries. Now to abolish it "in a single day" as someone said was done in West Africa,[102] would be both economically and socially disastrous. That much was certain. Not even the missionaries on the spot advocated this approach. Not unnaturally, the philanthropists tended to exaggerate the sufferings of the slaves in order to rouse the conscience of the British nation, which understandably was most sensitive on this subject. But slavery in these islands was not as harsh as it had been made to appear. Radical action therefore was inexpedient. That was how Salisbury looked at the problem. For him, it was a question of political decision based on expediency. Would it be expedient to make immediate decisions and damn the consequences, or would it be wiser to wait until the moment was ripe to act? That was the question. Salisbury was a very cautious man who curiously believed that a general Arab insurrection in Zanzibar would spread to many parts of the empire. This may have been a nonsensical assumption, but it must be admitted that in Africa alone, at this time, he was faced with explosive situations in the east, west, south, and north. To manufacture more difficulties in Zanzibar, as Curzon put it, would have been too adventurous for Salisbury's cautious spirit. So far so good. But Salisbury must be taken to task for totally subjugating the moral issues involved in any kind of slavery—which was after all the main concern of his critics —to all other considerations. Again, was his attitude not influenced by his natural sympathy for the ruling classes? After all, the Arab aristocracy represented in Zanzibar, so to speak, the kind of class which Salisbury himself had championed in England. His record as the secretary of state for India in the seventies shows also that he was sympathetic to the Indian princes. In the American Civil War we also find him supporting the propertied, slave-owning class of the south, but not because they were slave owners, but because of his fear of democracy. In West Africa, too, he showed that his sympathy was with Jaja of Oppobo rather than with the British merchants or even with Harry Johnston, whom he described as "a resolute but singularly lawless personage."[103] It is possible that his approach to abolition, *ab initio*, may have been affected by this attitude of mind.

Analogies may be misleading. But there is undoubtedly a remarkable consistency of sympathy in Salisbury's attitude toward those in authority. In Zanzibar, he went to great pains to be fair to the sultan; and when requested to extend the abolition decree to the mainland, he would not hear of it. He summed up his attitude in this dispatch to Hardinge:

> I believe it [slavery] to be an evil and desire its removal. But I think the abolitionist enthusiasts in England are in much too great a hurry. An institution so deep rooted in custom and religion cannot be pulled up hastily in an oriental community without producing much misery and some danger. I am not, therefore, inclined to hasten the process a bit more than necessity requires. Consequently, I should take the Proclamation of 1890 in its natural meaning and scope. It was a promise from Sayyid Khalifa, applicable to the whole of his dominions. I see no advantage in extending it beyond the ten mile strip. If we did so, we should extend the promise of compensation also: and both must apply to an indefinite tract of country—involving perfectly indefinite responsibilities and risks. A further reason for not extending the operation of the Proclamation beyond the ten mile line is that the abolitionists would press for abolition in British East Africa before we are ready for it and might conceivably set everything on fire.
>
> I expect considerable irritation on the part of both the French and Menelek when we conquer—if we conquer—the Khalifa's domain and it is impossible to predict where the political disturbance will extend and what will be its limits. So for the present we must avoid all cause of offence in your part of the world. The current of general politics at the present moment is anything but smooth. No sooner had we dodged round one big rock than the rapids hurry us against another. I say this

as a sort of apology for having restrained your martial ardour in the affair of the Ogadens. We cannot afford to have more than a limited area of heather alight at the same time. . . .[104]

This is sound commonsense; and it also summarizes Salisbury's general attitude.

Arthur Hardinge

Salisbury's attitude toward Zanzibar had the full support of Hardinge and Foreign Office officials. There was a feeling among these officials, especially the administrators in Zanzibar, that the Arab aristocracy, including the sultans, were treated unfairly: the assumption of a Protectorate in 1890 had robbed them of their political sovereignty; and the abolition of the legal status of slavery in 1897 had diminished their social influence. The admiration which they had for the Arabs was remarkable. Equally, they had a very low opinion of the black Africans.[105] Even in the composition of native administration, Hardinge preferred Arabs "and higher Swahilis."[106] Hardinge also preferred Arabs to Europeans. In fact, Kirk warned Lugard not to seek appointment in East Africa on this ground. Hardinge, indeed, was "building up an Arab Moh. [ammedan] governing class."[107] But after 1900, with the appointment of new British administrators a new trend of thought, based more on efficiency than on privilege, set in. This was made possible by the departure of the old guard. In 1900, Hardinge was transferred to Persia as British Minister; in 1901, Mathews died; and in 1902, Sayyid Hamoud died and was succeeded by his seventeen-year-old son, Sayyid Ali, predictably educated at a public school in England. This new trend should, of course, not be pushed too far. The Zanzibar revolution of 1964 has a long history! Sir Lloyd Mathews, the sultan's first minister, for instance, was English only in name—a fact admitted by Hardinge himself.[108] For many years he had lived among the Arabs and was said to confuse Oscar Wilde with Wylde, the philanthropist.[109] To him the abolition of slavery was "a regrettable necessity."[110] Hardinge shared a similar view. But he was particularly concerned with securing compensation for the slave owners. In a way his interest in this aspect of the question has a personal explanation. He belonged, on his mother's side, to the planter class who had been indemnified in Jamaica earlier in the century. Hardinge claimed that he wished the same kind of justice to be shown to the Arabs.[111] His objection to the antislavery legislation went further than that because his mother revealed that Hardinge saw nothing wrong with slavery; and, according to Kirk: "I have been told that he [Hardinge] *holds that man has no right to freedom, and a capitalist has as much right to buy and breed slaves as he has to keep horses.* [My italics.] I fancy Lord Salisbury, Curzon, and Balfour are all with Hardinge. So are the heads of the Foreign Office, except Hill who counts for little. . . . If I go to London next week I will make a point of teaching some of the opposition how to upset the scheme but it will count for little as the Government will use their majority to carry what they determined upon. . . ."[112] But Hardinge forgot that what was abolished in Jamaica was the whole institution of slavery, and that such a thing was not done in Zanzibar, thanks partly to his pleading the cause of the Arabs.

Hardinge was appointed consul-general in Zanzibar in May, 1894. He had served in Egypt under Cromer. He was now to succeed Portal who was his contemporary at Eton and had preceded him in Egypt. The two men, despite their apparently similar education and similar experiences, were very dissimilar in their approach to affairs in Zanzibar. While Hardinge assumed the role of the spokesman of the sultan's, Portal had pleaded in vain to have the sultanate abolished altogether. But immediately Hardinge was appointed to Zanzibar the trend was reversed. And since that date he had fought, with other Protectorate officials, a rear-guard battle against the Anti-Slavery Society and in favor of the Arab aristocracy. Since 1890 the Anti-Slavery Society had been vigorously demanding the abolition of slavery in Zanzibar and Pemba. When successive governments hesitated, they had set in motion a considerable pressure in Britain against the governments' policy which reached a momentum in 1895. Their agitation, reinforced by strong feelings in the House of Commons in May, 1895,[113] had forced the Rosebery government to pledge themselves to abolish the legal status of slavery in the Protectorate.[114] When Salisbury took office, Hardinge, despite the criticisms leveled at himself, pressed gradualism on the new foreign secretary, arguing that he was the only one "to plead" the cause of the Arabs and "to appeal on their behalf to English justice."[115]

There was considerable opposition to Hardinge in England. In December, 1895, Chamberlain had complained to Balfour that Hardinge was "very ready to make a case for slavery," and had suggested his promotion so that either Kirk or Lugard could replace him.[116] Had Zanzibar been under the Colonial Office, there is little doubt that Hardinge would have been removed. But apparently, Salisbury took no notice of this suggestion. One day Dilke confronted Hardinge on the terrace of the House of Commons and told him to his face that nothing would give him greater pleasure than to see the consul-general dismissed from his post—a sanction which Hardinge claimed he would rather face "than to act unjustly towards the Arabs."[117] In the House of Commons itself he was constantly attacked.[118] He survived because he had Salisbury's confidence. Toward the later part of his career, Salisbury tended to depend more and more on those pro-consuls on the spot whose opinions he valued. Hardinge was certainly one of these.[119] As Kirk put it: "Hardinge has the ear of Lord Salisbury and I doubt his advice and not mine will be followed." Hardinge too had the ear of Curzon. Wrote Kirk: "Curzon said 'We don't care about the slaves.' He and Salisbury too I believe only think how far they are compelled to go. They are out and out with Hardinge who is a college chum of Curzon's and Balfour's and talks to Curzon as George even at the Downing Street meeting."[120] He was also on very good relations with Sayyid Hamoud. The sultan, who owed his throne to Britain, was nothing more than a puppet until his death in 1902. He was fascinated by British habits and customs, and showed a willingness to anglicize his country. He even sent his son, Sayyid Ali, an offspring of his Swahili concubine, to Harrow. So partly because the sultan was a "good boy," and partly because of pure convictions, Hardinge amazed some of his contemporaries by appearing to defend—and did in fact defend—the institution of slavery. Four days after the abolition decree was published, he was praising the sultan's "vigor and promptness" in carrying out its provisions.[121]

In many ways Hardinge proved a success in Zanzibar. In 1899, for instance, he could report to Salisbury that "Our revenue is . . . advancing by leaps and bounds and notwithstanding all the troubles of this year, famine, cattle plague, etc., we are making good progress in every direction."[122] But he was quite unrepentant for his attitude on the slavery question. To him it still remained "a tiresome problem" which involved "no danger about it, in the sense of its leading to disturbances." He was more concerned with "keeping our pledges to the Arabs" than with the "pugnacity of the Church Missionary Society and United Free Methodists." "Of course," he concluded in another letter, "if we can really put it [slavery abolition in the mainland] off the better: the longer we delay it, the cheaper abolition will be."[123] It was not until October, 1907, and under a Liberal Administration, that abolition was extended to the mainland. By this time Salisbury and Hardinge were not around to influence events.

The story of Zanzibar is a good example of how the imperialism of conquest operated in nineteenth century Africa. Here, a strong, technologically advanced country of high power and scale—Britain

—under the banner of a self-proclaimed mission of suppressing the slave trade (out of which it had already made enormous profits), invades an agrarian country of low power and scale—Zanzibar— and in just over a generation found itself the de facto power in the country without drawing a sword. This is a classic example of Salisbury's pacific imperialism. Such a state of affairs, however, could not last indefinitely. The challenge of Germany to the status quo led to partition and conquest, and to the end of Omani hegemony in East Africa. After 1890, Salisbury's dealings with Zanzibar were concentrated on finding the least painful means of abolishing the institution of slavery. Unfortunately, he created the impression of accepting the principle of abolition only because of the pressure of the abolitionists in Britain.

Chapter VIII

"They Are Coming to Eat the Country"

Uganda provides another classic example of how the imperialism of conquest operated in nineteenth century East Africa. In the Bantu states of southern Uganda—especially in Buganda and Bunyoro-Kitara—there existed strong and centralized governments which functioned on principles intelligible—however remotely—to the British mind. The early British visitors to the lacustrine kingdoms had published detailed accounts of their experiences from which individuals derived practically all their knowledge about East Africa.[1] Speke, particularly, had propagated the erroneous doctrine of the Hamitic hypothesis which was to have a bright future for some years to come.[2] These expeditions had all started from the Zanzibar base. Their results are important in at least three respects. First, the geography of East Africa was placed in a comparatively correct perspective of Europe; second, they showed that however strong these African kingdoms might be, a technologically advanced European power could deal effectively with them; and third, they told horrible stories about the Arab slave trade and thus provided ammunition for abolitionists and humanitarians in Britain to rave in self-righteous indignation. Equally importantly, the celebrated missionary, David Livingstone, was to add his immense weight to the humanitarian pressure to abolish the slave trade in the East African hinterland when his *Last Journals* were published in 1874. Livingstone had come into contact with Baganda traders in the 1860s who exaggerated the size and importance of their country. He knew of the ivory and slave trade not only from reading Speke and Grant but by talking with Baganda and Arabs; he was informed of Muslim missionary activities in Buganda. And, at once impressed by Baganda and worried at what was going on, he began to consider seriously the prospects of evangelical work in Buganda.[3]

By the 1870s British representatives in Zanzibar had not only heard of Muteesa I's (Kabaka of Buganda) emissaries to the sultans but were aware of Egyptian efforts to annex Uganda to their Sudanese empire. John Kirk, particularly, did everything in his power to prevent such an eventuality, and worked to keep Buganda's communication with Zanzibar open.[4] H. M. Stanley who had visited Buganda in 1875 thought very highly of Muteesa and emphasized "the immense wealth of ivory to be obtained by those first in the field."[5] Stanley had come with the Bible in one hand and firearms in the other; the combination at once fascinated and frightened Muteesa. The history of Christianity in Buganda can be dated from Stanley's visit. Muteesa needed Stanley's arms to deliver him "from the Egyptians" and his Bible as a counterweight to the Koran as well as to the traditional gods.[6] With the failure of the Egyptian enterprise in Uganda and the success of the Mahdist revolt in the Sudan, any thought of invading or evangelizing East Africa from the north was abandoned. The commercial routes to the coast remained open, however, and the prominent position which Britian had acquired in Zanzibar and Mombasa meant that the future of Uganda in the new age of foreign influence must lie in that direction. In the beginning neither the coastal Arabs nor the Europeans had any stated policy of annexing Uganda. The Arabs wanted to trade and spread Islam; the Europeans wanted to replace the slave trade with "legitimate commerce, Christianity, and civilization." In their attempts to execute these aims, with Buganda as base, they undermined that kingdom's internal cohesion and paved the way for the conquest of Uganda. Having destroyed the religious and social basis for a strong African state, Islam and Christianity fought for the spoils with Christianity emerging as the winner. And since the conflict had resulted in the destruction of the Kiganda monarchy, Britain had to step in to hold the pieces together and protect the missionaries. Any other explanation of the conquest of Uganda is both unhistorical and superfluous. In Central Africa, as we shall see, missionary activities produced the same results as in Uganda.

Religion, Buganda, and the Conquest of Uganda
By the first half of the nineteenth century the struggle for mastery in the lacustrine region had swung in Buganda's favor. For the time being the kabakas of Buganda seemed to have adopted a consolidationist policy. But they also began to divert the boundless energy of their subjects toward opening up communication with the outside world, especially with the coastal people some eight hundred miles away. Buganda was a landlocked country situated on the equator on the northwest shore of Lake Victoria. With Bunyoro-Kitara to the northward humiliated, but still potentially dangerous,

Buganda's strategy apparently was to open up a trade route to the coast and prevent the same access to its old rival. In pursuance of this policy, Kabaka Suuna II had invited Arab traders to visit his capital in 1844. They brought with them firearms and a new religion which soon challenged some of the fundamental beliefs of the Kiganda religion.[7]

It was, however, during the reign of Muteesa I that Islam became a factor in Kiganda politics. The new monarch embraced Islam with remarkable enthusiasm. More Arabs were encouraged to visit Buganda. Muteesa introduced the Mohammedan Calendar, adopted Arabic dress, learned Arabic, built mosques, and between 1868 and 1878 he observed Ramadan. The two roles of kabaka and sultan did not mix well. He encouraged his chiefs to embrace Islam; and since in Buganda "the religion of the peasant is that of his immediate superior, that is of the man who has most power to cause him constant inconvenience,"[8] a substantial number of Baganda became Muslims by the 1870s.

Why did Muteesa embrace Islam? The Kiganda monarchy was at the height of its power at the end of Suuna's reign (ca. 1856). After Suuna things were not to be the same again. The rise of Buganda to its premier position over its neighbors had been attributed to the intervention of its numerous gods. Now, Muteesa felt himself strong enough to challenge these gods, thereby creating a religious crisis. Already he was a "Caesaro-Papist" to an extent undreamed of by Philip IV of France during the struggle for power within the *Respublica Christiana*. And now, against the canon of Kiganda tradition, he was attempting to turn himself into a god. The *bataka*, priests and mediums, like the medieval European clerics, attempted to use their spiritual powers to check the presumptions of the monarchy. Muteesa replied with repression and executions. When these failed to work, he saw in Islam a useful counterweight to the gods and their allies and against the *bataka*. To him the Arabs represented power—material, military, and spiritual.[9] And perhaps he saw in Islam a religion he could control to achieve political aims. Although he succeeded in maintaining trade links with the coast as well as in his broader policy of isolating Bunyoro-Kitara, he failed to control Islam in the way he had envisaged. By the 1870s, the new converts, aided by their Arab friends, had become a serious threat to monarchical and traditional authority and values. In 1876 Muteesa took the drastic step of executing over one hundred Muslim converts.[10] The spread of Islam was temporarily checked, the survivors of the purge for the moment cowed, although they were to reappear in the 1880s as a major force in politics.

Muteesa's flirtation with Islam and Arabs had brought Baganda in contact with the sultans of Zanzibar. By 1869 Sayyid Majid and Muteesa were exchanging presents, a relationship continued during the reign of Barghash. In the same period Khedive Ismail of Egypt and his European mercenaries were entertaining grandiose ambitions of extending Egyptian dominion over the equatorial lakes. John Kirk in Zanzibar, religious pressure in Britain, resistance by both Kabalega and Muteesa—all combined to force Egypt to abandon the project.[11] The Mahdist revolution finally made realization of the idea impossible.

These developments had important repercussions. They increased Muteesa's distrust of Arabs and Islam and paved the way for the entry of Christianity. Buganda was now introduced to the ideology of another power, a power which Baganda emissaries to the court of Barghash must have been aware was greater than that of Mohammedan Arabs. Baganda, therefore, were no doubt impressed by Stanley's boast at the court of Muteesa in 1875 "that the white men are greatly superior to the Arabs" and that "their book [the Bible] must be a better book than Mohammed's [Koran]."[12] Moreover, the destruction of Islamic influence had brought Muteesa back to the point from which he had started; the old conflict between him and the gods remained unsolved. This was exacerbated by the alienation of Muslim converts who were licking their wounds in private and waiting in the wings for a favorable opportunity to strike back.

The reception given to Stanley's famous letters published in the *Daily Telegraph* (November 15, 1875—although dated April, 1875) which led to the arrival of the first Protestant missionaries to Buganda (1878), appears to have temporarily eased Muteesa's internal problems. He accorded them warm welcome and in 1879 the Catholic contingent arrived. Muteesa was careful not to embrace Christianity to the extent he had embraced Islam. On the contrary, he subjected the operation of the new religion to careful scrutiny. The bickerings between Protestants and Catholics, although a puzzle to him and his people, enabled him, for some time, to keep the new religion in check. The adherents of Kiganda religion, however, opposed Christianity and seized the opportunity to renew their attack on Muteesa. The curbing of Islam was not followed up with the banning of Arab traders from Buganda. They still quietly extolled the virtues of Islam and did their best to discredit Christianity and the Europeans. The missionaries, too, extolled the virtues of Christianity and boasted to Muteesa that the Bible was "the source of England's greatness." And to counteract the material gains arising from dealings with the Arab traders, they attempted to impress Baganda with the basic skills of European technology. In addition, they taught reading and writing; they cured the sick, and preached with great force the Christian doctrine. They were not armed, did not trade, and were—so it semed—totally without fear. It is no surprise, therefore, that Baganda, eager for new knowledge and confronted with conflicting ideologies, fell "into the morass of a very profound intellectual confusion."[13] Nevertheless, Christianity rapidly gained adherents at the expense of Islam. Muteesa, like Barghash before him, was persuaded to pay an official visit to England. He was, however, prevented from undertaking the journey by the superstitions of his advisers. He therefore selected three commoners as envoys to Queen Victoria. These commoners were simply overwhelmed at what they saw in England and returned home—in spite of the predictions of the king's advisers—safe to tell their tale. British prestige soared.

Muteesa's much vaunted diplomatic skill was tasked to its limits. He had no longer power to impose a single faith on his people. Although he was not formally a Christian, growing numbers of his subjects were being baptized. Whether Muteesa knew it or not, the missionaries were undermining the social and religious fabric of Buganda. Caught in the confusion of the new times, and aware that any resolute action on his part would likely cause greater disintegration by far, he was forced to respond to a delicate position by prancing from one ideology to another. Having once embraced Islam and now anxious to be a Christian at any rate, before 1880[14] Kabaka Muteesa abandoned the leadership which traditionally was his. He did not, in the end, become baptized because the missionaries were strong enough to insist that he dismiss all his wives but one; because his advisers were opposed to such a stipulation; and because the mud-slinging between the Protestants and Catholics, their arrogance, their air of racial superiority and exclusiveness, and their bigotry and intolerance, caused Muteesa to adopt a lukewarm attitude toward the missionaries.[15] They seemed, however, to have had the opposite effect on a considerable number of his courtiers who embraced the new religion with great enthusiasm. But increasing obstacles to their work caused the White Fathers to withdraw temporarily from Buganda in November, 1882.[16] Nevertheless, Christianity gathered, rather than lost, momentum; and by 1884 about two hundred converts at Muteesa's court had been baptized.[17] Muteesa's efforts to restore his former authority over his subjects were doomed to fail. By flirting with the new religions he had irreparably damaged the monarchy and desecrated the sacred office of his illustrious ancestors for "the Kabakaship was essentially a religious office, linked with the living and the dead, with worlds visible and invisible, with the very world of Buganda."[18] A Muslim or Christian kabaka was a contradiction in terms. In Buganda, as in Zanzibar, the pacific imperialism of Europeans had fundamentally damaged the very existence of a powerful African state without firing a bullet. The Kiganda monarchy in its purest sense ended with Suuna; under Muteesa it was scorched; and under Mwanga II it was destroyed.

For the moment, Bunyoro-Kitara appeared to be doing better than Buganda. The accession of Omukama Chwa II Kabalega to the throne in 1870 had given that kingdom a new lease of life. Having won a long war of succession with the help of some Arab traders, he was far-sighted enough to force his new friends from his capital when they became too demanding. The result was that Islam was no factor in the state until after the establishment of British rule. The Christian missionaries, too, were barred from that kingdom until 1895. Kabalega was particularly suspicious of Christianity. He resisted Muteesa's efforts to interest him in their teachings, arguing that a religion that preached life after death was bound to be dangerous. He warned Muteesa to beware of such a doctrine because it implied that his father, Suuna, might rise from the dead and demand his throne back. On his part, he had no wish to surrender power to anyone—dead or alive. Unlike Muteesa, too, Kabalega was not involved in any conflict with Kinyoro gods or with their mediums. With the establishment of the *abarusura* (national standing army) and the ruthless persecution of the aristocracy, he had achieved by force what Muteesa had failed to achieve through adherence to a foreign ideology. Kabalega's troubles, however, began when, in 1872, the impetuous Samuel Baker annexed Bunyoro-Kitara to the Egyptian empire. He had reacted to this insolence with military action and forced Baker to retreat ignominiously northward after he had failed to hold his ground during the *Baligota Isansa* (the battle of Masindi, June 14, 1872). Baker's experiences were published in his totally untrustworthy book, *Ismailia* (1874), in which Kabalega was portrayed as a drunken, cruel savage totally opposed to Europeans and Christianity and who should therefore be brought to heel for the peace and regeneration of the lacustrine region. With the Mahdist victory in the Sudan, and given the geographical position of Bunyoro-Kitara, Kabalega was shielded from British attack so long as Buganda remained independent.[19]

Buganda could not remain independent for long. Muteesa died in 1884 and was succeeded by Mwanga II. An impressive amount of literature exists for Mwanga's reign.[20] The Christians welcomed the young prince's elevation.[21] The White Fathers returned to Buganda. Mwanga was very much unlike his father. Diplomacy was not his forte. He was too young, too inexperienced, and too undisciplined to cope with the momentous developments of his time. Few writers have anything good to say about him.[22] His position in Buganda's history has become analogous to that of King John in English history. It must be stressed, however, that the problems facing Buganda by the early 1880s cannot be explained solely in terms of Mwanga's personal inadequacies but more in terms of the economic, social, and religious disequilibrium brought about by the impact of Islam and Christianity.

After a short while on the throne, Mwanga discovered that the Christian converts were openly challenging his authority, thereby undermining the effectiveness of his office. Among other things they protested openly against his homosexual practices. The European missionaries rubbed the Buganda aristocracy on the wrong side in their enthusiasm to recruit more converts. By behaving like chiefs and attracting many of the youth to themselves, they posed a serious threat to the clientage system which was an important aspect of Buganda's social and economic organization. The Protestant mission particularly appeared to Mwanga to be politically motivated. It "was introduced to the court by a letter from the British Foreign Office and the kabaka looked upon it as an official embassy from Britain with more political support than the missionaries were willing to acknowledge."[23] Mwanga's Arab interpreters were constantly feeding him with their version of external affairs. He was informed of the quickening pace of European imperialism: the occupation of Egypt, the humiliation of Barghash, the Berlin conference (1884–85), and the 1886 Anglo-German Agreement which placed Uganda under the British sphere of influence.[24] These reports naturally frightened the young, carefree monarch.

He had to act to restore royal authority. He appeared to have grasped more clearly the ramifications and the disruptive influence of the new ideologies than his father. In October, 1885 news reached him that Bishop Hannington and his party were approaching Buganda through Busoga—the rear of the kingdom. Mwanga feared that the Europeans were planning something sinister. The resident Protestant missionaries apparently did not seek his permission to allow Hannington to enter the country. In Kiganda custom one had to be either a close friend or an enemy to enter another's compound through the rear. Consequently, as Hannington was not a close friend he was captured and executed as an enemy.

After this tragedy events sped to a cataclysmic confrontation. Between May and June, 1886 Mwanga ordered the burning alive of over one hundred Christian converts.[25] (The Catholics who perished in these funeral pyres were canonized by Pope Paul VI during his visit to Uganda in 1969.) The courage displayed by the Christians in marching boldly to their deaths and the subsequent actions of the survivors proved that Mwanga's last desperate effort to restore the Buganda of his ancestors had failed. The attitude of European missionaries to profess to forgive rather than to revenge the deaths of Hannington and the other Christians did not sound plausible to him. On the contrary, he was seized with consuming fear of vengeance. A series of natural disasters in Buganda added to his disquietude.[26] When therefore he learned of Stanley's expedition —ostensibly to him—to relieve Emin Pasha, he was convinced that the day of judgment was at hand. He was heard muttering endlessly to himself: "They are coming to eat the country."[27]

Stanley did not "eat the country." Captain Lugard did so in the name of the I.B.E.A.C. and Britain. Events between 1888 and 1892 are crucial but complicated. Briefly the picture was this: by 1888 four distinct parties—call them factions if you will—had emerged in Kiganda politics, all but one of them supported by foreigners. The first party comprised the ultra-conservative "Barons," the members of the *Lubaale* cult, who were convinced that "the foreign devils"—Europeans and Arabs—were out to undermine the very existence of Buganda. They had fallen out with Mwanga because of his initial flirtation with the missionaries and his distrust of them. There was the *Bawalabu* (Muslim) party supported by the Arab and Swahili traders who had been quietly regrouping since the purge of the 1870s. They still nursed ambitions of turning Buganda into a sultanate. The Protestants constituted the *Baengeleza* party and wished to see Buganda under Protestant, and by implication, English leadership. And the *Bafranza* party, the adherents to Catholicism, who wished to see Buganda led by Catholics, and indirectly, by France. It will be seen from these divisions that royal authority had been eroded.

In the beginning Mwanga had leaned toward the Catholics. But between 1884 and 1888 he had managed, in his own inimitable way, to isolate himself completely. The creation of military regiments—perhaps in imitation of Kabalega's *Abarusura*—in an effort to maintain his position served only to turn the new force against him.[28] In a last desperate attempt at survival he attempted, unsuccessfully, to maroon his regiments on an island in Lake Victoria (September, 1888). That was the last straw. The *Bawalabu* party seized the initiative, secured the cooperation of the other parties, and deposed Mwanga who, however, managed to flee from his kingdom. The Muslim-Christian coalition, breaking with tradition,[29] crowned Kiwewa (first son of Muteesa) as kabaka (September, 1888). The new monarch became a puppet in their hands. The deposition of Mwanga was followed by what has been described as an "oligarchical revolution" in the sense that the *locus* of power in the state was soon reversed. Appointments to chiefships now became the prerogative, not of the kabaka, but of the senior chiefs.[30] In short, the kabaka of Buganda became a constitutional monarch and thus ended for good the era of autocratic kabakas.

The oligarchical revolution was quickly followed by the Muslim revolution. The other members of the coalition were beaten in a surprise attack and forced to flee to Nkore (Ankole). The Muslims set up an Islamic state. When Kiwewa refused to be circumcized he was deposed (October 22, 1888); he ruled for only six weeks. The Muslims put prince Kalema in his place; Kalema performed the circumcision rites and thereby committed an abomination against Kiganda custom. This counter-revolution plunged Buganda into four years of civil war—during which period the country's economy suffered. The population was said to have decreased by two-thirds.[31] By 1889 the Christian parties, with the help of the missionaries, had succeeded in defeating the Muslims. Mwanga was restored to his throne but only on the understanding that he behave seemingly. Mwanga thus became for the Christians what Kiwewa and Kalema had been for the Muslims. On his defeat Kalema had fled to Bunyoro-Kitara. He was soon back in power (December 11, 1889) at the head of Kabalega's army under the command of general Rwabudongo. He ruled for nearly three months before being driven off again (February 3, 1890). He died shortly afterwards of smallpox. Politically the Muslims were finished but they continued to raid the Ssingo, Bulemeezi, and Kyaggwe portions of Buganda from their Bunyoro base. It was not until May 11, 1891, that the Muslims and their Banyoro allies were decisively beaten by Captain Lugard in collaboration with Baganda. By this time it has also become evident that the old "Barons" were finished as a political force.

The troubles of Buganda were not yet over. The first defeat of the Muslims paved the way for the consumation of the "Christian revolution"[32] which was briefly interrupted by Kalema. The Christian coalition soon ran into difficulties. The problem was a simple one and not altogether unexpected: which party should occupy the premier position on Buganda, Protestant or Catholic, England or

France respectively? The Baganda revolutionaries were by no means thinking of formally surrendering their sovereignty to foreigners. In reality, however, Buganda's sovereignty was a thing of the past. Equally importantly, the revolutionaries were now speaking in the idiom of Christian Europe, not of Buganda.

On December 13, 1890, Lugard had made an unauthorized entry into Buganda and had found the country in a state of anarchy. He had been sent by the I.B.E.A.C. to occupy Buganda and with it as base conquer the rest of Uganda. His force was insignificant, but this was counterbalanced by the anarchic situation that prevailed. Moreover, he gave the impression of being in a very strong position while, in fact, he was anxiously awaiting reinforcement from the coast. Lugard adroitly manipulated the warring parties as they manipulated him. He discovered that Mwanga seemed to favor the Catholics and, as a Protestant and an Englishman, his sympathies lay with the Protestants. It was Lugard who deliberately provoked the battle of Mengo of January, 1892—[33] a battle which was won by the Protestants only because of the maxim gun. His comment that he wished he "had had the luck to bag" Stanislaus Mugwanya, the Catholic leader, during the battle[34] is indicative of his sympathies. The victory of Mengo assured the Protestant minority the premier position in Buganda. Despite the Protestant boast that they won the battle it was clear that Lugard had won the game of manipulation in Buganda and was the de facto power in the country. On March 20, 1892, he forced Mwanga to sign a treaty placing his country under I.B.E.A.C. protection, in other words, under British protection. As a result of Gerald Portal's mission to Buganda,[35] the country was formally proclaimed a British protectorate (1894). The Kingdom of Buganda was abolished, *sensu stricto,* not in 1894, nor in 1967, but between 1888 and 1892.

The conquest of Buganda left Britain free to deal with the rest of Uganda. In 1891 Lugard had already brushed aside Kabalega's *abarusura* guarding the valuable salt mines at Katwe and established the client state of Tooro. With the withdrawal of the Tooro garrisons, Kabalega promptly reoccupied his lost province but was driven off once more when Colonel Colvile invaded Bunyoro-Kitara aided by a force of twenty thousand Baganda. By 1895 the Bunyoro army had been beaten and Kabalega had fled to northern Uganda.[36] In the same year Bunyoro, Nkore, Busoga, and Tooro were formally annexed by Britain. In 1897 Mwanga revolted in a vain effort to recover his lost independence. The British reacted by deposing him and setting up his infant son, Daudi Chwa, as the Protestant kabaka of Buganda. Two years later Mwanga and Kabalega were captured in Lango and banished. The Buganda Agreement of 1900 established the character of British rule in Uganda in the twentieth century.[37] Before 1900 Britain had begun the occupation of northern and eastern Uganda with its Baganda agents. By 1914 the occupation was completed although systematic administration started in Karamoja after 1919.[38]

The Missionary Conquest of Central Africa: "An Essay in Colonisation"

Aggressive European missionary evangelization in Africa during the nineteenth century started in central Africa. Their role in the imperialistic takeover of this region has been admitted by several authorities.[39] The missionaries themselves made no secret of their mission. Nowhere in Africa did they exert a more tremendous influence. They were aided by historical developments, the most important of which were the Shaka revolution in Zululand and the slave trade. The complex repercussions of Shaka's imperialism have been carefully analyzed.[40] Its importance to our study is that before the arrival of the missionaries the great migrations caused by the *mfecane,* the conquests and reactions, the usurpations and assimilations, the destructions, diseases, famine, had created a state of flux in central Africa. The Arab and Portuguese slave traders added to the general misery of the people by more barbarous acts of destruction and disintegration. The Zulu may have destroyed states, but they built stronger ones over their ruins. In contrast, the slave traders were neither state builders nor evangelists.

The European accounts from which we derive most of our knowledge painted Central Africa as the most accursed place on earth; and the slave trade was held largely responsible for the state of affairs. And yet it has been pointed out that European horror at the slave trade was hypocritical or, at best, naive because Europeans were, during the second half of the nineteenth century, the leading world buyers of African ivory and cocoa. The ivory was used, among other things, for manufacturing piano keys and billiard balls; while cocoa was extensively drunk in European homes. The desire to supply European markets with these items stimulated the slave trade.[41]

Until 1850 European knowledge about central Africa still remained insignificant. The Portuguese who had pioneered the field had exerted little impact outside the slave trade. By 1874 Livingstone, Stanley, Thompson, and Burton, to name only a few, had made Central Africa the best known region of Africa. Of these explorers David Livingstone was the most influential. At once a missionary, explorer, physician, administrator, botanist, and theoretician of the British empire, his heroic exploits, including the circumstances of his death, made him, within a generation, a household name in Christian Europe; and for Scotland, he was a darling son and a source of pride. His name, therefore, and the conquest of Central Africa are inseparable.

As an imperialist, Livingstone was strongly evolutionist. He was convinced that the black man was far below the white man in the evolutionary process. His development must lie in the advancement of the famous triad—"Christianity, commerce and civilization." The African was like a child who needed help; his culture and institutions were barbarous and should be swept away; he was, however, teachable (a radical opinion at the time, to be sure) and must be taught the right things, those things that would eradicate his "savage" heritage and uplift him to a higher and better existence. In short, Livingstone was not only a racist, even if a humane one, but a still stronger biological imperialist.[42] He was advocating a total revolution which would change the course of Central African history. This could not be achieved by preaching alone. It must be accompanied by commercial and military conquest as well as the settlement of white colonists. In his theory of empire, the venerable doctor differed little from Cecil Rhodes or Harry Johnston. Silva Porto's assertion, therefore, that "the Cross and the Sword, the former converting, the latter chastising, shall be the only engines of future redemption for the [African] people"[43] was a correct assessment of contemporary opinion although he neglected to include commerce in his chain of priorities. Livingstone, indeed, was speaking in the idiom of Victorian Britain and was listened to with respect and admiration. His death in 1873 increased his reputation and stimulated the missionary conquest of Central Africa. Missionaries and traders rushed there to continue his work.[44]

The reception given to these foreigners varied from one polity to another. Where they settled among societies troubled by slave traders or stronger neighbors they were viewed as protectors. Their centers became sanctuaries for refugees. Here we see the classic collaboration theme—the nonzero sum game—at work, for there existed mutual advantages for both parties. In some of these weak societies they found themselves—or worked to make themselves—as the de facto government usurping the role of the traditional rulers. In such situations they were at the center of political intrigues, commercial exploitation, and religious indoctrination. They were particularly successful among peasants who were terrified by aggressive and intrusive neighbors. Their prestige was enhanced by the performance of what appeared to the local population as incredible miracles. For example, they made "water effervesce by the addition of Fruit Salts"; they performed surgical operations; and through the use of "an anesthetic gained the reputation of being able to kill people and then restore them to life."[45] Their wealth, too, made them an economic power in their own right. They offered Africans paid jobs and thus diminished the importance of the slave trade.[46]

The members of the Blantyre mission, for example, intervened in the political and judicial processes of the Yao of the Shire Highlands to the extent that they acquired a position where no authority was strong enough to check their excesses. They became "a power in the land, and not a spiritual power only."[47] They were said to have executed an African and mercilessly flogged another to death.[48] In northern Malawi (Nyasaland) the "Livingstonia" mission was a fortified post which "became the main center of British influence" in those parts.[49] The Livingstonia Central African Company (later the African Lakes Company) founded by Scottish businessmen in 1878 made sure that man did not live by religion alone by supplying the material needs of the missionaries as well as engaging in the commercial exploitation of the region. "The policy of direct rule," writes Gann, "led the missionary into a serious moral predicament. The white preacher came to Africa as a bringer of Glad Tidings to teach the word of God to the benighted heathen. Now suddenly he became a ruler, able to impose godliness by word of mouth."[50] It is doubtful that they ever experienced such a crisis. For the Victorians any value system that did not conform to theirs was discarded outright without thought or analysis. Anything was better than the African rule with which they were confronted. And those who cared to make excuses argued that they were forced by circumstances "to be prophet, priest, and king rolled into one. . . ."[51] They exaggerated the degree of widespread chaos, instability, and destruction which necessitated the intervention of European forces to restore order.

But the missionaries in Malawi were not without successes. By 1890 over two thousand pupils were attending church schools. As advance agents of imperialism they also helped to soften the blow of the European impact. When Johnston visited Malawi (1889–90) he found that the "chief hold which we have over these regions comes from the quite extraordinary work done by . . . missionary societies." He continued: "The missionary is really gaining your experience for you without any cost to yourself. . . . They strengthen our hold over the country, they spread the use of the English language, they induct the natives into the best kind of civilization, and, in fact, each Mission Station is an essay in colonization."⁵²

Where the Europeans confronted strong African rule as among the southern Yao, in Matabeleland and Mashonaland (southern Rhodesia), they achieved no success and made little impact on the people before the conquest. The reason was obvious. These strong polities did not need their protection for survival. On the contrary, they were competitors with the missionaries for the protection of their weaker neighbors. Here the classic collaboration theme was absent. The zero-sum game operated because there was a clash of interests which would sooner or later lead to conflict. The attitude of Europeans to Southern Rhodesia justifies this interpretation. Because they did not have the confidence of the king and were not allowed a free hand to do as they liked, they adopted a hostile attitude toward the king and his country. They wrote about the country with a vengeance, distorting the picture of historical developments by propagating false rumors. They demanded the breakup of the state system if progress was to be made and argued that force was the only answer. Thus when the British South Africa Company (henceforth B.S.A.C.) forces invaded southern Rhodesia in 1890 a missionary wrote: "The hateful Matabele rule is doomed. We as missionaries, with our thirty years history behind us, have little to bind our sympathies to the Matabele people, neither can we pity the fall of their power." Of the Ndebele, wrote the same man: "The wrath of God" had fallen on them as a punishment for their rejection of Christianity.⁵³ And when Lobengula, successor to the great Mzilikazi, refused to allow a European prospecting company to operate in his kingdom, its leader wrote with contempt and hate:

> Oh ye spirits of deported negrophilists and followers of "Exter Hall" if only you could feel what is felt by us today, at the knowledge that we white men and *Englishmen* too, are under the thumb and utterly in the power of a lot of black scoundrels there is little doubt that your *"brotherly love"* for niggers would receive a serious check!! Brothers indeed! d . . . scoundrels!!. . . . To feel oneself under the power of a nigger is worse than being in prison and quite enough to bring on fever.⁵⁴

The point was well taken. Cecil Rhodes made sure that no such misfortune would happen to white men again. He made careful plans to provoke a conflict with Lobengula.

Mzilikazi had died in 1870, an obese, physically wrecked, but nonetheless a dignified and highly respectable, old man. His death had given rise to a disastrous civil war as a result of which Lobengula had emerged victorious.[55] Stories of his country's great mineral wealth, the good grazing land, fear of Transvaal intervention, and Lobengula's contempt for European ways, drove Rhodes to invade the country. Lobengula's efforts to play Boer against Briton and avoid a confrontation yielded few dividends. With the assistance of the Reverend John Moffat, who was assistant commissioner for Bechuanaland (Botswana), Rhodes persuaded Lobengula to sign two documents. By the first he undertook not to enter into treaty obligations with foreign powers without British sanction; and by the second—the so-called Rudd Concession—he gave away the mineral rights in his country to Rhodes's company for pittance. It was on the basis of the Rudd Concession that Rhodes secured the royal charter for his company in 1889. In 1890 he dispatched his "Pioneer Column" which occupied Mashonaland without Lobengula's sanction. The king did not contest the occupation. But eventually, in 1893, the inevitable clash occurred; the maxim gun proved where power lay, and Lobengula fled from his capital. He died in 1894 a refugee in some wilderness. And thus the history of the Matabele Kingdom came to an end. Or did it? By 1896 the Ndebele and Shona had regrouped and made a last desperate and bloody effort to drive the white men away. Their effort, though formidable, was not good enough.[56] Their defeat began the era of white supremacy in Zimbabwe (Rhodesia) which is today a major bone in the throat of black Africa.

In Barotseland the situation was somewhat different. Here was a powerful African state experiencing external and internal strains after the national revolution which had ended Makololo overrule.[57] In 1871 a European traveler called George Westbeech opened up profitable trade with the Barotse and broke up the commercial network of the great Ovimbundu traders. He gained the favor of the king and became a sort of royal adviser on European affaris. Here, too, the Gospel followed trade. During the civil wars of the 1880s it was Westbreech with his hunters and their guns who secured Lewanika on the Barotse throne. Consequently, he made sure that the king pursued a promissionary policy. Thus the Huguenot missionary, Francois Coillard (1834–1904), of Basutoland (Lesotho) fame, was formally received by Lewanika and his Council on March 23, 1886. By 1890 Coillard had succeeded in persuading Lewanika to seek the protection of England and subsequently to sign a treaty with the B.S.A.C. which gave Rhodes a free hand in northwestern Rhodesia.

Rhodes had reckoned that Lewanika's country was very rich in minerals and was determined to annex it. Coillard was delighted at the prospects of the imperialistic takeover of the country. He wrote: "I have no doubt that for the nation this will prove the one plank of safety. The Barotsi are incapable of governing, and, left to themselves, they would before long have annihilated each other."[58] Lewanika and his council had been led to believe that they had signed a treaty with Queen Victoria whereas, in fact, they had signed the company's document. Moreover, the gifts which Lewanika sent to Victoria never reached her.[59] Coillard, in short, had helped a commercial company rob Lewanika—his friend—of his sovereignty by default. It is not surprising therefore that when the Barotse discovered that they had been cheated, they regarded Coillard as a traitor and for some time were lukewarm toward the missionaries.

In northeastern Rhodesia it was the London Missionary Society who fought hard to reassure British paramountcy against Germany and Belgium. In collaboration with the African Lakes Company, they deposed, in 1891, a Lungu chief called Tafuna because he neither accepted dictation from them nor showed them respect. They destroyed Tafuna's villages and imprisoned him in Blantyre.[60] The missionary proceedings in Bembaland were even more bizarre. There was the case of a Bishop Joseph Dupont who proclaimed himself chief of the Bemba on the death of chief Mwamba. His intervention in the internal affairs of Bembaland precipitated the formal assumption of British sovereignty.[61] By 1901 the conquest of northern Rhodesia (Zambia) was complete.

Although it has been stated that between 1875 and 1885 the missionaries did not deliberately draw their governments to assume sovereignty in Central Africa,[62] the fact remains that, more than any other agents of imperialism, they prepared the way for the imperialistic takeover. Missionary enterprise simply presented the British government with a fait accompli. And given their celebrated exploits, their rationale for evangelizing Central Africa in the first place, and the spirit of Victorian Britain, any government which let them down did so at its peril.

Salisbury Restores British Initiative in Central Africa and Uganda, 1885–92

One great weakness of British imperial history in the nineteenth century has been the tendency to misinterpret African historical movements. Analysis of imperial conquest ought to focus less on theory and more on the contact of peoples. To emphasize developments in European diplomacy—which necessitates an almost total reliance on European official documents—in an effort to explain nineteenth-century expansion is to misplace priorities. Why did government officials write their dispatches, private letters, minutes, in the manner they did? What gave them the confidence to carve up African territories by merely looking at maps without reference to the owners? What sort of individuals, in any case, have provided us with our so-called historical "facts"? These, and similar other complex questions have not been emphasized by theoreticians of imperialism. They cannot be answered satisfactorily without examining the consequences of the slave trade, the impact of the European contact on the African peoples, and the European images of Africans.

Professor Seton-Watson's assertion that "Fashoda was bred on the Mekong River"[63] is misleading; so is that axiom of British imperial historiography which asserts that Africa was conquered simply to protest British interests in Egypt, and consequently, in India. We have seen that in East and Central Africa, Arabs, Europeans (travelers, traders, and missionaries) had prepared the ground for the imperialistic takeover well before the bombardment of Alexandria. By destroying the cohesiveness of African polities these forces found themselves in the saddle of affairs, a position they could only maintain so long as they successfully played the dangerous game of collaboration with the various groups within these polities. The question then is: how long would this unsatisfactory state of affairs have lasted before the metropolitan power stepped in? British missionaries and traders, for example, had powerful supporters in Britain. In the face of danger would the government let them stew in their own juice and hope to remain in power? Not even Bismarck could afford to ignore the plight of the German company in East Africa. Salisbury therefore intervened in Central Africa and Uganda to protect what private British enterprise had achieved. So long as the "pacific expansion of Englishmen" was progressing smoothly, he had no reason to intervene. When this was threatened by European intervention and African resistance, he stepped in to restore British initiative.

By annexing Bechuanaland in 1885 Salisbury made it possible for the Cape Colony to expand northward. The mineral revolution in South Africa (1886) made his action more significant. It convinced Rhodes that there was a lot of money to be made in Central Africa. Therefore Portugal must be prevented from joining its western possessions with those in the east; German expansion from southwest Africa (Namibia) must be stifled; so must Transvaal pretensions to Central Africa; the Boer republics must remain within the British empire; and efforts must be made to make Africa "all

British from the Cape to Cairo." Although Rhodes's view represented "a rough expression of his [Salisbury's] African policy as a whole,"[64] the prime minister realized that the risks were too high, especially in the 1880s. It would create awkward problems at home; it would dislocate the European balance with grave consequences for war. Salisbury therefore decided to share control and, through hard-headed diplomacy, protect his country's interests. Outwardly phlegmatic, cynical, and pessimistic, lacklustre Salisbury went about the conquest of Africa with a cool, calculated, unemotional, resolute, and quiet professionalism that pleasantly surprised Harry Johnston[65] and made him—at any rate, from the African's point of view—a very dangerous imperialist. Lord Salisbury, Henry Labouchere observed in the 1890s, was "a jingo" but there was "method in his madness."[66]

In Central Africa it is significant that Salisbury diplomatically secured for the jingoes what they wanted while giving the impression of being propelled by the awesome figure of Rhodes. He played this role of the reluctant imperialist for two reasons. First, he wished to avoid a European combination against Britain at a period when it felt itself isolated; second, the nature of domestic polities dictated restraint while conveying the impression that Britain must stand firm in the face of European competition, especially as British nationals were in the forefront of the religious, commercial, and in some areas, political control of Central Africa. It has been pointed out that even Portuguese pioneer companies were "financed by British capitalists."[67] Rhodes's willingness to bear the burden of conquest[68] made Salisbury's task easier in dealing with the House of Commons, but not with Germany or Portugal. The latter was a decedent power, not much of a threat to Britain, but it was backed by Germany and France.

In July, 1888 Salisbury declared Britain's exclusive claim to southern Rhodesia but was willing to neutralize Malawi and northern Zambesia.[69] But this was Livingstone's country and to abandon it, so it seemed, caused concern in many circles. In reality, however, Salisbury had abandoned nothing. He was waiting for something to happen. In January, 1889 Bismarck proposed colonial accommodation with Britain in return for an Anglo-German understanding in Europe.[70] He seized his opportunity, appointed the ebullient Johnston, in the same month, as consul to Mozambique with instructions to report on the extent of Portuguese control in the hinterland, and make treaties of friendship with the chiefs.[71] Before Johnston left for his post, he was instructed to proceed to Lisbon instead to work out "an understanding about frontiers which would keep the Portuguese out of the Shire Highlands and Central Zambesia."[72] The direct result of this diplomatic initiative, Johnston boasted, was "the establishment of British supremacy over British Central Africa."[73] But Johnston's package deal did nothing of the sort; it was more or less a confirmation of Salisbury's original offer.

Salisbury's reception of Johnston's agreement would suggest that he had changed his mind. According to Oliver, he "set in motion a slow and elaborately staged demonstration of British public opinion" against the proposed treaty.[74] Thus, when Lord Balfour of Burleigh informed Salisbury that "my Scottish friends don't like the Portuguese terms," he came into the open and bluntly replied:

> Neither do I . . . I don't want your Scottish friends to accept them. I want the Portuguese to know that I, too, have a strong public opinion behind me, and I am sending the Government a warning that they must not go too far.[75]

Scottish missionary opinion, emotionally attached to Livingstone's country, gave Salisbury overwhelming support. He suspended the negotiations and asked Johnston to return to his Mozambique assignment with powers to declare a protectorate over the disputed territories if the Portuguese threatened them. When the Portuguese crossed the Ruo frontier the order was executed. At the beginning of 1890 he was instructed to inform the missionaries that Portugal had given an undertaking to the British government not to settle the dispute by force.[76] On June 11, 1891 an Anglo-Portuguese treaty settled their difficulties in Central Africa.[77] And in the same year a British protectorate was proclaimed over Nyasaland. "The missionary occupation of Nyasaland," writes Oliver, "provided both the historical justification and the immediate pretext for the British annexation."[78] Rhodes made the administration possible by paying for it but the missionaries refused to be placed under B.S.A.C. rule.

Having diplomatically defended British interests in Central Africa and being aware that treaties without effective occupation and formal paramountcy were useless, Salisbury formally annexed these territories and left the military conquest to Rhodes and his company. The moving spirits in Central Africa may have been Rhodes and the missionaries; but without Salisbury's diplomatic, and indirectly military support, they would have achieved little success. He yielded no territories to the other powers; but he ended the Cape-to-Cairo idea both for the sake of European peace and British supremacy in East Africa.

In Uganda, too, Salisbury restored the British initiative. There is, however, scanty evidence that he had any clear idea of what to do about Uganda before 1890.[79] Here, unlike in Nigeria and southern Africa, private commercial enterprise was not proving an effective instrument of empire-building. And although the missionaries, having undermined the social fabric of Kiganda society, were experiencing difficulties in the 1880s, they were nevertheless in no danger. Nor did they ask for protection. Bishop Hannington was murdered in Busoga as a result of an injudicious decision on the part of the missionaries on the spot; the Uganda martyrs were Africans, not Europeans, and largely Catholics. What justification then had Salisbury for intervention? Of course if he was primarily concerned with the desire to protect Egypt, every other consideration would be of secondary importance. But nothing was done. He turned down Consul Holmwood's request to punish Mwanga, occupy Uganda and Equatoria, and protect the headwaters of the Nile.[80] Indeed Holmwood was asked to advise the missionaries to withdraw if they found their work intolerable.[81] This was a curious way to protect the headwaters of the Nile!

The 1886 Anglo-German Treaty did not state categorically that Uganda belonged to the British sphere of influence. Nor did the subsequent agreement of 1887 by which Britain and Germany undertook to "discourage annexation" in the rear of their respective spheres of influence, and agreed that if one party occupied the coast "the other could not, without consent, occupy unclaimed regions in the rear"[82] clarify the situation. On the contrary, this hinterland agreement was later to lead to misunderstanding between the two countries.[83] Considering the enterprise of British subjects in Buganda—which we have discussed—Salisbury may have been justified in assuming later on that the agreements of 1886 and 1887 had reserved Uganda for Britain.[84] But as Salisbury himself had pointed out in the case of Zanzibar: "keeping every other nation out" in the hope that Britain would move in later on was "a poor policy." As far as Germany was concerned, however, Uganda was a *res nullius*.[85]

Before Karl Peters's dash to Buganda in 1888 there was no other European power contesting paramountcy in that country with Britain. Salisbury had hoped, therefore, that the process of "pacific imperialism" would take its leisurely course. As was the case in other parts of Africa that was not to be. The German challenge altered his calculation. It also drove the missionaries to request imperial assistance to keep the Germans out; it gave Mackinnon the opportunity to renew pressure to grant his company a royal charter. Hitherto Salisbury had not been convinced that it was in the national interest, or politically and diplomatically prudent, to get actively involved in Uganda. In 1886 when the 1884 Clement Hill memorandum[86] urging the protection of the Upper Nile was resurrected by Holmwood Salisbury had sacked him and had refused to bring the proposal before the cabinet. He had even bluntly refused to involve his government with the expedition privately organized for the relief of Emin Pasha.[87]

Now, in 1888, when Mackinnon renewed his request for a charter Salisbury readily agreed to allow it. Why did he change his mind? The German irruption into Uganda threatened the informal influence which Britain had enjoyed in that country since the time of Speke and Grant. The collapse of the Kiganda monarchy in 1888 as a result of the Muslim-Christian impact had created a power vacuum which must be filled if the missionaries' safety were to be assured. How could this be achieved?

Just three years after the nightmare of the Liberals with regard to Khartoum, no British leader, let alone one of Salisbury's cautious spirit, would authorize a government expedition to the interior of Africa, eight hundred miles away from the coast. Should another disaster occur, how could he defend such a policy before Parliament and the British people? If he stated that he was protecting the headwaters of the Nile, the little Englanders and the Irish contingent would ridicule him. Henry Labouchere would be quick to point out to him that Khalifa Abdullah was protecting the headwaters of the Nile and would not welcome his assistance. Big Sir William Harcourt would roar himself hoarse in righteous indignation. In short, Parliament would not vote the money for the expedition.

There is no concrete evidence to suggest that Salisbury himself was particularly concerned with the Upper Nile at this stage. He knew now that pacific imperialism had its limits; that spheres of influence were useless without imperial presence of some sort; and that he had to do something to safeguard what British missionary enterprise had achieved. He turned to Mackinnon in the very faint hope that he might show half the enterprise of a Rhodes or two-thirds that of a Goldie. In his heart he knew, however, that this was impossible and prophesied that Mackinnon's company "will probably be bankrupt" sooner or later.[88] Nevertheless, once the charter was granted, Salisbury "egged on, urged on, advised, spurred and encouraged" Mackinnon to occupy Uganda.[89] Mackinnon, however, proved unequal to the task of empire-building in East Africa. He could not even deal decisively with Uganda and by 1890 he had gone bankrupt. The collapse of the company meant that it had failed in its primary function as an instrument of imperial strategy,[90] a fact admitted by Salisbury with much propriety.[91]

Salisbury was back to the beginning. What, then, was to be done? He resorted to what he knew how to do best: a diplomatic defense of British interests in Uganda. In 1889 he suggested arbitration to Count Hatzfeldt as a practical way of settling Anglo-German differences in East Africa, a gesture which the German ambassador viewed quite correctly, as Salisbury's "only one way of obtaining an early settlement, which would attain the object, . . . without exposing him and his Government to attacks; which might be awkward on account of too great compliance with our wishes. . . ."[92] In January, 1890 Germany accepted this idea of arbitration.[93] In March, 1890 Salisbury passed this information to Sir Lewis Pelly, a director of the I.B.E.A.C., who had earlier expressed concern as to the difficulties facing the company.[94] This notion of arbitration is very fundamental to the understanding of Salisbury's attitude to the negotiation.

On March, 1890, Bismarck was sacked by the Kaiser. The architect of the German nation had, for some time, been tottering toward his fall; and his departure was seen by Ambassador Malet as presenting an excellent opportunity for settling the points at issue. He wrote to Salisbury:

> Sir Percy Anderson has a difficult task before him but, in a general way, I suspect that the German Government are even more anxious than we are to get all the African questions in dispute between us definitely settled. It would be a feather in the cap of the new Govt., while failure would be ascribed to the absence of the master directing mind of Prince Bismarck.[95]

It is fair to assume that this dispatch may have persuaded Salisbury to allow the arbitration proposal to fade out gradually so that London and Berlin could sort out their differences directly. Moreover a general settlement would be more likely to embrace wider issues which an arbitrator would not have been allowed to touch. But Salisbury had other reasons for expecting a favorable settlement. Anderson, who left for Berlin early in May to prepare the ground for arbitration with his opposite number, Dr. Krauel, had made so much progress in their discussions that arbitration appeared unnecessary. In fact, Hatzfeldt was told on May 10 that the only outstanding differences related to the delimitation of districts west of Lake Nyassa.[96] Indeed the German Foreign Ministry had not been exactly unreasonable in the territorial disputes in East Africa, and had, on occasions, bent over backwards to help Salisbury. In 1888, Baron Holstein had literally implored him not to go so far in meeting German wishes in Zanzibar as to endanger his parliamentary position in Britain since Germany preferred him at the Foreign Office to anyone else.[97] In 1889 Herbert Bismarck had told a British emissary that "the commercial value of East African enterprise was altogether fictitious," and Euan-Smith was convinced that the Germans "would be ready to go very far to meet any proposition . . . that would result in a final solution of East African difficulties."[98] When, therefore, in May, 1890 Salisbury made it plain to the Germans that Uganda was, without doubt, in the British sphere of influence,[99] the Germans who "had no serious hopes of acquiring Uganda."[100] yielded on this point.[101] In fact as Krauel put it to Anderson: "Uganda at least as far South as one degree south was in the British sphere."[102] Indeed during the Anderson-Krauel discussions, the Kaiser himself, although he was denouncing Stanley as "an adventurer who was prepared to sell himself to the highest bidder," and with whom he would have nothing to do, yet was urging

> General Caprivi that it was of the highest importance that Your Lordship's [Salisbury's] position in Parliament would not be weakened and had asked him to bear this in mind as a first condition in the negotiations. Africa His Majesty said was not worth a quarrel between England and Germany.[103]

Such was the confidence that Salisbury inspired in Berlin that there was dismay when they learned that he no longer commanded a majority in Parliament in July, 1892; and such their sincerity that some, ignorant of the subleties and nuances of the British Constitution, went so far as to make eccentric suggestions which, they believed, would make it possible for Salisbury to remain in power.[104]

Diplomatically speaking therefore, unlike the Anglo-French negotiations—which were going on in West Africa at that time, almost *pari passu* with the Anglo-German negotiations in the east—Salisbury was negotiating from a position of strength. Evidently the Germans had shown all their cards while Salisbury still reserved some of his in his own hands. The surprise offer of Heligoland[105] settled matters; it was a brilliant piece of diplomacy and an opportunistic one. But the goodwill he inspired in Germany also placed a special responsibility on his shoulders to live up to expectations: he ended the "Cape to Cairo" dream—to the dismay of Rhodes, Kirk, and Mackinnon.

The thesis of the opportunism of the Heligoland offer is further strengthened by Salisbury's letter to Malet in which, less than a year earlier, he had declared himself in opposition to such a course.[106] Nevertheless, the convention of July 1, 1890, procured a vast East African empire for Britain for the loss of Heligoland and the Cape to Cairo route. Salisbury, indeed, did not personally care for Heligo-land.[107] Undoubtedly it was an unfavorable agreement for the Germans who, in the words of Baron Eckardstein, "had got Heligoland at the cost of disproportionately important concessions in East Africa."[108] Germany gave up claims to Zanzibar, Uganda, Witu, and some other acquisitions by Karl Peters. The German public ignorantly held Count Hatzfeldt responsible for such a curious bargain, whereas the blame, according to Eckardstein, lay with the Kaiser and his erratic whims.[109] Eight years later, Lascelles reported the Kaiser as saying, with reference to the cession of Heligoland:

> It is true that you . . . gave up Heligoland, but you got a great deal in exchange, in fact about ten blacks to every one white man I found in the island. I replied that I believed that we did not complain of the arrangement, although I was not sure that a large black population was much of an advantage. "Oh", said the Emperor, "when they become too numerous you get up a little war and have a lot of them knocked on the head."[110]

Queen Victoria, on the other hand, strongly objected to battering away any part of her empire on any pretext whatever; and she was only placated on the undertaking of Salisbury to promise that the transaction would not constitute a precedent.[111]

The Heligoland Agreement ended the partition of East Africa and surrendered Uganda to Britain. The military occupation of the country was another matter. Until this was done the agreement was a useless scrap of paper. If the protection of Egypt was Salisbury's whole point in the negotiations, he was sufficiently acquainted with the rules of the game to know that military occupation was the only means to safeguard treaty obligations. If that was the case, why did he not dispatch an imperial occupation force? The Dervishes, for example, were not a party to the arrangement. Nor were the French. There was a danger of attack on Uganda from the north either by the Dervishes or, for that matter, by the French should they establish their mastery on the Upper Nile. Mwanga was no longer hostile—temporarily at any rate, as he owed his throne to the missionaries—but he was no party to the agreement either. Kabalega was hostile to both Buganda and Britain. He had occupied the Buganda capital in 1890 for some three months; he might possibly attack again in the future in his drive to refound the ancient empire of Kitara.[112]

Meanwhile the bankruptcy of the I.B.E.A.C. had meant that it was on the point of folding its operations. But in October, 1891 the

Church Missionary Society and some private individuals contributed the sum of £25,000 to help the company toward "the maintenance of the Uganda control."[113] Lugard, an employee of the company, who had been fighting to keep Uganda British, was therefore asked by his employers to soldier on till the end of the year in the hope of imperial assistance and "ultimately . . . recoup their immediate bosses."[114] Although Salisbury expressed his satisfaction at the generous gesture made "for this important object,"[115] no government support was offered.[116] Without the missionaries and public opinion generally the company would have abandoned Uganda.[117] Once more Salisbury had demonstrated a very curious way of retaining the headwaters of the Nile for which he is said to have labored so hard throughout the partition of Africa. Admittedly, he pleaded for the construction of the Mombasa–Uganda railway, running over six hundred miles from the coast to the Kenyan side of Lake Victoria and passing through difficult and hostile country,[118] partly for the purpose of maintaining Britain's position in Uganda. Inevitably the building of the railway would take time, and was, in fact, completed in 1902 after the conquest of the Sudan was over. There was no guarantee, therefore, that Salisbury was master of historical forces. When he fell from power in July, 1892 no practical protection had been given to the headwaters of the Nile. Indeed, as Sanderson has admitted: ". . . so long as the Tana-Juba hinterland remained open, nothing that happened in "Uganda" could give complete security to the Upper Nile."[119]

The War Office and the Uganda Base, 1894–99
The position in Uganda when the earl of Rosebery became foreign secretary in 1892 was something like this: the company was to withdraw at the end of the year and Uganda would be left unprotected; Bishop Tucker and the missionaries had sworn to remain in their posts "whatever may be their fate"; Lugard, too, had declared "that as an officer holding H.M.'s Commission he has pledged his own honor and that of the British nation to remain there forever," and in fact, had "annexed two other provinces larger than [B]uganda" which he garrisoned with Sudanese troops for the "honor of the British nation."[120] Lugard, of course, was bluffing. He could not last long without imperial assistance. By September 1 he was on his way to England and the courageous Captain Williams was left in command with a token force.[121] It was Rosebery's government which retained Uganda to the detriment of his party[122] especially as the Liberal cabinet of 1892 were, on the whole, not interested in the

headwaters of the Nile;[123] and a Liberal foreign secretary, Earl Grey, who in March, 1895 gave the bellicose warning against French proceedings in the Upper Nile.

By 1894 it had become an open secret that France was determined to have a footing on the Upper Nile.[124] The Grey warning may have irritated the French. It did not, however, cause them to withdraw although under the administration of a civilian, M. Liotard, they remained quiet at Ubanghi.[125] The War Office, in fact, had always doubted the French ability to achieve their dream of a stronghold on the Upper Nile.[126] Salisbury did not share their doubt. In 1895, when he was pressed to sanction the reconquest of the Sudan, he replied: "If I could recommend such a result, I should lay down that there must be no forward movement in Egypt till our railway had reached the lake . . . if we allowed such a proceeding, we shall certainly have a French forward movement on the Upper Nile: but if we had reached the lake, I think we might make such an enterprise impossible."[127] Much should not be made of this document when it is remembered that the railway had been in the planning stages for about five years and no one was sure that it would be completed in the next five years.

In a letter to the duke of Devonshire Salisbury rejected the thesis that he maintained British presence in Egypt in order to protect the route to India and, by implication, had to occupy Uganda as part of this strategy.

He wrote:

> I do not see that the Mediterranean has more than a secondary interest. Malta can take care of itself. Egypt is quite unaccessible from the Red Sea—and the route to India is only five days shorter by the Canal than by the Cape. These considerations are important no doubt: but not in the first degree. What our huge fleet is doing or expected to do in the Mediterranean is one of the mysteries of official strategy.[128]

This very important document is reinforced by Salisbury's instruction to the Defence Committee in 1898:

> I am directed by the Marquess of Salisbury to inform you that, in view of the possibility of a war between this country and France, he has under his considerations the question of the position in such an eventuality of the East Africa Protectorates under the Administration of this Department, which have a seaboard, namely, the East Africa Protectorate itself, and that of Zanzibar, including the island of Pemba.

Salisbury wished to know if it would be possible or desirable, during war, and in accordance with articles 10 and 11 of the Berlin Act, to place these Protectorates "under the rule of neutrality."[129] Once more, he has shown that he had no use for the East Africa base strategy as a positive act of policy. It would certainly have been odd for the man credited with the acquisition of East Africa purely for its strategic value to advocate such a course. Indeed, the committee quickly pointed out to him that to declare these territories neutral would be to the positive advantage of France in war time. Furthermore, though there was little military disadvantage in neutralizing Zanzibar and Pemba, in accordance with article 11 of the Berlin Act, such a course would deprive England of the ports of "Mombasa and Kismayu as bases for warlike operations."[130]

In the meantime the French had decided to reinforce their activities in the Upper Nile. In 1896 Liotard was replaced by a soldier, Captain Marchand. At once French troops on the Upper Ubanghi began to be steadily increased.[131] The War Office, therefore, had good reason to infer that the honeymoon was over and that the French were threatening to march on the Nile Valley toward Fashoda, with the aim in view of supplanting "British and Egyptian interests" with their own, and of interrupting "the continuity of British influence between Egypt and Uganda."[132] To forestall the French thus became the paramount concern of the War Office especially as their greatest difficulty was the time factor. To organize an expedition from England would raise two problems: public attention would at once be drawn to it and the whole business would be exaggerated out of all proportions; and second, the long distance between the Upper Nile and England was such that the French were bound to reach there before them. It was suggested that Uganda would be more to the purpose because there "we possess a base from which an expeditionary force could be rapidly and secretly despatched to the Upper Nile." Moreover, it was argued that,

> an English force operating from Uganda would find itself upon the Nile with its resources unimpaired and with greater facilities for movement than would be the case with an expedition of any other nationality. It would be in closer touch with a permanent base, and this superiority would be even more manifest if a depot were formed at Wadelai and held by Sikhs.[133]

As later events were to show, the War Office grossly underestimated the difficulties.

There were of course several ways of asserting British paramountcy on the Upper Nile. Britain could come to terms with France and convince the latter to recognize its claims. But Salisbury knew that France was not in a cooperative mood. The cooperation of Abyssinia could be sought. The third course would be to come to an arrangement with Leopold II of the Belgians (as was in fact suggested by M. Van Etvelde). Or, to operate from Uganda toward the Nile Valley, making treaties and asserting British sovereignty, with or without the cooperation of Menelek and Leopold. Sir John Ardagh of the War Office suggested the last course. The only difficulty, he feared, was that Uganda would be denuded "temporarily while troops to replace the force were on their way from the coast." But he warned Salisbury that if no action was taken, "we may soon hear of a belt of French Treaties from Ubanghi across the Nile to Abyssinia" in view of Menelek's military activities in the neighborhood of Sobat; of the French advance toward Fashoda; and of the Congo state's toward Wadelai.[134]

Here was an important question of imperial policy for decision as Hill immediately recognized. "It will be seen that they open up questions of Imperial policy," he minuted to Salisbury, "which will require very careful consideration and might lead to very important results." He also suggested, and Salisbury concurred, that the matter must be brought before the cabinet.[135] The important point for the cabinet to decide was what step, if any, in the light of the War Office memorandum, "should be taken to prevent France cutting off our chance of free communication from Uganda to Egypt."[136] Hill, in fact, did not hide his disapproval of the Uganda routes. He summed up his views:

I hesitate to differ from military experts, but it seems to me that sufficient account has not been taken of the extreme difficulty of transport at present between Mombasa and Uganda. As the railway advances and we get carts on the Sclater road, the difficulties will diminish; but I am afraid that we are not yet in a position to find the carriage which a body of Indian troops requires.

It is necessary to do more than allude to the other difficulties of expense and the reluctance of the Indian Government to spare troops, for they might be overcome if the importance of the service demanded it.

Without these, or some other troops as support in Uganda, it would probably be thought too risky to let a body of the Protectorate troops go off north. One officer might get down the Nile for some distance safely, and make treaties; but it would be a dangerous mission, and treaties without occupation would meet with scanty respect. . . .

The conclusion seems to be that a race against France with a sufficient force to maintain even a semblance of effective occupation would be a costly and hazardous operation, and, if she is in earnest in her intention to advance, would run a great chance of being too late; while an attempt to restrain France by diplomatic means is a question of policy depending upon how far we are prepared to back up such an attempt.[137]

Once more, Hill had been right. A diplomatic defense of imperial interests was not good enough; it must be backed up by force.

What action the cabinet decided to take on the War Office memorandum is not clear. But on March 26 Major Macdonald accepted an offer to lead a treaty-making expedition toward the north, with instructions to occupy Fashoda before the French.[138] It was not, however, until June 18, 1897, that Macdonald left for Mombasa.[139] By this time Dongola had already fallen; and preparations were being made to advance on Khartoum. After a chequered progress, Macdonald was joined by the Uganda-Sudanese contingent whom he described as being in "a somewhat low state of discipline."[140] Within a few months some of them had, in fact, bolted back to Uganda.[141] But instead of satisfying their grievances Macdonald proceeded without them and stressed the employment of Indian troops in Uganda.[142] The result was that the grievances of the deserters became widespread among those who remained behind, and in October they mutinied.[143] It was not until March, 1898 that the mutiny was suppressed and Macdonald was back, as it were, to the point from which he started.[144] In July he confessed to Salisbury that he would be unable to reach Fashoda by the end of October and that, in any case, Major Kitchener would be there before him. He nevertheless hoped to reach Lado by the end of September and requested that a gunboat be sent there to meet him —his intention being to join hands at Fashoda with the column operating from Egypt;[145] and thereby preventing "foreign Powers from establishing themselves in the Basin of the Nile between that river and Abyssinia."[146] "It would be of little service," minuted Salisbury. "The situation may have changed before the orders reach him."[147] Khartoum fell in September but Macdonald continued his treaty-making expedition. In December, however, he confessed that he could go no further because of insufficient materials and requested permission to reinforce and still proceed "to join hands with Egypt."[148] But instructions had already gone out that the expedition should return.[149] On January 27, 1899, Berkeley, the British representative in Uganda, was informed that Macdonald had been instructed to undertake no further costly expeditions on the Ugandan frontier.[150] On March 4 Macdonald and his staff arrived back safely at Mombasa; Macdonald returned to England on April 15.

Barrington and Salisbury aptly provided the assessment of the Macdonald mission. In Barrington's opinion, "he had succeeded in making treaties with a lot of tribes—but that seems to be all that he has accomplished."[151] To which Salisbury observed: "He has certainly not been a success. Indeed he might repeat the General Confession to us with much propriety."[152]

When Salisbury left office in 1892 no effective protection had to be given to the headwaters of the Nile. When he returned to office in 1895, he turned his attention to the construction of the Uganda railway. The decision to invade the Upper Nile from the Uganda base was hatched at the War Office and sold to him in 1897, at a period when he was devaluing the strategic value of the so-called "route to the east." The histories of the Macdonald mission and that of Marchand expose the futility of the headwaters of the Nile in the protection of the British position in Egypt. Kitchener's occupation of Fashoda, and not Salisbury's diplomatic defense of Uganda, secured British hegemony in Egypt. And Salisbury knew it.

PART IV

Egypt and the Sudan 1885–1900

Chapter IX

Salisbury Drifts Awhile
in the Nile Valley, 1885–96

The events which led Britain to muddle into Egypt in 1882 are well known. So are the repercussions of the occupation. The Mahdist revolution and the sacking of Khartoum in 1885 had widened the Suez Crisis. The solving of the Egyptian question, therefore, became intricately connected with the status of the Sudan. The liberals who had steamed their war into Egypt and had mismanaged the Khartoum Crisis were at their wits' end and must have been greatly relieved when Gladstone's second ministry fell in 1885.

On June 11, 1885, Salisbury formed his first ministry and became his own foreign secretary. Though this was a stopgap government, it became obvious that Gladstone's Egyptian bondage was no less Salisbury's. It seems to have been a canon of Victorian political behavior that foreign affairs ought to stand above party politics. Salisbury immediately set out to clean up the mess left by Gladstone. In August Sir Henry Drummond Wolff was sent to Constantinople to open negotiations with the sultan, the paper sovereign of Egypt. Salisbury's instruction to Wolff is clearly unequivocal: "Our diplomatic task is twofold: to obtain the arrangements necessary for our work in Egypt now; secondly, in leaving it, to secure the privileged position which will pay us for our blood and treasure."[1] These were hard terms, neither the French nor the sultan were likely to accept. But between 1885 and 1887 Wolff worked tirelessly to win the sultan over and secure a settlement. The final convention, however, was not signed by the sultan in deference to French objection. What perturbed France, prima facie, was Salisbury's insistence on Britain's unlimited period of reentry into Egypt in case of emergency.[2] In reality, however, the French did not seriously desire British withdrawal. British presence in Egypt protected the French investments against the emergence of African nationalism which might attempt to fill the vacuum left by the British. The French barked but did not bite; they used the Suez Crisis to embarrass Britain diplomatically and to try to win territorial concessions elsewhere.[3] British governments were in possession of this evidence and would have been stupid if they succumbed to the French blackmail. Salisbury decided to pursue a policy of drift.

With the failure of the Wolff Convention in 1887 it became obvious that the Egyptian question could not be settled by diplomacy; an immediate military settlement was also ruled out as impracticable and unsafe. Salisbury therefore decided to drift along and play a waiting game. In fact he had no other choice. Though public opinion was against the evacuation of Egypt,[4] there was equally no strong public pressure to push him along in the direction of a bold policy. The memories of Gordon were still so fresh in people's minds that, even if such a pressure existed, no sane government, let alone one with a precarious parliamentary majority, would have attempted to execute a forward policy in the Upper Nile.[5] Moreover, the tight-fisted financial policy of the Treasury and the House of Commons practically ruled out such a policy.[6] And Sir Evelyn Baring,[7] pursuing a purely parochial policy, and behaving as if the Egyptian problem had no wider significance, set his face against a forward policy. He argued that so long as England occupied Egypt there was no danger of a Dervish threat to his ward.[8]

Salisbury, indeed, did not need to be restrained from pursuing a forward policy in Egypt or the Sudan. He had already deprecated such a course. As soon as France had vetoed the Wolff Convention, he wrote to Lyons:

> We cannot leave the Khedive to take his chance of foreign attack or native riot: and the French refuse to let us exercise the necessary powers of defence, unless we do it by continuing our military occupation. I see nothing for it but to sit still and drift awhile: a little further in the history of Europe the conditions may have changed: and we may be able to get some agreement arrived at which will justify evacuation. Till then we must simply refuse to evacuate. . . .[9]

And about three years later he wrote to Cromer in connection with the Sudan:

> Whenever you have money enough to go to Khartoum, the resources of civilization will be adequate to the subjugation

of the country. If you leave them for the present where they are they can destroy nothing, for there is nothing to destroy. They cannot erect any domination which shall make the conquest of them a formidable task, for they have, practically speaking, neither cannons nor machine-guns, nor even the ammunition for ordinary rifles. Surely, if you are not ready to go to Khartoum these people were created for the purpose of keeping the bed warm for you till you can occupy them.

And with reference to the Italian claims on the Upper Nile, he said:

I have felt that we must reconsider our enmities and friendships as far as Egypt is concerned. The doctrine that Egypt lost all claim to the places evacuated five years ago; and that Italy will acquire a claim if "in process of self-defence," she is called upon to occupy those places, makes it evident that Italy is the most formidable enemy that Egypt has at present to face.

If that be so, the Dervishes are rendering us a service in keeping Italy out. . . . We should therefore think twice before bringing their domination to an end. But if you have money to go to Khartoum, the argument ceases to have any application.[10]

From these extracts certain facts emerge: first, Salisbury's attitude was characterized by what may be described as a non-policy; second, only money prevented him from authorizing the reconquest of the Sudan; and third, Italy, and not France, was then Britain's principal enemy in the Upper Nile.[11]

Rosebery, by virtue of the Anglo-Congolese Agreement of May 12, 1894, and more significantly, by the Grey Declaration of March, 1895, may have adopted a more positive approach in the Nile Valley than Salisbury. But one thing is clear: neither of them had an Egyptian or Sudanese policy. Both behaved like a dog in the manger: while they were not ready to reconquer the Sudan, they contrived to prevent anyone else from undertaking the task. They succeeded because of Britain's command of the sea;[12] because the *France-Russe* proved to be a paper tiger, not in the sense of their combined military strength, but in the sense that Russia appeared unwilling to risk a war with England, and probably with Germany as well, and all because of the Sudan;[13] and because the kaiser's anxiety to draw England into the orbit of the Triplice, and Salisbury's masterly but evasive reaction to Berlin's solicitations, did not make it possible for French governments—usually with serious internal problems and perpetually on the edge of collapse—to call England's bluff. France therefore resorted to the tactics of making England's position in Egypt uncomfortable, and of extracting concessions here and there, whenever possible, without dragging the relations of the two countries to the point of war, until the Fashoda incident. The question of the Upper Nile was therefore of great diplomatic importance in this period, as Professor Sanderson has ably demonstrated.[14] But this is not to admit, as Sanderson does, that Salisbury's decision to advance on Dongola was the result of developments in European diplomacy.[15]

In March, 1895 the Grey Declaration had resurrected the dormant difficulties in the Upper Nile. In April Rosebery seized the occasion to put certain questions on the matter to Cromer. He wished to know (1) what the Egyptian government's attitude was to a possible French advance toward the Upper Nile; (2) whether the Egyptian government themselves were anxious to advance on Dongola; and (3) whether or not the French would find it difficult to occupy the Bahr-el-Ghazal.[16] To (1) Cromer replied that the Egyptian government was very much worried by French proceedings in the Upper Nile. To (2) he said that the khedive's ministers generally favored the reconquest of the Sudan up to Khartoum, but had refrained from pressing the matter because they believed—quite correctly—that he (Cromer) was averse to a forward movement for the present. He added:

> I have always been so afraid of the soldiers and others getting the bit in their teeth and running away with one, that I have persistently put forward the objections to the adoption of a forward policy. . . .[17] The Sudan is worth a good deal to Egypt, but it is not worth bankruptcy and extremely oppressive taxation. . . . In all Egyptian matters we have for the last twelve years been continuously moving round in a circle, and we always arrive at the same conclusion—namely, that we must either yield to the French and make the best terms we can with them, which, under the given conditions, must of necessity be very bad terms for us, or, if we take any decisive step on our own account, we risk a very serious quarrel with France.

It was therefore left to the cabinet to decide if the Sudan was worth a war with France. Then "it will be quite time enough to slip the leash when responsible politicians think that the time for coursing the hare has come." At the same time, Cromer made his own position clear:

Eleven years ago I said that the ultimate solution of the Egyptian question would depend on the relative naval strength of England and France. At the time no one believed me. I hold to that opinion more strongly than ever now. The force of circumstances much more than the faults of any Ministry or of any individuals has drawn us into a situation which renders war a not improbable solution of the whole mess.
. . . I wish the works at Gibraltar were finished.

He warned that if France established itself in the Upper Nile, a British reconquest of the Sudan would no longer be a practical proposition. He went on:

More than this, it is obvious that if any civilized Power holds the waters of the Upper Nile, it may in the end be in a position to exercise a predominating influence on the future of Egypt. I cannot, therefore, help thinking that it will not be possible or desirable to maintain a purely passive attitude much longer.[18]

What, then, should be done? Cromer rejected outright evacuation but contented himself by saying: "If we do not move backward, we must sooner or later move forward. The only question, if this view be allowed to obtain, is, when and how we shall move forward."[19]

To the third question he replied that his military advisers believed that France could easily capture the Bahr-el-Ghazal.[20] But, like Salisbury before him, Rosebery refused to be drawn into a forward policy because of the expense it would involve.[21]

The Salisbury Cabinet and the Emergence of "The New Policy" toward the Sudan, 1895–96

When Salisbury returned to power in July at the head of a huge majority he showed no inclination to move backward or forward. He steadfastly pursued his earlier policy of "drifting awhile."[22] And when in August the government was asked by an opposition member to define their Egyptian policy,[23] Curzon could only reply, amid ministerial cheers, that "H. M. G. will not be driven, tempted, or cajoled into any sudden action with regard to our policy in Egypt."[24]

But that, precisely, was what happened in the next few months. The government was constantly cajoled into opting for one policy or the other—to move backward or forward. The first rumblings came from an unusual quarter. In July Mr. Money[25] produced a long pamphlet in which he forcefully set out the pros and cons for the evacuation of Egypt, and finally settled for evacuation.[26] Such a pamphlet was quite harmless so long as it did not see the light of day. Consequently Cromer, Barrington, and Salisbury strongly advised against its publication especially as Money was a civil servant.[27] But on March 10, 1896, the article appeared in two French papers, including the *Matin*.[28] It was indeed an embarrassing situation for Salisbury and Cromer. Money claimed that the publication of the article was "a perfect puzzle to me";[29] but there was reason to believe that he knew what he was doing.[30] Nevertheless, Cromer made sure he was severely reprimanded by Salisbury.[31] Later on he insisted that Money should be retired.[32]

The Kaiser, too, saw the succession of the new Ministry, as well as the crisis in Turkey, as opportune to try to blackmail England into the Triplice. In a conversation with Colonel Swaine he warned that France and Russia were planning something sinister against England in the Mediterranean and the Sudan. "For Italy," he said, "I plead for your sakes as much as for hers in the Mediterranean and the Sudan. . . . With reference to the Sudan, keep your eyes on Obock." He also revealed that France and Russia were "plotting something in the Red Sea," and warned England and Italy to "be wide awake to counteract any such move on the political chess-board, for there you two stand alone. We have no interests in those parts."[33] But though Salisbury considered this dispatch important enough to have it discussed by the Cabinet, he appeared not to have been influenced at all by the Kaiser's revelations. In fact, he later on confided in Devonshire that the Kaiser was merely trying "to bully us into accepting the Triple Alliance."[34] And Devonshire himself remarked that "the German Emperor is a young man to whom it may be best to speak pretty plainly."[35]

Another pressure for a forward policy came from Italy. On July 19, the delimitation of Egypto-Italian frontiers between Baraka and the Red Sea was completed and the agreement was signed on behalf of the Italian government by General Baratieri.[36] By the above agreement the actual lines of demarcation were to be left to the officers to be appointed by the respective governments to conclude the delineation on the spot.[37] In August General Ferrero, the Italian Ambassador, suggested to Salisbury the possibility of Anglo-Italian cooperation in smashing Abyssinia "which imposed a barrier to the extension of Anglo-Egyptian influence toward the Upper Nile and the equatorial lake."[38] Salisbury carefully evaded any discussion of the suggestion.[39] And by September the delineators[40] appointed in accordance with the July agreement confessed their inability to reach any final conclusion.[41]

On October 12 news reached Salisbury that the Italians had defeated an Abyssinian force at Debra Ailat.[42] He was unmoved by the news.

Meanwhile Salisbury had been restraining himself from losing his temper over the antics of Leopold II. Since the Congo Treaty of 1894 Leopold's territorial appetite in the Upper Nile had been very much sharpened. In August, 1895 the king arrived in England and gave audiences to several individuals, including Salisbury. These audiences as a rule began either at 6:30 a.m. or 8:30 a.m.— a practice which led Salisbury to remark: "There are advantages in being an Englishman."[43] The purpose of Leopold's interview with Salisbury was to ascertain the foreign secretary's attitude toward the Upper Nile. Salisbury's report of this interview reveals his cynicism and distrust of the Belgian king:

> After 10 mins. of Brussels exhibition and other matters [he wrote to Bigge[44]], the King of the Belgians plunged into the valley of the Nile: and we remained there for more than half an hour. His language was very mysterious: he spoke much of a unique crisis; and an opportunity that would never return. What he wished England to do was to throw herself into the arms of France, not caring about Germany. France he said carried Russia with her: and Russia carried Germany: so that if we had France, we had Germany of necessity as well.[45]

Leopold boasted that he was very popular in France; and wished Salisbury "to fix a date for evacuating Egypt," the aim being to win France's favor especially if England should decide "to annex China to the Indian Empire" at little or no cost.[46] As to what would become of the Nile Valley in such an eventuality, he suggested that England should induce the khedive to hand it over—as a concession—from Khartoum upwards "to some person who was 'au courant' of the affairs of Africa." Leopold, said Salisbury, "was too modest to mention who that person was." He went on:

> I do not imagine he thought so badly of me to suppose I took all this seriously: but I think he is anxious to raise some discussion about the valley of the Nile to which France should be a party. He is at some mischief. From his constantly dwelling on his own popularity at Paris and from the fact, which he conjectured, that Belgium refuses to accept the Congo—I suspect that he is making some arrangement to sell to France the succession of the Congo State—together with any rights of ours which he can lay hold on in the valley of the Nile. He was most solemn in warning me not to throw away this chance of ex-

tending the British Empire over the greater part of Asia.

I shall make no other record of the conversation than this— as I think it had better not be sent to the Legation. His feeling against Germany and in favor of France was very marked. . . . I never made any direct answer: only saying that the matters he spoke of were of extreme interest. Much of our time was passed in alternately complimenting each other.[47]

Undaunted, Leopold procured yet another interview with Salisbury. This time he placed his cards directly on the table, and showered the prime minister with what the latter called "extraordinary confidences." Leopold proposed that Abbas II should lease to him, under British influence, the region controlled by the khalifa. Then, he (Leopold) would subdue the Mahdists, make better soldiers out of them, and then hand them back to England to be used as it thought fit. But he suggested that England could use them to put the Armenian massacres to an end.[48] That such curious suggestions should emanate from so intelligent a man is indeed surprising; and the fact that he expected to be taken seriously is even odder. It was the kind of opportunity which Salisbury never let pass without a jibe. "The idea of an English General at the head of an army of Dervishes marching from Khartoum to Lake Van, in order to prevent Mahometans from ill-treating Christians," he commented, "struck me as so quaint that I hastened to give the conversation another turn lest I should be betrayed into some disrespectful commentary." Throughout the interview Salisbury skillfully avoided the obvious traps intended to lure him into indiscretions regarding his Sudanese policy. Leopold was forced to give up the attempt, and in Salisbury's own words, "retired (with a shower of compliments, but) in despair."[49]

Salisbury's taciturnity in regard to his policy in the Nile Valley should surprise no one. It was in line with his general attitude to political developments. Nothing had happened in the Nile Valley to justify any positive action. He was disinclined to manufacture difficulties for himself by "discussing disagreeable contingencies."[50] As he put it in 1887: "Whatever happens will be for the worse and therefore it is to our interest that as little should happen as possible."[51] This flagrant pessimism—traceable to his childhood days—is of the greatest importance in trying to assess Salisbury's attitude to imperial and domestic issues. Perhaps Chirol[52] was right when he wrote: "Lord Salisbury seems to be keeping his own counsel with regard to the Egyptian question."[53] And if he had any plans for the Sudan—which is doubtful—he breathed not a word to anyone, not even to Cromer.[54]

It was in fact left to the pro-consul to ask his chief to state his Sudanese policy.[55] Then came the reply:

> You will get a telegraphic answer in a few days about the chance of our wishing to spend money in reconquering the Sudan. If I could recommend such a result, I should like to lay down that there must be no forward movement in Egypt till our [Uganda] railway had reached the Lake. If we allowed such a proceeding, we shall certainly have a French forward movement on the Upper Nile: but if we had reached the Lake, I think we might make such an enterprise impossible.[56]

The implication here is obvious: there was no immediate possibility of reconquering the Sudan; and second, the Uganda railway would have the negative utility of checking any French forward movement on the Upper Nile (which it did not do). In other words, this document could hardly be posed as evidence—as has generally been the case—that the main purpose of the railway was a mere strategic plan for the recovery of the Sudan besides keeping the French out.

Cromer at once telegraphed his concurrence with Salisbury's view.[57] Indeed, he had secured the kind of assurance he had longed for. For financial reasons, he was no enthusiast for the immediate recovery of the Sudan. In fact, he later admitted that he had anticipated the military solution of the Nile problem taking place some twenty-five years after the abandonment of the Sudan.[58] He knew that Egypt's financial position, though much improved, would still be inadequate both for the construction of the reservoir—a project very much after his own heart—and a Sudanese expedition without financial assistance from England. He assumed that this assistance would not be forthcoming. In November he got the green light to proceed with his reservoir project[59] (the cabinet having decided on October 29 that an advance to the Sudan was not on).[60] In effect, the cabinet had postponed the recovery of the Sudan indefinitely.

Meanwhile a strong rumor gained ground in Egypt that England was planning to pull out of the country. Cromer at once requested the prime minister to deprecate such a course publicly.[61] On January 18, 1896, Salisbury stated categorically that British policy had not changed and that the "report may be due to the threats which the German Emperor is understood to have used in private."[62] He followed this up with a long summary of his interview with Courcel on the issue. This revealed nothing new—except that France was as wooly-headed as England as to what to do about

Egypt. But significantly, Courcel reaffirmed that Paris had no intention of demanding evacuation "because France had large investments in Egypt, and Egyptian securities would certainly fall in value if we [the British] went." "Hanotaux," Salisbury concluded, "has also sent me a message through a private friend that 'they wanted very little'—we shall see."[63] In fact Hanotaux's message read: ". . . we want very little. At present our grievance is chiefly a sentimental one. It irritates us to be so completely ignored. Some recognition of our right to be heard would be sufficient."[64] This apologetic attitude was the main weakness of the French case. As in his negotiations with Germany over East Africa, Salisbury here had a strong diplomatic position. This was what was lacking in the West African negotiations.

Paris and London were therefore anxious to leave the Nile problem alone.[65] The Porte's secret attempts to reopen it fizzled out when the whole thing came into the open.[66]

Indeed, it served Salisbury's interests to play down developments in the Nile Valley at this time. He had too much on his plate: the Jameson Raid had brought England's reputation, in foreign eyes, to a low ebb; the "Kaiser Telegram" had driven England and Germany farther and farther apart; the Venezuelan Crisis had, in itself, the potentialities of a grave danger—delicately being averted by informal negotiations;[67] the Armenian Crisis had forced Salisbury to concentrate his attention eastwards;[68] and, moreover, efforts were being made to settle Anglo-French differences in West Africa. Salisbury therefore had, of necessity, to play things down in the Nile Valley.

But such an attitude could not be kept up for long. He was not the master of events. Two important developments were already forcing his hand.

Khalifa Abdullah
In the summer of 1885 Khalifa Abdullah succeeded the deceased Mahdi as the Dervish leader. A ruthless and ambitious man, he had always cherished the thought of invading Egypt, but soon he discovered that he could not, for the present, fulfill his ambition because he was already fully occupied. But yet he found time to harass the frontiers of Egypt by occasional raids. By the close of 1886 he had occupied Sarras, a district only thirty miles south of Wady Halfa; but he withdrew after a few months. He returned in 1887 but was driven out on April 27. He returned once more and succeeded, by September, in permanently holding the place. For two years he raided the district between Wady Halfa and Assouan.

"These repeated attacks," says an official report, "spread terror far and wide among the population of the Nile Valley."[69] In 1889 five thousand fighting Dervishes, led by Wad-el-Njumi, and supported by thousands of followers, attacked an Anglo-Egyptian force; but on September 3 they were defeated by General Grenfell at the battle of Toski, seventy miles north of Wady Halfa.

At the same period, Osman Digna, master of the eastern Sudan, was holding sway over the Red Sea Littoral, and practically put Suakin in a state of siege. It was not until the spring of 1891 that Suakin was temporarily relieved after he had been defeated at Afafit. Two years later, the restless Dervishes struck again. This time they carried out a successful raid on the oasis of Khargeh. They penetrated two hundred and thirty miles into Egyptian territory and carried off eleven prisoners and a considerable amount of property, returning to their base without loss. Encouraged by this success, another party of Dervishes—three hundred strong—under Osman Azrak, raided the post at Murat Wells (November 12, 1893) lying half-way between Korosko and Abu Hamed. They lost twenty-nine men and were forced to withdraw. Ever since this raid, continues the report, "the southern frontier district has constantly been kept in a state of disquietude and alarm owing to repeated rumors of intended raids."

In 1894 it was reliably reported that the khalifa had planned a double campaign in the following spring. He not only intended to capture Wady Halfa but also Tokar. But two Italian victories—the first at Kassala (July, 1894), and the second at Agordat (December 21, 1894) disrupted his plans. These were very important victories indeed for the Dervishes were reduced to inactivity for some time. The khalifa adopted a waiting policy.[70]

By the close of 1895 he began to show signs of renewed activity. In December he summoned all Mahdists to unite "and fight against infidels and God's enemies," because "God, in his Holy Book," had commanded them to "support religion and be not divided." He wished for friendly relations with all his neighbors.[71]

On December 10 the Dervishes raided the village of Adendan, twenty-five miles north of Wady Halfa. This was followed, on January 30, 1896, by another raid at Old Sarras. In these raids nineteen persons were killed; several prisoners and cattle were carried off. It had, in fact, proved impossible to check these periodic raids. And, "based on Dongola, they [the Dervishes] have been able to strike almost at will and to escape with impunity," the official report continues, "while, in spite of all efforts to intercept them, contraband convoys carrying lead and powder have reached Dongola with the connivance of the nomad Arabs living in the vicinity of the Nile Valley." By February rumors of intended Dervish movements became rampant. On February 26 intelligence reached British authorities in Egypt that merchants who had escaped from Berber nine days before had reported that a body of seven hundred Dervishes had been ordered to attack the post at Murat Wells; while a second force had been sent to Kokreb, eighty-five miles from Suakin; and a large force was advancing from Omdurman toward Dongola.

There was nothing defensive in all these Dervish movements. They terrorized the riverain population. The situation, admitted the report, had "become intolerable" and had perhaps "afforded ample grounds for an advance along the Nile Valley with the object of depriving the Dervishes of Dongola," the base of their operations. The several defeats of the Italians by Abyssinia had made the case for such a course more compelling. It goes on:

> But in the meantime, emboldened by the reverses suffered by the Italian arms at the hands of the Abyssinians, the Khalifa abandoned his passive attitude on the Atbara and caused Kassala to be invested with an army of 10,000 Dervishes.
>
> The grave situation thus created threatened the safety of Egypt, and called imperatively for active measures to be taken without delay. To have left matters alone, and to have awaited the issue of the struggle between the Italians and the Dervishes, would have been most impolitic.
>
> In the event of a successful attack on Kassala, or even if the Italians should for military reasons be compelled to withdraw from the place, it may be predicted that an outbreak of fanaticism will ensue, and that the attack of the Khalifa's forces, encouraged by the prestige of a victory, real or imaginary, over Europeans, will fall with full force upon the Khedive's dominions.[72]

This Cabinet Memorandum—one of several reports (and perhaps, the most important one) which determined the cabinet's course of action—has, hitherto, not been quoted or analyzed in any published work. It does, however, put a different complexion on the generally accepted view that the Mahdist threat to Egypt played no part in the decision to advance on Dongola. Certainly it was not the only reason, or indeed, the main reason for the advance, since this memorandum was discussed by the cabinet only after the first authorization of the advance; but it played a significant part in determining and justifying the limits of further action. Indeed, the conclusion of the above report was the burden of Cromer's own argument in December, 1895.[73]

Italy's Capacity for Defeat

The second development concerned Italy. We saw that on December 12, 1895, the Italians scored a victory over an Abyssinian force at Debra Ailat. This victory, however, proved to be a flash in the pan. On December 7, 1895, General Baratieri was soundly beaten by the Abyssinians at Amba Alagi. Thus, Amba Alagi avenged Debra Ailat; and the Italians, far removed from their base, found their position untenable. As soon as the news reached Kitchener, the sirdar of the Egyptian army at once suggested that a couple of battalions should be dispatched from Suakin to occupy Kassala.[74] This was not a difficult military operation, but Cromer feared "that, if once a forward movement is begun, it is difficult to see how far it will lead." Moreover, as the Italians had not asked for help he advised that it would be wiser to "wait until either we are asked to afford it, or until events occur which, in English and Egyptian interests, would render such action imperative." He was not in the least anxious to "pull the chestnuts out of the fire for Italy," or Germany, for that matter.[75]

Cromer's advice was well taken. But in January, 1896 Salisbury learned that the Dervishes and Abyssinians, though bound by no convention, had agreed to deliver simultaneously the final blow to Baratieri's forces.[76] Fearing the possibility that the Dervishes might also attack Kassala, Salisbury advised "a demonstration in the vicinity of Wady Halfa," for the purpose of creating "a diversion" (provided Cromer raised no objections).[77] Cromer, like Kitchener and other military authorities, strongly objected to a "mere demonstration." They believed that, if Egyptian troops simply advanced and then retired, the Dervishes would gain considerably in prestige, "more especially in the event of any actual collision which would certainly ensue if the advance took place from Wady Halfa." Moreover, a demonstration would be of no value to the Italians; they therefore advised "that whatever ground is taken from the Dervishes must be permanently held." Cromer himself feared the opposition of Egyptian ministers to help Italy "unless, at the same time, Egypt obtained some incidental advantage." If, however, Salisbury was determined on some action, he suggested that an advance could be made from Wady Halfa in the direction of Suada, "or, perhaps, even to Dongola," where the Dervishes had a force of eight thousand men; or, alternatively, an advance could be started from Suakin in the direction of Felik, "or even to Atbara," where cooperation might be obtained from the Italians. He favored the latter route as the more effective and cheaper way of helping the Italians.[78] On January 14 Salisbury replied that, so long as no indications existed that the Dervishes were marching on Kassala, it would be better to wait.[79] This decision appeared to have temporarily paid off, for Cromer immediately telegraphed a report from Suakin which stated that the khalifa's forces, under Ibrahim Khalil, had suffered a defeat at the hands of the Degheain and Kiana Arabs. "An insurrection at Omdurman is expected," he wrote excitedly. "The aspect of affairs in the Sudan may be materially altered if this news proves to be correct."[80] Nothing of the kind happened at Omdurman.

On December 16, 1895, Sanderson had had an interview with Ferrero during which the latter had put forward his government's request for permission to occupy Zeyla "for moral effect."[81] But Salisbury had refused to give any such permission. He minuted:

> I adhere to the policy laid down in my letter. I am content to give leave for them to pass. No doubt Menelik might, if he chose, say that this was a breach of neutrality and quarrel with us. Such a risk we might readily take.
> But to admit Italian soldiers to occupy Zeila is to declare ourselves the allies of Italy in her war against Menelik. . . .[82]

A week later Sanderson had another interview with Count Metternich who "came to pump" him on the same question. The Italians, said Metternich, only wanted to land two hundred men at Zeila for two or three days. This, they believed, "would produce immediately a great moral effect." Sanderson doubted that any moral effect could result from such a demonstration; on the contrary, he feared the result would be to attract "an attack upon the British Protectorate." The proposal, he wrote, "seemed to me one of the coolest proposals that could be found in the annals of diplomacy."[83] Evidently, the Foreign Office had no intention of offering any material assistance to the Italians.

But once more the Dervishes forced Salisbury's hand to come to some decision. In February they attacked an Italian military post in the neighborhood of Kassala, but were beaten off after a skirmish. It was, however, believed that they were contemplating an attack on Kassala itself with five thousand men.[84] The evidence that Salisbury was looking for was slowly coming in. He at once asked for the opinions of Egyptian military authorities as to the necessary course of action should the Italians evacuate Kassala.[85] Meanwhile, Crispi's attempt to secure help having failed, he warned Salisbury that he would authorize the evacuation of Kassala.[86] Egyptian authorities felt very concerned about the situation. They proposed that a force should be dispatched from Suakin to occupy a position at the junction of the Khor Langeb and the Khor Baraka. They also felt that it was essential to occupy Kokreb, on the Berber road, with another force. These measures were intended to prevent the Dervishes marching on Kassala. "If an advance is made," wrote Cromer, "they consider that there should be no subsequent retreat, and I fully agree with them." He added: "That the Dervishes should be allowed to reestablish themselves at Kassala, is on every ground, most undesirable. Prompt action is necessary if anything is to be done."[87] Salisbury saw the implication of this recommendation; and after consulting the War Office, he wrote to Cromer:

> Military authorities here consider that occupation of posts you mention could not be effected without a conflict, and that if subsequently attacked and surrounded by Dervish forces operations for their relief on a considerable scale would be necessary.
>
> H. M. Govt. are doubtful whether they are justified in running the risk of such contingencies in return for a merely nominal advantage. This country has no great interest in the occupation of Kassala. The Khalifa's power tends steadily to decrease,[88] and under these circumstances the obvious policy is to await events. Until we are masters of the Valley of the Nile, Kassala has little value. When we are in possession of that region, it will be easy to deal with it.[89]

Once more Salisbury had refused to shift his position. But his reason is unmistakably clear: any advance on the Sudan would only be undertaken primarily for the interest of Britain; and the interest of Britain meant the possession of the Nile Valley. We saw earlier that in February, the Dervishes had planned to occupy simultaneously Kassala, Kokreb, Dongola, and Murad. These were hardly the activities of a power facing a steady disintegration. And though Cromer said that "too great weight should not be attached to these reports," he admitted "that some hostile movement, of which the probable objective is Kassala, is contemplated."[90] Privately he wrote to Salisbury: "This matter is very serious. If we decided to advance we shall be at the mercy of circumstances which will very probably draw us into further operations."[91] Evidently, Cromer was not thinking in terms of the reconquest of the Sudan. But he did recognize the overwhelming military arguments in favor of the relief of Kassala. Moreover, it would be impolitic to allow Kassala to fall into Dervish hands; and it would also be undesirable to feel unconcerned "whilst the Italians are beaten as I greatly suspect they will be." Nevertheless, his main objection to an advance was financial. He explained:

> We are tied hand and foot by international fetters and if we again get into financial difficulties we shall be more or less at the mercy of the French. On the whole I would stand the risk and go on, but the question is one of great difficulty and I venture to urge very careful consideration before decision is taken.

He also requested guidance in dealing with the Italians and added: "We ought to make some capital out of it with the Italians and indirectly with the Germans who have always wanted to help Italy."[92] This of course shows that Cromer, at any rate, did not believe that European considerations would be an important factor in reaching the decision to advance. But to drum up diplomatic noises about helping Italy might have an added advantage.

On March 1 the Abyssinian army routed Baratieri's forces at Adowa.[93] And on March 2 the Dervishes were before Kassala. The khalifa ordered all trade between Berber and the Nile frontier, and between Berber and Suakin to be stopped.[94] On March 10 they completely surrounded Kassala and cut off all communication with Asmara. The situation was precarious; but Kassala was expected to withstand a siege for three months. The garrison at Adigat was in a more serious plight. The soldiers could hold out for only forty days, after which, they would be beyond redemption.[95] It will be seen, therefore, that the belief that the Dervish power was steadily declining had little justification. News of these developments focused the public's attention on the Nile Valley. It was no longer a question of private concern between the powers that be. What next was anybody's guess.

The New Policy

On March 4 Kaiser William formally requested Salisbury to help Italy in her difficulties.[96] On March 6 he refused to comply; and on March 8 he also turned down a similar appeal from Italy.[97] But on March 12, after consulting the military authorities, the cabinet decided to send a military expedition to Dongola.[98] This meant, in effect (as we shall see), that they had initiated the reconquest of the Sudan. It was a dramatic, but in a certain sense, not a sudden change of policy. Since 1895 all developments pointed to the inevitable conclusion that, sooner or later, England would have to move backward or forward in the Nile Valley. What was lacking was a good opportunity to justify such a course. The Italian appetite for defeat provided it.

Salisbury was by no means anxious to undertake a forward policy but circumstances beyond his control forced his hand and he decided to take his opportunity. Historians have much difference of opinion on this point; but contemporaries had no illusions as to the meaning of the decision of March 12. What they wanted to be told—but were not for some months—was that the government was irrevocably committed to recover the Sudan. Nevertheless they assumed that that was the case. This decision is of great interest and needs pursuing further. Since July, 1895 continuous pressure had been brought to bear on Salisbury to declare his policy in the Nile Valley; and he had consistently refused to commit himself. The decision of March 12, therefore, took some people unaware; but it was hardly the "bolt from the blue" that Rodd said it was.[99] What reasons did Salisbury give for authorizing this advance? And how did the cabinet react to this new policy?

In his telegram of March 12, Salisbury stated that the measure was taken in order to help Italy; he also admitted that it would be to Egypt's advantage since it would "tend to dispel any disposition to attack Egypt which may have been created among the Dervishes by the recent defeats suffered by Europeans at the hands of the Africans."[100] To Lascelles he made the same point, but added:

> Supposing an attack on Kassala were successful, or even if military reasons should compel the Italian Government to withdraw their troops from Kassala, clearly an outbreak of fanaticism may ensue, and Khalifa Abdullah's influence may be considerably augmented, while the Dervish troops will be encouraged to attack the frontiers of Egypt, to defend which may cause serious trouble.[101]

To Ford he explained the immediate events leading to the decision: first, Ferrero called on him and stated that over ten thousand Dervishes were advancing by Sabderat in the direction of Keren, and had asked for help. Apparently Salisbury had refused to commit himself; and on March 11 the ambassador called again and pressed the same view. This time, Salisbury decided to summon a cabinet "who, after careful deliberation and consultation with their military advisers, have decided to authorize an advance of Egyptian troops up the valley of the Nile as far as Dongola."[102] But in a private letter to Cromer he frankly set out the reasons behind the decision:

The decision to which the Cabinet came yesterday was inspired specially by a desire to help the Italians at Kassala; and to prevent the Dervishes from winning a conspicuous success which might have far-reaching results. In addition *we desired to kill two birds with one stone, and to use the same military effort to plant the foot of Egypt rather farther up the Nile. For this reason we preferred it to any movement from Suakin, or in the direction of Kassala, because there would be no ulterior profit in these movements.* [My italics.] Also we wanted to avoid the risk of having to cross swords with the Abyssinians which might take us far. But the main object was to relieve the stress on Kassala. For this reason publicity was essential—and indeed would have to be carried even to a certain amount of bluffing.

We have made no official statement of our intention. I have told the Ambassadors that we sanctioned an advance to Dongola. We do not hold ourselves bound to go so far if the difficulties are serious—and if our object can be attained with a less advance. We do not wish to have to send more English troops into Egypt if we can help it, because such a step would involve diplomatic explanations. But of course, if necessary, it must be done. . . . For general reasons which I have spoken before I could have wished that our friends the Italians had less capacity for being beaten, and would have let us wait two or three years more till we were quite ready in the Valley of the Nile. But it would not have been safe, either from an African or European point of view to sit quite still while they were being crushed. . . .

I forgot to add that a mere demonstration is almost impossible under our form of Govt. The House of Commons asks questions which must be answered. If we say that our movement is a mere demonstration and that we mean to return without doing anything Osman Digna will not be frightened. But an objective, however conditional or contingent is an answer.[103]

Nowhere, in any published work, has this document been printed in full. But it had been used to serve various purposes and various contentions. As printed here, however, one learns several things which will keep one's judgment in perspective. First, the Italian disaster provided the occasion for the advance. Second, it was decided to use the opportunity to initiate the reconquest of the Sudan as far as possible, but with Dongola as the first objective. Third, Abyssinia must not be antagonized since such a development might complicate matters. Fourth, Salisbury was unprepared to sanction the advance when he did, but had had to do so on political grounds, And fifth, a mere demonstration might embolden, rather than frighten, the Dervishes into attacking Egypt. Here, then, are the main reasons behind the cabinet decision of March 12. All are important and should not be seen in isolation. In a private letter to Chamberlain he confirmed the sheer opportunism of the whole venture. He argued that if a mere demonstration had been approved, "we shall miss a good opportunity" and "lose seriously in credit."[104] And in another letter from Beaulieu he revealed that the ambition of other European powers in the Upper Nile was an added incentive to seize the opportunity when it came.[105]

The cabinet have been unfairly treated in their handling of the Dongola decision. Their so-called confusion has been very much exaggerated.[106] They may not have known all the facts and figures about the Sudan; but their subsequent pronouncements show that they knew what they wanted, even if they did not want the same things. After the cabinet meeting Chamberlain and Balfour together discussed the Dongola expedition and communicated their conclusions to Salisbury. If Dongola was captured and the inhabitants, disgusted with the *Mahdiya*, "welcome our advance . . ., we may very properly go further to Khartoum, and gradually restore the Sudan to Egypt and to civilization." But if the khalifa was found to have popular support and could offer "a very serious resistance, involving immense efforts, both military and financial, on the part of Egypt, and carrying with it great responsibilities for this country," they advised a consolidationist and waiting policy at Dongola "until the time is ripe for further advance." In either case the Egyptian military authorities should be warned to exercise great caution since the British government would be blamed for any mishaps that might arise, and perhaps find themselves in a position in which "we should have to come to the rescue with a British army and I suppose that, besides other consequences, the Government would be deserted by its followers."[107] Obviously, the two ministers were determined to avoid a repetition of Gordon's disastrous Sudan adventure. Obviously too, they were very much worried about the inevitably adverse response of public opinion should any disaster occur.

But Lansdowne and Hicks-Beach did not appear to have been enthusiastic about reconquering the Sudan and would have happily, if given a free hand, endorsed Cromer's plan of an advance in the direction of Kassala.[108] One, however, gets the definite impression that the cabinet, as a whole, were terrified at the thought of an ambitious reconquest of the Sudan. They were therefore inclined to exercise excessive caution. In a private letter to Chamberlain Salisbury summarized his, and indeed, the cabinet's aims, fears, and anxieties:

We must advance with cautious steps. I should like to lay down that the troops should never get ahead of the point where they can be supplied by rail and river. If we stick to this rule, we can keep whatever we take: for I presume that wherever we are we can hold our ground against an attack of the Dervishes if our supplies are quite secure. The available money must determine how long our strides are to be: and also an element in our calculation will be the defensive power of the Dervishes. Neither of these are as yet quite known quantities.

We have counsellors who press us, and will press us towards two opposite extremes, which must be equally avoided. One set of counsellors will urge us to be satisfied with a demonstration and then to go back again. We shall lose seriously in credit if we do this: and we shall miss a good opportunity. The other extreme is what Kitchener and his friends will urge on us—to press forward without regard to the security of our supplies, or to our power of paying our way as we go along. This extreme is worse than the other: for it may lead to disaster as well as discredit. I earnestly pressed on Lansdowne that he must be prepared to sit heavily on Kitchener and on his own military advisers. He is so fully sensible of the danger that he leans rather in the other direction, and wishes to return after a demonstration in order that he may not expose Kitchener to temptation.[109]

The cabinet members were, in general, for a slow and cautious reconquest of the Sudan. They were not sure that their final aim would be achieved. But they were determined to avoid previous mistakes.[110] They could not calculate how long the reconquest would take; but at least a start had been made. In an important cabinet memorandum, Lansdowne made these points more clearly. "The time has come," he wrote, "when it is absolutely necessary that the War Department should receive definite instructions as to the eventualities for which it is expected to be prepared in the Nile Valley." He explained that the Italian difficulties at Kassala and Adigat provided the occasion for the advance; but he also reaffirmed that the "ulterior object was to restore a portion of her lost territory to Egypt." He went on:

Our language to the other Powers and to Egypt has, however, been inconsistent with the idea that a successful feint in the interests of Italy was all that we intended. I assume therefore, that we shall not be able to stop short of the achievement of something which will permanently advance Egyptian interests in the Nile Valley, or at all events be a substantial step towards such an advance. *The minimum will be a short extension of the Wady Halfa-Sarras Railway; the maximum, the complete reconquest of the Soudan.* [My italics.] It is impossible to say at this moment where it may be found convenient to stop—there are several unknown quantities in the calculation.

These included the ability of Italy to resist the Dervishes and its future policy in the Nile Valley; the reaction of the Egyptian government to the advance; the kind of opposition which the advance might generate; and the possibility of foreign complications. But taking a brighter view of things, Lansdowne emphasized the point that "our ultimate aim" was "the reconquest of the Soudan." He therefore recommended the early occupation of Dongola provided adequate preparations were made. The occupation, he believed, "would be not only valueless but a positive weakening of the Egyptian frontier" unless it was conceived "as a step towards the subjugation of the Soudan." To carry out this policy, Abu Fatmeh, a region only forty miles from Dongola, should first be occupied; and to strengthen the frontier, Akasheh should be occupied and the railway extended beyond Sarras. Having laid down his plan of campaign, Lansdowne dealt with the detailed preparations for the advance. One other thing that punctuated the whole argument was the almost obsessional concern with caution. Nevertheless, he was prepared to allow Kitchener to occupy Dongola at once if he could do so "with his own troops" and "with absolute safety."[111]

A few days later Cromer summarized the situation, as he saw it, with impeccable accuracy:

What we want to do is, I think, pretty clear. We want (1) to get, sooner or later, to Dongola; (2) to resist the almost inevitable pressure to go further than Dongola.

As to the first point, now that we are in for the business, there can, I think, be no question of stopping short of Dongola.

As to the second point, something must, of course, depend on circumstances. For instance, a revolution may occur in the Sudan. Moreover, I quite recognize that Dongola cannot be the final halting place; eventually Khartoum will have to be recovered. What I mean is that the Egyptian Government, with its present military and financial resources, cannot go further than Dongola at present. There must therefore, so far as can at present be judged, be a very long halt at Dongola—perhaps of two or three years—in order to enable preparations to be made for any further advance. . . .

The military question is in reality a financial question, and looking at the general Egyptian tangle, it is quite impossible to separate the financial from the political question. They are inextricably woven together. . . .

The prayer which I have to address to you is this: "Save me from the English Departments. . . ."

In 1884, we succumbed to the Treasury; we have in consequence suffered ever since, and we are suffering now, for most of our financial troubles are due to the measures adopted in 1884. Now I rather fear the War Office. Let me implore you to deliver me from their hands.[112]

Did Salisbury then initiate the reconquest of the Sudan in March, 1896? The answer, indeed, must be yes. The fact that the cabinet confirmed, as subsequent developments showed, that their first objective was the occupation of Dongola, implied—as both Cromer[113] and Lansdowne[114] easily realized—an inevitable step toward the recovery of Khartoum. Salisbury, too, as we have seen, had made the same point. So had Balfour and Chamberlain. The recent discussions on Salisbury's motive for sanctioning the advance on Dongola have tended to clothe in mystery and academic quibbling what, otherwise, was a plain issue. Historians are of course known to manufacture difficulties for themselves. There is no reason why Salisbury's private and official justification of the Dongola advance should not be accepted as correct. To understand Salisbury's motives, one must, first of all, understand the character and principles of the man himself; one must also grasp the circumstances under which he took his decision. Salisbury always kept his mouth shut until he had made up his mind; and once he had decided on any course of action he was unequivocal, within the limits of the governing principles of international diplomacy, in explaining his motive. He made it plain that the decision to advance on Dongola was forced on him by circumstances beyond his control. The psychological reasons against a mere demonstration, as he later realized, were only too obvious; the uncertainty of a favorable public reaction to a bold policy was at the back of his mind. But he also realized that, for political reasons and other interests, something had to be done. He could not be expected to expend Anglo-Egyptian resources just to pull the chestnuts out of the fire for Italy without receiving any benefits for his labors. Therefore, trusting on luck and on hunch, and at the same time, urging the necessity for adequate preparations to avoid the mistakes of old, he authorized a slow and cautious reconquest of the Sudan, leaving the options open to proceed as far as circumstances would permit. After all he, and the British people, had longed for an eventual recovery of the Sudan. The opportunity, if missed, might never come again. He put this point succinctly to Ford:

> We had for some time recognized that some measures for driving back the Dervishes and recovering territory which had fallen into their hands would sooner or later be necessary. . . . Considerations which were not without their importance, but which were of secondary character, had made us wish to defer for some time longer the commencement of any such operation. On reflection we were of opinion that these considerations were overruled by the important suggestions of the Italian Ambassador.

The Italian request, he said, determined his decision "not in respect to its ultimate policy, but in respect to the time and opportunity that was selected."[115] Salisbury, indeed, was aware that the Italians were nobody's fools. When, in March he had asked for a public expression of gratitude from Italy, the duke of Sermoneta, the new foreign minister, had refused to comply, not only because such a statement would be very embarrassing to Italy, but also because "the motive for the advance in the direction of Dongola had originated in the desire of serving British interests although such a policy might indirectly benefit other countries" friendly to England. The duke did not "for a moment blame England for pursuing such a policy for he entertained the highest respect and admiration of a country whose actions were guided by practical considerations."[116] No explanations could be more frank and intelligible than these. Any attempt, therefore, to attribute some other motives to Salisbury's action can hardly be justifiable.[117] What is of more academic interest is what convinced the prime minister that the British electorate would view favorably a decision to advance on Dongola with all that implied.

Chapter X

"The Foreign Office War," 1896–98

Contemporaries indeed were never in doubt as to the real meaning of the Dongola decision. They merely demanded from the government a public confirmation of what everyone knew. Since the death of General Gordon in 1885 and the ignominious British retreat from the Sudan (following a few years after the Majuba disaster), there had been an undercurrent of opinion that Gordon must be avenged to restore British prestige. In April, for instance, the *Westminster Gazette* had stated that the advance on Dongola was undertaken purely and simply "to crush the Khalifa, reconquer the Soudan, and assert the right of Egypt over the Bahr-el-Ghazal."[1] Mr. Charles Williams went further:

> When the third Government of the Marquis of Salisbury entered upon its first real session with a majority so large as to leave it no excuse for failing to do its clear duty for fear of consequences in home politics, the word was given to do what had long been waiting to be done. The excuse afforded was the defeat of the Italian force at Adowa by the Abyssinians. . . . If there had not been one excuse there would have had to be another, for the thing had to be begun before long.[2]

The dangers and difficulties of such a policy were obvious; but British opinion, nevertheless, was overwhelming in support of the government's policy. Looking back on the Sudan advance, Brodrick[3] had remarked: "I have never remembered a step taken by any ministry and carried to its conclusions which secured so universal a commendation as this advance into the Soudan."[4] Public opinion certainly did not force Salisbury into the Sudan. But he had gambled on its backing of his policy and must have been amazed at the support he got.

The reconquest of the Sudan was guided by the ground rules laid down by Salisbury. He knew what he was getting into and was scared of adverse consequences. In West Africa and East Africa, for example, he had made concessions where, in his opinion, they were absolutely necessary. In the Sudan he discovered that he had no room for maneuver. His hands were tied. As he saw it the Upper Nile was a special case and in a class by itself. He realized only too well the diplomatic implication of the famous Grey Declaration of March, 1895; he did not lose sight of the domestic political implications either. The Grey warning, as a contemporary had pointed out, "bound Lord Salisbury to make war on one of the Great Powers of Europe in the event of certain circumstances arising."[5] This was a grave responsibility to inherit, especially for one who claimed to be a man of peace, on coming to office. If France violated the warning and occupied any portion of the Upper Nile, and Salisbury did nothing, Britain would lose disastrously in prestige in the eyes of the world; at home the consequences might be even graver. After all the Unionists considered themselves, with apparent pride, as the party of empire. Now to fail to do what the Liberals had committed themselves to do in the interests of that empire would indeed be odd. This partly explains Salisbury's uncompromising attitude during the Fashoda crisis.

But the Upper Nile was also believed to be inextricably linked with Egypt, territorially and politically—what in fact, has been described as "the organic unity of the Nile Valley."[6] Salisbury therefore knew that British mastery in the Upper Nile meant also her complete mastery in Egypt. He would be rid of French nibbling interference; Germany would no longer wield the *baton Egyptien*. But in 1895 he was at a loss as to what to do about Egypt or the Upper Nile. Indeed, as late as 1897, he had confided in Sanderson: "Egypt is argumentatively a tough nut to crack."[7] Cromer, too, appeared to have been of the same view. The Egyptian question, in its larger aspects, was insoluble, he had written; but "a general recognition of its insolubility would in some degree, constitute a paradoxical semi-solution."[8] Salisbury's statement, particularly, is significant. It could be interpreted to mean that methods other than arguments were needed.

There are numerous books on the military aspect of the Sudan campaign. In this chapter and the next we will emphasize the diplomatic and political aspects of the conquest. Attention will be focused on Salisbury—the man at the helm—to determine how he reacted to the great pressures under which he was working.

The Diplomacy of Conquest: The Road to Dongola, March to September, 1896

There is no doubt that by authorizing the advance on Dongola Salisbury had altered the course of British policy toward the Sudan. He was able to do this precisely because English opinion was on his side; and his impregnable parliamentary majority was an added advantage. For purely local reasons, this was exactly the policy which Cromer had all along dreaded. But Salisbury was acting in the interests of imperial policy as a whole as Cromer himself admitted.[9] So, from the beginning the foreign secretary and his proconsul were looking at the problem from different angles. Cromer's efforts to reverse the course of British policy in the Sudan is well known.[10] His repeated telegrams home, strongly arguing his own point of view, tended to complicate further what had been described—unfairly in my opinion—as the cabinet's confused handling of the Sudan question.[11] And the inability of the Italians to make up their minds whether or not to evacuate Kassala caused Salisbury to appear more vacillating than he really was.[12] He had given full publicity to the policy of helping the Italians; if they felt no longer threatened, then, he had no choice but to rescind his decision. Another difficulty with which he had to contend was the hostility of the khedive, though, as Cromer pointed out, this hostility could be overcome.[13] Salisbury, indeed, treated the khedive shabbily. It did not occur to him to consult the supposed ruler of Egypt before announcing the Dongola expedition. And when reminded of this, he merely retorted "The Khedive is a new danger for which I was not prepared. It did not exist when I was last in office."[14]

At Cromer's suggestion, Salisbury had authorized the Egyptian government to apply to the *Caisse de la dette publique* for a credit of £500,000 to enable it to prosecute the Dongola expedition.[15] The application was supported by a majority decision of the *Caisse* and the money accordingly granted.[16] But a successful French appeal against this decision meant that the money had to be refunded and that England should assume financial responsibility for the war. The French success proved, in the end, to be as great a blunder as their earlier decision not to participate in the bombardment of Alexandria in 1882. Salisbury was later to claim, as we shall see, that because the Sudan was conquered with English money and men, no one else had a right to interfere in its affairs.

Meanwhile Cromer's repeated telegrams had driven Salisbury to summon another cabinet to consider the expedition in depth. This time Wolseley and Grenfell were invited to attend. It was reaffirmed that the broad objects of the expedition were to help the Italians and "to restore to Egypt a portion of her lost territory." They also agreed "that an advance should take place beyond the Murad Wells" and Akasheh occupied "without delay, with the avowed intention of a further movement on Dongola." Dongola was not to be taken in haste. The railway should first be advanced to Akasheh and afterwards to Abu Fatmeh. These details were temporarily to be kept secret. The only public announcement necessary would be "to state that an advance is about to be made to Akasheh with Dongola for its objective." This cautious policy was adopted because "the above scheme of operations appears to be more prudent and less likely to give rise to either military or financial difficulties than an attempt to take immediate possession of Dongola." They also decided to remove the control of the war from the War Office. Cromer and Kitchener were empowered to direct the operations under Salisbury's superintendence.[17] The reconquest of the Sudan has therefore been rightly described as "the Foreign Office War."[18]

When on March 20, Kitchener, Wingate, and Slatin Pasha started for Wady Halfa, the advance on Dongola had begun.[19] Its popularity in England was counterbalanced by its unpopularity in France and, even, in Egypt. The khedive, for instance, opposed it in private, but pretended to support it in public. His grievances were that he was not consulted before the decision was taken, and that the operation was dictated by Italian, rather than Egyptian, interests.[20] But the truth was that Abbas II, in collusion with Egyptian nationalists—who believed in Egypt for the Egyptians—had all along opposed the British occupation of their country and hated the prospect of its occupation of the Sudan.[21] Early in 1895 they had stirred up disturbances the seriousness of which led Alfred Milner to suggest the desirability of a British coup d'etat in Egypt. The purpose of the coup would be to remove Abbas II and replace him with someone willing to support England for the "excellent work" it was doing in that country.[22] And during the Dongola advance Dawkins[23] described the Egyptian reaction thus:

> Native press very bad here, due to inspiration from Palace and to belief in what will please the palace. I am always on the side of a policy of contempt (perhaps not the best but only possible one with British public opinion behind) but we may be forced out of it when caricatures of the Queen are published as habitually breaking Commandment No. 7, and her blood being "made of microbes zizi"[?][24]

But Cromer tended to minimize the strength of the opposition. "If we are successful, and notably if we get to Dongola," he wrote, "the opposition will be silenced; but it will gain greatly in strength if things turn out otherwise."[25] Cromer, indeed, failed to realize that the Egyptian opposition was much more deep-rooted than that. And earlier, he had consoled himself with the discovery that "the Khedive hates the Sultan more than he does us. . . ."[26]

French opposition[27] to the advance emanated, of course, from considerations of imperial strategy and national prestige. Neither Courcel nor Berthelot was satisfied with Salisbury's explanations.[28] What they wanted, however, was, as usual, not exactly clear. There was the well-worn talk of the occupation of Egypt being "distasteful to French public opinion"; and there was the usual request for devising "some method of soothing our just susceptibilities, or some compensatory arrangement."[29] And as they got no satisfaction on these points, Berthelot, perhaps for domestic effect, leaked out to the press, in the form of a communiqué, the interview he had had with Dufferin[30] after they had agreed that the discussion was "entirely officious and not official."[31] Part of the reported conversation read as follows:

> Le ministre des Affaires Entragéres a fait connâitre, au conseil qu'il avait recu hier, de l'Ambassadeur d'Angleterre en France, une lettre l'informant du projet d'une expedition militaire á Dongola.
>
> Dans un entretieu qu'il a en ensuite avec Lord Dufferin, M. Berthelot a demandé à celui-ci des renseignements sur les causes et le but de ce projet et a appelé son attention sur la gravité de ses conséquences.[32]

Dufferin particularly took exception to the expression "gravité de ses conséquences" especially as the excited French press interpreted the passage "as containing a menace addressed to England, not merely by the Foreign Office, but by the Council of Ministers."[33] Expectedly Berthelot repudiated all responsibility for the leakage. He also assured Salisbury that he intended no menace over Egypt.[34] Obviously, the leakage was a calculated piece of political gambit intended to reassure the French public that the weak Meline Ministry was capable of pursuing a tough policy in foreign affairs. Courcel himself admitted that he could not defend the reasonableness of "the outburst of violent feeling which was produced in Paris by the news of our advance towards Dongola."[35] In general, the French government, unlike the French people, behaved decently over the Dongola expedition with all that it implied. Both Hanotaux and Courcel were disposed to leave the Egyptian problem alone.[36] It must be noted, however, that Berthelot took serious objections to the expedition. He said: "We had just been making an approach to a better understanding, when suddenly this new phase of the Egyptian question was going to separate us further than ever." He added that if Britain "went to Dongola, it eventually meant the occupation of Khartoum" which "implied the indefinite prolongation" of the occupation of Egypt.[37] But soon afterwards Berthelot fell from power; and his successor, Hanotaux, appeared to be pursuing an opposite policy. He saw "no serious matter in dispute between our two govt's." and "was ready to encourage us to advance up the Nile, for he believed that the undertaking in which we were now engaged would compel us to come to an understanding with France." In other words, as he explained, he was giving England a long rope to hang itself in the Sudan, for the Sudan had always "become the grave of every adventurer who had tried to subdue it." France, he said, "had ceased to be aggressive," "and she did not seriously desire any future extension of dominion."[38]

There is strong evidence to suggest that Hanotaux did not want any more disputes over Egypt. He showed no enthusiasm over winning the *Caisse* suit, and made it plain that he regretted the outcome.[39] In fact, he attempted, unsuccessfully, to adjourn the decision. Early in November, 1896 he sent a confidential message to Salisbury through Sir E. Vincent, who was visiting Paris, that England and France should jointly agree to adjourn the suit indefinitely. "The object of this queer move," remarked Salisbury, "is to announce to the world that, as between England and France, the hatchet is buried in Egypt." Hanotaux was adopting this attitude, he said, to make the sultan yield to the powers by killing his "belief that Egypt is an obstacle to the cooperation of England and France." "I am skeptical as to these preferred reasons," he went on, "though I can suggest no other explanation of the proposal. But the proposal itself appears to me innocent."[40] The matter was referred to Cromer who, believing that England would "win the law suit," advised that, as "we cannot now count on German and Austrian support," it would be worthwhile to ask Hanotaux to make a public announcement of his intention first, and then Salisbury would give an immediate assent.[41] Salisbury concurred.[42] But Hanotaux, fearing a trap, refused to comply and the proposal fell through. England lost the law suit. One may be tempted to conclude that Hanotaux was desirous of improving relations with England but got little encouragement. But it must be remembered that in 1897, when Salisbury was nursing one of his regular bouts of influenza in the Riviera, he had used the opportunity to procure an interview with Hanotaux. During their tête à tête, he had proposed to the French minister the setting up of an arbitration tribunal, consisting of two neutral powers, to settle all Anglo-French difficulties. And though Hanotaux accepted the proposal in principle, he tended to see obstacles at every corner. Salisbury's attempt to get his friend Courcel to interest his chief in the proposal also failed.[43] His attitude had the effect of confirming Salisbury's belief that the French were aware that their case, especially in the Nile Valley, was a bad one. Nevertheless, unlike Lebon, Hanotaux did not particularly object to the British possession of the Sudan.[44]

In June, therefore, Salisbury had the courage to inform Courcel that the reconquest of the Sudan was incomplete until the Egyptian flag floated once more over Khartoum,[45] thus confirming Berthelot's fears. France swallowed this statement for several reasons; but the principal one was that the Egyptian policy of the *France-Russe* was bankrupt. The two countries were not only actuated by different aims in this matter, but also their opposing views with regard to the Ottoman empire had brought their relations to a low ebb.[46] France refrained from pushing the Upper Nile question to extremes. Instead, it resorted to the tactics of seeking compensations elsewhere, and redoubled its efforts especially in West Africa where it had caught England on the wrong foot. She had also other means of nullifying English efforts on the Upper Nile. By the end of 1895 it had been decided in principle to dispatch Marchand to that region. It was not, however, until June, 1896 that Marchand left Paris on his mission. Leopold's "incognito residences at Paris which rather exercised the ingenuity of the diplomatic world,"[47] as Salisbury put it, was also another indirect way of putting pressure on England. But he was determined to beat them at this game. He wrote to Cromer:

> More direct intimation of the same kind [i.e., Leopold's activities] have reached me from France. You have doubtless heard of the scheme of French colonial politicians for territorially uniting their possessions in the Upper Congo with Obok on the Red Sea. I never quite understood how the intervening stretches of Abyssinian and Shoan territory would be dealt with: possibly it will be by compensation. But this absurdity received more countenance when the French Ambassador hinted to me several times that the French would like to carry their territory [from the French Congo State] across the Nile Valley in the neighbourhood of Bahr-el-Ghazal. The Italians

have more than once warned me of French designs in this quarter and have (characteristically) suggested as a remedy that they should be allowed to occupy Khartoum. In short the Nile Valley is in the diplomatic market and considering how much Egypt depends on the Nile we can hardly keep her from bidding at the sale.[48]

Salisbury, in fact, was an early bidder. On March 23 he had already received news of the fall of Akasheh without opposition.[49] Akasheh was an early conquest; but early conquests often raise false hopes and false confidences. So he determined to leave nothing to chance. He had already stressed the importance of railway and river transport in an "inglorious mode of warfare" which one was driven to wage by "fellaheen or finance."[50] Lansdowne also was equally of the same opinion and emphasized the importance "of a gradual advance, accompanied by the extension of railway communication."[51] On April 1 Salisbury deprecated Kitchener's removal of troops from the Red Sea coast. He also objected to any premature introduction of British or Indian troops and was against Kitchener's purchase of five thousand camels because of the cost involved.[52] He knew he had to sit pretty tightly on the sirdar. As Wingate informed Milner "in confidence," he and Kitchener were anxious to take Khartoum in 1896 as soon as they heard of the Dongola advance.[53] But early in April, Kitchener was reporting that the Dervishes were "very strong." He was, however, confident that he could hold his own.[54] This new intelligence further justified the need for caution.

On Friday, April 24, the cabinet met again to discuss the expedition. Two things occupied their attention: the need to provide an adequate force; and the fear of "a financial embarrassment in Egypt" which might place England "at the mercy of the Powers as we were in 1885." They therefore unanimously agreed not to go beyond Dongola for the time being and not to employ English troops unless absolutely necessary. Some even urged that if it was not safe to go as far as Dongola, Kitchener should be instructed not to go that far. He was only to occupy what places he could "with reasonable safety." "But at the bottom of this somewhat odd recommendation," Salisbury remarked, "there lies what I think is the only difference of opinion—and it is only a very slight one— existing in the Cabinet. Two or three members think that if Dongola cannot be achieved without an expeditionary English force, it ought not to be achieved at all." He dissociated himself from "so positive a view" and carried the majority of the cabinet with him. He reaffirmed "that Dongola must be occupied" with an English force if absolutely necessary.[55]

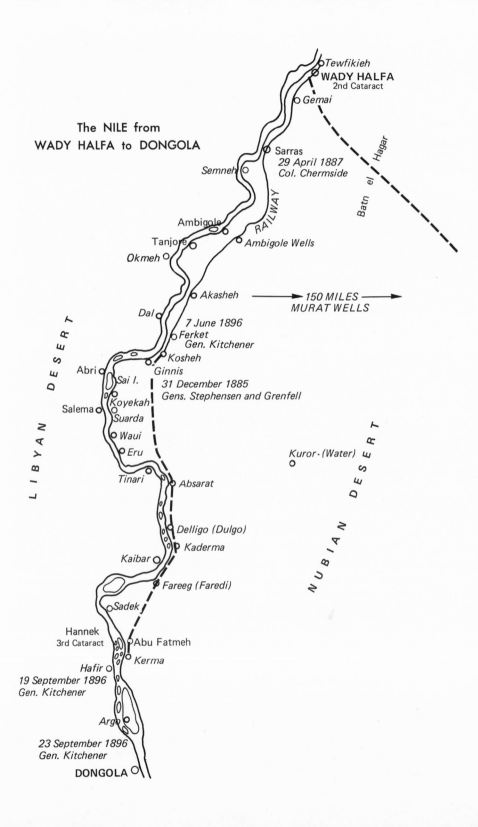

The NILE from
WADY HALFA to DONGOLA

Tewfikieh
WADY HALFA
2nd Cataract

Gemai

Sarras
29 April 1887
Col. Chermside

Semneh

Batn el Hagar

RAILWAY

Ambigole

Tanjore

Ambigole Wells

Okmeh

Akasheh

→ 150 MILES →
MURAT WELLS

Dal

7 June 1896
Ferket
Gen. Kitchener

Kosheh

Abri

Ginnis

Sai I.

31 December 1885
Gens. Stephensen and Grenfell

Koyekah

Salema

Suarda

LIBYAN   DESERT

Waui

Eru

Kuror - (Water)

Tinari

Absarat

NUBIAN   DESERT

Delligo (Dulgo)

Kaderma

Kaibar

Fareeg (Faredi)

Sadek

Hannek
3rd Cataract

Abu Fatmeh

Kerma

Hafir
19 September 1896
Gen. Kitchener

Argo

23 September 1896
Gen. Kitchener

DONGOLA

Right from the start the cabinet had been extraordinarily cautious in their handling of the Sudan campaign. The reason was obvious: they were all determined to avoid a repetition of the disaster of 1884–85. After all, at one time or another, they had used the Gordon episode to discredit the Liberals. They were naturally afraid of being paid back in their own coin. Moreover, a disaster of a similar magnitude could spell political death for some of them. It could usher in a revulsion against imperial expansion in general among the electorate—a revulsion more serious and more soul-searching than anything that happened as a result of the Boer War. Equally, a successful result would be a feather in the cap of the government which would further discredit the opposition. These were some of the realistic political terms in which Salisbury and his cabinet conducted the expedition. To survive they decided to pick their runs in singles rather than in boundaries. Some spectators, like the *P.M.G.*, might grumble at the idea of "Conquest by Procession"; others, like the *Daily Mail*, might resort to slow hand-clapping; but as far as the cabinet was concerned, the end justified the means. In the end they were proved right; and those who had upbraided them for their supineness were now to shout themselves hoarse in praise and in joyous ebullition of jingoism.

When Kitchener resolved to start for Dongola on July 10 so as to take full advantage of the rising river,[56] there was much consternation in government circles. Salisbury at once summoned the Cabinet Defence Committee, and after their deliberations, he wrote to Cromer:

> Several of my colleagues are still impressed with the fear that Kitchener meditates an expedition into the wilderness at the head of a string of camels. I do not share their apprehension—though I have as much horror of the camel as they have. I do not think, however, that any such project is in your mind. . . .
>
> These apprehensions were not the mere tremors of the civilian.

Indeed, Wolseley, "fully persuaded that the Sirdar was bent on a camel raid," had suggested his replacement with "some great English general" because "It is not wise to put a man in command of troops and tell him to follow one plan when he prefers another." On political grounds, "The suppression of the Sirdar was not pressed" by the cabinet; "but the fear of his going forward without waiting for the completion of his line of communication was genuinely felt: and would be very reasonable if his intentions were as they were represented to be." Kitchener was overruled.[57] Cromer was very much perplexed by what he called "the dragging tactics of London," but he admitted that it was essential not to run any unreasonable risk. Kitchener, he said, was contemplating no camel raid; the railway would reach Akasheh by early July, and at about the same time, the materials for continuing the line would arrive. July, too, would be favorable for crossing the cataracts by steamship. He therefore saw "no reason for delaying the advance." He also asked for Indian troops to be dispatched to Suakin so as to liberate the Egyptian garrison there.[58] This was accordingly done and the troops placed under the command of Colonel Charles Egerton.[59] They reached Suakin in June and left after the fall of Dongola.[60]

In May Wolseley had officially repudiated any responsibility on his part relating to the conduct of the war.[61] And, in order to quiet many anxieties among his colleagues, with regard to Kitchener's proceedings, Salisbury insisted that the sirdar should submit to him a weekly progress report written every Monday morning.[62] In July, however, Kitchener surprised the Dervishes at Firket. They showed some resistance but collapsed under pressure.[63] In the same month an outbreak of cholera among the sirdar's troops carried away many lives; but on September 23 he was able to defeat the Dervishes at Dongola. The khalifa's forces did not make a fight of it and hurried off at Kitchener's approach.[64] The sirdar, however, hoisted the Egyptian flag on the old Mudirieh at Dongola.[65] And so the birth place of the Mahdi passed into Anglo-Egyptian hands. The first stage of the reconquest of the Sudan was over; and Cromer said so with apparent relief. "The campaign in the Soudan," he wrote to Salisbury, "so far as I can make out, is virtually at an end."[66]

"Conquest by Procession": From Dongola to Khartoum, September, 1896 to September, 1898

After Dongola, the Dervishes were driven back to Berber, Metemmeh, and Omdurman. Whatever the khalifa's plans for not making a stand at Dongola, the loss of this territory was a great blow to the Mahdist cause. Dongola was perhaps the richest province of the Sudan. Strategically and psychologically, it was an important victory.[67] The fall of Dongola had all along been expected. By July both Kitchener and Wingate were urging Salisbury to authorize the occupation of Abu Hamed as soon as Dongola was taken. But he instructed them "not to advance up the Nile beyond Meravi, where the course of the Nile is again interrupted by rapids."[68] The soldiers, however, had a strong advocate in Milner.[69] Egyptian ministers, like Milner, were also unanimous in their demand for a further advance. Cromer himself admitted that there were no insuperable military objections to such a course. "The question," he said, "is wholly a financial one."[70] Earlier, Dawkins had "put before Cromer the idea of England loaning the money [to Egypt] for the expedition, and taking a mortgage on the Sudan." Cromer and Palmer had then opposed the suggestion, and Dawkins had remarked:

> I thought it better to let it drop, but he will have to come back to it *if* Kitchener exceeds his estimate (unlikely) or *if* the Court of Appeal goes against us (to my mind not unlikely).[71]

Dawkins let the proposal drop; and "Lord over-baring,"[72] always wedded to his own ideas, instead produced a memorandum in which he argued that Egypt should pay "the whole bill and that in return England who rushed Egypt into the business should use her gigantic credit on behalf of Egypt." This plan should only be adopted if the *Caisse* suit went against England. He requested Salisbury's permission to come to England and develop his ideas before the cabinet. But Salisbury put the memorandum in the waste paper basket and informed Cromer that he was not in the least disposed to discuss unknown contingencies. Dawkins was delighted. He wrote to Milner:

> Cromer is furious. . . . Cromer is now pondering how far he can work other members of the Cabinet more or less behind Salisbury, and get his views understood and supported although his memorandum is pigeonholed. He will go home rather despondent, very irritated and a little desperate. You must see how much you can help.[73]

Cromer did go to England as he proposed to do but predictably failed to get his way. He returned to Egypt jublilant, however, rather than desperate. "Do you know I have come back not caring a rap whether this I-I Court decides for us or not," he confided in Dawkins. "If they decide against us let's have another policy and a bigger one. The English gov't. will obviously help us in meal or in malt, let's get all we can and go on with the Soudan if Kitchener's men can do it." Cromer, said Dawkins, was now prepared "to jettison his proposals . . . although he professes to feel bound. *Litera Scripta manet.*" [My italics] [74]

It is not known what promises Cromer brought back from England. But it is fair to assume that he must have been assured that a further advance was on. On his return to Cairo, Kitchener begged Cromer to support him in his resolve to occupy Berber and Abu Hamed in 1897. He believed he could achieve this objective without British help. He also impressed on Cromer the danger of Menelek's intervention in the Upper Nile. The French, he said, had sent a strong mission to the Lion of Judah and were pressing him to recognize their sphere of influence in Equatoria. The khalifa, too, had appealed to Menelek to support him in repulsing the infidel invaders of his country.[75] Already disposed to "go on with the Soudan," Cromer dispatched the sirdar to London to put his case before Salisbury and Hicks-Beach, and to ask for the sum of £500,00 toward the cost of further operations.[76]

Meanwhile, Cromer tried to persuade Salisbury to authorize an immediate advance. He reminded his chief that he (Cromer) had calculated on remaining "two or three years at Dongola," but events had rendered further operations necessary. The Dervish power was not as great as it was feared to be, and "the military success has been more complete" than was contemplated. Moreover, the expense of the expedition had been negligible. The soldiers, he said, were therefore pressing for a speedy conclusion of the war so as to prevent the Dervishes from recovering from their recent defeat. And "the financiers," he concluded, "say that the period of expectation is particularly costly."[77] There is no doubt that Salisbury was impressed by these arguments. But anticipating opposition from the House of Commons,[78] and perhaps from Hicks-Beach, to financing the operations with English money, he refused to commit himself for the time being. His fears were unfounded. But there were better reasons for recommending some rest at Dongola as Wingate, the advocate of a bold policy, was now to realize. He confessed that he had become convinced that "the cessation of the expedition immediately we had secured the province [Dongola]" was wise because the "troops were tired out, clothing had become rags and everyone wanted some rest." He therefore suggested that the railway should first be pushed to Abu Hamed by June, 1897, before occupying Berber early in the following September.[79]

On November 9 Kitchener arrived in London and easily persuaded the cabinet to approve the expenditure of £500,000 for further operations.[80] The money was to be spent mainly on railway construction and gunboats. The cabinet's action was in itself a clear admission that the capture of Khartoum was on the cards. It was only a question of time and of calculation. Kitchener's handling of Hicks-Beach was a remarkable performance. Flushed with victory on his arrival in London, and with added confidence as major-general,[81] he mounted a swift campaign against the chancellor.[82] When they finally met the sirdar got what he wanted without much trouble. Salisbury and Balfour were also present at this meeting. The former was far from unhappy that things had gone Kitchener's way. But he asked Cromer to keep the military objective secret, and if he must speak of it, to say that it was not proposed to go beyond Abu Hamed. "For the present our objective is to give strategic security to the position we have already occupied," he concluded, "and to do it in a manner which shall be of permanent advantage to trade. Avoid as far as you can using any official and formal phrase which can be quoted as proving that Dongola is part of Egypt."[83] He also instructed Cromer to conceal the military objective from the khedive and his ministers.[84] Abbas II's opposition to British policy was well known to Salisbury. Indeed, in October, Cromer had reported that the Mussulman population had thrown in their lot with their khedive. This open demonstration of hostility, he said, was their way of expressing their sympathy for the Turkish massacre of Christians. And the result was that "any political opposition which may have previously existed against Great Britain has now become distinctly more Islamic in its character."[85] Undoubtedly, Salisbury must have been influenced by this development to refrain from making his plans known to the khedive. Kitchener's organizing ability, his superior weapons and gunboats, would have been useless in the face of a general Arab rebellion against their invaders. The possibility of this development which had restrained Salisbury from adopting a drastic action in Zanzibar, also impressed on him the need for caution in the Sudan. Add to this the machinations of other European powers in the Upper Nile and the picture is complete.

In financial matters, too, Hicks-Beach was a constant worry to him. He complained to Chamberlain: "The influence which the Gladstonian garrison at the Treasury have upon Beach's mind is very disastrous."[86] This was no exaggeration. It was this "garrison" which had caused Beach to kill the Suez Canal Shares scheme; in East Africa he got some tough talking to from Salisbury before he approved the expense for the Uganda railway; and now, in the Sudan, "well—Beach is Beach," to borrow Chamberlain's remark.[87] In October he had warned that if the *Caisse* suit went in France's favor, he would only approve of a part of the money being loaned to Egypt, and it would be left to the Egyptian government to find the rest.[88] In fact, Hicks-Beach saw the Sudan question simply as a business transaction. His argument was clear and simple: if England paid for the occupation of any territory, then it was only just that it administered it and did not hand it over to the Egyptian government.[89] In other words, he was asking for a mortgage on the Sudan, the idea already put before Cromer by Dawkins, another financial expert. And when this idea began to take root, Beach's objections to the advance diminished. He wrote enthusiastically to Salisbury: "The Soudan news looks like business," and advocated finishing off the war at once.[90] When, however, Kitchener presented the bill of £500,000 for a further prosecution of the war, Beach's mind had not yet been changed; and when the sirdar carried the chancellor with him, the prime minister's joy was unrestrained. He wrote to Cromer:

> His [Kitchener's] campaign against the Chancellor of the Exchequer was not the least brilliant and certainly the most unexpected of all his triumphs. But all his strategy is of a piece—the position was carried by a forced march and a surprise. In fact I had to give my approval at the end at a moment's notice when the train by which Kitchener was to go away was already overdue. I need not say I was very glad to do so: and the Cabinet, to whom the matter was stated on Wednesday, entirely approved. As soon as the French find out what he [Kitchener] is after, we shall have an ebullition. But I do not think we need fear that it will be any violent until the railway has reached Abu Hamed: and we are preparing to go further: so we have time before us.[91]

He went on to say that he could do nothing to prevent the Italians from evacuating Kassala; and that he anticipated no immediate trouble from France and Russia despite the fact that

> The French, and some of the German papers use language as if formal steps were to be taken quickly by France and Russia to raise the Egyptian question. There was the same talk in the early Summer; but I do not believe it. What the French might do, if the matter lay wholly with them, is incalculable. Their policy depends on the vote of an Assembly whose impulses vary with the changes in the weather. But France will not act without Russia; and Russia shows no sign of any hostile action as yet. But of course we shall know more when we see how our next step is taken.
>
> My impression is that when you get to Berber, you will stay there some little time. You will acquire some breathing space to bring your revenue up to the point necessary for further execution: and the temptation to survey a line from Berber to Suakin will be irresistible. But of course your steps may be hastened by the advance of some other Power towards the Upper Nile.[92]

Earlier, Salisbury had also stated that he did not view seriously the possibility of some "French explorer" taking "effective occupation" of "some spot in the Nile Valley," and that even if Britain took Khartoum, France would bark but not bite. But he also warned that by hurriedly "destroying the Dervish power we are killing the defender who is holding the valley for us now."[93]

Once more he had stated categorically that the capture of Khartoum was on, but still adhered to the maxim: "Slow and steady wins the race." In fact, in November he informed the queen that the cabinet's approval of the Korosko-Abu Hamed railway construction "was equally important whether for the protection of the territory already reconquered or to provide a base for a further advance to the south."[94] This cabinet decision removed his earlier fear that the difficulty of communications between Dongola and Khartoum "appears to be one of the principal obstacles to continuing the advance."[95]

Early in December the Court of Appeal upheld France's contention and Cromer requested the British government to repay the money in the form of a loan to Egypt.[96] On the same day Salisbury consented to the request.[97] But on December 9 Hicks-Beach voiced his opposition to lending the money to Egypt. "I decidedly object to the policy . . . of strengthening our position in Egypt by becoming her banker," he wrote to Salisbury, "and I do not think it could be justified in Parliament." Cromer, he said, was "on the wrong track."[98]

In January, 1897, Kimberley, who had replaced Rosebery as the Liberal leader in the Lords, asked for a clarification of the government's Sudanese policy because "we have heard from other sources that the object was to retrieve the honour of this country by reconquering the Soudan."[99] Salisbury declined to give the details of his policy because, he said, "other people," especially the khalifa, would "overhear what I am saying to the noble Lord." But he repeated

> that one of the objects for which we occupy Dongola was because it was on the highway to Khartoum—(cheers)—and that we do look upon the occupation of Khartoum sooner or later as the objective to which we are urged alike by our desire to efface something of what took place ten years ago, and also by our desire to extirpate from the earth one of the vilest and cruellest despotisms which has ever been seen, something compared to which the worst performances of the worst minions of the palace at Constantinople are bright and saintly deeds, and because we desire to pour

into the lap of Egypt those countless treasures of industry and commerce which the fertile Valley of the Nile is prepared to carry down as of old, if we only remove the cruel hand which has hitherto stifled the industry of the Egyptian and the Sudanese people. (Cheers) I am very importunate in every desire I have had to speak with the utmost frankness to the noble Lord.[100]

A most un-Salisbury like speech, except in eloquence, it does seem; but despite some un-Victorian aspects of his nature, Salisbury was essentially a Victorian and a patriot. The Victorians earnestly believed in the superiority of their civilization over alien cultures; the later Victorians believed that the rule of the khalifa was the cruelest on earth and some of them were determined to destroy it; and most of them were convinced of the wealth of the Nile Valley. Salisbury was no superman and he certainly shared most of these views. Nowadays, however, better researches have revealed that the khalifa's rule was not as cruel as the Victorians believed;[101] and no one now seriously believes that the Nile Valley was exceptionally rich in the last century. But the Victorians did not have this knowledge. In trying to assess their attitudes to imperial expansion, therefore, the temptation to judge them on the basis of our modern knowledge must be resisted. Some imperial historians still seem unable to realize this fact.

In February Hicks-Beach ended any remaining doubts about the government's policy when he told the Commons that, since England compelled Egypt to abandon the Sudan, its responsibility was to recover the Sudan for Egypt. He stated "that Egypt could never be held to be permanently secured so long as a hostile power was in occupation of the Nile Valley up to Khartoum. (Cheers)" In the same speech he bitterly attacked the French for not allowing "us a free hand in Egypt,"[102] and sparked off a diplomatic row. Harcourt, Morley, and Dilke repeated their ineffectual performances of 1896[103] and the government romped home with a majority of 112.[104] Dejectedly, Dilke was to admit "that the policy of the Conservative party on this question had changed since 1888."[105]

On two counts therefore Salisbury's judgment had been proved wrong: the cabinet had shown no fight over authorizing the money for further advance; and the Parliament of 1897 had proved to be more imperialist than that of 1896.[106] The press, too, almost unanimously supported him; and some, furiously roared for total vengeance. Among the majority of them Cromer's unashamed proclamation that "the shade of Gordon [is] beckoning us on to Khartoum," had had a tremendous impact. On the home front, therefore, Salisbury had a free hand with regard to his Sudanese policy. And even Cromer, who had objected to the Sudan venture, appeared now to be a zealous convert.

On the foreign front things were not so rosy. In 1896 Salisbury had decided, at Hicks-Beach's suggestion,[107] to send a mission to Abyssinia with the aim in view of securing Menelek's neutrality in the Sudan war.[108] Rodd was selected for the mission; and though he was able to sign a treaty to this effect in May, 1897,[109] there is little evidence to suggest that the treaty amounted to much. It has been suggested that this was because Salisbury's price for securing Abyssinian neutrality was regarded at Addis Abbaba as niggardly in comparison to what other powers, especially France, were prepared to pay.[110] Salisbury, indeed, was unenthusiastic about the mission from the start.[111] But in March, 1897 he confided in Cromer: "I am afraid by all accounts we shall have to fight rather harder for Khartoum than we imagined. The alliance between the Dervishes and the Abyssinians is very surprising. It does not look now as if your railway to Abu Hamed will be finished before the Nile begins to fall: and that we can do nothing till next year."[112]

The French attitude was worrying because of its sheer uncertainty. But it must be reiterated that initially the French government had shown no disposition to be nasty. As early as 1895, Hanotaux had suggested a general and cordial settlement of all Anglo-French differences.[113] But as no definite proposals were made, Salisbury had remained skeptical as he explained to Dufferin:

> Courcel comes here occasionally. Nothing could be more charming than he is: but he carefully avoids all questions on which we might possibly differ. Not a word about the valleys of the Nile, the Niger or the Mekong. It is not my affair to bring these matters into conversation; for in each of the three valleys we are in possession, and one of the beatitudes of the *possidentes* is that it is to their interest to hold their tongue.[114]

In December, 1896, despite the fact that Salisbury had hinted once more to Courcel that Britain eventually hoped to occupy Khartoum,[115] the French were still assuring him in the beginning of 1897 that they were disposed to let the Nile question lie low. Hanotaux, however, made it plain that he would oppose the advance on Khartoum "on financial grounds."[116] Anglophobe papers in France and Egypt demanded strong and positive action from their government;[117] but Hanotaux remained professionally cool.

He assumed this attitude, according to Monson, because he had a weak case.[118] Monson was perhaps right. The weakness of the French case did not revolve on the justice or injustice of their claim, but on the simple fact that their policy on the Nile Valley was bankrupt. In February, 1897 Courcel wished to know from Salisbury why it was that England and France could not come to terms in the Nile Valley. But when asked to state the French terms he became evasive.[119] Earlier, Cromer had reported a long interview with Courcel which did not "advance[d] matters much." He complained that the French ambassador "does not know his subject. The result is that he can only deal in generalities"; and all Courcel's talk of settling Anglo-French differences *d'en haut* instead of *d'en bas*, Cromer dismissed as "very clever, French & unpractical."[120]

By 1897, however, the French had discovered a new ground for complaint in Hicks-Beach's attack of their attitude during the Dongola vote.[121] It was an uncompromising speech, which even the king of Austria confessed to be "rather strongly worded."[122] The speech had a disastrous effect on French public opinion, and Courcel believed that it had imperiled the position of M. Faure and Hanotaux. "Why do you wish to plunge so beautiful a country into revolution?," he demanded from Salisbury. The foreign secretary denied any such intention but still upheld Beach's views. The ambassador was once more asked to state what they wanted; and once again, he evaded the question. Salisbury wrote to Monson:

> I failed, as usual, in ascertaining what they want. I asked two or three times "Mais donc que voulez vous je fasse?" but I never got anything but a rigmarole for an answer. More gushing confidences, more elaborate solicitations, more ceremonious consideration—these are the only things which I can induce him to specify. He wants me to delineate a sort of diplomatic Carte du dendre after the fashion of Madame de Rambouillet. I cannot induce him to make any practical proposition. I asked him to fancy himself in my place—what would be the first telegram he would send to Lord Cromer? But I could get no answer. It is very embarrassing. My impression is that they know that nothing can be done in the direction of their desires. The state of the facts, not we, offer a hopeless obstacle. But they have to satisfy the ignorant politicians of the Assembly! And they think it will be possible to go through a show of profound deference and affectionate consideration which will be taken by the Assembly as a sufficient substitute for practical concessions. But how is it possible to maintain an attitude of diplomatic bowing and scraping when you have at your side

a very free press and a freer House of Commons? I despair of any permanent improvement of our relations on this subject. But can we do anything to damp down the present indignation? It is very difficult. If I made a speech for that purpose, now, it would necessarily have the appearance of knuckling down in consequence of their fury—which would make trouble here, and would make the French quite insupportable.

He went on to give other reasons why it was inadvisable to make a fresh speech on the question, and added:

Any course obviously taken for the purpose of pleasing France is very irritating to Germany and the irritation may be inconvenient, if at the time or a short time afterwards an opportunity should occur of giving practical expression to it. So much does this reaction follow as a matter of course, that the Austrians are glad of Beach's speech because they will have less difficulty than they have hitherto had in persuading Germany to behave well to us.[123]

This gem of a private letter reveals at once the strengths and weaknesses of Salisbury's diplomatic position in relation to the Nile problem; more than this, it demonstrates the pitiably hopeless state of French diplomacy in the Nile Valley. This is important. When Salisbury caught Germany in a similar mess in East Africa in 1890, he took the lion's share of the loot. The same thing was to happen all over again in the Nile Valley. Indeed, in this scramble for Africa, it was only in West Africa that Salisbury countered the most serious foreign competition. Here, the French had a fair case and Salisbury admitted it; here, too, they showed great enterprise and industry. Salisbury realized this also and was resolved to share; but even then, England did much better than France in the partition of West Africa. It is of course fashionable nowadays to claim that Salisbury deliberately sacrificed territories in the west in order to strengthen his country's position in the Nile Valley. As we saw earlier, there is not an ounce of evidence to support this view, especially between 1895 and 1898. No amount of concession would have reconciled France to the British occupation of Egypt. Salisbury had come to know this by 1895. And perhaps this was what Dawkins had in mind when he wrote: "I don't believe myself that you can come to any terms with France over Egypt short of evacuation and a kind of Dual Control, and I pray this may be avoided."[124]

The French, in any case, demanded no concession and instead decided, with Russian support, to oppose England's lending money to Egypt. But their opposition was not viewed seriously since

England had no undertaking prohibiting her from lending money to Egypt up to the amount of £1 million.[125] Indeed, until the fall of Khartoum the French government made no further serious attempt to raise the Nile question despite pressure from public opinion. This fact was confirmed by Monson in 1898:

> They will continue to say and do everything spiteful that they can devise; but they will go no further. It would be inconvenient for them to hear our answer if they were so rash as to propose one.
>
> The glamour of, and the enthusiasm for, the Russian Alliance, have faded away.[126]

It must be noted, however, that when, in 1897, it was suspected that Hanotaux might propose the inclusion of the Nile and the Niger in a general settlement, Salisbury had expressly forbidden such a course.[127] But French adventurers, of course, had other ideas. In May, 1897 they were quite busy in western Abyssinia and were reported to be preparing to cross over to the Nile. And though they were carefully watched by Menelek, it was feared that they might plant French flags at some uncomfortable place in the Nile Valley, "and thus drawing their Gov't. in, for the protection of the national flag."[128] This fear did not materialize from the expected quarter. It was left to Marchand to make it a reality.

Meanwhile Kitchener was preparing for the next stage of the advance. The Dervishes, too, were preparing to resist him to the last. Reports which reached London convinced Salisbury that the khalifa had a formidable army and that his power was far from declining as was originally thought.[129] This knowledge increased his caution. When, therefore, the *Standard* and other papers vigorously urged the government to take Khartoum without delay, he was quick to warn Cromer "not to commit yourself to any plan of the kind as it is very unlikely to be sanctioned here."[130] Once more, he had got public opinion wrong, for two days later he was writing joyfully to Cromer that the Dongola vote "passed here without exciting any serious opposition or indeed attracting much notice."[131] His real reason, however, was that he was determined not to run any risks and consequently refused to authorize an immediate capture of Khartoum until the railway had progressed far enough.[132] Moreover, he believed—with Sanderson—that, for financial reasons, there was no harm in delaying "the completion of the job."[133] In May, 1897 the railhead reached Abu Hamed. But he was still "not quite free from disquiet as to your [Cromer's] plan for future action." He went on to give reasons why Abu Hamed should not be taken in 1897, and characteristically concluded:

. . . then, if you are established, *en l'air*, at Abu Hamed or Berber and any accident happens to your camels, Kitchener and his army may possibly survive it; but the sensation here will be enormous. Every kind of expert will write or speak to prove indefatigably [?] that not a single soldier will return alive. The fire will be skillfully stoked by the House Guards. And my fear is that the pressure to send a British expedition to relieve you will become too strong to resist— especially as it will be pushed by every kind of royal and professional influence. . . . Could we not destroy Kassala and leave it?[134]

But Cromer and Kitchener were determined to occupy Abu Hamed during the summer, and quickened the work on the railway. In June the sirdar produced a memorandum in which he argued that the occupation of Abu Hamed was necessary "in order to protect the railway and enable the larger gunboats to cross the cataracts with security."[135] Cromer also argued that Egyptian troops could take Abu Hamed without difficulty, and should occupy Berber afterwards since the Mahdist power there showed signs of collapse. But he added that if they should prove strong at Berber, "then the only thing to do is for the Egyptians to occupy the positions they will then hold, and await events." He refused to employ English troops on climatic grounds, the English battalion sent to Dongola in 1896 having proved useless.[136] Salisbury succumbed to these arguments; and on August 7 Abu Hamed was captured. The Dervishes unexpectedly abandoned Berber as well and retired to Mettemeh. Cromer and Kitchener wished to press home their advantage and in October requested authorization to dislodge Osman Digna and Mahmud from their positions on the Atbara (after which the Egyptian force should retire to Berber); to continue the railway to Berber; and to occupy Mettemeh with the help of some friendly Jaalins if the gunboats proved ineffective.[137] These recommendations were passed on to Lansdowne who raised no objections to the first and second, but regarded the last with apprehension.[138] Salisbury therefore instructed Cromer to use his own judgment in the matter.[139] Soon it became known that the Dervishes held Mettemeh in force and had no intention of retiring. Their camp also was out of range of the gunboats. Cromer was forced to conclude that "any idea of a further advance this year may, in my opinion, be now completely abandoned."[140]

On the same day Kitchener tended his resignation on the grounds that his position at Berber was untenable; that Mahmoud, the kahlifa's cousin, was commanding "a force of Dervishes of better fighting qualities and far greater numerical strength than we have ever met before"; and that "the financial authorities appear to be unable to grant what I think necessary for military efficiency."[141] On October 22 Cromer telegraphed privately to Salisbury that the sirdar's "nerve has gone. This is very awkward."[142] "It is abundantly clear that the reconquest of the Soudan is beyond the military and financial resources of the Egyptian Gov't.," he wrote in another letter. "In moments of retrospection I tear my hair over the hurried decision of March, 1896. It has upset all my calculations and introduced an entirely new factor into Egyptian politics." He advised that the soldiers' demand to push on must be resisted. He also revealed that "my Sirdar is a changed man," and did not resign purely on financial grounds.[143] Cromer was right. What worried Kitchener most, as he explained privately to Dawkins, was the delay in taking Khartoum,[144] an event described as the "dream of Kitchener's life."[145]

On October 24 he withdrew his resignation. By this time, too, Wolseley and Ardagh were strongly stressing the importance of the capture of Khartoum in the winter of 1897–98.[146] Salisbury, on the other hand, wished the operation undertaken in the following year:

> Both Lansdowne and I disagree in this view [he wrote]
> . . . I only know one argument in its favor—the possibility that if we wait another year, we may find that the French have anticipated us by setting up a French Principality at Fashoda. It is of course as difficult to judge what is going on in the Upper Nile as to judge what is going on on the other side of the moon.

He felt that it would be unlikely that the French would set up such a principality, and from a technical point of view, he refused to

> believe that any adventure of Liotard or Brazza would affect our title to whatever, in the Nile Valley between Lado and Khartoum, is not Egyptian. But the technical considerations will not go for very much. If ever we get to Fashoda the diplomatic crisis will be something to remember: and the "what next" will be a very interesting question.[147]

Kitchener read the situation differently. "We ought to push on to Khartoum this winter," he argued, because "the French are now working hard to forestall us on the Upper Nile, and if they do so we may have to face serious complications with them when we attempt the job in the autumn of 1898."[148] Surprisingly, Cromer came down heavily against the sirdar. The Egyptians, he pointed out, could not do the job without English help; and he personally did not favor the idea of employing English troops "either now or at any future time." The importance of the occupation of the Sudan, though of considerable interest to Egypt, was grossly exaggerated. England had only a leasehold of Egypt and it was not wise for her therefore to make any sacrifices in men or money just to recover the Sudan for Egypt. The government must be blamed for rushing into the Dongola expedition in the first instance. Did he not protest against that policy then? If his advice had been taken, "the present dilemma" would "have been avoided." He was opposed to any further advance until things had quieted down on the Indian frontier and until the railway had reached Assouan or perhaps Berber. The season was not favorable for any operations. "What is it, after all, we want in Africa?," he asked. It was not to acquire "large tracts of useless territory which it would be difficult and costly to administer properly." It "is to trade with Central Africa. For the purposes of the trade, it would certainly be preferable that no portion of the waterway of the Nile should be in the hands of an European Power." The government, to protect this trade, should reach some arrangement "with Menelek, who is a most important factor in the situation." It was questionable if it was wise for the government to be "drawn by a combination of public pressure and military arguments into further and more remote enterprises." England could always capture Khartoum before any other power; and, in any case,

> for all important commercial purposes the French are, to a great extent, already forestalled, for the trade of the regions for which there is now some competition, must in the end almost inevitably find its way either to Uganda, or else via Berber or Dongola to Suakin or Alexandria. I should add that my belief is that the importance of the trade in question is not so great as is often supposed.[149]

What can one make of these arguments? The cabinet, indeed, must have been puzzled as they considered Cromer's memorandum in the afternoon of November 16. Was it not Cromer who had been pressing them, since the fall of Dongola, to authorize a further advance? Was he not shouting in public that the ghost of Gordon was "beckoning us to Khartoum"? Did he not advocate the occupation of Abu Hamed even before the railway reached there? Cromer wrote as if the occupation of the Sudan was authorized solely for the capture of the trade of that region. But this was not the whole truth. He ignored the international and local complications of the Sudan question. Was Cromer not aware that an attempt to come to an understanding with Menelek had not been exactly successful? The cabinet must have asked themselves these questions and many more. That they did not share his views was evident, for they not only authorized the capture of the Atbara, but also in June, 1898 were unanimous in their determination "to follow up the thrashing which we hope we will give the Khalifa." Nevertheless, what worried the cabinet most of all, and to some extent, Cromer, was the fear toward the end of 1897 that the Dervishes were more formidable than Kitchener's past victories would indicate. The prospect of a successful Dervish counter offensive, with its domestic and international consequences, was uppermost in their minds.[150] On Christmas Day, 1897 Cromer put this point bluntly to Salisbury:

> I greatly fear that, whether we like it or not, an expedition to Khartoum next year will be almost unavoidable. It is no longer a question of anticipating the French on the Upper Nile. The real question, as I pointed out in the memorandum I sent to you some little while ago, is whether the Egyptian army can hold the territory which has already been acquired. The difficulties which arose directly there were reports of a serious Dervish advance have certainly brought home to my mind the precarious nature of the situation. We have to occupy a very extended position with an army which is neither very strong in point of numbers nor very trustworthy—and this with a formidable enemy in unpleasantly close proximity.[151]

It is of course now well known that the formidable nature of the kahlifa's army was exaggerated by contemporaries.[152] But Cromer's attitude to the Sudan adventure was confused. Toward the close of 1896 he was reported to have said:

> I wanted [by his speech at the Turf Club] to knock on the head *the wholly erroneous idea* that I disagreed in the Soudan policy of the Gov't. *I did not and do not disagree.* My contention was that, mainly on financial grounds, the action was premature; but I quite recognize that in English political life one cannot always choose one's opportunity.[153]

The fitting commentary on this letter was provided by Curzon himself: "I suppose one might say that Lord Cromer's memory was a little short. But it is more flattering to ourselves to feel that we have converted him."[154] Cromer's memory indeed was short in this matter. But it must be admitted that he was genuinely worried at the prospect of a financial embarrassment to Egypt—a fear worsened by Beach's parsimony. "I always feel afraid," Cromer wrote to Salisbury, "that some morning I shall have to explode a mine under the Chancellor of the Exchequer's chair."[155]

By November, 1897 arrangements were completed by which Egyptian troops occupied Kassala and the Italians finally withdrew.[156] This did not ease the military situation. The Dervishes were showing more fight than anybody had thought possible;[157] and Kitchener and Cromer were forced to ask for English troops for the capture of Khartoum.[158] But Beach still had some reservations, and advised against trying "a forward policy in too many places at once" because of impending difficulties in India, Crete, and South Africa. He did not wish the mistakes of 1878-80 when "our Afghan and Zulu misfortunes were the main cause of our defeat in 1880"—to be repeated. "I don't want," he said, "to add a Khartoum expedition to our present engagements."[159] Like Cromer, it is indeed difficult to form a precise opinion about Beach's intentions. In public he appeared to be advocating a forward policy; in private his view oscillated like the English weather. Compare the following letter he wrote to Salisbury a few months later to his views above. Now, having suggested that the Sudan war should be finished off at once, he added:

> It would be obviously advisable that Kitchener should be able to follow up the thrashing which we hope we will give the Khalifa. Ought he not to be asked whether the condition of the Nile and his means of transport beyond the railhead are such as to enable him to do this if he was sufficiently strengthened by English troops, and if so, what force he would require in addition to that for which Cromer has already asked and which I assume will be sent. I would take his opinion and not that of the War Office, and if he said the thing could be done I would send out the force he might ask for.[160]

Salisbury was delighted at what appeared to be an apparent conversion of Beach to a forward policy. He tried at once to summon a cabinet but failed to get them together at a short notice. But he assured Cromer that the "extract expresses their general view."[161] Cromer, too, appeared to have swallowed his own objections to a forward advance. "It looks as if the settlement of the Soudan business would be forced on us at once," he wrote. "Indeed, if we once begin to send English troops the sooner the whole thing can be settled and the troops brought back the better."[162]

In January, 1898 Kitchener became convinced that the "battle of the Soudan may be fought at Berber."[163] But for three months nothing was done. The movements of the Dervishes were anxiously followed; their intentions studiously analyzed.[164] Kitchener did not know what the next step would be. "I am perplexed by the situation here," he telegraphed to Cromer; and, curiously enough, faced with a military situation, asked a civilian for advice.[165] Wisely, Cromer advised him to exercise patience and use his discretion.[166] Salisbury concurred: "The Sirdar may count on the support of H. M. Gov't. whichever course he decides on adopting."[167] After a considerable amount of indecision,[168] Kitchener stormed the Dervishes at the Atbara, and completely routed them after severe fighting. Mahmoud, the Dervish commander, was taken prisoner.[169] Superior weapons, and not Kitchener's tactical skill, had done it.

The victory of the Atbara paved the way to Omdurman. No more objection to a bold policy was heard from any corner. Salisbury waited patiently and anxiously. By now his timorous handling of the Sudan adventure had become for him a determined resolve to settle the Egyptian question. And this, he told his family, was "the one point which all others must subserve."[170] Five months later—on September 3—the news of the victories of Omdurman and Khartoum reached him.[171] The opportunity he seized in March, 1896 had paid dividends after two uneasy years. The Sudan had been reconquered. The Egyptian problem had yet to be solved beyond doubt.[172] The final solution should be sealed at Fashoda and the Bahr-el-Ghazal.

Chapter XI

Salisbury and Fashoda, 1898

The greatest failure of Khalifa Abdullah was perhaps his inability to muster a general Pan-Arab-cum-Abyssinian active cooperation against their foreign invaders. The Mahdi might have achieved such a result had he lived. The khalifa's despotism and his increasing reliance on his own people—the western Sudanese—alienated otherwise friendly provinces. He was of course working against immense odds; but nevertheless, both as a leader of his people and as a soldier, he must be pronounced a failure. It is not always realized that contemporaries visualized the Sudan as sprawling from the Nile across to the North of West Africa. Strictly speaking, the "Western Soudan" was supposed to be Mahdist. There is little evidence to suggest that the khalifa seriously sought the active involvement of these western African Moslems in his cause.[1] Had he successfully united these Moslems—a difficult task, to be sure—even now, the story would have been different. Nor did he seek the active participation of other African nationalists, like Kabaka Mwanga, and Omukama Kabalega. Had he done this and got some support, Britain would have been forced to fight on three fronts—in West Africa, in East Africa, and in the Sudan. Whatever their faults, and whatever barbarities they may have committed, these African leaders had one thing in common: they were all fighting for their independence. Had they shown any sense of unity and purpose in their opposition to British interference in their affairs, the French, and possibly the Russians, out of purely selfish motives, would have been only too willing to distribute arms all round. They did so in Abyssinia with devastating results; and the Italians were the sufferers. This lack of coordination was the whole pattern of African resistance to alien rule. In fact, it is fair to say—without being derogatory to either side—that Britain won her African empire on the cheap. She was not really tested. Indeed, her only serious test in Africa was provided by the Boers—an organized and determined people, who exposed wide open the military weaknesses of the *Pax Brittanica*. Had the khalifa and his emirs shown half the sense and shrewdness of the Boer leaders, even without modern weapons, it is doubtful if the Sudan would have been so cheaply conquered. Certainly Kitchener was no military genius. The battle of the Atbara exposed his obvious weaknesses. It is not surprising that he regarded this battle as the decisive event in the reconquest of the Sudan. In 1900 he charged headlong into the Boers and was beaten. Kitchener, it has been truly said, reconquered the Sudan through a minute attention to details. He possessed rare courage; but so did the khalifa, Mahmud, and Osman Digna. But he had other things which they lacked: an organizing ability backed by superior weapons. Moreover, he had an abundance of luck. "Lucky Kitchener" was a truism which few Victorians bothered to note. But reading between the lines one can detect that Salisbury did. He saw the danger of a spontaneous, if not united, Arab resistance against their alien invaders; he knew the weaknesses of the British land forces; and he knew that other European powers were not ignorant of these weaknesses. Above all, Britain was friendless in Europe. He had the rare ability of seeing all these developments as of a piece. That cannot be said of some of his colleagues, or of the British public, for that matter. That was why he despised the jingoes as people who were governed by their hearts rather than by their heads. He did not despise them for wishing to increase the extent and power of the empire. As he saw it, they were out to fight everyone for everything, useful and worthless, in the sacred name of patriotism and national honor. He would have none of that. That was one of the reasons why he took firm control over imperial expansion in Africa; and that is why he merits this study. Salisbury the ace diplomatist is well known; but Salisbury the imperialist—curiously enough not everyone yet accepts him as one—is a much more interesting character.

British Opinion and Fashoda: Attitude of Salisbury

In the year 1898 British jingoism reached its apogee; in the same year Salisbury was at the height of his career. Omdurman and Fashoda had made him the most popular man in Britain. Britain's standing in the world was high; and Salisbury, undoubtedly, was the most important man in Europe. Omdurman and Fashoda represented the triumph of the Imperial Idea over the Manchester School. In June, 1898 the Niger Convention had settled Anglo-French difficulties in West Africa and added large tracts of territory to the British empire. Omdurman meant that Britain would have an undisputed sway in the Sudan, and consequently, in Egypt.

But France would not have it that way. On September 7 it became known that Marchand had definitely reached Fashoda some two months earlier.[2] The implications were only too obvious: were he to be allowed to stay, Britain would have been prevented from reaping the full fruits of its victory.[3] Such a development would also have been universally interpreted as another example of Salisbury's obsequious submission to the French. Salisbury would have lost disastrously in prestige for being too cowardly to enforce the Grey Declaration. The French would have grown pig-headed and the whole enterprise would have been universally acclaimed as the result of French cleverness and enterprise. Moreover, the rickety Brisson ministry would have had a long lease of life. These were the stark realities which Salisbury did not lose sight of as Kitchener and Marchand stood face to face at Fashoda.[4] His handling of the situation stemmed fundamentally from his conception of Britain's right to title in the Nile Valley vis à vis the other powers. Here, unlike West and East Africa, he simply resolved not to share control. His main contention was simply that: between 1884 and 1885 the Mahdi conquered the Egyptian Sudan and became its undisputed master. But Egypt never renounced its claims to that region. On the contrary, it had been making preparations since then aimed at a future reconquest of its lost provinces. The Sudan, therefore, unlike the other regions of tropical Africa, could not be regarded as a *res nullius*. This logically meant that no other power, except the Porte, who was the supposed overlord of Egypt, had a right to occupy any portion of the Upper Nile. But England, by the occupation of Egypt in 1882, had assumed the direction of that country's affairs. France had been invited to participate in the bombardment of Alexandria, but had declined to do so. By its refusal it had, willy nilly, disbanded the *Condominium* and thereby lost its political right in Egypt. When England became master of Egypt in 1882, it also became, ipso facto, master of the Sudan. And as it forced the Khedive to abandon the Sudan temporarily, it was in honor bound to recover those provinces for Egypt and for it. When, and how, this would be accomplished would be determined by a complex of circumstances. Meanwhile, the Dervishes were, in his words, "keeping the bed warm" for Egypt.[5] Whether or not this argument was valid in international law is beside the point.[6] Salisbury never moved an inch from this position. In East and West Africa he had no comparative argument to advance. Therefore, to understand Salisbury's attitudes to imperial issues in Africa, the reader must bear this important fact in mind. True, there may be other reasons why he resolved not to share the Egyptian Sudan with anyone else; but they must all be subordinated to the above argument which Salisbury himself had called "the Egyptian theory."[7] Of these other reasons, one may mention the strategic value of the Sudan. A look at the map of Africa will show that a hostile power in complete command of the Sudan could be a great nuisance to British possessions in East and West Africa, and more importantly, to Egypt. The hostile power, it has been said, by controlling the flow of the Nile, could easily throttle Egypt. If France, for instance, acquired a substantial sphere of influence in the Sudan, its power to make the British occupation of Egypt uncomfortable would be great. Britain, more and more, would be subject to the blackmail of the Triplice. By authorizing the advance on Dongola in March, 1896, Salisbury, far from pandering to the wishes of Germany or Italy, was in fact attempting to rid himself of this difficulty in the event of a decisive reconquest of the Sudan.

Another reason was advocated by Cromer and accepted by Salisbury. This may be called the *commercial theory*. As far as Cromer was concerned a major reason for the reconquest of the Sudan was to make it possible for Egypt "to trade with Central Africa"; and "for the purposes of trade it would certainly be preferable that no portions of the waterway of the Nile should be in the hands of an European Power."[8] In several speeches Salisbury countered the arguments of those who believed that the Sudan was commercially worthless, by laying stress on the importance of the riches of the Nile Valley.[9]

Fourth, Salisbury wanted a monopoly of the Sudan because of the state of public opinion. The rise of the Mahdi had caused the death of Gordon. This event overnight turned an otherwise eccentric English General into a national hero and a symbol of the indomitable spirit of Victorian England. "Gordon must be avenged," had become a national credo. Moreover, the Wolseley expedition of the eighties had cost the British taxpayers £4 1/2 million.[10] To allow any power, even the Porte, to occupy the Sudan would have been thoroughly detestable to public opinion. It was, in a word, to invite disaster. And though public opinion showed no particular interest in the Nile Valley in the 1880s,[11] by 1898 it had become hysterical and almost rabid about that region.

Now, in September, 1898, as the British rejoiced at the reoccupation of Khartoum and the avenging of Gordon, a French force was reported to be at Fashoda. Joy turned into fury. The jingo press went wild. "Pass along, Please"; "A United Nation"; "Worse things than War"[12]—these were typical of their editorial comments. Even the Liberal press joined the chorus and the already tenuous party divisions now became indistinguishable. The *Daily News* saw the situation as "A Plain Issue," by which it meant that Marchand must withdraw unconditionally.[13] The more levelheaded papers advised the Frenchman to withdraw "voluntarily" but "quickly";[14] others quietly hinted to the French government to avoid humiliation by recalling their gallant "traveler."[15] The right wing *Morning Post* showed an extravagant jingoism comparable to the *Daily Mail*'s when it asserted that Marchand must withdraw or England would fight. To abandon the national policy of England, it added, "would mark the extinction of that spirit which has made Great Britain what she is, and has created the British Empire."[16] And to dismiss the false rumor propagated by Dilke and the *Manchester Guardian*[17]—that Salisbury was contemplating a retreat over the Fashoda issue—the *Westminster Gazette* gave this solemn admonition to France, and indirectly to Salisbury: ". . . we beg France not to allow admiration for Lord Salisbury's 'tact and moderation' to persuade them that Fashoda may become a second Tunis or Madagascar."[18] The *Standard,* the Tory paper, was more blunt:

> Lord Salisbury has one overwhelming advantage—he commands, on this occasion, the support of every class and section in the country. Liberals and Radicals are as enthusiastic as Ministerialists in inviting him to enforce the principle so admirably formulated by Sir Edward Grey. But the strength of the national conviction is the measure of the Prime Minister's responsibility. Great is the opportunity, but grievous will be the burden of blame if ministers do not rise to the height of the emergency.[19]

In general, the press was of the opinion that England was not master of the Nile Valley until it was in occupation of Fashoda. Their grievance against France was not due merely to the single incident of Fashoda. It was the cumulative result of feelings, rightly or wrongly held, that France had consistently behaved badly toward England in colonial matters, and that Salisbury had not shown sufficient firmness in dealing with it. Some reiterated that England had given way in Siam, Tunis, Madagascar, and West Africa. They were tired of "graceful concessions." France should be told: "Thus far and no farther."[20]

It was not only the press that cried for action. Rosebery, for instance, lent his influence to their demands when he openly urged the government to be firm and when he claimed to have personally authorized the Grey Declaration.[21] On October 19, even Hicks-Beach jumped on the bandwagon declaring that there were "worse things than war."[22] The speech was drowned in cheers. Campbell-Bannerman called Beach a "swashbuckler" and accused him of using provocative language. Beach countered this accusation with a hard-hitting speech at Bristol. He dismissed "this cant of the talk of provocation," and accused the Liberals of "priggish diplomacy that is too polite to say exactly what it means."[23] Implicit in Beach's Tynemouth speech was the belief, generally shared by the public, that a war with France would result in a swift victory for England due to the preponderance of its naval power.[24]

The independent *Daily Graphic* argued that a war with France was inevitable and urged that the sooner it was fought the better.[25] Other papers, too, strongly advocated a preventive, rather than a defensive, war,[26] especially since it was rumored that France was mobilizing its naval squadron.[27] Warrant officers were said to be itching for a war as a means of distinguishing themselves and thus paving their way for promotion.[28] Goschen, Chamberlain, and Devonshire were said to have argued that Fashoda had afforded the opportunity of permanently crippling such a dangerous rival as France.[29] And the Kaiser deliberately put out the information that England was determined to attack France as soon as possible.[30] It was not surprising therefore that the *Daily Mail* told its readers, with apparent delight: "Our Ships and Men Getting Ready for the Word 'Mobilize'." It was indeed generally believed that the government was spending a lot of money on war preparations.[31]

This background is necessary for it sets the circumstances under which Salisbury, not of his own making, was forced to handle the Fashoda affair. It also demonstrates the impact of domestic opinion on foreign affairs. Obviously, Salisbury did not need to be converted to a strong line. His views, often operating independently from that of the nation, had this time coincided. And it was a formidable combination. But this proved to be both his strength and his weakness. It strengthened his diplomacy; but it also tied his hands. His answer to the French, therefore, was simple and direct: there was no question of negotiation while Marchand remained at Fashoda. From this position he never wavered. And during the critical weeks (September 25 to November 4,

1898), he kept calm and uncommunicative, while the newspapers kept the issue alive. Indeed, during this Fashoda incident he remained at Schlucht where he was holidaying. Report after report poured into the Foreign Office boxes from Monson, Rodd, and Kitchener; but an examination of the documents shows that his replies were few and far between.

The message remained the same. Even when he returned to England the volume of correspondence did not materially increase. The private letters to the ambassadors, as well as to his cabinet colleagues, which make the "Salisbury Papers" a mine of information depreciated appreciably. Between September and December, 1898 Monson received only two important letters; Cromer received two or three; and most of his colleagues received none. The queen wrote more than she received. It was this situation which forced Monson to complain that he was "dreadfully hurt at never hearing from you [Salisbury], and he is not satisfied at being told that your silence is due to your perfect confidence in him."[32] But Salisbury could only retort: "What a plague his susceptibilities are! Writing to Ambassadors generally does harm. However I will try to put some verbiage together for tomorrow."[33] And when he did write, it was nothing of importance.

This attitude demonstrates the essential Salisbury. He believed he had a good case. The cabinet was behind him. So was the country. At Fashoda, the French were in a weaker position. In military terms, England was accepted to be stronger than France. From all reliable sources he had learned that Russia would not fight over the Nile Valley.[34] The diplomatic crisis suited the Triplice. If anything, they would probably support England against France—perhaps not openly—though at a price.

In the rest of Africa there were hardly any remaining territories to barter. French internal politics was still unstable. The Brisson ministry was as weak as the first Labor government under Ramsay Macdonald. Fashoda, indeed, was much more than "a lesson in Sea Power," as has been suggested.[35] From almost every angle France was at a disadvantage. So, as Salisbury saw it, there was nothing much to be said: Marchand must go. He did not wish to humiliate France further by making rambunctious speeches or writing fiery dispatches. He did not believe in kicking an opponent when he was down. Hence, he did not belong to the war party— the preventive war school—to which many of his colleagues belonged. If he believed at all that France would fight over Fashoda—which is doubtful—then he was on the side of the defensive war school. In any case, British war preparations were negligible.[36]

It is possible that Salisbury was looking far ahead to the period when Fashoda would have receded into history. Perhaps he was reckoning that when this happened, no word or action of his would make a rapprochement impossible. He may have been anticipating the Entente Cordiale which took place a year after his death. But this may be giving him more credit than he deserved or more foresight than he merited. But it is a fact that Salisbury was inclined to move closer to France than to Germany.

Egypt had always stood in the way. The reconquest of the Sudan would inevitably settle the Egyptian question; a purely diplomatic victory against France over Fashoda would sooner or later destroy the big dream of a French empire running uninterruptedly through tropical Africa, from west to east. Naturally France would feel hurt; but time heals all wounds. If these were his thoughts, then, he was justified in the end. Disregarding his own personal characteristics for the moment, this is perhaps the only construction to be put on his attitude during the Fashoda crisis. This also explains his much quoted speech after the French had formally announced the withdrawal of Marchand. In this classic speech he cleverly upheld the strength of British diplomacy while not depreciating that of France. He also practically gave the French government the sole credit for resolving a dangerous situation. He had, in effect, presented what was, by all accounts, a French humiliation as a substantial French victory.[37] It was a remarkable performance. But the English press, especially *The Times*, was not equally high-minded. "We are under no anterior obligation to her [France]," *The Times* wrote, "for withdrawing from a place in which she never had any right to be."[38]

Salisbury also rejected publicly the substantial demand for a Protectorate over Egypt. And on December 16, at the Constitutional Club, he turned up in a lecture mood. Here he summarized his diplomatic methods and hit out at his jingo critics and warmongers. Evidently, he had the past few months in mind. The critics of reticence in diplomacy, he said, "are as unreasonable as Pharaoh." He proceeded to enumerate the virtues of reticence and regretted that some of his colleagues had indulged in too much plain speaking. "The dangerous temptation of the hour," he added, "is that we should consider that rhapsody can be made an adequate substitute for calculation."[39]

The Sealed Instructions: Calculation versus Rhapsody

Rhapsody indeed has never been a good substitute for calculation. The British press might go wild over their successes against the khalifa and the French. But these successes were not won by chorus singing. They were won by sheer calculation. Kitchener's victories, Salisbury had himself emphasized, were "achieved by the application of the most businesslike consideration to his enterprise." He did not indulge in the language of "talk talk."[40] Salisbury's diplomatic victory at Fashoda was achieved precisely in the same way.

One could easily get the impression that Salisbury simply sat back and did nothing while the martial mood of the nation rose to feverish heights. This impression is not entirely wrong. But there was something else. Long before Omdurman he had anticipated the Fashoda crisis. He had calculated its magnitude and had taken adequate measures to contain it. He knew that when the chips were down he would not, as in West Africa, be caught out of place. That was why he could afford to sit still and watch in cynical amusement, but also with disquiet, between September and November, 1898, while the newspapers called for war.

On November 30, 1895, the bourgeois ministry, which came to power a few weeks earlier, gave their official blessing to the Marchand mission. Apparently this question had already been discussed by the previous ministry without reaching any decision. It was left to Berthelot, Dufferin's "Old Chemist," to authorize the Marchand mission.[41] It was, however, not till June 26, 1896, that Marchand left Paris as *Commissaire du Gouvernment en Mission Speciale*. His brief included the occupation of Fashoda *"en permanence."*[42] From then onwards the Intelligence Division of the War Office tried as best it could to follow his progress. Between 1896 and the autumn of 1898 numerous and conflicting reports concerning his whereabouts were transmitted to the Foreign Office. Activities of other European powers in the Upper Nile were also closely watched and reported.[43] In February, 1897 the War Office impressed Salisbury with the necessity for an English expedition from Uganda designed to checkmate the French.[44] It was also known by this time that the French government had applied to the Congo Free State for permission to make use of its railways for transporting troops and war materials.[45] By November it was rumored that Marchand and his party had been massacred by the Dinkas or the Azendres.[46] But this proved to be untrue. Nevertheless, conflicting reports as to the fate of Marchand were regularly carried by English and continental papers.[47] In April the French were reported to have "actually crossed the Nile."[48]

These reports appeared not to have worried Salisbury. He was convinced that the simultaneous advance of Kitchener and Macdonald from the north and south respectively would keep any French threat in check. Moreover, the Dervishes could be trusted to look after them as he explained to Cromer:

> . . . such indications as we have are not favourable to the idea of the French having moved any force, even a small one, into the Nile Valley. In the first place, the Dervishes are there. We heard of them beating off the Congolese from Regaff some months ago. In the second place, we have heard of no force moving up the Ubangi—the only road of approach—still less of food or munitions both of which would be sorely needed. I suspect that all these comings and goings to the Court of Abyssinia have in view the opening of some communication with the White Nile through Abyssinia: but such an idea need not worry us—for if we captured Khartoum next year, we should be in ample time to prevent any invasion of the river banks from the East. Also I doubt the value of such taking possession.
>
> If Liotard gets to the mouth of the Bahr-el-Ghazal and makes a treaty with a chief—I doubt whether on purely technical grounds he can be held to have established an effective occupation against us, who duly communicated to Paris the Anglo-German Agreement in 1891, and received no protest. Moreover Edward Grey's bellicose protest in the House of Commons was conveyed to Paris in due diplomatic form.

But he regretted that

> Macdonald has had a serious mishap. He was to have met 300 Sudanese from Uganda; and they have declined to go. The curtain has fallen on the denoument of this incident: and we have not heard from him since he left rail-head.[49]

In November Monson expressed grave concern about "the possibility of the French planting their flag at Fashoda," and wished to have his chief's opinion.[50] But he was merely told that "our policy with respect to the valley of the Nile has in no degree changed."[51] Nevertheless, Salisbury began to show signs of anxiety. Early in 1898 he attempted to reach a rapprochement with Russia over China by refusing to take a strong line over the Russian seizure of Port Arthur. The attempt produced no results.[52] There was, however, nothing to fear since the *France-Russe* left much to be desired.

In fact, he had already sent a formal note to Hanotaux in the previous December "in regard to the exclusive sphere of influence claimed by England in the Basin of the Upper Nile."[53] This note was unheeded. On the contrary, the French press began to discuss vigorously the Marchand Mission. But Hanotaux carefully avoided any allusion to it or to the Upper Nile.[54] By January, 1898 the French expedition had not yet got to the Nile. In fact it was believed that if they managed to get there it would be with a diminished force because of the scarcity of food supply.[55] But in March the War Office warned that "if the star of any of the contending Powers in these regions [the Upper Nile] may be considered as rising in the ascendant, it is that of France, and not of Great Britain, the Dervishes, or the Congo Free State."[56]

The War Office was wrong. The battle of the Atbara was practically to seal the fate of Mahdist hegemony in the Sudan; and it left the final thrust on Khartoum in no doubt and thus made England the strongest power in the Upper Nile. Hicks-Beach was perhaps the only one who would have been satisfied to wait awhile and consolidate before going farther south.[57] But Salisbury and Cromer were planning far ahead. They were disturbed by the rumors which grew stronger and stronger that Marchand was uncomfortably near to Fashoda.[58] But there were some, like Lord Granby,[59] who saw no cause for anxiety. "Kitchener," he said, "always comes to the front when wanted . . . If there is a French 'exploring' expedition at Fashoda, as they say there is, they must feel rather awkwardly situated."[60] Salisbury, however, left nothing to chance. In May he reminded the khedive that, as a result of the Tel-el-Kebir victory, Britain had "acquired by conquest complete control over" the Egyptian government and "cannot allow that control to be disputed."[61] Obviously, he was preparing the ground for the impending claims to title over Fashoda. Cromer, too, argued in a long memorandum that, after the fall of Khartoum, Kitchener would proceed toward Fashoda so as to accomplish what Macdonald had failed to do.[62] A further stage in Salisbury's calculation was the theory that English and Egyptian flags should fly side by side at Khartoum to avoid "a good deal of diplomatic hamper."[63] He followed this up by getting the cabinet to remit the £800,000 loaned to Egypt to defray the cost of the Dongola expedition.[64] This was a clever move because it meant that he could claim later on that the Sudan was conquered with English money and men.

Meanwhile, the French had staked their claims on the Upper Nile. Marchand was believed to be at Fashoda; and France claimed Wadai, Dafur, and Bahr-el-Ghazal, as well. They also talked of a *"trait d'union"* from Djibuti to the Nile. The Bahr-el-

Ghazal was claimed in the hope that it would be occupied by Marchand. "This policy," said a War Office report, "was foreshadowed in the 'Annuaire de l'Armes Coloniale' 1898, page 29" where it was stated:

> Le Capitaine Marchand est aujourd'hui sur le Nil: nil doute qu'il ne le descendre bientot, reliant ses itine raires a ceux des Missions de Bonchamp et Clochette, venant par l'Abyssinie.
>
> Le Nil deviendra un fleuve franco-abyssinien dans sa partie Septentrionale, et nous serons alors en bonne posture pour reclamer l'evanuation de l'Egypte par les Anglais.[65]

The Bonchamps expedition was hoped, therefore, to make the Djibuti connection possible. This development perhaps caused Salisbury to play his trump card. The basic ideas did not originate from him as is generally thought. They were Cromer's[66] which he adopted almost word for word. To forestall French and Abyssinian ambitions in the Upper Nile, strictly secret instructions were given to Kitchener. After the fall of Khartoum, he was required—provided no insuperable military objections intervened—to dispatch at once two flotillas from Khartoum; a relatively large one was to go up the White Nile, and the smaller one to go up the Blue Nile. The officers to command these expeditions were to be carefully chosen from Englishmen serving in the Egyptian Army. The White Nile flotilla, the more important of the two, might preferably be commanded by Kitchener in person. Both, however, were to fly English and Egyptian flags; and both commanders were given identical instructions. They were to defend themselves if attacked, but were warned not to provoke any conflict themselves should they meet with a French or Abyssinian force. The officer commanding the Blue Nile flotilla was to proceed up river as far as Roseres, some distance beyond Karkoj; and if he should find the Abyssinians in effective occupation of the river before his arrival at Roseres, he was to stop where he was, establish a post outside the territory occupied by the Abyssinians, hoist British and Egyptian flags, inform the Abyssinian commander that the frontier question would be settled by their respective governments, and then await further orders. The limit of the expedition would be Roseres because cataracts began at that spot. But if the Abyssinians were not contacted, he was to go as far as Famaka—which was believed to be the head of the cataract. The officer commanding the White Nile flotilla should contemplate two contingencies: he might find that the French had occupied some spot; or more likely, he might find the Abyssinians. If he found a French flag flying he was to protest against the presence of a French force, and formally to claim the territory occupied by them in the name of Britain and Egypt. He must not be provocative; but must defend himself if need be. He should establish posts both up and down the stream, and opposite to the French post. And if, from a military point of view, he considered it prudent, he should pass by the French posts and proceed farther up stream. Should the Abyssinians be encountered instead, he should adopt the same procedure, but using a modified language. There would be no formal protest, but he was to act like the commander of the smaller flotilla. The composition of forces to accompany the flotillas was left to Kitchener's discretion. He was, however, advised to collect a large force both for better impression on their opponents and for immunity against attack. As soon as the expedition left Khartoum the Ugandan authorities should be warned so that the two parties might possibly make a junction. Telegraphic communications from Khartoum should also be established as far south as possible.[67]

These are the salient points contained in Salisbury's famous sealed instructions. The ideas, strictly speaking, were Cromer's, but the letters were written in Salisbury's handwriting. They were thoroughly discussed by the cabinet and approved by the queen before being sent out. Kitchener was specifically told not to open them till he had taken Khartoum. The secrecy surrounding these orders was such that it was not until September that Monson was formally informed of them, and even then, on request.[68] Throughout the remaining stages of the Sudan campaign, Kitchener, Hunter, and Rundel carried one of these sealed orders in the lining of their tunics.[69]

On August 18 a group of refugees reported that a French party was at Fashoda.[70] And on August 27 Kitchener learned from Duem, on the White Nile, that a party of Europeans at Fashoda had established themselves in the buildings which used to be government offices.[71] Omdurman fell on September 2; five days later Kitchener and Hunter set out southwards with their instructions.[72] There was nothing else Salisbury could do. He had done his share and could afford to sit back and await developments. The rest was left to the sirdar; and he proved a most worthy ambassador.

Salisbury and Delcasse

By issuing the sealed orders Salisbury had, implicitly, transferred the Sudan business from the soldiers to the diplomats. From September 7 to November 3 the Fashoda affair held the field. Initially,

Delcasse proved conciliatory.[73] And until the famous meeting [74] at Fashoda was made public on September 25 he consistently denied any knowledge of the exact whereabouts of Marchand "but let it be assumed that he is at Fashoda."[75] Obviously he knew more than he was prepared to release.[76] He was studiously avoiding a showdown. After the fall of Khartoum, he had congratulated the British government on their success.[77] He also knew that he had a poor hand to play. He specifically told Monson that Marchand "had been enjoined to consider himself as an emissary of civilization without any authority whatever to decide upon questions of right" between the two countries. He also implored Salisbury to instruct Kitchener not to cause any local difficulties should he encounter Marchand.[78] Salisbury's reply was anything but conciliatory though it appeared to leave a loophole:

> If M. Delcasse should revert to this subject, I request you to point out to him that, by the military events of last week, all the territories which were subject to the Khalifa passed by right of conquest to the British and Egyptian Governments. H. M. Govt. do not consider that this right is open to discussion, but they would be prepared to deal in the manner suggested by His Excellency with any territorial controversies now existing in regard to those regions which are not affected by this assertion.[79]

Delcasse's reaction to this dispatch was noncommittal. He read it "3 or 4 times" and "said that he had no fault to find with its 'redaction,' except that the expression 'territories subject to the khalifa' was vague, and that he for one did not know the extent of them."[80] But in another interview with Monson he rejected Salisbury's view that the French had no right to be at Fashoda. Monson merely restated Salisbury's argument and warned that any French incursion "into the Upper Nile Basin would be considered by us an unfriendly act." At this juncture Delcasse asserted that "as a matter of fact, there is no Marchand Mission," and that in any case, "France had not only never recognized the British sphere of influence in the Upper Nile region, but that M. Hanotaux had, in the Senate,[81] openly protested against the Grey Declaration."[82]

Meanwhile Kitchener was sending home reports of his proceedings including a long account of his meeting with Marchand.[83] Salisbury instructed Monson to read all Kitchener's telegrams to Delcasse "but without leaving copies with him."[84] He also approved Kitchener's handling of a difficult situation.[85] After reading these dispatches Delcasse reserved his comment until he had consulted his cabinet.[86] The cabinet, in turn, refused to take any action until they had received Marchand's own version of the events. They therefore asked permission to contact Marchand.[87] "H. M. Govt. cannot decline," Salisbury replied, "to assist in forwarding a message from the French Agent in Egypt to a French explorer who is on the Upper Nile in a difficult position."[88] But he also warned that this decision:

> does not imply the slightest modification of the views previously expressed by them [H.M.G.]. You should add that, whether in time of Egyptian or Dervish dominion, the region in which M. Marchand was found has never been without an owner, and that, in the view of H. M. G., his expedition into it with an escort of 100 Senegalese troops has no political effect, nor can any political significance be attached to it.[89]

Evidently, Salisbury was in no mood for compromise. "Firm as a Rock,"[90] was indeed an accurate assessment of his attitude toward the Fashoda impasse.

Naturally, this attitude aroused very strong resentment in France.[91] Conciliation began to give way to defiance; and a simple dispute was imperceptibly acquiring the makings of a war which neither Salisbury nor Delcasse was anxious to wage. By September 28 Delcasse had become determined, and even obdurate. He declared that the abandonment of the Sudan in 1884, ipso facto, made the country a *res nullius*. Britain therefore could not lay claim to it on behalf of Egypt. He warned that French public opinion was dangerously excited over the issue. "Do not drive me into a corner," he protested, "do not ask me for the impossible." He assured Monson that he had no wish to "break with England over Fashoda"; but Monson replied that he "feared the possibility of such an event." Then Delcasse issued this threat: "We shall not in that case stand alone, but I may say again I would prefer England to that other for our ally." And Monson concluded that the die was cast.[92] Certainly the French minister knew that he was already beaten. But in diplomacy it often pays to assume a tough posture. Salisbury did not consider Russian participation in a war over Fashoda a probability. The recent Anglo-German Convention settling in advance the future in Portuguese colonies in Africa had improved relations between the two countries.[93] Nevertheless, Delcasse declared unofficially, not quite in the fashion of Edward Grey, that Kitchener, "by establishing a post on the Sobat, committed what is, if not an act of war, at all events a more than unfriendly act." He asserted that to evacuate Fashoda unconditionally "would be the humiliation of France, and neither this nor any other Ministry could submit to such a course. They would look upon any formal demand to retire as an ultimatum, and would reject it."[94] This interview had the desired effect on Monson. "I see no possibility of our arriving at any solution," he confessed privately; "but I quite admit that if the French gave way the Govt. would be turned out at once. They make it a question of national honour; and I need not say what that means here."[95] On the following day he warned that Delcasse was not "bluffing" but "thoroughly meant what he said."[96]

Salisbury appeared to have been unimpressed. But he carefully avoided formally demanding the recall of Marchand. Instead, he reacted by instructing Kitchener to make Marchand's position "as untenable as possible." No "reinforcements or munitions of war" should be allowed to reach him; and until he was prepared to quit Fashoda he should not be furnished with food supplies "except in case of extreme necessity."[97] Delcasse protested that this policy of starving Marchand out of Fashoda was "an act of barbarity."[98] Salisbury, indeed, was relentless in making his victory complete. To counteract the argument that Kitchener had no authority to act on behalf of the khedive south of Omdurman, Abbas II and his ministers were to "be induced, as far as possible, to initiate the orders given to him, or at least to confirm it [? them]"[99] Abbas II had no choice but to comply.[100]

Monson, as usual, had overestimated French preparedness to fight. On October 3 Prince d'Arenberg, one of the leaders of the colonial group, indicated that he would like his country to renounce its claim over Egypt. He also admitted that by its refusal to participate in the occupation of Egypt in 1882, France had already renounced its claim to that country.[101] On October 5 Courcel had an inconclusive interview with Salisbury lasting two hours. Both stated their usual case; and Courcel's implied facesaving formula "that both sides should give out that negotiations were going on on future territorial delimitations" was rejected outright. In fact, Salisbury claimed to have done France a favor by saving the Marchand Mission from certain destruction at the hands of the Dervishes. "We separated without coming to any conclusion," he concluded, "for I had no communication to make . . . & he made no suggestion of any arrangement by which the right could be reconciled with the present pretensions or desires of France."[102] French resistance began to weaken gradually. Delcasse was said to have admitted "that the material interests of France are not so much engaged in this question."[103] In general,

France was not disposed to fight England over Fashoda. Monson explained:

> . . . everything conspires at this moment to disincline the French to a quarrel. Their internal condition is in the last degree one of unrest. Confidence in their institutions, in their public men, *and even in their army,* has been grievously shaken. Confidence in their lately acquired ally is no longer secure; and with all these incentives to a pacific attitude, they have still further present in their mind the certainty that the apotheosis of their resurrection from the abasement of thirty years ago, the glorification of the rehabilitation of France, which is to be displayed before the world in the International Exhibition of 1900, will be ruined by the disturbance of the general peace of Europe, and that a wider-reaching catastrophe to the entire well-being & prosperity of France will be symbolized by the downfall of the project.[104]

Undoubtedly, this knowledge encouraged Salisbury's determination not to compromise. Kitchener's announcement at Fashoda that he had placed the country under martial law was immediately approved. "I presume," Salisbury observed, "that no opposition would be offered should M. Marchand elect to retire by the way he came."[105] But the French explorer felt that it was impossible to retire by this original route.[106] Nevertheless, from now onwards, there began to appear strong indications that he would be recalled. The *Matin,* supposed to be the organ of the French Foreign Office, and which had earlier adopted a strong line on this issue, now became markedly reconciled to the policy of withdrawal. French policy in the Upper Nile, it stated, "has been actuated solely by the necessity of obtaining a commercial outlet for Central Africa, and in no way by a desire to thwart English policy in the valley of the Nile."[107] The following day it argued that "The abandonment of Fashoda is perfectly compatible with national honour." Then, it launched a savage attack on the colonial group for their imprudence in saddling France with useless and extravagant territories—practically inaccessible from the French possessions on the Atlantic coast—and "annexations in the mountains of the moon, which might, for all the good they do to us, as well be in the moon itself." It ridiculed the "hungry . . . appetite" of "the Colonial Party for the acquisitions of fresh black territories, and for the responsibility of governing more cannibal tribes."[108] This was odd, coming from the *Matin;* and a perfect example of political turncoat. It was, of course, the practice during this era of imperial expansion for individuals, governments, and pressure groups to employ all sorts of arguments to hide their inability to get what they wanted. The French used the same tactic during the Niger negotiations; Salisbury did the same during the Say-Barruwa line controversy; and the Kaiser himself was perhaps more adept than anyone else in employing this device. The *Matin*, therefore, was indeed using what Malet once described as "the well-worn formula that Africa was not worth quarreling about."[109] And yet in West Africa Britain and France were at each other's throats; over Fashoda they reached the brink of war; and Britain actually fought a costly war over South Africa! Commenting on the *Matin* article, Monson wrote:

> If a hint from the Govt. has inspired this article, the writer has carried out his instructions with vengeance; and it will be interesting to observe whether this is but a solitary note, or whether the cry will be taken up by the whole pack.[110]

Of course, the whole pack did not join in, but it was obvious that Salisbury had outgamed Delcasse. On October 11 Monson had an unofficial and private interview with the French minister, during which, for the first time, he became serious. He was irritated, he said, by the bellicosity of the English press which had made "the international situation much more dangerous." But Monson was inclined to the belief that his frame of mind may have been due to cabinet criticism of his handling of the Fashoda diplomacy. Delcasse hinted that he might retire from politics and warned "that another Minister would not be so accomodating."[111] One important fact, however, emerged out of this interview: Delcasse was willing to order Marchand's recall provided the discussion on territorial delimitations would begin immediately following his retreat. Delcasse, concluded Monson, would eventually authorize evacuation "if we can build him a golden bridge for that retrograde movement."[112] On the same day *La Depeche Coloniale* proposed the exchange of poor little Gambia for the poor, but strategic, Fashoda.[113] Salisbury took no notice. On October 14 President Faure's brother-in-law, a medical doctor, was reported to have told "his patient, a member of the Chancery, that the President had exclaimed that he wished Marchand were in the Inferno, or anywhere else than Fashoda!"[114] The Parisian press, however, though comparatively moderate, did not yet give up the fight. Some of them still "advocated the intervention of Russia in the dispute, and intimated that this is the moment for that Power to show that she is not going to continue to be the sleeping partner of the alliance."[115] But this was wishful thinking since Muraviev had let it be known that Russia could be of no assistance to France in the Fashoda dispute. His excuse was that the Russian fleet was ice-locked, and therefore inoperative, for some four or five months during the winter.[116] On hearing this news Salisbury exclaimed: "I thought as much. The Czar's ministers never give anything for nothing."[117]

However, following Delcasse's hint that Marchand would withdraw, Salisbury appeared to have relaxed his rigid attitude and proposed to refer the next step to the cabinet.[118] But nothing appeared to have happened. On the French side, the unfounded rumors that Salisbury was anxious to conciliate over Fashoda led Delcasse to delay Marchand's recall.[119] Concerning these rumors, Fitzroy noted in his diary:

> The idea of a section of the British public that Lord Salisbury's resolution is in need of strengthening, shows very little knowledge of the sagacious statesmanship that is often masked by the play of his placable and pessimistic intelligence. He has been able to tackle & lay at rest several dangerous questions, because he had the wisdom to see and the courage to tell the nation that there are some controversies better closed than kept open until we can enforce extreme rights. With an Empire like ours, concentration of effort should be the watchword of British policy, and it is because Lord Salisbury realizes this that he has made of Africa an object lesson of firm and comprehensive management.[120]

On the English side, the uncompromising speeches of Devonshire and Beach tended to frustrate Salisbury's diplomacy and increase French irritation.[121] In France, too, Delcasse was accused of weakness; but he still believed that it would be an "unparalleled calamity" for England and France to come to blows over Fashoda. Monson merely retorted that the Marchand Mission "had been a deliberate attempt to obstruct our advance up the Nile Valley, and to intercept our line of communication between North & South Africa, the establishment of which, as all Europe knows, is the object of our policy."[122] In fact, Salisbury's reply to Delcasse's obvious conciliatory postures was to call out the reserve Fleet and to authorize naval preparations.[123] On October 23 the *Matin* thought it fit to print an interview with M. Bonvalot, the African explorer, in which it was admitted that the Marchand Mission was a mistake.[124]

By the middle of October there had begun to arrive conflicting reports of French war preparations. One purported to come from a "regular employ of the French Colonial Office," known to the

War Office as "A," who stated that the French army was unready for any war.[125] A week later General Brackenbury reported that France was secretly mobilizing her navy and urged that Britain should be prepared for a preventive rather than a defensive war.[126] There is, however, little evidence to show that French preparations were not purely defensive measures.[127]

On October 25 Salisbury received the substance of a note purported to have been sent to Delcasse by Muraviev. It reads as follows: "Do not give England any pretext for attacking you at present. At a later date an opportunity will be found by Russia for opening the whole question of Egypt." "My own opinion," commented Monson, "is that Count Mouraviev neither categorically refused, nor contingently promised, the support of Russia in the present emergency."[128] Queen Victoria felt very concerned about this development and urged Salisbury to find out from the Russians if the rumor was true.[129] Salisbury advised against such a course:

> If we asked Russia she would give us an answer as should induce us to give way—that is to say she would frighten us as much as possible. This would be quite consistent with her holding exactly the opposite language to the French: for a war now would be inconvenient to her. She wishes to stop it: but whether it is stopped by France yielding or England yielding she does not care . . . Italy must go with us. Germany will probably try to levy blackmail.[130]

Obviously frightened herself, the queen blamed poor Monson for the news. "I think Sir E. Monson has been frightened by these reports," she wrote, "I do not believe them." She accused Monson of excessive gullibility and requested Salisbury to find a modus vivendi. "Pray see Sir F. Lascelles who leaves today and is so sensible & well informed," she concluded.[131] The queen, who since the crisis had been advocating firmness mixed with caution,[132] was now strongly against "a war for so miserable and small an object."[133]

Perhaps it was this fervor of imaginary Russian interference, and rumors of French naval preparations[134] that caused Salisbury to summon a cabinet on October 27. At this cabinet ministers showed much difference of opinion in discussions that lasted a long time. They, however, reaffirmed "that, so long as the French flag flew at Fashoda, it was impossible that this Government would enter upon any territorial discussion." And though they would certainly enter into discussion after Marchand's recall, "we could give no agreement with respect to the nature of the territorial arrangement to which your Majesty's Government could consent." They also decided that the fleet should be got ready for war.[135] This, indeed, was a drastic step. It is difficult to say whether Salisbury was one of the hawks or one of the doves. What is certain was that the cabinet were determined to yield no ground to the French. Individual ministers, too, made their positions clear. Chamberlain was said to have accused Salisbury of being too weak to "choose the right moment to strike like Bismarck did at Ems,"[136] and to have warned that no "graceful concessions" would be tolerated.[137] So did Curzon.[138] Hicks-Beach, Balfour, and Devonshire were also dead against any concessions.[139] Goschen was said to be in favor of war.[140] Lansdowne, like Queen Victoria, would gladly give France only a commercial outlet on the Nile.[141] Perhaps, Salisbury was in agreement with Lansdowne; but even so, he was outnumbered. It is, however, difficult to see how he could be "firm as a rock" and yet be unprepared to fight a war should Delcasse call his bluff. Consequently, on October 29, Fitzroy[142] received draft proclamations calling out reserves of officers and men,[143] and by October 31 six proclamations covering the entire War Office machine were ready.[144]

Meanwhile, France was suffering from one of her regular doses of internal crises. Events began to move with almost breathless rapidity. By October 25, the war minister had resigned; and the overexcited Monson reported the probability of a military coup d'etat.[145] The following day, the Brisson ministry resigned; a new government took over three days later with Delcasse still retaining his portfolio. On October 26 Britain alerted the Mediterranean squadron after Monson had reported French naval preparations.[146] And on October 27 the cabinet decision was duly conveyed to Courcel. Salisbury made it plain that to enter into negotiations would be to admit the legality of Marchand's position. Courcel, of course, rejected the implied illegality of the explorer's position but hinted that France had discovered that Fashoda, after all, could not supply it "with the outlet to the Nile which she was anxious to obtain and that therefore was useless to her." Salisbury retorted that whatever be the case Marchand had no right to be where he was and must withdraw unconditionally.[147] Courcel protested that this "would not conciliate public opinion in France," and demanded unofficial assurances that negotiations would follow withdrawal "to gratify the French public, even though it might turn out that it could not be continued without waiting for information appointing a Mixed Commission or some other excuse."[148] Salisbury merely observed: "I cannot give him any unofficial assurances. I cannot ascertain, still less predict, the bend which the Cabinet will take on any issue which is not fully before them."[149] Delcasse, however, insisted that Britain wished to humiliate France. He hinted to Monson that he might be forced to seek German assistance who "would not be averse from coming to an understanding with France for this end." This warning led him "to the execution of a coup, which he had undoubtedly prepared for my benefit." The gist of the plot was as follows: Delcasse produced documentary evidence that the Russians "would associate themselves with any step ('toutes les demarches')" which France might decide to take. He had refused to print this document in the Yellow Book because he wished to keep down the inevitable excitement arising from such a course.[150] The message was obvious: by insisting on France's humiliation, England was risking a hostile combination of European powers. Unusually, Monson took no fright at such a disastrous prospect. It was a good thing the document was not published, he bluffed, because England would have regarded it "as a menace" and would have treated it accordingly.[151] The curtain went down. Delcasse's ingenious plot received no applause.

On the contrary, Marchand behaved foolishly. He decided, on his own account, to go to Cairo with Captain Baratier, leaving Germain in charge at Fashoda.[152] Salisbury seized his opportunity and acted at once. Kitchener was instructed to reply, if Marchand desired to return to Fashoda, "that no gunboat is likely to leave Khartoum for the south for some time."[153] This was another way of saying that he should be prevented from returning to Fashoda. Delcasse was furious and sent feverish orders that the two officers must return to their posts.[154] The French press, on the other hand, blamed Delcasse—unfairly—for authorizing Marchand's "escapade."[155] Kitchener executed his orders and the Fashoda crisis was practically over. On November 2 Salisbury tightened the screw further:

> I have to observe that, as the railway from Wady Halfa to Berber is a military line not open to the public, Major Marchand and Captain Baratier should, if they apply for permission to travel on it, be requested to explain in a note what is the object of their journey to Fashoda, and what course it is their intention to take on arrival there.[156]

This was not necessary, for on the same day the Dupuy cabinet decided to give up.[157] The Fashoda crisis was over. Commonsense had triumphed to the relief of everyone. Salisbury's reply to a letter from Chamberlain congratulating him on his brilliant victory was very indicative of the man. "I think the conduct of our affairs has been successful," he wrote, "but I entirely decline to accept the exclusive credit of the result for I depended largely upon the assistance of several members of the Cabinet at various times."[158] Fashoda, nevertheless, remains Salisbury's greatest diplomatic triumph and indeed "an object lesson of firm and comprehensive management."

Chapter XII

Bahr-el-Ghazal and Equatoria, 1898–1900

Fashoda was a decisive victory for Salisbury. Looking back on this episode, however, it is difficult not to admire the attitude of Theophile Delcasse. Throughout the crisis he was operating in an impossible position. The domestic instability caused by the Dreyfus-Esterhazy-Zola scandal had weakened the French government and was weakening its effectiveness in foreign policy.[1] It had also increased French chauvinism and could possibly have led the government to seek redemption in another foreign venture. European diplomats in Paris, reported Monson, were increasingly worried at the "disquieting possibility" of this happening. Monson was concerned particularly at "the susceptibility of the French warrior, who in view of all the supposed attacks on his honour may be inspired with the idea of vindicating [?] at the expense of perfidious Albion."[2] A month later he wrote that France's "relations with other countries are becoming abnormal" and France itself was becoming "a standing menace to Europe." He feared a military coup which would "be followed by a foreign war."[3]

Salisbury dismissed these fears as "gloomy forebodings" and mere "conjectures."[4] From his diagnosis of the situation France was isolated in Europe. The British navy was supreme. He was leading a united cabinet and a united country while France was faced with growing anarchy. The possibility, therefore, of a French showdown over Fashoda was remote. Delcasse appears to have seen the situation similarly. Salisbury demanded an unconditional French surrender and got it. And in one of those exasperating minutes of his to which historians tend to attach undue importance, Salisbury summed up the new territories added to the British empire, de facto if not de jure, as "wretched stuff."[5] Why was he prepared to fight a European war over some "wretched stuff"? The theory that he was merely protecting the route to the east appears to me farfetched. Salisbury had real grievances against France.[6] He was convinced that, in the Upper Nile crisis, right was on his side. A resolute solution of the problem when the French had been caught on the wrong foot would rid him of the French bone in his throat and end once and for all the unjustified accusation of "graceful concessions." A firm stand against Belgium at Bahr-el-Ghazal and Equatoria would secure the inviolability of the Nile Valley and solve the Egyptian problem.

It is not surprising, therefore, that Salisbury displayed his usual obstinacy in the Upper Nile and took a calculated gamble. His actions were motivated by political considerations primarily domestic and personal. The dignity with which the French cabinet accepted their humiliation is praiseworthy. Certainly it was French commonsense which triumphed at Fashoda, not England's. Salisbury's speech announcing the recall of Marchand, and his subsequent admonition of his colleagues and the press to do more calculations and less talking, were in themselves an admission that Britain's conduct over the Fashoda crisis left much to be desired. He and the queen appeared to be the only two people in England who kept their sense of proportion.[7] But their hands were tied by public opinion which sincerely believed that France, by her unfriendly attitude toward England's imperial ventures, asked for, and got, what it deserved. It was, indeed what one London paper called "Homemade Humiliation."[8] Salisbury, consistently derided for his supposed "graceful concessions," found himself in an impossible position. Having initially assumed a resolute attitude, he turned the Fashoda incident—quite unwittingly—from one of rightful ownership to title to one of national honor. France swallowed its pride. And war was averted. Salisbury did not prevent the war. Delcasse did. That was why the British foreign secretary saw no joy in victory. He was "a peace minister condemned by the perplexities of the time to live under the shadow of war."[9] M. de Staal, not always a reliable observer, nevertheless saw the situation clearly. The queen wrote in her *Journal*:

> M. de Staal spoke very sensibly, as he always does: lamented over the imprudence of the French, and said Lord Salisbury had been placed in such a difficult position, owing to the extraordinary feeling of unanimity in this country on the Fashoda affair, which had prevented his giving [way] at all, to facilitate matters.[10]

"Lord Salisbury is a Classic"

After Delcasse had ordered Marchand's recall, he carefully avoided alluding to Anglo-French relations either in the Nile Valley or elsewhere.[11] The French, initially, tended to forget the whole affair. Salisbury's Mansion House speech was well received; but they still waited anxiously for the major speech at the Lord Mayor's Banquet on November 9.[12] This was to be the famous "Dying Nations Speech."[13] It descended on the French with a bang. Those who believed that England was bent on humiliating France concluded that their worst fears had been justified. In their fury they seemed not to have cared that Salisbury had also come decidedly against annexing Egypt. Monson wrote excitedly to his chief:

> I think I may say that you have established a funk here: and the French had received a very considerable shock. . . .
> Your speech has frightened people here. At first, I am told, there was a disposition to assume that among the "nations en decadence" you meant to include France; but reflection, and study of the context, have corrected this misapprehension.[14]

But only in some quarters. Monson explained in an official dispatch:

> There is no doubt that this country has been intimidated by the attitude of England. Frenchmen had not realized what their position would be if their neighbour across the Channel whom they had been used to flout with comparative impunity suddenly gave them to understand that the limit of toleration had been reached. . . .
> They had . . . counted upon the support of an ally [Russia] who, I cannot myself doubt, led them on up to a certain point with words of encouragement, and then explained that she had nothing at this moment at their service but sympathy.
> France appears to be staggered, and in consequence calls herself humiliated. I should like to think that the feeling of resentment will be transitory, but the contrary is, I fear the more likely.[15]

The speech, in fact, got a mixed reception in French newspapers, most of which were suspicious of Salisbury's intentions. The *Petit Journal* feared "the simple opportunism" of his attitude which made him more dangerous than Chamberlain despite the fact that the former "renounces the idea of using the Fashoda incident as the pretext for an immediate war." The *Matin* believed that the armament of which Salisbury talked about was directed against France. The *Evenement* sniffed "a sour smell of fog" from the speech. And the *Radical* said that Salisbury had a modest triumph over a British audience "exalted enough to demand the proclamation of a Protectorate over Egypt." But Blowitz, *The*

Times celebrated Paris correspondent, quoted a friend of his—a French statesman, "who, although not now in office, has held office in the past and may hold office again"—as saying:

> Lord Salisbury is a classic. It was not for nothing that he was the coadjutor, the friend, perhaps the disciple, of Disraeli. He knows it is necessary to act on the imagination of peoples, that oracles were listened to with respect and credulity which were not always evoked by utterances that were clear, and that stones carved in the form of the Sphinx outnumber those erected to the god of the Sun. He delivered a speech, therefore, that is positively Sibylline.[16]

Certainly Salisbury did not intend to include France among the category of *nations en decadence*; but the speech was poorly timed. The bitterness of the Colonial party against Britain was intensified. Openly they began to agitate for a Franco-German anti-British colonial alliance.[17] The rampant chauvinism of the English press tended to make matters worse. As Monson pointed out, the French press was moderate in comparison.[18] But Delcasse was very upset by England's attitude. He carefully avoided any allusion to the Marchand mission, and his demeanor was "one of significant taciturnity."[19] Monson was worried. The "patronising tone now adopted in public in England," he complained, "which virtually amounts to a pedagogue lecture to a flogged schoolboy—let this be a lesson to you not to be naughty again, is likely to exasperate the French." He was, however, convinced that the French government would "not throw out the Niger Convention, and that it will be passed by the Chamber *sub silentio*."[20]

How did Salisbury handle this new situation? We saw that between November and December he had made three speeches—all intended to reassure France of England's good intentions—but without much luck. Fashoda, like Egypt before it, stood in the way. Fashoda may have practically solved the Egyptian problem; but it certainly had created a new problem for European peace. Salisbury's immediate reaction showed that he anticipated trouble. He wrote to the Defence Committee:

> I am directed by the Marquess of Salisbury to inform you that, in view of the possibility of a war between this country and France, he had had under his consideration the question of the position, in such an eventuality, of the East Africa Protectorates under the administration of this Department, which have a seaboard, namely, the East Africa Protectorates itself, and that of Zanzibar, including the island of Pemba.

Salisbury wished to know if it would be possible, or desirable, during war, and in accordance with articles 10 and 11 of the Berlin Act, to place these Protectorates "under the rule of neutrality."[21] Once more, Salisbury had shown that he had no use for the East Africa base strategy as a positive act of policy. It would certainly have been odd for the man credited with the acquisition of East Africa purely for its strategic value to advocate such a course. Indeed, the committee quickly pointed out to him that to declare these territories neutral would be to the positive advantage of France in wartime. Furthermore, though there was little military disadvantage in neutralizing Zanzibar and Pemba, in accordance with article 11 of the Berlin Act, such a course would deprive England of the ports of "Mombasa and Kismayu as bases for warlike operations."[22]

In a particularly difficult interview with Courcel the magnitude of French indignation was brought home to Salisbury. The French ambassador, his old friend, "was in a very bad temper, and tried to get up a wrangle," he noted. "He kept constantly throwing down challenges to me which I as constantly refused to pick up."[23] This interview concerned the territorial delimitations which were to follow in the wake of Marchand's evacuation. But Salisbury observed:

> My impression is that we can hardly touch the matter again till Marchand is well out of the premises. Then I think we must make a serious effort to ascertain what territories were under the Khedive, and what were under the Khalifa—if there were any differences between the two categories [?]: and also some reliable account of the watershed between [the] Nile and [the] Congo, and the upper portions of the affluents of the Nile. This information, when we have it, may enable us to ascertain (1) what we have a right to on the Egyptian theory. (2) What we have a right to on the Common Conquest theory. (3) What sort of rights of occupation the French have any where established: and (4) what portions of the country it is worth our while to take.
>
> We have been so anxious to establish our position against the French, that we have half pledged ourselves to liabilities which will furnish subjects of penitent reflection to the Treasuries both of England and of Egypt. But till all this information is obtained and assimilated I do not see that we can enter upon any useful negotiations with the French. For the present the crisis has terminated favourably.[24]

So indeed it had. But there had been no significant change in Salisbury's standpoint. Marchand must leave "the premises," and sufficient information must be gathered, before any negotiations could take place. This would necessarily take some time and France would have to be patient. It had no choice. Indeed, Frenchmen believed that since England had won a significant victory over Fashoda, France was honor bound to evacuate its posts in the Bahr-el-Ghazal since refusal to do so might result in a war it was ill-prepared to fight. France, they said, "must resign herself to the fact that England's navy is incomparably superior to her own." Moreover, "France cannot pretend to face at the same time the German army and the English navy without ruining herself."[25] But as a seasoned diplomat was to remark: "she is steadily ruining herself."[26] Nevertheless, Fashoda had taught France to take stock of its position. A report on the estimates of the Ministry of Foreign Affairs revealed this. The report frankly accepted that the firmness of the English tone had caused the recall of Marchand. France preferred peace to war. "It was not the fault of our diplomacy," it insisted, "that the interests of France were not better safeguarded!" but because for twenty-eight years French military preparations were mainly directed toward the war of revenge. They did not foresee dangerous situations arising from the colonial sphere. In the future, France must coordinate its foreign and colonial policies more effectively. This would involve a better understanding between the foreign and colonial departments. "It must be understood also," it concluded, "that the relations between France and other Powers must unavoidably be influenced by events which have their origins in the necessities of Colonial policy. . . ."[27] Salisbury realized this development a decade before France. That was one of the reasons he had kept a firm control over imperial affairs, especially in the trouble spots of Africa. And that helped him to win the decisive victory at Fashoda.

In December M. Paul Cambon replaced the experienced and highly respected Baron de Courcel as French ambassador to the Court of St. James. During his ambassadorship, Courcel had maintained an especially close relationship with Salisbury. But unlike the latter, he had little knowledge of African affairs. This always placed him at a disadvantage in their discussions. In matters concerning the principles of high diplomacy, however, he showed such mastery and delicate professionalism as was perhaps unequalled by any diplomat of his day. When the baron decided to retire from the diplomatic service Delcasse found it difficult to get a worthy successor. It was even rumored that Hanotaux was in the running. But at last Delcasse settled for Cambon, generally regarded as an Anglophile. Salisbury had his reservations about the new man. In 1897 he had described Cambon as "an evil influence" when am-

bassador to the Porte.[28] Salisbury did not live to see the Entente
Cordiale; but Cambon's behavior between December 1898 and
March 1899, at any rate, seemed to have justified the prime minister's assessment of him. Ostensibly he was all that he was supposed
to be; but his private dispatches home show that either he was not
an Anglophile after all, or he had little confidence in the good faith
of England not to spring a surprise attack on France.[29] Perhaps
historians are simply unfair to Cambon. England's failure to de-
mobilize[30] even after Marchand had left Fashoda on December 11 certainly justified Cambon's fears. Salisbury's explanations
for failing to do this were most unconvincing.[31] On March 15,
1899, Salisbury himself admitted that Cambon was worried by the
deteriorating relations between England and France to the point
of fearing a war.[32] Delcasse, too, was so impressed by this fear that
he considered it necessary to warn Monson that a French naval
defeat by England would not necessarily mean the end of
France.[33] From France also there were reports of defensive war
preparations.[34] In England, the Admiralty, unprepared to relax
their military readiness,[35] forced Salisbury to go along with them.
The truth therefore was that neither Delcasse nor Salisbury wanted
a war. But the mutual suspicion between French and British "war
lords," as well as the exaggerated reports of their respective ambassadors, made vigilance and preparedness essential for national
safety.

Cambon's initial interviews with Salisbury dealt with generalities. The Fashoda affair did not crop up. The first of these was held
at Windsor Castle where, in Salisbury's words, "he gave me a very
interesting lecture on French philosophy during the last two centuries"; the second took place in London where Cambon dwelt on
"a full explanation of the difference between the principles of
French and English colonial administration."[36] But on January 11
Cambon formally communicated the evacuation of Fashoda to
Salisbury. This presented a good opportunity to discuss Anglo-
French differences in the Upper Nile. Cambon brought up the
question and Salisbury was willing to discuss it. But "I thought it
better at once to say that there was one point upon which opinion
in England was very strongly and steadily fixed," the prime minister explained, "and that was the objection of this country to share
with France political rights over any portion of the valley of the
Nile."[37] Since this was what Cambon wanted to discuss, Salisbury
was in effect asking him to retreat on this point before anything
was said. Indeed, he made it plain that England would not "recognize any rights of France over any part of the territory situated

upon the eastern slope of the watershed between the Nile and the Ubanghi." He would however grant France commercial outlet on the Nile, not as a favor, but on the principle of normal policy. The outlet "must be commercial, not political"; and "no part of it could be under the French flag." Cambon did not question these observations and left the impression that "the French had abandoned the idea of asking that their flag should float in any part of the valley of the Nile." Cambon, however, was only interested in the delimitation of the territories to the north and northwest of the Bahr-el-Ghazal, most of which, he claimed was ownerless. He contended "that a line could be found, starting from the southeastern end of Tunis, passing to the east of Lake Chad, leaving Darfur to Egypt, and then separating the Bahr-el-Ghazal from the Ubanghi." He also observed, and Salisbury assented, that "the extravagant protectionist policy" of France which, however, "was visibly slackening," was the main cause of the strained relationship between England and France.[38] This conversation went according to pattern. Once more, it was all take and no give on Salisbury's part. But at least the discussions had begun.

The details of these negotiations are not of paramount interest to us.[39] But the Anglo-French Declaration of March 21, 1899, is important for several reasons. It sealed the settlement of the Egyptian question. It shows that Salisbury never for once weakened in his resolve to establish British mastery in the Nile Valley. The reason for seeking this mastery is of course an open question. But as he saw it the whole thing was part of the process which the fin de siècle imperialism of European powers had brought about. If anyone must be master of the Nile Valley at all, then it must be England. It possessed the better right to title in that region than any other power. This claim may be right or wrong; but that was how he saw it, and most of his countrymen agreed with him. The agreement also demonstrates a lack of ambiguity of attitude in Salisbury's handling of territorial delimitations in Africa. Once he had got what he considered important he was inclined not to bother about the rest. The same was true in East and West Africa. His reasoning was simple and based on practical, and not ideological, considerations: in the scramble for Africa, Britain got the lion's share. It was therefore undesirable to ruin any prospect of a peaceful settlement by insisting on the possession of territories with, at any rate, no ostensibly important values; or if the title to which could not be reasonably established. Moreover, besides the obvious accusation of greediness which would be leveled at it, and the international and internal dangers that would arise therefrom, Britain might run the danger of overtaxing the strength of its empire.[40] This was a commonsense argument. That he held such a view did not necessarily make him an antiimperialist at heart—which would be an absurd thesis considering his role in the partition of Africa— as contemporaries like Morley, Labouchere, and Stead never tired of pointing out—a view which hitherto had not been suppressed as it ought to have been. Contemporary critics, infuriated by Chamberlain's so-called *volte face* in joining the Tories, went to absurd lengths to get even with the colonial secretary. It became fashionable for opposition journals—the *Westminster Cartoons* being the most bizarre example—to portray Salisbury as a cosy and innocent little Englander at heart, being bamboozled and dragged along into the dangerous pathways of imperial expansion in Africa by "Brummagen Joe" to some, by the "Columbus of Birmingham" to Labouchere, and by "Josephus Africanus" to his admirers. The validity of these views, born out of political jealousy, has never been tested or even questioned. Chamberlain may have had the acquisitive propensity of a magpie; but to make him the sacrificial lamb of British imperialism is unfair. He did not become colonial secretary until 1895. A decade before that he had been constantly in the political wilderness. During the same period, both under Salisbury and Rosebery, large tracts of territory had been added to the British empire. Indeed, the so-called "stock-jobbing imperialism" of the late nineties was nothing more than a consolidationist imperialism of a new kind, based as it were, on the pacification or delimitation of claims already broadly established. And as we saw in West and East Africa, and now in the Sudan, Salisbury was far from following Chamberlain's lead in dealing with these imperial questions. Outwardly, Salisbury might appear quiet and retiring, and oftentimes gave the impression of being uninterested in what went on. But this would not be a correct assessment of the man himself. True, he was a compromiser by nature, and was convinced that compromise was the essence of diplomacy. He conducted European diplomacy in the same fashion in which he ran his household and his cabinet. To him the same principle, within reasonable limits, applied. When this much is said, Salisbury also combined these characteristics of serenity and easy-goingness with an imperious and obstinate nature which often puzzled his critics. In 1886 Randolph Churchill became too officious and was humorlessly allowed to axe himself; in 1898 the French were equally humorlessly allowed to humiliate themselves. Compromise, in his view, was not weakness. But compromise was not limitless. His contemporary critics were shocked at his resolution during the

Fashoda crisis. The French, as Monson pointed out, were simply "staggered."

Salisbury's compromising propensity once more became apparent after he had secured the mastery he sought for in the Nile Valley. Hicks-Beach also appeared to be getting over his earlier bellicosity. He wrote to Salisbury:

> . . . how far up the Nile Valley are we to claim against the French? We have, I believe, recognized the Congo State at Regaf & Lado. Is there any reason why we should not admit the French to some point on the Nile between us & the Congo State?—perhaps at Meshra-er-Rek, which, if the Sirdar's gunboat has occupied it, might thus be exchanged for Fashoda. . . .
> I suppose, also, that the Nile navigation would be free.[41]

Cromer, on the other hand, appeared to have acquired more appetite for territories during the Fashoda crisis. He rejected any suggestion to maintain the status quo in the Upper Nile. He was quick to remind Salisbury that if the French really wanted a *debouche sur le Nil* after the evacuation of Fashoda, "they have only to stay where they are and they will have attained their object" since "they hold the greater part of the Bahr-el-Ghazal Province and have established posts on the principal affluents of the Nile." But he admitted that Britain was in a position to throttle French trade, "supposing there to be any trade to throttle, which is not certain," "unless they come to terms with us." He added:

> It may be an open question of what "the valley of the Nile," over which we claim authority consists, but it can hardly with reason be said to be limited to a short distance from the banks of the main stream; from the point of view of physical geography, the term may more reasonably be held to comprise those portions of the Bahr-el-Ghazal Province now occupied by the French. . . .
> I hold very strongly that, if we accept anything less than the Ubanghi watershed as our frontier, we should insist on a valid *quid pro quo* in return for our concession.

At the same time, he urged Salisbury to insist, following the precedent established by the French themselves in Tunis, "that we should be no longer hampered by all the vexations and obsolete restrictions by which we are at present bound." The moment to be blunt with them was ripe because there was little doubt of the general drift of English opinion. It may be that it is inclined to go rather far in the direction of insistence on British claims & views; but, however this may be, it seems a pity not to utilize the favourable breeze in order to get the ship more or less to harbour. It seems also pretty certain that if a question of war—though personally I disbelieve in the French fighting—we are stronger than they. Would it not be advisable to take advantage of such an exceptionally favourable combination of affairs?[42]

Earlier Cromer and Kitchener had demanded that Britain should secure all the territories running from Darfur to Lake Chad,[43] which in effect meant the isolation of the French Congo from French West and North Africa.[44] Salisbury rejected the demand.[45] But in December Cromer pressed him to keep two objectives in view in any discussion with Cambon: first, to find a formula which would rid the Sudan of internationalism, the bane of Egypt; and second, "to devise a plan which will give some legal sanction to legislative and administrative measures. If these two problems are solved I do not much care about the rest." Nevertheless, it would be necessary to determine the geographical extent of the Nile Valley. And even if England was not interested in a particular territory, it should be careful to choose its neighbor. If, for example, the warlike Dinkas came under French influence, they would likely organize a formidable force which would give England infinite trouble.[46] Meanwhile the negotiations progressed slowly. And in February Cromer suggested that Wadai should be secured as a buffer state.[47] Salisbury dissented:

> I do not see how we can make out a case for demanding Wadai. It certainly is not in the valley of the Nile: it cannot be treated as part of the road from Darfur to Sokoto, because the agreement of last June[48] giving the North, East, & South shores of Lake Chad to France cuts across any such communication. The Senoussi [?] argument will hardly stand alone. The French might as well claim that all Roman Catholic countries ought to belong to France. On the other hand the claim that the whole of Darfur shall belong to Egypt is clearly sound: and Cambon knows that we shall insist on it. I agree with you that North of Lat.15° we have no great interest in the question of territory. Cambon presses that instead of the watershed or crest of the Gibestan mountains, which according to the general principle we should follow, we should follow the North-Eastern foot of them. I do not at present see that we have much interest in that question. I hope we can so phrase our

assent to this part of the delimitation as not to hurt the feelings of the Sultan, whose dominion over Tripoli is a great deal
more real than his dominion over Egypt: and therefore we
should not interfere with his hinterland more than we can
help. It would be better also not to offend the Italians—whose
claim is simply grotesque.[49]

Compare this dispatch with the series of exchanges with Chamberlain toward the final stages of the Niger Convention. The parallel
is unmistakable. It demonstrates the same sense of notions of undoubted rights, of shady claims, of compromise and of proportion,
which can be easily misinterpreted, but which always guided him
in making decisions. As in West Africa, he had made no major concessions to France, but he had refrained from pursuing shady
claims. Cromer, in fact, did not want Wadai; but he objected to the
French having it either.[50] Nevertheless, Salisbury advised him to
"be moderate, for if your demands are excessive we may find it
hard to defend our frontiers both on the spot and in Parliament."[51]

The Sudan Convention business was transacted by the Foreign
Office with little or no interference from outside. Chamberlain,
who had been indisposed since January, did not participate in the
issues referred to the cabinet, though he was kept abreast with
developments by Lord James of Hereford. Even when he resumed
his duties he felt too weak and depressed to bother about the
Sudan.[52] And until the convention was signed Salisbury constantly
maintained that England would not share the Nile Valley with any
other power.[53] The ease and swiftness with which this arrangement was concluded baffled British Military Intelligence.[54] But it
is known that Salisbury had warned Cambon on March 20 that he
was leaving for Nice.[55] This must have hastened the agreement.

In the "Chamberlain Papers" there is a memorandum on the
Sudan Convention credited to Salisbury, and dated March 22,
1899, a day after the agreement was signed. Why he felt the need
to write such a memorandum is not clear. In it he argued a case for
the retention of the whole of Darfur if the French got Wadai.[56] It
is probable that Chamberlain may have had objections to aspects
of the convention.

At Delcasse's request the Sudan Convention of March 21, 1899,
was officially regarded as a declaration annexed to the Niger Convention of June 14, 1898.[57] He adopted this procedure so as to en-
sure its passage through the French Chambers.[58] This Declaration
insured beyond doubt England's mastery of the Nile, and curiously
enough, helped to make possible the *Entente Cordiale.* From the
start Salisbury knew what he wanted and finally succeeded in get-

ting it. He summed up the result of his labors: "It keeps the French entirely out of the Nile and restores to Egypt the province of Darfur."[59]

After March 1899, Anglo-French relations remained very cool for awhile. There is no evidence to suggest that France nurtured a revenge; but Delcasse was no longer able to work closely with Monson. He studiously kept aloof and said as little as possible.[60] And when he did speak, it was to represent England as the guilty party in the territorial disputes with France[61]—an accusation which Salisbury vehemently objected to. "I am rather impressed with the impudence of Delcasse," he wrote, "in representing us as the guilty parties in refusing a settlement of the smaller controversies that separated the two nations." If he raised the question again Monson was instructed to remind him of how France had invaded Madagascar "& excluded our commerce" despite a solemn undertaking not to do so. France also had urged England to abolish its Consular Courts, "undertaking to do the same for us at Zanzibar; but when we, somewhat weakly, allowed the abolition of the Courts at Madagascar she had laughed to scorn our request that she would do the same at Zanzibar." In West Africa it had refused to go to arbitration; in Siam it had made "persistent efforts to drive the Siamese into a war by extravagant claims to set up rights of protection." Now, having been so consistently beastly to England, "they have nothing to urge but our hesitation to grant them two favours to which they have no real right whatever. I suppose we shall have Hanotaux back before the year is out. The change will not be for the better."[62]

For the first time Salisbury had spelled out in detail his grievances against France. And he made sure that Delcasse got the message. Obviously, he had all along been very hurt by the nagging accusations of "graceful concessions" in Madagascar, Tunis, Siam, and West Africa. Was Fashoda and Bahr-el-Ghazal therefore a calculated revenge, or merely a determination not to allow the Upper Nile to become another Madagascar, Tunis, Siam, and West Africa? This is an open question, but it has an element of truth in it.

Repercussions of the Congo Treaty of May 12, 1894

The Bahr-el-Ghazal province was generally accepted to be that enormous region in the west of the Sudan with features like a right-angled triangle, though irregularly shaped. It was well-watered and fertile. On the north it was comprised by the Bahr-el-Arab and Bahr-el-Ghazal rivers; on the east by the White Nile between its junction with the Bahr-el-Ghazal and the Albert Nyanza;[63] and on the southwest by the Nile-Congo watershed.

The first European governor, under the Egyptian government of this province was the Italian, Gessi Pasha. He rid the place of slave dealers, and in 1878 suppressed the revolt of Zuberhr Pasha's son, Suliman, making his camp Dem Suliman (Dem Zubehr) into the capital of the province. On Gessi's death in 1881 he was succeeded by (Frank) Lupton Bey, a one time captain in the Red Sea merchant trade. A year later Mahdism first spread into this area. It started first at Liffi and by the end of 1882 had engulfed the whole province. In 1884 the Bahr-el-Ghazal surrendered to the Mahdi, thus signifying the end of the Turkiya in that region.

The equatorial province stretched from the Albert Nyanza to Lado, its capital. In 1879 this region was placed under the charge of Emin Bey[64] by Gordon. And by the end of 1882 it was the only region still out of sympathy with the Mahdist cause. Nevertheless, it soon was forced to follow the example of the others, and Emin managed to switch position from being Gordon's governor of Equatoria to being the Mahdi's captive governor of Darfur for twelve years.

This was the position when, on May 24, 1890, the so-called Mackinnon Treaty granted to Leopold II sovereign rights in the region around the Bahr-el-Ghazal. In the same year the Congo state decided to send Captain Van Kerckhoven on a commercial expedition to the Equatorial province. The expedition set out from Stanley Pool toward the middle of February 1891; by July 1892 its history had become obscure. But by September Kerckhoven was reported to be on the Nile.[65] Indignant protests in the English papers against the action of the "Congo filibusters in the British sphere of influence" followed hot on this news. But Kerckhoven indeed did not reach the Nile; nor did any member of his expedition.[66] In any case, Leopold claimed that the Agreement of 1890 also conferred on him sovereign rights in the Nile Basin. This claim was repudiated in turn by Salisbury and Rosebery. Indeed, they both refused to recognize the treaty as binding on the British government.[67] Subsequent French activities in the Nile Valley, however, were to force Rosebery to renew, as it were, the treaty which he had found unacceptable. The result was the Anglo-Congolese Agreement of May 12, 1894. It was signed at Brussels by the representatives of the British government and the Congo state. Rosebery made sure that notes were exchanged to state categorically "that the parties to the agreement do not ignore the claims of Turkey and Egypt in the Basin of the Nile."[68] Leopold, in fact, had only a leasehold of these territories during his lifetime.[69] Right from the beginning a combination of circumstances made it impossible for Leopold to exercise his rights in these territories. Toward the end of 1894 the Belgians were reported to be in the Bahr-el-Ghazal, where they were frantically collecting treaties from the leaders of Taimo. The khalifa, on hearing of these activities, sent a strong force in October 1894 to reoccupy the province. The Belgians withdrew, deserting the chief of Taimo, Sheikh Hamed, who in turn sided with the Dervishes and handed over to them the treaties he had made with the Belgians. France and Germany, too, realizing the implications of the Congo Treaty, made it impossible for Leopold to utilize the greater part of the territories leased to him. Nor did Leopold's attempt in 1896 and 1897 to consolidate his hold on these territories prove successful. During these years two expeditions, under Dhanis and Chaltin, organized piecemeal in three columns, were dispatched by the Congo state toward the Nile but achieved no practical results. The position was that, by 1898, the Congo state could boast only of a precarious footing on the Nile at Regaf.[70]

Now, after the evacuation of Marchand from Fashoda, the Belgian king resurrected his hitherto dormant rights under the Congo Treaty—thus presenting Salisbury with a new problem. With the Dervishes broken, Leopold's troops were able to occupy effectively certain places in the Upper Nile. These included Regaf, Kero, Lado, and Wadelai. They also infiltrated into certain territories further north. When Salisbury protested to Brussels against these activities, Leopold simply replied that the Congo Treaty was, as far as he was concerned, still valid. Salisbury did not altogether reject this assertion. Indeed, Monson was informed that the treaty still was operative.[71] At this time also, a handful of Abyssinian, Russian, and French explorers began to intensify their activities in these regions. In June or July 1898 an Abyssinian force led by a Russian, and probably more than one French, officer had been reported to have arrived at the mouth of the Sobat and to have planted a flag there. French steamers also had brought three months' provisions destined for Fashoda. Enclosed in an iron barge, the provisions included one small cannon. In fact the French had already established a fort at Meshar-er-Rek, and three on the Souch River. They were however believed to have established none on the Bahr-el-Arab or the Bahr-el-Ghazal. But indications pointed to the fact that they were attempting to join hands with Marchand at Fashoda. Salisbury had already taken steps to make this impossible. Moreover, the flag they had planted at the junction of the Bahr-el-Ghazal and the Bahr-el-Gebel had been unceremoniously removed by the Dervishes; but they could still obtain supplies at Meshra-er-Rek from the Jang country, with whom they had concluded treaties.[72]

These activities really did not threaten the British position; and after Marchand's recall they became even less important; but the fear that the French might join hands with the Belgians to cause trouble gave cause for further anxiety. And early in 1899 Chamberlain suggested the possibility of compensating France in the Bahr-el-Ghazal in return for their allowing England a free hand in Newfoundland.[73] Apparently Salisbury rejected the suggestion for two reasons: he had no wish to share the Nile Valley with France: and second, he considered the Congo Treaty still operative. Already the *Independence Belge* and the *Petit Bleu* had published letters purported to have been inspired by Leopold, recommending the handing over of the Bahr-el-Ghazal to the Congo state as the best means of solving Anglo-French differences. It was also claimed that Salisbury had already consented to concede Bor to Leopold.[74] This was followed by an article in the *Fortnightly Review* urging that the dispute should be handed over to boundary experts.[75]

Salisbury did not view any of these suggestions favorably. In April 1899 he produced a memorandum of his own on the Congo Treaty. He began by frankly admitting its validity, but he also confessed that "the case is undoubtedly complicated," and that though Britain had neither repudiated nor invalidated the treaty, "many things have happened since it was signed." He went on:

> The avowed consideration for the lease was the strip from Tanganyika to Nyanza; but there were two other considerations, which for obvious reasons could not be formally mentioned. The French threatened the Bahr-el-Ghazal from the west; the Dervishes held their hands on it from the north. The lease was given to the Congo State in order that they might keep out the one and the other from the Valley of the Upper Nile for us; but the Congo State gave us no such considerations. Under the threats of Germany, they failed to convey us the strip. Under the threats of France, they promised not to occupy the Bahr-el-Ghazal; and consequently, they became perfectly useless for the purpose of repelling the Dervishes. We have lost our strip altogether; we have had to move the French out of the Bahr-el-Ghazal ourselves; and we have had to destroy the power of the Dervishes ourselves. While the French and the Dervishes were in occupation, the Congo Govt. said nothing of the lease, and made no effect to occupy; but now that the cost and peril of removing both France and Dervishes has been assumed by us, then the Congo State, after five years of silence, bethinks itself of the lease; and asks that we shall give it what we have won, free from all the obstacles by which in 1894 it was beset. This can hardly be.

Because of these considerations, Salisbury argued, the treaty would be modified but not invalidated. The matter would be closely studied and more information gathered before negotiations would begin. The negotiators, when the time came, would bear two things in mind: first, that in 1894 Egypt exercised only a dormant right in the Bahr-el-Ghazal. To have done otherwise would have been "a physical impossibility" at the time. But these rights "have been revived at our cost and by our action. We have the right, which we shall surely exercise." The negotiators would therefore "insist on the reservation of the rights of Egypt made in the Convention." Second, Leopold, "purely for his own convenience, and without any sanction from us," had chosen not to exercise his treaty rights, thereby avoiding "heavy responsibilities." "It is clearly our right to imitate him," he concluded, "and defer for a similar period giving any effect to the Convention, so long as it is convenient to us to do so. Therefore, there is no hurry in coming to any decision."[76]

Here, as indeed in the entire Sudan question, Salisbury was convinced that he had a watertight case and that right was on his side. Lansdowne's view of the dispute was more accurate. He said: "I wish we had taken the point in 1894 that the lease *by* us of the Bahr-el-Ghazal region and the lease *to* us of the 25 Kilometre strip were interdependent. The omission I fear weakens the argument now, althou' it does not destroy its force."[77] Salisbury also was aware that the balance of power was to his advantage. Therefore, the Congo threat could be ignored especially as an arrangement had been reached with France. No one seriously believed that the Congo state could achieve what France had failed to do. Britain was master of the Nile and would make sure that Leopold did not get too ambitious. But the dispute dragged on until 1906 when Britain was obliged, under a Liberal government, to cut the Congo state's communication with the Nile, and thus brought the wily Leopold to heel. Nevertheless, the king of the Belgians was still astute enough to salvage the so-called "Lado Enclave."

The Status of the Sudan: Argument for Conjugate Sovereignty
We saw earlier that Hicks-Beach tended to treat the Sudan venture as a business transaction and had steadfastly fought against the expenditure of English money without receiving an adequate quid pro quo.[78] He had not objected to the advance on the ground of principles. He had made his position clear to Salisbury as early as 1896: "If . . . the Powers would not allow Egypt to use her money in reconquering her lost provinces," he had asked, "why should H. M. Govt. hand over the provinces to Egypt if conquered by British

taxpayers' money & troops?"[79] This was a very valid point as he proceeded to explain:

> I feel sure that the H. of C. would not so much mind paying, if we announced that we should hold and administer the Soudan, or any part of it, until Egypt could pay the cost of its recovery. And surely it would be a strong position to take up against French policy: for we should be forced into it by their hostility, and it would really rest with them to terminate it.

Unless this was done, he warned that the Commons would strongly oppose the lending of £500,000 to Egypt should the *Caisse* suit be lost.[80] As we saw earlier, too, the idea of putting a mortage on the Sudan had been preached and accepted among the financial experts in Egypt. Salisbury's attitude was noncommittal. But when he authorized further advance in 1897 Dawkins saw a glimmer of light. "What is most significant in Lord Salisbury's telegram, & wherein I think I see the result of your teaching," he wrote to Milner, "is a parting injunction not to 'use any form of phrase which may imply that Dongola is part of Egypt.' This is very good, and is thoroughly accepted by Cromer & Palmer."[81] But when eventually the *Caisse* suit went against England, he was forced to the conclusion that, because of international complications, it would be impracticable for England to seize the Sudan for itself.[82] Hicks-Beach, however, was not so sure. He required Milner's opinion and received the comforting reply:

> My own view is that the ulterior effects of that decision are much exaggerated by the Press. [It would, he believed], leave things pretty much where they were. . . .
> As regards Dongola, it is quite clear that it was never one of the Assigned Provinces, that is to say the Provinces, the taxes of which are directly payable to the Caisse. Though I never had any doubt on the point, I have looked it up, & you may take this as absolutely certain.
> It follows that the Egyptian Government may play ducks & drakes with the revenue of Dongola, & of all the other Sudanese Provinces as much as it pleases. The Caisse has no sort of control over them. . . . [He therefore advocated the] starting of a separate Sudan Budget . . . kept entirely distinct from the Revenue & Expenditure of Egypt.[83]

Armed with this assurance, Beach asked for authorization to state in Parliament "that Dongola is held by H.M. Govt. as a pledge for any money which they advance."[84] But Salisbury, fearing khedival objections and international complications, referred the matter to Cromer. He wanted to know how the Egyptian government would react to such an announcement; whether or not the original decree pledged Dongola to the bondholders, and, ipso facto, to the *Caisse*; and supposing Dongola was so pledged, but Britain was to argue that the decree was annulled by the abandonment of Dongola in 1883, "has anyone, except the *Caisse*, a right to dispute our ruling?"[85] He was, in any case, convinced that Britain could always "paralyse the action of the *Caisse*, having regard to the recent Judgement."[86] Cromer replied that (1) he feared the opposition of the khedive but not that of the Egyptian ministers. But he advised that they ought to be consulted before hand; (2) no decree ever pledged the Sudanese revenue to the bondholders; and (3) he feared it was a mistake to suppose that Britain could always paralyze the *Caisse*'s action. And though he concurred in Beach's proposal, he nevertheless was opposed to it purely on diplomatic and political grounds: France would resent such an announcement and nobody could foresee what action she would take as a result. He concurred with it only on the ground that he was convinced that France and Russia had no intention of raising the Egyptian question. "Should it be considered that I am wrong in assuming this much," he concluded, "it becomes more doubtful whether the adoption of such a policy is advisable."[87]

Hicks-Beach was therefore temporarily overruled. But once it became pretty certain that Khartoum would be captured by the autumn of 1898, Cromer and Salisbury gradually reverted to his ideas. In May, 1898 Salisbury quietly reminded Abbas II that England had "acquired by conquest complete control over the action of the Govt. of the Khedive [and] cannot allow that control to be disputed."[88] In June Cromer assented to Salisbury's proposal that "we might advantageously hoist the two flags[89] together as a useful means of pressure pending a settlement." Cromer, however, admitted "that if we can obtain all we practically want without a radical change of the political station of the Soudan, this will perhaps be the best policy to adopt, although there are some obvious attractions in the alternative project." But he also recognized that "the alternative project"—the Egyptian administration of the Sudan— would be a great financial burden unless England could be called upon to help.[90] A day later he made his position clearer in a private letter. He requested that a parliamentary announcement was necessary to the effect "that, in consideration of the military and financial sacrifices we have made, we reserve complete liberty of action as regards the future of the Soudan."[91] Salisbury still objected to a public announcement. He wrote:

> I do not think that Parliamentary announcement would be wise. It would produce a storm of questions and accusations, which would possibly rouse French feeling, and might provoke some other Power to blackmail us. I should deprecate any public announcement till Sirdar is inside Khartoum.[92]

Earlier, he had intimated to Cromer "that we may soon be at the parting of the ways in Soudan affairs, and that our general lines of policy may have to be shifted"; and Cromer, in reply, had suggested two solutions: one was the separation of the Sudan from Egypt; and the other was the governing of the two countries as one.[93]

In July Cromer arrived in London bringing with him a lengthy memorandum dealing with the future of the Sudan. He expected to return to Egypt by September and was anxious to have the cabinet's decision on the subject. He urged them to take into account, before coming to any decision, the effect of their policy on local Egyptian feeling. He conceded that evacuation of Egypt was out of the question and that this meant continuous khedival opposition to English rule. The only way to counteract his influence—usually based on "appeals made to sentiments of race hatred and religious fanaticism"—was to raise the material prosperity of the common people. And in pursuance of this course, he was "very anxious to revert as soon as may be to a policy of fiscal reform which still affords a wide scope for action." And as to the Sudan, he knew that many difficulties existed in relation to the adoption of a forward policy; but he deprecated any "halting mid-way in the execution of our Soudan policy." The future was uncertain; there might be trouble with Menelek; caution was therefore essential and the reoccupation of territories should be limited to those absolutely necessary for the execution of general policy, in other words, to those "mainly to the banks of the White Nile and a portion of the Blue Nile." It would also be desirable to humor Abbas II by floating English and Egyptian flags side by side at Khartoum after its fall. This would be a temporary measure. "In reality," he continued, "the hoisting of the British flag would only give outward and visible expression to a *de facto* position which already exists." "The Khedive knows perfectly well that neither in Egypt nor in the Soudan can he take any important step without the consent of H.M. Govt." Menelek, he said, had already been asked to deal directly with Britain in

Egyptian matters. Nevertheless the two flag idea was necessary to bring

> the political theory into harmony with the realities of the situation. It would emphasize the fact that the Khedive is not free to act in the Soudan without the consent of his senior partner. It would afford a salutary warning to the Sultan, and it would be a clear indication to the French and the Abyssinians that the control of the Nile is more an English than an Egyptian question.[94]

There is no indication of how the cabinet reacted to these proposals which they examined on July 27. But it is generally assumed that they accepted the basic ideas. Indeed, on June 27 the Committee of Ways and Means had passed a government resolution which stated "that it is expedient that the grant-in-aid of £7,988,021 to the Government of the Khedive of Egypt should not be repaid."[95] Salisbury's generosity was by no means disinterested. He wanted to strengthen his hands in dealing with the anticipated difficulties with France, and possibly with the khedive, after the fall of Khartoum. But Abbas II was merely told that the decision was taken to help his government and on the understanding that they "would be able to provide for all [future] expenses connected with the prosecution of the Soudan expedition."[96] In July Salisbury showed his hand. In an important memorandum he made out a strong case for the establishment of a conjugate sovereignty in the Sudan. This was a revolutionary idea and had no precedent in international law. Consequently, he asked the lord chancellor, Lord Halsbury, to decide if there was "anything repugnant to the theory or practice of international law in this conjugate sovereignty."[97] Indeed, Salisbury's memorandum was a formalization and improvement of the arguments of Hicks-Beach and Cromer which we have been examining. Its originality, however, rests on the fact that he thought out the two flag idea, or in other words, conjugate sovereignty based on the right of conquest. He started by placing the chequered history of the Sudan in perspective. He admitted the Mahdi's victories of the early eighties had caused the disappearance of the Egyptian flag in the Sudan. The position then was that

> The Soudan was conquered, *and by the avowal of the Egyptian Government itself had ceased to form part of Egypt.* Hence therefore all the rights and liabilities, in whomsoever vested, which had been borne, and continued to be borne, by Egypt, no longer weighed upon the Soudan.

Thirteen years have passed away and the fortune of arms has been reversed. The Khalifa's capital is, we hope, about to pass into the hands of the Anglo-Egyptian army. It will pass by the right of conquest.

The conquered territories "should pass without limitation or reservation" to the victors. But in the peculiar case under consideration, who would properly be called the victors? England or Egypt, or both? He admitted that a legist would decide in favor of Egypt to dispose of the territories as it liked, but added:

I am only contending that such a disposal is not obligatory: that it is entirely at the discretion of *the actual conqueror*. For many reasons it would not be convenient to renew the Egyptian character of these formerly Egyptian provinces: for the task of governing Egypt under the manifold hindrances of its international obligations, drives the English advisers of the Khedive to despair.

To declare them to be conquered by Great Britain, and therefore to be a portion of the Queen's Empire, might be strictly agreeable to fact. But it would give great offence: it would be bitterly resented by the Moslem population, with the Khedive and the Sultan at its head: and it would involve responsibilities which a British government answerable to Parliament would not willingly undertake.

The only alternative would be that the reconquered country should be held, as it has been conquered, by the joint forces of Great Britain and of Egypt. The two flags would then float side by side: the duties of Govt. would be performed by both Govts. conjointly, acting in such a manner and through such organs as they should arrange by agreement between them: and presenting a conjoint individuality to Foreign Powers with whom they would communicate in the usual way. . . . There is no precedent for such an agreement. . . . But I think it would be popular in this country.

He knew that there would be objections to the theory, but it had also advantages; in any case, it would serve as a temporary measure till the attitude of England and of Europe generally to Egypt had been more accurately defined.[98]

The originality of this theory must have puzzled Halsbury's legal mind. He, however, dismissed Salisbury's argument as "inaccurately, or at all events inadequately stated" in terms of international law, because the rule did not apply to part of a territory, but to a state in its entirety. He explained:

I think it is untrue to say that the bare possession of a part of the territory of a State extinguished the character of that territory as forming a part of the territory from which it is withheld by the power of the sword. I think when the power of the sword is withdrawn the *status quo ante* revived with all its obligations and interests both public and private.[99]

In a subsequent judgment Halsbury admitted that there was nothing in international law to prevent the application of Salisbury's theory in the Sudan.[100]

On August 2 the substance of Salisbury's theory was formally communicated to the khedive.[101] And by November Cromer had completed a draft Anglo-Egyptian Agreement based on it, which he submitted to Salisbury.[102] The few alterations made on this original draft—alterations attributed to Kitchener—were intended to depreciate further the authority of the khedive.[103] But Salisbury and Cromer raised no objections and the final draft was signed on January 19, 1899.[104] This arrangement, better known as the *Condominium*, and described by Cromer as "a status hitherto unknown to the law of Europe,"[105] was indeed a curious bargain. It was the product of Salisbury's acute mind and compromising mentality which sounded well on paper, but did not work out in practice. Indeed, it could with justice be described as fraudulent since the powers of the khedive and the sultan were nominal. The "conjoint individuality" that Salisbury talked about logically presupposed an equal sharing of power. But this was not to be: and, in fact, was not intended to be so. However, the moral and legal aspects of the agreement do not concern us at present; and in any case, nobody challenged it at the time.[106] However, it must be admitted that Salisbury had flouted the authority of the Porte and the khedive with impunity. Indeed, before the agreement was signed he insisted that Egypt and the Sudan should be separated as far as possible: that the Sudan's governor general should take his orders directly from Cromer and should be warned against the dangers "of excessive centralization," because "Too great a centralization is . . . exposed to the danger of that mania for paper-piling, which is the endemic pest of British departments."[107] But Salisbury also did not wish the khedive to be too much involved in Sudanese affairs. In fact, Cromer admitted that the first article of the *Condominium* agreement was deliberately couched "in such a manner as to expressly exclude the recognition of Egyptian rights, except as regards such territories as might be reconquered by the combined action of the British and Egyptian Govts."[108] And on

January 20 Salisbury instructed Crawford[109] to inform Macdonald "that, as his expedition is purely British, it is preferable where possible to avoid hoisting the Egyptian flag in the districts where he visits."[110] The following day Kitchener was formally appointed the governor general of the Sudan and instructed to take his orders from Cromer and Salisbury, and to keep the former fully informed of developments in the Sudan.[111]

In the Sudan therefore one was not only confronted with the revolutionary idea of sovereignty but also with the absurd situation that while parts of the same country would be ruled by the so-called *Condominium*, other portions were ruled solely by England. Such a development did not make for unity. True, for obvious reasons neither Egypt nor the Sudan was directly annexed; but in both countries, especially in the latter, Britain maintained an authority which was as good as if they had been annexed. And this authority was maintained by force. This is interesting, for the Egyptian question, it has been written, "could not be solved by force; it could be solved only by compensation and good will," and it was not even solved by Fashoda.[112] Unless by the Egyptian question the writer meant something other than the undisputed and de facto British supremacy in Egypt and the Sudan, the Nile problem was solved neither by compensation nor by good will, but by force.

Notes

CHAPTER I

1. H. Maxwell, *Life and Letters of . . . the Fourth Earl of Clarendon* (London, 1913), 11, p. 359; Algernon Cecil, "Salisbury," in *British Foreign Secretaries* (London, 1927), p. 279.
2. Gwendolen Cecil's *Life of Robert, Marquis of Salisbury*, 4 vols. (London, 1921–23). Although she carries the story only to 1892, hers is still the best biography.
3. But he saw in W. E. Smith the supreme embodiment of this endowment. See Cecil, *Salisbury*, 4, p. 216.
4. Ibid., 1, p. 70; Arthur Bauman, *The Last Victorians* (London, 1927), p. 63.
5. A. J. P. Taylor, *From Napoleon to Stalin* (London, 1953), p. 122.
6. Lugard Papers, vol. 40 (Kirk), Sir John Kirk to Flora Shaw, Sept. 4, 1895 (Private).
7. Cecil, *Salisbury*, 2, p. 237.
8. For studies of life at Hatfield see Cecil, *Salisbury*, 1; A. S. (Alice Cecily Cecil), *Hatfield 1887, 1903*, typed and deposited in the Bodleian Library, 1964; Blanche E. C. Dugdale, *Family Homespun* (London, 1940); Viscountess Milner, *My Picture Gallery, 1886–1901* (London, 1951); Viscount Cecil of Chelmwood, *All the Way* (London, 1949); A. S., *A Memory, 1887–1947* (of J. E. H. Cecil, 4th Marquess of Salisbury, 1861–1947) (1950), private circulation, Bodleian Library, Oxford.
9. Dugdale, *Family Homespun*, p. 106.
10. Viscountess Milner, *Picture Gallery*, p. 79.
11. Ibid., pp. 41–42.
12. Ibid., p. 79.
13. Cecil, *Salisbury*, 1, p. 56; Cecil, *Biographical Studies of the Life and Political Character of Robert Third Marquis of Salisbury* (printed for private circulation), p. 49.
14. Lady St. Helier, *Memories of Fifty Years* (London, 1909), pp. 266–68.
15. Arthur Mee, *Lord Salisbury; The Record Premiership of Modern Times* (London, 1901), p. 101.
16. Lady Frances Balfour, *Ne Obliviscaris* (London, 1930), pp. 147–48.
17. Cecil, *Studies*, p. 20.
18. Viscountess Milner, *Picture Gallery*, p. 79.

19. Mee, *Salisbury,* p. 83.
20. Percy Colson, ed., *Lord Goschen and His Friends: The Goschen Letters* (London, 1946), pp. 97–99.
21. The Sudan is excluded because of its anomalous position.
22. H. J., and Hugh Massingham, eds., *The Great Victorians* (London, 1952) only grudgingly accepted him as one of the great Victorians, pp. 465–78.
23. *Westminster Gazette,* Aug. 24, 1903, editorial.
24. *Fortnightly Review,* 80 (Oct., 1903); "Lord Salisbury" by Sidney Low, pp. 562–75; cf. *Nineteenth Century and After,* 53 (Sept., 1903), no. 319, p. 524.
25. Rosebery at the Oxford Union Society, Nov. 14, 1904, in *Oxford Miscellaneous: Report of Proceedings and Speeches,* Bodleian, Oxon, no. 8715.
26. *National Review,* 2 (May, 1908), "The Late Duke of Devonshire," by Bernard Holland, citing Salisbury, p. 400.
27. The Earl of Midleton, *Records and Reactions, 1856–1939* (London, 1939), p. 108.
28. Salisbury to Devonshire, July 10, 1902, cited in full in Bernard Holland, *The Life of . . . Devonshire,* 2 vols. (London, 1911), 2, p. 279.
29. See *infra,* pp. 155–68.
30. Cecil, *Salisbury,* 2, p. 21.
31. See *Westminster Gazette,* July 5, 1895, "Lord Salisbury's Blazers"— leading article.
32. Cecil, *Studies,* p. 39.
33. *Review of Reviews,* 17 (1898), p. 228.
34. French ambassador to London of Anglo-French parentage.
35. Salisbury Papers (henceforth S.P.), 26 (to France, 1878–80), Salisbury to Lyons, Dec. 16, 1879, no. 66; see also S.P. 59 (to Paris, 1887–92), Salisbury to Same, Feb. 5, 1887, no. 63.
36. S.P. 64 (to Germany, 1887–92), Salisbury to Malet, Feb. 16, 1887, no. 2.
37. Ibid.
38. Marquess of Salisbury, *Essays—Foreign Politics 1861–1864* (London: J. Murray, 1905), p. 143; J. A. Spender, *The Public Life,* 2 vols. (London, 1925), 1, p. 46.
39. F.O. 800/17 (Lascelles Papers), Salisbury to Bertie, Dec. 4, 1895.
40. S.P. 64, Same to Same, Royat, Sept. 1, 1888, no. 32.
41. Ibid., Same to Same, Jan. 24, 1888, no. 17.
42. S.P. 59, Salisbury to Lytton, Sept. 23, 1890, no. 96.
43. Victor Morrier was the son of Sir Robert Morrier, H. M.'s ambassador to St. Petersburg. Victor was serving at this time as a member of the Boundary Delimitation Commission and kept his father informed of developments.
44. S.P. 74 (to and fro Russia, 1890–92), Salisbury to Morrier, Feb. 11, 1891, no. 91.
45. Frances Balfour, *Ne Obliviscaris,* p. 294.

46. He was Davy Cyssell, the Welshman, who had accompanied Henry VII to England, and from whom he probably inherited his dark complexion.

47. For Salisbury's diplomatic practice see Cecil, *Studies*, section 2; L. M. Penson, "The Principles and Methods of Lord Salisbury's Foreign Policy," in *Cambridge Historical Journal*, 5, no. 1 (1935); Penson, *Foreign Affairs Under the Third Marquess of Salisbury* (London, 1962); Penson, "The New Course in British Foreign Policy, 1892–1902," in *Transactions of the Royal Historical Society*, 4s., 25 (Mar., 1942); H. Temperley and L. Penson, eds., *Foundations of British Foreign Policy: From Pitt (1792) to Salisbury (1902)*, (Cambridge University Press, 1938), select documents; J. A. S. Grenville, *Lord Salisbury and Foreign Policy; the Close of the Nineteenth Century* (London, 1964), esp. pp. 11–23. Those interested in studying the question more deeply are referred to what are, in effect, Salisbury's blueprints for English foreign policy—(1) Marquess of Salisbury, *Essays—Foreign Politics 1861–1864* (London: J. Murray, 1905), esp. pp. 151–231; (2) Marquess of Salisbury, *Essays—Biographical, 1861–1864* (London: J. Murray, 1905).

48. S.P. 55 (to Egypt, 1887–92), Salisbury to Baring, Feb. 15, 1889, no. 41.

49. Ibid., Same to Same, Nov. 15, 1889, no. 49.

50. Ibid., Same to Same, Aug. 31, 1890, no. 58.

51. A good account of England's differences with Portugal (1889–91) is contained in Cecil, *Salisbury*, 4, pp. 257–76.

52. F.O. 84/1969, H. H. Johnston to Sir V. Lister, Apr. 5, 1889, cited in Roland Oliver, *The Missionary Factor in East Africa* (London, 1952), p. 125.

53. See Arthur Marsden, "Britain and the 'Tunis Base', 1894–99," in *E.H.R.*, 79 (Jan., 1964), no. 310, p. 86; C. W. Dilke, *The Present Position of European Politics*, cited in Stephen Gwynn, and G. M. Tuckwell, *The Life of . . . Sir Charles Dilke*, 2 vols. (London, 1918), 2, p. 245.

54. Salisbury, *Essays—Foreign Politics*, p. 155.

55. Ibid., p. 156.

56. F.O. 800/1 (Sanderson Papers), Salisbury's Minute to Sanderson, July 30, 1895.

57. S.P. 119 (to France, 1895–1900), Salisbury to Dufferin, July 26, 1895, no. I.

58. Cecil, *Studies*, p. 43.

59. Midleton, *Records and Reactions*, p. 106.

60. Dilke Papers, B.Mus.Add.Mss., 43944 (Foreign Affairs), note by Dilke; see also the *Liverpool Daily Post*, Dec. 2 and Dec. 5, 1898.

61. *The Times*, June 30, 1898. "Lord Salisbury on Foreign Affairs."

62. S.P. 119, Minute by Salisbury (n.d.).

63. Lord Newton, *Retrospection* (London, 1941), p. 34.

64. S. Gwynn, ed. *The Letters and Friendships of Sir Cecil Spring-Rice,*

1859–1918 (London, 1929), 1, Rice to Stephen; Oct. 30, 1898, p. 263.

65. Ibid., Same to Same, Mar. 21, 1896, pp. 202–3.
66. The Earl of Ronaldshay, *Life of Lord Curzon* (London, 1928), 1, Salisbury to Curzon, June 27, 1895, pp. 234–35.
67. Milner Papers, vol. 191, P. Gell to Milner, July 22, 1898 (Supl. Copy).
68. H. W. Lucy, *Later Peeps at Parliament*, "Smoking Room Confidences" (London, 1905), p. 133.
69. Ibid., p. 129.
70. Frances Balfour, *Ne Obliviscaris*, Lady Frances to G. S., Sept., 1894, p. 231.
71. Ronaldshay, *Curzon*, 1, Curzon to Salisbury, June 20, 1898, p. 251.
72. Midleton, *Records and Reactions*, pp. 105–7.
73. Viscountess Milner, *Picture Gallery*, p. 227.
74. Lucy, *Later Peeps at Parliament*, pp. 431-32.
75. *Fortnightly Review*, vol. 80 (Oct. 1903), p. 570.
76. See J. Gallagher, and R. Robinson, "The Imperialism of Free Trade," in *Economic History Review*, 2s., 6 (1953), no. 1, pp. 1 ff.
77. The term was invented by Dr. C. R. Fay, cf. *C.H.B.E.* (1940), 2, p. 399.
78. Cited J. R. M. Butler, "Imperial Questions in British Politics, 1868–1880," in *C.H.B.E.*, 3 (1959), p. 42.
79. Cecil, *Salisbury*, 2, p. 302.
80. S.P. 21 (Miscellaneous, 1878–80), Salisbury to Temple, Sept. 2, 1878 (private copy).
81. Ibid., Salisbury to Sir Stafford Northcote, Aug. 22, 1878 (private copy). He was referring to Asiatic Turkey.
82. S.P. 26, Salisbury to Lyons, August 10, 1878, no. 2.
83. Cited in Richard Koebner, "The Concept of Economic Imperialism," in *Economic History Review*, 2s., 2 (1949), no. 1, p. 25.
84. S.P. 26, Salisbury to Lyons, Nov. 12, 1879, no. 58.
85. D. A. Low, "The British and Uganda, 1862–1900" (Oxon Ph.D. thesis, 1957), pp. 105–7.
86. Cited in Edward Salmon, *The Marquis of Salisbury* (London, 1901), p. 73.
87. Sir Charles Dilke, *Problems of Greater Britain*, 2 (London, 1890), p. 172.
88. Cited in Viscount Chilston, *Chief Whip* (London, 1961), p. 126; T. P. O'Connor, *Memoirs of an Old Parliamentarian*, 2 vols., 2 (London, 1929), p. 120.
89. *Q.V.L.*, 3s., 1, p. 262; *C.H.B.E.* 3, p. 156.
90. C. W. Dilke, *The Present Position of European Politics* (London, 1897), p. 282.
91. Cited F. D. Lugard, *The Dual Mandate in British Tropical Africa* (Edinburgh & London, 1922), p. 13.

92. *Hansard*, 4s., 25, June 1, 1894, cols. 150–52; see also L. A. C. Raphael, *The Cape to Cairo Dream* (New York, 1936), p. 337.
93. Cecil, *Salisbury*, 4, p. 226.
94. Cited in full in Cecil, *Salisbury*, 4, pp. 225–26, 228.
95. See, for example, his last speech on imperial affairs at the Albert Hall, *The Times*, May 7, 1902; see *D.N.B.*, Second Supplement, 1, p. 340.

CHAPTER II

1. J. A. Hobson, *Imperialism: A Study* (London, 1902); V. I. Lenin, *Imperialism: The Highest Stage of Capitalism* (London, 1916).
2. For some of the most important of these theories see J. A. Hobson, *Imperialism: A Study;* V. I. Lenin, *Imperialism: The Highest Stage of Capitalism;* C. J. Hayes, *A Generation of Materialism, 1871–1900* (New York, 1941); Ronald Robinson and John Gallagher with Alice Denny, *Africa and the Victorians: The Official Mind of Imperialism* (London, 1961); Joseph A. Schumpeter, *Imperialism and Social Classes* (Harvard University Press, 1951), trans. by Heinz Norden and edited by Paul M. Sweezy.
3. For further details see G. N. Uzoigwe, *The Slave Trade and African Societies*, Monograph and Report Series, no. 3, 1971 (Center for Afro-American Studies, University of Michigan, Ann Arbor).
4. For further details see R. Robinson, J. Gallagher, and A. Denny, *Africa and the Victorians* (London, 1961); Gallagher and Robinson, "The Imperialism of Free Trade," *Economic History Review* 2d series, 6, p. 1 (1953); idem, "The Partition of Africa," *New Cambridge Modern History*, 11 (Cambridge University Press, 1962), chap. 22.
5. For a legal opinion on this subject see U. O. Umozurike, "International Law and Colonialism in Africa: A Critique," *East Africa Law Journal* 3, I (1970), pp. 47–82.
6. Cited in W. W. Rostow, *British Economy in the Nineteenth Century* (Oxford, 1948), p. 108.
7. Rostow, *British Economy*, 108 ff. has a useful section on "Economic Factors and Politics," esp. pp. 137–40.
8. *Nineteenth Century*, 45 (Greenwood, "The Cry for New Markets," Apr., 1899, no. 266), pp. 538–47.
9. Ibid., 38, see two articles on "New British Markets" by Holt S. Hallett, pp. 236–46, and C. E. D. Black, pp. 247–60, Aug., 1895, no. 222; and one by Lugard, Sept., 1895, no. 223, pp. 442–54.
10. J. L. Garvin, *The Life of Joseph Chamberlain*, 3 vols., 3 (London, 1932–34), pp. 448 ff., 465–67, 531–32; *Hansard*, 4s., 22 (Mar. 12, 1894), col. 102. For Britain's economic history in the nineteenth century the following works have been consulted: J. H. Clapham, *An*

Economic History of Modern Britain, 1887–1914 (Cambridge University Press, 1958); W. W. Rostow, *British Economy;* W. H. B. Court, *British Economic History 1870–1914* (Cambridge University Press, 1965); W. Ashworth, *An Economic History of England 1870–1939* (London, 1960); Henry Pelling, *Modern Britain* (London, 1960), pp. 14–29 esp.

11. Robinson, in *C.H.B.E.*, 3, p. 161.
12. Annual Report of London Chamber of Commerce, April 20, 1893, cited in F. D. Lugard, *The Rise of Our East African Empire*, 2 vols. (London, 1893), 1, p. 380.
13. *Hansard*, 4s., 36, Feb. 14, 1895, cols. 698–99; *Annual Register*, 1895, pp. 38–40; George Bennett, ed., *The Concept of Empire: Burke to Atlee 1774–1947* (London, 1953), pp. 311–13.
14. *The Times*, May 24, 1895.
15. Spender, *Life, Journalism, and Politics*, p. 79.
16. *Annual Register*, 1896, p. 205; cf. also Bennett, *Concept of Empire*, Nov. 25, 1896, p. 316.
17. *The Times*, Feb. 15, 1896.
18. Ibid., Sept. 16, 1896.
19. Ibid., Sept. 18, 1897.
20. Ibid., Sept. 13, 1898, "Economic Imperialism," leading article.
21. *Fortnightly Review,* vol. 70, E. R. Farraday, "Some Economic Aspects of the Imperial Idea" (A paper read before the economic section of the British Association, Sept. 9, 1898), Dec., 1898, pp. 961–67.
22. *P.M.G.*, July 5, 1899, editorial, "Why We Seek Tropical Colonies."
23. F. D. Lugard, *The Dual Mandate in British Tropical Africa* (London, 1922), 43–47; cf. also Lugard, *Rise of E. African Empire*, 1, pp. 381–82.
24. Sir Henry Johnston, *The Story of My Life* (London, 1923), p. 241, reporting interview with Chamberlain.
25. M. Paul Leroy Beaulieu, the political economist.
26. *The Times,* July 29, Aug. 13 and 15, 1898. Benjamin Kidd, "The Control of the Tropics."
27. Enclosure in Chamberlain Papers (henceforth, J.C.P.), Charles Marston, "Mr. Chamberlain's Scheme of Preferential Tariffs: An Address to the Members of the Wolverhampton Literary Club on October 6, 1903," p. 5.
28. D. C. Paige et al., "Economic Growth: the Last Hundred Years," in *Economic Review*, July 1, 1961, p. 35, cited in Court, *British Economic History*, pp. 3–17; see also Ashworth, *An Economic History*, pp. 3–24; Rostow, *British Economy*, pp. 20–24.
29. Court, *British Economic History*, pp. 3–17.
30. See *Edinburgh Review*, vol. 182, no. 373, July, 1895 for a review of these Commissions, pp. 1–26; cf. Court, *British Economic History*, pp. 17–32. For a discussion on the Agricultural depression see F. A. Channing, *The Truth about Agricultural Depression* (London, 1897);

and for a good analysis of the Great Depression, see Rostow, *British Economy,* pp. 58–89, 145–60, 180–221.

31. *Annual Register,* 1895, 119–20.
32. Pelling, *Modern Britain,* p. 14.
33. Ashworth, *An Economic History,* pp. 138–62. For discussion on foreign competition see P. T. Moon, *Imperialism and World Politics* (New York, 1927), 25–28; Marston, "Mr. Chamberlain's Scheme," pp. 3–14; *Nineteenth Century,* 40, Sir Frederick Young, "Commercial Union of the Empire," July, 1896, no. 233, pp. 27–33; ibid., 45, J. W. Cross, "British Trade in 1898: A Warning Note," May, 1898, no. 267, pp. 850–56; *Contemporary Review,* 76, Ritortus, "The Imperialism of British Trade," (i) July, 1899, no. 403, pp. 132–52; (ii) Aug., 1899, no. 404, pp. 282–304; *Monthly Review,* 6, J. H. Schooling, "British Commerce, 1881–1900," Jan., 1902. no. 16, pp. 40–58; *Times,* May 24, 1895; ibid., Sept. 16, 1896, "Foreign Trade"; and ibid., Sept. 15, 1897, "British Trade and Foreign Competition"; Clapham, *An Economic History,* pp. 1–71; Berard, *British Imperialism,* pp. 62 ff.; G. D. H. Cole, *A Short History of British Working-Class Movement 1789–1947* (London, 1947), pp. 224–28.
34. Ashworth, *An Economic History,* p. 139.
35. Marston, "Mr. Chamberlain's Scheme," p. 6; Pelling, *Modern Britain,* pp. 14–15.
36. Clapham, *An Economic History,* p. 37.
37. Marston, "Mr. Chamberlain's Scheme," p. 6: Pelling, *Modern Britain,* pp. 14–15.
38. These statistics are enclosed in Milner Papers, vol. 442; "Memorandum on British and Foreign Trade and Industry, 1903" (Cd. 1761), 403 ff.
39. *Contemporary Review,* 80, Feb., 1899, no. 398, pp. 218–22.
40. *The Times,* Sept. 13, 1898, "Economic Imperialism," leading article; ibid., Feb. 15, 1896, "The Commercial Value of Africa," p. 15.
41. *National Review,* 43, L. J. Maxse, "Cobden and Cobdenism," July, 1904, pp. 861–70.
42. Marston, "Mr. Chamberlain's Scheme," pp. 9–11.
43. Milner Papers, vol. 442, "Memorandum on British and Foreign Trade and Industry, 1903" (Cd. 1761), Summary I, p. 16. Table showing distribution of (*a*) exports of all British produce; (*b*) exports of manufactured and partly manufactured articles among principal protected, and other countries and colonies.
44. Milner Papers, vol. 442, Summary I, p. 16.
45. *Contemporary Review,* 74, Lord Farrer, Dec., 1898, no. 396, pp. 810–36.
46. Ibid., 75, Feb., 1899, no. 398, pp. 218–22.
47. Ibid., 74, J. A. Hobson, "Free Trade and Foreign Policy," Aug., 1898, no. 392, pp. 167–80; cf. J. A. Hobson, *Imperialism: A Study,* 3d. ed. (London, 1938), pp. 28–40. Compare his analysis with the official

charts and statistics cited in this study. See also *Contemporary Review*, 72, M. G. Mulhall, "The Trade of the British Colonies," Nov., 1897, pp. 697–708.

48. Milner Papers, vol. 190, Benjamin Kidd to Milner, pp. 15, 16, 20, Jan., 1896.

49. Cited in Marston, "Mr. Chamberlain's Scheme," p. 6. This was a pretty high percentage out of a population of around thirty-seven million.

50. *National Review*, 45, Apr., 1905, no. 266, p. 320.

51. Ashworth, *An Economic History*, p. 3.

52. See *The Times*, May 24, 1895; ibid., 2, Mar., 1897; ibid., June 19, 1897.

53. *The Times*, June 19, 1897.

54. *Fortnightly Review*, 80, Oct., 1903, p. 569; H. D. Trail, *The Marquis of Salisbury*, 2d ed. (London, 1892), pp. 110–11.

55. S.P. (*Quarterly Review* articles) Apr., 1865, no. 234, pp. 540–74.

56. Cecil, *Studies*, p. 86; "Negotiation and Retaliation: The view of the late Lord Salisbury," N.U. no. 297, 1904 (Publication of the Conservative Central Office). It reviews Salisbury's speeches from 1879 to prove that he was a retaliationist, and quotes a letter by Lord Robert Cecil to *The Times* (Jan. 13, 1904) supporting this view.

57. F. A. Channing, *Memories of Midland Politics, 1885–1910* (London, 1918), p. 38.

CHAPTER III

1. *Quarterly Review*, 156, "Disintegration," credited to Salisbury, no. 312, Oct., 1883, pp. 562–65, 595.

2. Baumann, *Last Victorians*, p. 127, citing Salisbury.

3. R. C. K. Ensor, "Some Political and Economic Interactions in Later Victorian England" in *Trans. R. Hist. Soc.*, 4s, 31 (1948), pp. 26–27.

4. Algernon Cecil, *Queen Victoria and Her Prime Ministers* (London, 1953), p. 334; C. Cecil, *Salisbury*, 5 (draft), p. 5. This unpublished volume is deposited at Christ Church Library, Oxford. It is not a finished work.

5. *The Times*, May 10, 1900; cf. *National Review*, 24 (Feb., 1895), no. 144, pp. 771–82.

6. *Annual Register*, 1899, p. 94.

7. *The Times*, May 10, 1900.

8. S.P. (Sec.'s Note Bk., 1881–87), June 28, 1883.

9. Ibid., Aug. 27, 1883.

10. Ibid., Feb. 14–16, 1884.

11. Ibid., Salisbury to Lord Mayor, Sept. 10, 1885.

12. Ibid. (Sec.'s Note Bk., 1887–93), Salisbury to Mr. Arnold White, Feb. 15, 1887 (confidential).

13. *Q.V.L.*, 3s., 1, p. 169.
14. Cited in R. Robinson in *C.H.B.E.*, 3, p. 168.
15. H. H. Johnston, *The Story of My Life* (London, 1923), p. 218.
16. Ibid., p. 241.
17. Ibid., p. 221.
18. R. Oliver, *Sir Harry Johnston and the Scramble for Africa* (London, 1957), p. 141.
19. *The Times*, June 30 and Nov. 15, 1898; May 10, 1900. Spender, *The Life of . . . Sir Henry Campbell-Bannerman* (London, 1923), 2 vols., 1, pp. 257–58; *Contemporary Review*, 68, Percy A. Hurd, "The New Imperialism," Aug., 1895, pp. 171–83.
20. J. A. Spender, *Life, Journalism and Politics*, 2 vols. (London, 1927), 1, pp. 78–79.
21. Neil Malcolm, "On Service in the Uganda Protectorate," *Blackwood's Magazine*, 166, Nov., 1899, no. 1009, p. 631.
22. M. Victor Berard, *British Imperialism and Commercial Supremacy* (London, 1906), p. 42.
23. B. Webb, *Our Partnership* (London, 1948), p. 140.
24. Kennedy Jones, *Fleet Street and Downing Street* (London, 1920), p. 105.
25. Thomson, *England in the Nineteenth Century, 1815–1914* (London, 1964), p. 188.
26. Ernest Barker, *Political Thought in England* (London, 1915), pp. 146, 185–86; cf. G. M. Young, *Victorian England: Portrait of an Age*, 2d. ed. (Oxford University Press, 1960), p. 177.
27. Phillip Guedalla, *Mr. Churchill: A Portrait* (London, 1941), p. 31; Spender, *Life, Journalism and Politics*, p. 74.
28. The practical result of these Acts was that two million voters were added to the existing three million. For details, see Richard and Hunt, *Modern Britain*, p. 228, or any other good text book.
29. *Commerce*, Aug. 28, 1895, editorial.
30. The early Winston Churchill would fit well into this category.
31. Cited in Terence Ranger, "The Last Word on Rhodes?", in *Past and Present*, July, 1964, no. 28, p. 120.
32. The king of Benin was said to have been "taken round in irons by Sir Ralph Moore and exhibited at Brass and elsewhere," Lugard Papers, vol. 41 (Kirk), Sir John Kirk to Lugard (n.d.).
33. Ibid.
34. A. L. Kennedy, *Old Diplomacy and New 1876–1922: From Salisbury to Lloyd-George* (London, 1922), p. 84. It will be noted that, after Fashoda, confidence in the government returned as the bye-election results testified, *Annual Register*, 1899, p. 3.
35. Cf. "The Evolution of Joseph Chamberlain," in *Spectator*, July 3, 1936, p. 7; or as Chamberlain put it: "It is not I that change, but circumstances"; cited in *Westminster Gazette*, July 22, 1895, p. 2.
36. Cf. Publications of the Conservative Central Office, Sept., 1897, no. 37; *Pall Mall Gazette*, July 8, 1895; cf. also *The Times*, Jan. 17,

1895; *Pall Mall Gazette,* July 2 and 8, 1895; *Standard,* July 5, 1895; *Morning Post,* July 8, 1895; *St. James's Gazette,* July 16, 1895; *Colonies and India,* July 20, 1895.

37. *The Times,* Jan. 18, 1895, Campbell-Bannerman at Greenwich.

38. S.P. 138 (to Turkey, 1895–1900), Salisbury to Currie, July 27, 1895, no. 4. He wrote: "The elections are a great surprise. Our most trusted prophets did not venture far beyond fifty. . . ."; Cecil, *Salisbury,* 5 (draft), p. 31.

39. J.C.P. (Heresford), Chamberlain to Lord James of Heresford July 18, 1895.

40. Cf., for example, A. G. Gardiner, *The Life of Sir William Harcourt,* 2 vols. (London, 1923), 2, p. 367. *Contemporary Review,* 74, Aug., 1898, no. 392, pp. 290–96; *Quarterly Review,* 182, Oct., 1895, no. 364, pp. 538–67; *Nineteenth Century,* 38, 1895, no. 81, p. 119; *Blackwood's Magazine,* 158, July, 1895, no. 957, pp. 146–56; *Pall Mall Gazette,* Nov. 13, 1895.

41. Cited in *Nineteenth Century,* 38, Aug., 1895, no. 222, p. 181.

42. Ibid., pp. 177–87.

43. *Pall Mall Gazette,* Aug. 3, 1895, editorial.

44. Ibid., Aug. 15, 1895, "A Battle Bleat," editorial citing *Daily News.*

45. *National Review,* 24, Dec., 1894, no. 142, p. 456.

46. Maccoby, *English Radicalism,* p. 198.

47. Ibid. For similar conclusions see Elie Halevy, *Imperialism and the Rise of Labour, 1895–1905* (London, 2d ed. 1951), p. 7; *E.H.R.,* 81, J. P. D. Dunbabin, "Parliamentary Elections in Great Britain, 1858–1900: A Psephological Note" (a general survey, not detailed), Jan., 1966, no. 318, pp. 92–99.

48. *Quarterly Review,* 182, "The New House of Commons: The Triumph of Conservatism" (survey carried by the *Pall Mall Gazette* Office), 1895, no. 364, pp. 538–67.

49. S. Maccoby, *English Radicalism, 1886–1914* (London, n.d.), p. 205.

50. *Pall Mall Gazette,* July 31, 1895, "In Explanation of Victory by an 'Independent Inquirer'."

51. See, for example, Halevy, *Imperialism,* p. 4.

52. *Quarterly Review,* 182. Oct., 1895, no. 364, p. 542.

53. Ibid., 185, Jan., 1897, no. 369, pp. 269–93; *Blackwood's Magazine* 158, July, 1895, no. 957, pp. 137–45.

54. *National Review,* 36, Jan. 1901, pp. 735–44; cf. also Spender, *Life of Bannerman,* 1, p. 294. Bannerman whose majority was slashed to 630 confessed that "Glasgow is damnable"; Blanche Dugdale, *Arthur James Balfour, First Earl of Balfour: 1848–1905* (London, 1939), p. 236.

55. In Wales the Unionists won eight seats as against two in 1892.

56. Dugdale, *Arthur Balfour,* p. 236.

57. *National Observer,* July 20, 1895, encl. in J.C.P. (Vol. 4/9, Colonial Policy, 1895–97).

58. The Liberal landslide of 1906 demonstrated that they could and did.

59. *Quarterly Review,* 189, Jan., 1899, no. 377, pp. 241–65.
60. S.P. (Balfour), Balfour to Salisbury, Jan. 5, 1901.
61. F.O. 800/145 (Lansdowne Papers), Salisbury to Lansdowne, Sept. 1, 1900 (private).
62. See, for example, Baumann, *Last Victorians,* pp. 77–80; Lucy, *Diary of Salisbury Parliament 1886–1892,* p. 419; How, *Salisbury,* p. 300.
63. *Quarterly Review,* 189, Jan., 1899, no. 377, p. 248.
64. See Barbara W. Tuchman, *The Proud Tower: A Portrait of the World Before the War, 1890–1914* (New York, 1966), p. 4.
65. *Fortnightly Review,* 64, H. D. Trail, "Lord Salisbury's Triumph," Sept., 1895, p. 359.
66. G. M. Young, *Arthur James Balfour* (London, 1963), p. 169.
67. Cf. *Nineteenth Century,* 46, Sir Wemyss Reid, "The Newspapers," Nov., 1899, no. 273, p. 848.
68. Kennedy Jones, *Fleet Street and Downing Street,* p. 106, citing Professor Saintsbury.
69. R. A. Scott-James, *The Influence of the Press* (London, 1913), p. 216.
70. Kennedy Jones, *Fleet Street,* pp. 106–7.
71. Scott-James, *Influence,* pp. 26–43.
72. Kennedy Jones, *Fleet Street,* p. 289.
73. Ibid., pp. 96–97, 146, 150.
74. *The Times,* Sept. 24, 1900, or any other daily.
75. S.P. (Middleton), Middleton to Schonberg MacDonell, May 1, 1896.
76. Sometimes some of these politicians wrote the leading articles in their favorite papers.
77. Scott-James, *Influence,* pp. 211–13.
78. Ibid., p. 320.
79. Cf. Kennedy Jones, *Fleet Street,* pp. 289 ff.; Scott-James, *Influence,* p. 28.
80. Dugdale, *Balfour,* p. 158. The personal attacks on Chamberlain by the *Standard* and the *New Review* just before the 1895 election nearly drove him into premature retirement, see Devonshire Papers, pp. 340, 2607; Devonshire to Chamberlain, Apr. 17, 1895, 340, 2608; Chamberlain to Devonshire, Apr. 19, 1895.
81. The Earl of Oxford and Asquith, *Memories and Reflections 1852–1927,* 2 vols. (London, 1928), 2, p. 233.
82. S.P. 101 (Misc., R-S, 1895–1900), Rawless to Salisbury, Jan. 5, 1899 and Minutes by Broderick, no. 2; Barrington to Rawless, Jan. 10, 1899 (copy and private), no. 4.
83. Asquith, *Memories and Reflections,* 2, p. 236, citing Spender.
84. S.P. (Victoria), Salisbury to the Queen, Dec. 19, 1895, Tel.
85. S.P. 100 (Misc., M-P, 1895–1900), Malet to Salisbury, Nov. 15, 1898, no. 20, encl. speech by duke of Bedford, Malet's brother-in-law, no. 21.
86. *Quarterly Review,* 96, Oct., 1902, no. 392, p. 655.

87. *The Times*, Aug. 24, 1903.
88. *Quarterly Review*, 156, Oct., 1883, no. 312, p. 567, *G.D.D.*, 1, Count Herbert Bismarck to Prince Bismarck, 4, Mar. 22, 1889, pp. 374, 404–5.
89. Spender, *Public Life*, 1, p. 78.
90. See Chilston, *Chief Whip*, p. 52; Cecil, *Studies*, pp. 25–27; Young, *Victorian England*, p. 134.
91. Kennedy, *Salisbury*, p. 349.
92. For details, see Oliver, *Missionary Factor*, p. 126.
93. S.P. 51, Salisbury to Wolff, Feb. 23, 1887 (private), no. 149; Cecil, *Salisbury*, 4, pp. 41–42; cf. S.P. 64, Salisbury to Malet, Feb. 16, 1887, no. 2.
94. S.P. 55, Salisbury to Baring, Dec. 28, 1888 (private), no. 37.
95. S.P. 74, Salisbury to Morrier, Jan. 19, 1887 (private), no. 50.
96. Cited in Mee, *Salisbury*, p. 25.
97. *Hansard*, 78, Jan. 30, 1900, col. 28.
98. *The Times*, Aug. 2, 1895, cf. *Maccoby, English Radicalism*, pp. 226–27, 277.
99. *Edinburgh Review*, 182, Oct., 1895, no. 374, p. 525.
100. *The Times*, Nov. 20, 1895.
101. *Fortnightly Review*, 66, Oct., 1896, pp. 602–14.
102. *Nineteenth Century*, 37, June 1895, no. 220, pp. 1027–35. For the position of the Irish parties see O'Connor, *Memoirs of an old Parliamentarian, op. cit;* T. M. Healy, *Letters and Leaders of my Day* (London, 1928) in two vols. Important source material for the Irish struggle; F. S. L. Lyons, *The Irish Parliamentary Party, 1890–1910* (1951).
103. Succeeded Rosebery as Liberal leader in the Lords in 1896.
104. Dilke Papers, B.Mus.Add.Mss. 43941, Nov. 4, 1896; see also *Hansard*, 4s., 75, July 28, 1899, cols. 661, pp. 652–53; ibid., 45, Feb. 8, 1897, col. 22; ibid., 53, Feb. 8, 1898, cols. 23 and 32; ibid., 66, Feb. 7, 1899, col. 18; ibid., Feb. 8, 1898, col. 23; 45, Feb. 8, 1897, col. 22.
105. See Campbell-Bannerman Papers, B.Mus.Add.Mss 41224, Ripon to Bannerman, Sept. 30, 1899. Same to Same, June 2, 1900 (private); Same to Same, Oct. 26, 1900 (private); cf. Bannerman to Ripon, Oct. 8, 1899, Oct. 27, 1899, June 1, 1900 (private), Oct. 29, 1900, (private), and Nov. 7, 1900 (secret).
106. *National Review*, 24, Dec., 1894, no. 142, pp. 454–56; cf. the introduction to Roy Jenkin's *Mr. Balfour's Poodle* (London, 1954), where he analyzes the relative strength of the parties in the Lords.
107. Mee, *Salisbury*, p. 24.
108. Ibid.
109. Lucy, *Peeps at Parliament*, p. 117.
110. Asquith, *Fifty Years of Parliament*, 1, p. 50. For discussions of jingoism see *National Review*, 32, Jan., 1899, no. 191, pp. 631–41; *The Times*, Jan., 1899, 18, 19, 20, for the celebrated Morley-Cham-

berlain debate on the meanings of jingoism and little Englandism.
G. P. Gooch, "Imperialism," in Charles Masterman, ed., *The Heart of the Empire* (London, 1901), pp. 301–11.

111. An extreme example of the nature of jingoism of this period was that of Mr. J. E. A. Sergeant, a solicitor practicing at Alford, who wrote to Salisbury advocating the partition of France—"Giving to Belgium a slice—Britain to have again, her domain—her provinces—Italy also a slice." F.O. 83/1367, Sergeant to Salisbury, Sept. 3, 1895 (private). He did not receive an acknowledgment of his letter.

112. H. W. Lucy, *A Diary of the Unionist Parliament 1895–1900* (London, 1901), pp. 45, 145; cf. Baumann, *Last Victorians*, pp. 262–65; O'Connor, *Memories*, 2, 74–79; Wolff, *Rambling Recollections* (London, 1908), 2, p. 113; *South Wales Daily News*, Aug. 27, 1897, editorial.

113. Gwynn and Tuckwell, *Charles Dilke*, 2, p. 256.

114. "Imperium et Libertas," said Winston Churchill, "is the motto of the Primrose League, and it may also be the motto of Progressive Toryism," R. Churchill, *Winston S. Churchill*, 1 (London, 1966), p. 408.

115. Crane Brinton, *English Political Thought in the Nineteenth Century* (London, 1933), p. 146.

116. F.O. 800/148 (Curzon Papers), Mr. Neville Bruce to Curzon, Apr. 21, 1898.

117. S.P. (Palmer), Selborne to Salisbury, Oct. 11, 1895.

118. Barotseland (Loziland).

119. F.O. 800/176 (Bertie Papers), Cecil Rhodes to Bertie (?) July, 1899.

120. See *Nineteenth Century*, 45, no. 263, pp. 10–19; cf. Spender, *Campbell-Bannerman*, 1, pp. 224, 257–58.

121. *Edinburgh Review*, 192, Oct., 1900, no. 394, pp. 537–38.

122. See *Review of Reviews*, 17, Jan.–June, 1898, pp. 222–35.

123. Mee, *Salisbury*, p. 39; W. Brook Smith, *"Lord Salisbury"* in *Makers of Modern Britain* series (London, 1903), no pages; *Daily Telegraph*, July 14, 1902; *Fortnightly Review*, 80, Oct., 1903, pp. 574–75; Salmon, *Salisbury*, pp. 74–75, 82–83; Mee, *Salisbury*, p. 40; *Quarterly Review*, 96, no. 392, p. 656; *Daily Telegraph*, Aug. 24, 1903.

124. *The Times*, July 16, 1902; *Ibid.*, July 14, 1902.

125. Mee, *Salisbury*, p. 39.

126. F.O. 83/1379, encl. *Hansard*, 4s., 34, June 13, 1895, col. 1103.

127. J. A. Spender and Cyril Asquith, *Life of Lord Oxford and Asquith*, 2 vols. (London, 1932), 1, pp. 141, 146; *Annual Register*, 1899, p. 2; J. L. Hammond, "Colonial and Foreign Policy" in *Liberalism and the Empire* (London, 1900), 161–71; Bullock and Maurice Shock, ed., *The Liberal Tradition: From Fox to Keynes* (London, 1956), p. 233; *Annual Register*, 1897, pp. 205–6; Richard Burdon Haldane, *An Autobiography* (London, 1929), p. 93.

128. See Robert Rhodes James, *Rosebery: A Biography* . . . (London, 1963), p. 284.; Elizabeth Langford, *Victoria R. I.* (London, 1964), p. 566.; Viscount Morley, *Recollection*, 2 vols. (London, 1917), 2, pp. 88–89; *Annual Register*, 1900, pp. 161–65. On Nov. 6, 1900, *The Times* estimated the Lib. Imps. to be around 81 M. Ps.

129. Asquith, *Fifty Years*, 1, p. 270; Bennett, *Concept of Empire*, pp. 326–27; Hobson, *Imperialism*, p. 234; James, *Rosebery*, p. 418; Campbell-Bannerman Papers, B.Mus.Add.Mss., 41218, Bannerman to Grey, Nov. 19, 1900 (private); cf. ibid., Grey to Bannerman, Nov. 17, 1900 (private).

130. See Channing, *Midland Politics*, p. 177; James, *Rosebery*, p. 410; Spender, *Life, Journalism & Politics*, 1, p. 56; Horace G. Hutchinson, ed., *Private Diaries of Sir Algernon West* (London, 1922), 315; 332; Morley, *Recollections*, 2, p. 891; *Blackwood's Magazine*, 166, Aug., 1899, no. 1006, p. 304.

131. For a useful discussion on the various opinions on the empire in the later nineties see A. F. Madden, "Changing Attitudes and Widening Responsibilities, 1895–1914" in *C.H.B.E.*, 3, pp. 339–54.

132. *Edinburgh Review*, 192, no. 393, July, 1900, p. 247.

133. See Peter Fraser, *Joseph Chamberlain: Radicalism and Empire, 1868–1914* (London, 1966), 14; *Review of Reviews*, 21, Jan.–June, 1900, p. 443; Gwynn and Tuckwell, *Charles Dilke*, 2, p. 310; Haldane, *Autobiography*, 3; *P.M.G.*, Jan. 26, 1899; *Daily News*, May 10, 1900; Gardiner, *Harcourt*, 2, pp. 27–30; *Hansard*, 4s., 40, May 8, 1896, col. 964; Goldwin Smith, *Reminiscences* (N.Y., 1910); *Contemporary Review*, 67, Goldwin Smith, "The Manchester School," pp. 377–89; C. A. Bodelsen, *Studies in Mid-Victorian Imperialism* (N.Y., 1925); J. A. Marriot, *Modern England 1885–1939*, 2d ed. (1941), p. 109; Campbell-Bannerman, *House of Commons*, Dec. 6, 1900.

134. S.P. (*Quarterly Review* articles), Jan., 1863, no. 12.

135. Haldane, *Autobiography*, pp. 94–100; Asquith, *Fifty Years*, 1, pp. 219–22; W. S. Blunt, *My Diaries* . . . *1888–1914*, 2 vols. (London, *1918–19*), 1, p. 399. Dilke Papers, B.Mus.Add.Mss., 43941, "Memoirs," Jan. 29, 1893; Campbell-Bannerman Papers, 41224, Bannerman to Ripon, Oct. 29, 1900 (private); F.O. 800/6 (Lascelles Papers), F. H. Villiers to Lascelles, Jan., 1896 (private). *C.H.B.E.*, 3, Robinson, loc. cit., p. 132; *Hansard*, 4s., 37, Feb. 28, 1896, col. 1406 (Labouchere); ibid., 38, Mar. 3, 1896, col. 802; Spender, *Life, Journalism, Politics*, 1, p. 56; Spender, *Great Britain, Empire.* . . . , p. 119; Dilke Papers, 43916, Hyndman to Dilke Feb. 9, 1899. *Hansard*, 4s., 40, May 8, 1896, col. 958, James, *Rosebery*, p. 403; West, *Diaries*, p. 332.

136. See Midleton, *Records and Reactions*, p. 105; Asquith, *Fifty Years*, 1, pp. 270–71; Brinton, op. cit., p. 146; *C.H.B.E.*, 3, p. 341; W. F. Monypenny, *The Empire and the Century* (London, 1905), pp. 5–

6; *Blackwood's Magazine*, 164, July, 1898, no. 993, p. 161; Spender, *Britain, Empire, Commonwealth*, p. 81; Balfour, *Ne Obliviscaris*, Lady Salisbury to Frances Balfour, Nov. 26, 1895, p. 271; James, *Rosebery*, 256. *Pall Mall Gazette*, Oct. 23, 1900; F.O. 633/II, Cromer to Morley, Aug. 26, 1902; Chilston, *Chief Whip*, pp. 86–87.

137. Thomson, *England in the Nineteenth Century*, p. 157; Frank Hardie, *The Political Influence of Queen Victoria, 1861–1901*, 2d ed. (Oxford University Press, 1938); E. F. Benson, *Queen Victoria* (London, 1935); Long, *Victoria R. I.*, op. cit.; R. J. Evans, *The Victorian Age, 1815–1914* (London, 1950), p. 354.

138. A. P. Newton, *A Hundred Years of the British Empire* (London, 1940), p. 245.

139. See Evans, *Victorian Age*, p. 362; Hardie, *Political Influence*, p. 174; Gardiner, *Harcourt*, p. 198; Balfour Papers, B.Mus.Add.Mss., 49683, Queen Victoria to Balfour (Nice), p. 27 Mar. 1898 (Tel.); Frederick Ponsonby, *Recollections of Three Reigns* (London, 1951), p. 73; Almeric Fitzroy, *Memoirs*, 2 vols. (London, 1925), entry on Oct. 7, 1899, p. 19.

140. K. Young, *Arthur Balfour*, Balfour to Lady Elcho, Nov. 2, 1895, p. 175; *Q.V.L.*, 2s., 3, pp. 47, 105, 113, 135, 137–39, 157.

141. Ponsonby, *Three Reigns*, pp. 12, 39; Hardie, *Victoria*, pp. 142–82; *D.N.B.*, op. cit., p. 339.

142. James, *Rosebery*, pp. 235 ff.; C. J. Lowe, *Salisbury and the Mediterranean*, p. 93; Longford, *Victoria*, p. 518. Balfour Papers, B.Mus. Add.Mss., 49691, Salisbury to Balfour, Oct. 21, 1900, no. 106.

143. Jenkins, *Dilke*, p. 144; Gardiner, *Harcourt*, 2, p. 198; The Marquess of Crewe, *Lord Rosebery* (London, 1931) 2, pp. 400–401; Robinson in *C.H.B.E.*, 3, p. 160.

144. F.O. 800/1 (Sanderson Papers), F.O. Minutes, Oct. 31, 1895.

145. A recent study has ably demonstrated the influence of domestic politics on French expansion in Africa. See Roger Glenn Brown, *Fashoda Reconsidered; The Impact of Domestic Politics on French Policy in Africa, 1893–1898* (Johns Hopkins Press, 1970).

146. *Quarterly Review*, 96, Oct., 1902, no. 392, pp. 652–54.

CHAPTER IV

1. Cited in K. O. Dike, *Trade and Politics in the Niger Delta 1830–1885: An Introduction to the Economic and Political History of Nigeria* (Oxford University Press, 1956), p. 18.

2. Ibid.

3. Eric Williams, *Capitalism and Slavery* (London: Andre Deutsch, 1964).

4. J. E. Flint, *Sir George Goldie and the Making of Nigeria* (Oxford University Press, 1960), pp. 21–22; Cherry Gertzel, "John Holt" (un-

published Oxford Ph.D. thesis, 1959), p. 4; cf. C. W. Newbury, ed., *British Policy towards West Africa: Select Documents, 1786–1874* (Oxford University Press, 1965).

5. *Parl. Pap.*, 1892 (C. 6701) 56, Salisbury to Dufferin, Mar. 30, 1892, pp. 775–802; *Times*, June 30, 1898; cf. "Devonshire in Glasgow," ibid., Oct. 19, 1898.

6. Ibid.

7. For analysis of the report see, J. D. Hargreaves, *Prelude to the Partition of West Africa* (London, 1963), pp. 64–78; Dike, *Trade and Politics*, pp. 166–81. The text of the report is printed in *Parl. Pap.*, 1865, V (412), iii; cf. Newbury, *British Policy*, pp. 529–30; G. E. Metcalf, ed., *Great Britain and Ghana; Documents of Ghana History, 1807–1957*, pp. 305 ff.

8. Sir Charles Bower Adderley (later the first Baron Norton 1814–1905), was later to support Irish Home Rule as well as the colonial policy of Chamberlain.

9. Lord Edward Stanley (later the fifteenth Earl of Derby) was an opponent of all colonial military adventures.

10. Metcalfe, *Great Britain*, p. 305.

11. Dike, *Trade and Politics*, p. 181.

12. C.O. 267/285, F.O. to C.O., Oct. 9, 1865.

13. C.O. 267/303, F.O. to Admiralty, Oct. 11, 1869.

14. C.O. 147/21, Kimberley's Minutes of Nov. 15, 1871.

15. C.O. 147/23, Kimberley's Minutes of Aug. 6, 1872.

16. Metcalfe, *Great Britain*, p. 361.

17. Ibid.

18. C.O. 879/3 (formerly C.O. 806), Memo of Mar., 1874.

19. For the nature of the expansion which took place in this period, see Dike, *Trade and Politics*; A. A. B. Aderibigbe, "Expansion of the Lagos Protectorate 1863–1900" (unpublished London University Ph.D. thesis) 1959; Metcalfe, *Great Britain*; Gertzel, "John Holt"; *Parl. Pap.*, 1892 (C. 6701) 55, pp. 775 ff. Salisbury to Dufferin Mar. 30, 1892; F.O. *Confidential Print* (5284), Memo by H. P. Anderson, July 28, 1886; F.O. to Liverpool Chamber of Commerce, Dec. 30, 1891, *Africa Pamphlets etc.* (Rhodes House Library, Oxford).

20. *Parl. Pap.*, 1892 (C. 6701) 56, Salisbury to Dufferin, Mar. 30, 1892, p. 778.

21. Newbury, *British Policy*, p. 31.

22. For French military operations in West Africa see A. S. Kanya-Forstner, *The Conquest of the Western Sudan: A Study in French Military Imperialism* (Cambridge University Press, 1969).

23. *Parl. Pap.* 1892 (C. 6701) 56, Salisbury to Dufferin, Mar. 30, 1892, p. 778.

24. *Times*, June 30, 1898.

25. P.R.O. 30/29/55, Clarendon to Admiral Harris (private), Oct. 21, 1869 (copy).

26. *Times*, June 30, 1898.

27. F.O.C.P. (5284), Memo by H. P. Anderson, July 28, 1886.
28. E. T. Raymond, *Portrait of the Nineties,* chap. 1.
29. See Gertzel, "John Holt," p. 43; *Times,* Aug. 1, 1895; *Quarterly Review,* July, 1899, vol. 190, no. 379.
30. R. Robinson, J. Gallagher, and A. Denny, *Africa and the Victorians,* pp. 33–41, 379 ff.
31. Cf., for example, E. D. Morel, *The Affairs of West Africa* (London, 1902), pp. 10, 12, 21, 25–26; M. Kingsley, *Travels in West Africa* (1897), Appendix I, pp. 631–80; the proceedings of the various Chambers of Commerce; and newspapers and periodicals of the period.
32. Hargreaves, *Prelude,* p. 29 (footnote).
33. *The Times,* Feb. 15, 1896, July 29, Aug. 13 and Aug. 15, 1898.
34. Cf. D. Wellesley, *Sir George Goldie* (London, 1934), p. 21; FO27/3370, R.N.C. to C.O; C. Newbury "Victorians, Republicans and the Partition of West Africa," in *Journal of African History* III, 3 (1962), pp. 497–98.
35. F.O. 2/34, Palmerston's Minutes of Apr. 22, 1860.
36. Robinson and Gallagher, *Africa & Victorians,* p. 379.
37. Newbury, *"Victorians,"* pp. 497–98. Jean Stengers, "L' Imperialisme colonial de la fin du XIX siecle: Mythe ou Realite," Ibid.
38. F.O. 83/1536, W.O. to F.O. Nov. 24, 1897 (inclosures & minutes).
39. A. N. Cook, *British Enterprise in Nigeria* (Pennsylvania, 1943), 83; Dike, *Trade and Politics,* pp. 202–6, 209; J. B. Webster and A. A. Boahen, *The Revolutionary Years: West Africa Since 1800* (London: Longmans, 1967), pp. 202–4.
40. Henri Brunschwig, "French Exploration and Conquest in Tropical Africa From 1865 to 1898," in L. Gann and P. Duignan, eds., *Colonialism in Africa 1870–1960,* vol. 1 (Cambridge University Press, 1969), pp. 133–36; Kanya-Forstner, *Conquest,* pp. 28–34, 43–50; Hargreaves, *Prelude to Partition,* chaps. 3 and 4.
41. Brunschwig, "French Exploration," pp. 141–51; Kanya-Forstner, chaps. 3 and 4.
42. Hargreaves, *Prelude,* pp. 310–13; idem, "Toward a History of the Partition," pp. 103–5; Flint, *Sir George Goldie,* chap. 3.
43. See, for example, M. E. Townsend, *Origins of Modern German Colonialism, 1871–1885* (N.Y., 1930); H. R. Rudin, *Germans in the Cameroons, 1884–1914* (New Haven, 1938); A. J. P. Taylor, *Germany's First Bid for Colonies* (London, 1938); W. O. Aydelotte, *Bismarck and British Colonial Policy* (Philadelphia, 1937); P. Gifford and R. Louis, eds., *Britain and Germany in Africa* (New Haven, 1967).
44. Aydelotte, *Bismarck,* pp. 18, 25–26; E. Eyck, *Bismarck* (Zurich, 1944), 3, pp. 394–424.
45. Taylor, *Germany's Bid,* pp. 6, 18; *The Struggle for Mastery in Europe, 1848–1918* (Oxford, 1954), p. 25; Robinson and Gallagher, *Africa and the Victorians,* chap. 6.

46. See Townsend, *Origins*.
47. H. A. Turner, "Bismarck's Imperialist Venture: Anti-British in Origin?," in Gifford and Louis, *Britain and Germany*, pp. 52–53.
48. Hargreaves, *Prelude to Partition*, pp. 316–28; Dike, *Trade and Politics*, pp. 214–15; R. Louis, "Great Britain and German Expansion in Africa, 1884–1919," in Gifford and Louis, *Britain and Germany*, chap. 1; Turner, in ibid., chap. 2.
49. Geary, *Nigeria Under British Rule*, pp. 170–71; Dike, *Trade and Politics*, pp. 206–7; Flint, *Sir George Goldie*, pp. 23–25.
50. Dike, *Trade and Politics*, pp. 207–14; Robinson and Gallagher, *Africa and the Victorians*, p. 167.
51. F.O. 84/1879, Goldie to Salisbury, Aug. 15, 1885.
52. Geary, *Nigeria Under British Rule*, p. 179.
53. Dike, *Trade and Politics*, p. 212.
54. Cook, *British Enterprise in Nigeria*, pp. 84–85.
55. *Parl. Pap.*, 1892 (C. 6701) 56, p. 778; cf. C.O. 96; Minutes by Knatchbull-Hugessen, Feb. 18, 1873, p. 104.
56. S.P. 26, Salisbury to Lyons, Aug. 10, 1878.
57. Hargreaves, *Prelude*, pp. 201–12.
58. F.O. 27/2414, Lyons to Salisbury, March 31, 1879.
59. S.P. Salisbury to Lyons, Nov. 12, 1879, no. 58; G. Cecil, *Salisbury*, 4, p. 251.
60. See, for example, Hargreave's "Towards A History of the Partition of Africa," *J.A.H.*, pp. 99–100.
61. Cecil, *Salisbury*, 2, p. 234.
62. F.O. 72/2418, F.O. to C.O. Nov. 22, 1879.
63. S.P. 26, Salisbury to Lyons, Nov. 29, 1879, no. 60.
64. Gallagher and Robinson, "The Imperialism of Free Trade," in *Economic History Review* (London, 1953), 6, 2s., no. I, p. 3.
65. S.P. 26, Salisbury to Lyons, Dec. 16, 1879, no. 66.
66. S.P. 8, Lyons to Salisbury, Dec. 1, 1879, no. 85.
67. S.P. 8, Lyons to Salisbury, Dec. 3–4, 1879.
68. S.P. 59, Salisbury to Lytton (written at Puys), Sept. 19, 1890, no. 95.
69. Robinson and Gallagher, *Africa and the Victorians*, pp. 379 ff.
70. C.O. 87/116, Minutes on F.O. to C.O., Aug. 4, 1880.
71. Robinson and Gallagher, *Africa and the Victorians*, p. 163.
72. Hargreaves, *Prelude*, pp. 265–71.
73. *Parl. Pap.*, 1892 (C. 6701) 56, pp. 778.
74. C.O. 147/52, F.O. to C.O., Nov. 25, 1882.
75. Hargreaves, *Prelude*, pp. 301–2. For Britain's relations with the Congo see Roger Anstey, *Britain and the Congo in the 19th century* (Oxford, 1962); cf. also Jan Vansina, *Kingdoms of the Savana* (Wisconsin, 1966).
76. Robinson and Gallagher, *Africa and the Victorians*, p. 163.
77. Hargreaves, *Prelude*, p. 308.
78. Roger Louis, "Sir Percy Anderson's Grand African Strategy, 1883–1896," in *E.H.R.*, 81 (1966), pp. 292–314.

79. F.O. 84/1654, Memo by Anderson, June 11, 1883.
80. F.O. 84/1655, Lister to Paucefote, Nov. 29, 1883.
81. Hargreaves, *Prelude,* p. 315.
82. Ibid., p. 313.
83. Cited in Kanya-Forstner, *Conquest,* p. 126.
84. S. E. Crowe, *The Berlin West African Conference* (London, 1942), pp. 124–29.

CHAPTER V

1. Crowe, *Berlin-W. African Conference,* pp. 124–29.
2. Ibid., pp. 152–75.
3. Ibid., pp. 3–4, 103.
4. Ibid., pp. 192–93.
5. Ibid., p. 194.
6. Ibid., p. 177.
7. For West Africa see for example, Michael Crowder, ed., *West African Resistance: The Military Response to Colonial Occupation* (London, 1971); B. O. Oloruntimehim, "Muhammad Lamine in Franco-Tukulor relations 1885–1887," *Jour.Hist.Soc.Nig.* (*JHSN*), 4, no. 3 (1968); Martin Legassick, "Firearms, Horses and Samorian Army Organization, 1870–1898," *J.A.H.,* 7, 1 (1966), pp. 95–115; R. Griffiths, "Samori Toure," *Tarikh,* 1, 4 (1967); Obaro Ikime, "Nana Olumu: Governor of the Bini River," *Tarikh,* 1, 2 (1966); T. N. Tamuno, "Some Aspects of Nigerian Reaction to the Imposition of British Rule," *JHSN,* 3, no. 2 (1965); P. Igbafe, "Ovonramwen and the Fall of Bini," *Tarikh,* 2, 1 (1968); J. D. Hargreaves, "West African States and the European Conquest" in *Colonialism in Africa.*
8. R. Oliver and J. D. Fage, *A Short History of Africa* (London, 1962), p. 203; Gallagher and Robinson, "Partition of Africa," *Cambridge Modern History,* pp. 618–64.
9. See J. C. Anene, *Southern Nigeria in Transition 1885–1906* (Cambridge University Press, 1966), chap. 2.
10. For official accounts of events in Asante after 1874 see C.O. 879/ 42, 43, 44, 49, 62. The best study of Asante resistance is J. K. Fynn's "Ghana-Asante" in Crowder, ed., *West African Resistance,* pp. 19– 52. See also David Kimble, *A Political History of Ghana* (Oxford University Press, 1963), pp. 279–329.
11. For the official account of the affairs in the Northern Territories see C.O. 879/54, 58, 64.
12. C.O. 879/54, African (West), no. 569, 776; C.O. 879/55, no. 570, 327; cf. *Parl. Pap.,* 1899 (C. 9388) 60, pp. 9–181; ibid. (C. 9391), Evidence and Documents, pp. 183–682; *Parl. Pap.,* 1898 (C. 8922) 59; La Ray Denzer, "Bai Bureh"; in *West African Resistance,* pp. 233–64.

13. Yves Person, "Samori" in *West African Resistance*, pp. 111–41; Kanya-Forstner, *Conquest of Western Sudan*, pp. 183–89; Griffiths, "Samori Toure," loc. cit., Legassick, "Samorian Army Organization," loc. cit.

14. Hargreaves, "West African States" in *Colonialism in Africa*, p. 206, and fn. 2.

15. Oloruntimehim, "Mahmadou Lamine" in *West African Resistance*, pp. 80–106; cf. idem. in *JHSN*, loc. cit.

16. Kanya-Forstner, "Tukulor" in *West African Resistance*, pp. 53–77; cf. idem., *Conquest of Western Sudan*, chap. 7.

17. David Ross, "Dahomey" in *West African Resistance*, pp. 144–67; B. I. Obichere, *West African States and European Expansion* (Yale University Press, 1971), chaps. 3 and 4.

18. Geary, *Nigeria Under British Rule*, p. 33.

19. Robert Smith, "Ijebu" in *West African Resistance*, pp. 170–94; A. B. Aderibigbe, "The Ijebu Expedition, 1892: An Episode in the British Penetration of Nigeria Reconsidered" in T. O. Ranger, ed., *Historians in Tropical Africa* (Rhodesia, 1962); idem., *Expansion of Lagos Protectorate*.

20. Obaro Lkime, "Nigeria-Ebrohimi," in *West African Resistance*, 203–28; idem., *Merchant Prince of the Niger Delta* (N.Y., 1968); idem., "Nana Olumu" in *Tarikh*, loc. cit.

21. Roland Oliver, *Sir Harry Johnston and the Scramble for Africa* (London, 1957), chap. 4; Dike, *Trade and Politics*, chap. 10; J. C. Anene, "Jaja of Opobo" in *Eminent Nigerians of the Nineteenth Century* (London, 1960), pp. 17–25; Geary, *Nigeria Under British Rule*, Appendix 1, pp. 278–94; J. B. Webster and A. A. Boahen, *The Revolutionary Years: West Africa Since 1800* (Longmans, 1967), chap. 13; Cherry Gertzel, "Relations between Africans and European Traders in the Niger Delta 1880–1896," *J.A.H.*, 111, 2 (1962), pp. 361–66.

22. *Parl. Pap.*, 1896 (C. 7977) 59, pp. 363–88; A. C. Burns, *History of Nigeria* (London, 1929), pp. 168–71; Flint, *Goldie*, chap. 9; F.O. 83/1442, A.P.S. to F.O. March 28, 1896.

23. *Parl. Pap.*, 1898 (C. 8677) 60, pp. 97–155. This was originally circulated as C. 8440 in Aug., 1897. See also Burns, *History of Nigeria*, pp. 178–87.

24. S.P. (Goschen), Goschen to Salisbury, June 14, 1897 (private).

25. Lugard Papers, vol. 41 (Kirk), Kirk to Lugard (n.d.).

26. *Parl. Pap.*, 1898 (C. 9124) 62, pp. 367–94; ibid., 1899 (C. 9529) 63, pp. 395–416.

27. Geary, *Nigeria Under British Rule*, p. 201.

28. For the nature of resistance by the Sokoto Caliphate in our period see, Flint, *Goldie*, chap. 11; D. J. M. Muffett, "Sokoto Caliphate," in *West African Resistance*, pp. 268–95.

29. This is the burden of D. J. M. Muffett's *Concerning Brave Captains*

(London, 1964), cf. idem., "Sokoto Caliphate" in *West African Resistance.*

30. For details see G. N. Uzoigwe, *The Slave Trade and African Societies,* Center for Afro-American and African Studies, University of Michigan (Monograph and Report Series, no. 3, 1971).
31. Robinson and Gallagher, *Africa and the Victorians,* p. 175.
32. J. E. Flint, "Nigeria: The Colonial Experience From 1880 to 1914," in *Colonialism in Africa,* op. cit., p. 225.
33. Robinson and Gallagher, *Africa and the Victorians,* pp. 163–89, 300–306.
34. Historians of West Africa agree on this point. See, for example, Flint, *Goldie,* chaps. 3 and 4; Hargreaves, *Prelude,* chaps. 6 and 7; Anene, *Southern Nigeria,* chap. 2.
35. *Parl. Pap.,* (1886) 55.
36. *London Gazette,* June 5, 1885.
37. F.O.C.P. (5284), Memo by H. P. Anderson, July 28, 1886.
38. Flint, *Goldie,* chaps. 5–7.
39. Kanya-Forstner, *Conquest of Western Sudan,* chap. 7.
40. S.P. 59, Salisbury to Lyons, Feb. 5, 1887.
41. Ibid.
42. S.P. 56, Egerton to Salisbury, Aug. 5, 1887, no. 46; Same to Same, Dec. 22, 1887, no. 55; S.P. 57, Lytton to Same, Dec. 12, 1888, no. 78, Dec. 20, 1888, no. 84.
43. For Salisbury's views in the seventies, see S.P. 26, Salisbury to Lyons, Nov. 12, 1879, no. 60; and Dec. 16, 1879, no. 66.
44. *Parl. Pap.,* 1892 (C. 6701) 56, Salisbury to Dufferin, Mar. 30, 1892.
45. Ibid.
46. Ibid. I have merely given the salient points in these negotiations. For more details see Obichere, *West African States,* chap. 2. For the official documents relating to these negotiations cf. F.O. 403/85, "France in West Africa, 1884–89"; S.P. 57, Lytton to Salisbury, Dec. 26, 1888, no. 87; S.P. 58, Same to Same, Jan. 14, 1889, no. 1; Feb. 26, no. 11; Egerton to Salisbury, June 27, 1889, no. 29, and Lytton to Same, July 11, 1889, no. 31.
47. Cited in Cecil, *Salisbury,* 4, p. 323.
48. *Parl. Pap.,* 1892 (C. 6701), 56.
49. Mr. E. Phipps and Sir Joseph Crowe represented Britain; MM. Hanotaux and Hausmann represented France.
50. F.O. 27/3273, Salisbury to Dufferin, May 12, 1896, no. 139 Africa.
51. *Parl. Pap.,* 1893–94 (C. 7108) 109, *Gold Coast. Anglo-French Bound. Agreements.*
52. Ibid. (C. 7026).
53. Ibid. (C. 7230).
54. F.O. 27/3273, Salisbury to Dufferin, May 12, 1896, no. 139 Africa.
55. Ibid.; F.O. 27/3277, Salisbury to Same, Jan. 31, 1896, no. 1

Africa (Tel.); F.O. 27/3274, Dufferin to Salisbury, Feb. 1, 1896, encl. Dufferin to Berthelot of same date, no. 17 Africa.

56. F.O. 27/3274, Dufferin to Salisbury, Feb. 3, 1896, no. 19 Africa.
57. Mr. H. Howard (of the Paris Embassy) represented Britain and was assisted by Sir Augustus Hemming of the C.O., soon to proceed to British Guiana as M.H.'s Governor. M. Larrony represented France, and was assisted by M. Roumme.
58. F.O. 27/3273, Salisbury to Dufferin, May 12, 1896, no. 139 Africa.
59. S.P. 116, Salisbury to Dufferin, Feb. 7, 1896 no. 34 (bound out of order); cf. F.O. 27/3273, Same to Same, Feb. 7, 1896, no. 33 Africa (correctly bound).
60. F.O. 27/3274, Dufferin to Salisbury, Feb. 8, 1896, no. 21 Africa, *Report*.
61. Ibid.
62. Ibid., Dufferin to Salisbury, Feb. 15, 1896, no. 22 Africa, *Report*.
63. Ibid., Anderson's Minutes on above.
64. Ibid., Salisbury's Minutes on above.
65. Hertslet, *Map of Africa by Treaty*, vol. 11, p. 572.
66. Waddington's comment referred to the "light soil" section.
67. F.O. 27/3273, Salisbury to Dufferin, Feb. 21, 1896, no. 56, Africa.
68. F.O. 27/3274, Dufferin to Salisbury, Mar. 3, 1896 (confidential) no. 41 Africa; cf. S.P. 114, Duf. to Salisbury, Nov. 2, 1895, no. 12.
69. Ibid.
70. Ibid., Same to Same, Feb. 28, 1896, no 46, Africa: Same to Same, Mar. 5, 1896, no. 47 Africa; cf. S.P. 114, no. 34.
71. S.P. 119, Salisbury to Dufferin, Mar. 3, 1896 (copy), no. 2.
72. F.O. 27/3374, L.O. to F.O., Dec. 3, 1897.
73. S.P. (Chamberlain), Chamberlain to Salisbury, Dec. 8, 1895 (private).
74. J.C.P. (Salisbury), Salisbury to Chamberlain, Dec. 10, 1895 (secret).
75. S.P. (Chamberlain), Chamberlain to Salisbury, Dec. 16, 1895 (private).
76. J.C.P. (Salisbury), Salisbury to Chamberlain, Dec. 23, 1895.
77. F.O. 27/3274, Dufferin to Salisbury, Feb. 18, 1896, no. 24 Africa encl. extract from the *Temps* of Feb. 17, 1896.
78. Ibid., Same to Same, Feb. 19, 1896, encl. extract from *Figaro* of Feb. 19, 1896.
79. Cf. F.O. 27/3273, no. 33 Africa for these treaties.
80. Lt. Fergusson was a black officer of Afro-American descent in the Gold Coast Colonial Service.
81. F.O. 27/3274, Dufferin to Salisbury, Feb. 23, 1896, no. 31 Africa, encl. *Report:* cf. F.O. 27/374–75 for the reports on the examination of these treaties and the minutes thereon. I have only given a cross-section of the French objections.
82. Ibid., Same to Same, Feb. 28, 1896, no. 33 Africa, *Report*.
83. Ibid., Anderson's Minutes on Dufferin's no. 33 Africa, *Report*.

84. Ibid., Anderson's Minutes on Dufferin's no. 37 Africa, *Report.*
85. Ibid., Anderson's Minutes to C.O. on Dufferin's no. 53 Africa, *Report.*
86. Ibid., Anderson's Minutes to C.O., on Dufferin's no. 55, Africa, *Report.*
87. F.O. 27/3300, Anderson's Minutes on Sanderson's draft dispatch, March 11, 1896.
88. F.O. 27/3273, Salisbury to Dufferin, Mar. 20, 1896, no. 91 Africa, reporting Sanderson's conversation with Courcel.
89. Ibid.
90. Ibid., Same to Same, Mar. 28, 1896, no. 103, Africa.
91. F.O. 27/3277, Sanderson to Dufferin, Feb. 17, 1896, tel. no. 4, Africa.
92. S.P. 114, Dufferin to Salisbury, Mar. 6, 1896, no. 36.
93. F.O. 27/300, C.O. to F.O., Mar. 1, 1896 (secret).
94. Ibid., Anderson's Minutes (Mar. 12) on Sanderson's draft dispatch (Mar. 11).
95. Ibid., Salisbury's Minutes on same.
96. Ibid., Anderson's Minutes (Mar. 13) on same.
97. F.O. 27/3275, Dufferin to Salisbury, April 30, 1896, no. 69, Africa, *Report.*
98. Ibid., Anderson's Minutes (May 2) on same.
99. Ibid., Sanderson's note to Salisbury (Oct. 16, 1897) *re.* same. Anderson died in July, 1896.
100. Ibid., Salisbury's Minutes on same.
101. Ibid., Dufferin to Salisbury, May 8, 1896, no. 75 Africa, encl. *Report.*
102. Ibid., Anderson's Minutes (May 9) on Dufferin's no. 75 Africa.
103. Howard's proposal was that since the 1890 Agreement and the Siamese Agreement of 1896 provided for the determination of Anglo-French spheres of influence to the west of the Niger, France should be bluntly told that there was no need to discuss the Say-Barruwa Agreement, or to permit any interference in Lagos.
104. F.O. 27/3275, Salisbury's Minutes on Dufferin's no. 75 Africa.
105. F.O. 27/3273, Salisbury to Dufferin, May 12, 1896, no. 139 Africa.
106. F.O. 27/3274, Dufferin to Salisbury, May 23, 1896, no. 88 Africa, *Report.*
107. Ibid., Salisbury's Minutes on Dufferin's no. 88 Africa.
108. S.P. 114, Dufferin to Salisbury, May 15, 1896, no. 48.
109. F.O. 27/3301, C.O. to F.O., July 13, 1896.
110. Ibid., Everett's Memo of July 23, 1896.
111. Sir Clement Hill was the head of the African Department of the Foreign Office in succession to Sir Percy Anderson.
112. F.O. 23/3301, Hill's Minutes (Aug. 13, 1896).
113. Ibid., Salisbury's Minutes on same.
114. Ibid., C.O. to F.O., Sept. 26, 1896, encl. Memo by Maxwell and F.O. Minutes.

115. Ibid., C.O. to F.O., Sept. 14, 1896.
116. Ibid., F.O. to C.O., Oct. 1, 1896 (immediate).
117. Ibid., Minutes by Sanderson on same and approved by Salisbury.
118. F.O. 27/3276, Howard to Salisbury, Aug. 5, 1896 (confidential), Memos.
119. Ibid., Everett to Hill, Aug. 12, 1896.
120. F.O. 27/3301, Memo by Everett Nov. 19, 1896, with enclosures.
121. Ibid.
122. F.O. 27/3301, C.O. to F.O., Nov. 27, 1896.
123. Ibid., F.O. to C.O., Nov. 30, 1896.
124. For Goldie and Nupe see Flint, *Goldie*, chaps. 3 and 4.
125. F.O. 27/3273, Salisbury to Gosselin, Dec. 1, 1896, no. 273 Africa; F.O. 27/3335, Salisbury to Monson, Jan. 12, 1897, no. 9 Africa.
126. F.O. 27/3275, Monson to Salisbury, Dec. 27, 1896 (confidential) no. 236 Africa; S.P. 114, Same to Same, Dec. 27, 1896, no. 70.
127. Ibid., F.O. Minutes on Monson's no. 236 Africa; F.O. 27/3335, Salisbury to Monson, Jan. 12, 1897, no. 9 Africa.
128. F.O. 27/3301, Everett to Hill, Dec. 31, 1896 (private).
129. Ibid., F.O. Minutes on above; F.O. 27/3335, Hill's Minutes of Jan. 19, 1897.
130. F.O. 27/3335, Salisbury to Monson, Jan. 12, 1897, no. 6 Africa.
131. Ibid., Hill's Minutes on Salisbury's no. 6 Africa.
132. F.O. 27/3368, R.N.C. to F.O., Mar. 9, 1897 (urgent).
133. Ibid., Hill's Minutes (March 9).
134. F.O. 27/3335, Hill's Minutes of March 10, 1897.
135. Ibid., Hill's Minutes of March 11, 1897; F.O. 27/3368, Scarborough to Hill, Mar. 9, 1897.
136. F.O. 27/3335, Salisbury to Monson, Mar. 12, 1897, no. 44 Africa.
137. Ibid., Same to Same, April 13, 1897, no. 86 Africa.
138. F.O. 27/3368, C.O. to F.O., Mar. 22, 1897 (encl. Tel. from Maxwell).
139. Hill, for example, noted the shadiness of Britain's claim to Mossi.
140. F.O. 27/3368, Hill's Minutes on C.O. to F.O. of March 22, 1897.
141. F.O. 27/3338, Gosselin to Salisbury, April 5, 1897, no. 98 Africa.
142. F.O. 27/3368, Sanderson to Salisbury, April 10, 1897 (draft).
143. F.O. 27/3335, Salisbury to Monson, April 27, 1897, no. 103 Africa.
144. F.O. 27/3338, Gosselin to Salisbury, June 26, 1897, no. 195 Africa.
145. Ibid., Hill's Minutes on Gosselin's no. 195 Africa.
146. F.O. 27/3335, Salisbury to Gosselin, June 29, 1897, no. 176 Africa.
147. S.P. 114, Monson to Salisbury, July 6, 1897, no. 62.
148. F.O. 27/3370, C.O. to F.O., June 26, 1897.
149. Ibid.
150. F.O. 27/3370, Hill's Minutes of June 30, 1897.
151. Ibid., Hill's Minutes of July 8, 1897.
152. Ibid., F.O. to R.N.C., July 23, 1897 (most confidential).
153. Ibid., R.N.C. to F.O., July 27, 1897.

154. Ibid., Hill's Minutes on above.
155. F.O. 27/3371, C.O. to F.O., Aug. 4, 1897; Selborne to Salisbury, Sept. 3, 1897; cf. S.P. (Palmer).
156. Ibid., F.O. to C.O., Aug. 5, 1897 (immediate and confidential) and Minutes.
157. Ibid., Hill's Minutes of Aug. 4, 1897.
158. Ibid., Salisbury's Minutes on above.
159. Ibid., Sanderson to Salisbury, Aug. 5, 1897.
160. Ibid., Salisbury's Minutes to Sanderson.
161. S.P. 114, Monson to Salisbury, Sept. 3, 1897, no. 74.
162. Ibid., Same to Same, Sept. 5, 1897, no. 75; F.O. 27/33339, Same to Same, Aug. 28, 1897 no. 253 Africa.
163. F.O. 27/3335, Salisbury to Monson, Sept. 4, 1897, no. 259 Africa.
164. S.P. 114, Monson to Salisbury, Oct. 12, 1897, no. 80.
165. F.O. 27/3335, Salisbury to Monson, Sept. 10, 1897, no. 265 Africa.
166. There are numerous instances of this. See, for example, F.O. 27/3371, C.O. to F.O., Aug. 4, 6, and 13, 1897; ibid., F.O. to C.O., Aug. 19, 1897; F.O. 27/3335, Salisbury to Monson, Sept. 16, 1897, no. 271 Africa.
167. For these protests see F.O. 27/3371–74; F.O. 27/3437–40.
168. F.O. 27/3371, F.O. to C.O., Aug. 19, 1897 (draft).
169. Ibid., C.O. to F.O., Aug. 14, 1897 (confidential).
170. Ibid., C.O. to F.O., Aug. 25, 1897 (confidential) and Encl. (secret).
171. Ibid., Hill's Minutes on above.
172. Ibid., Salisbury's Minutes on Same.
173. Ibid., Hill's "Memo on Meeting of Committee on Niger Hinterland Question," Sept. 2, 1897. Copy initialled by Salisbury.
174. J.C.P. (Imperial Affairs. Niger Negotiations), Selborne to Chamberlain, Sept. 8, 1897 (confidential). This conference was also attended by Hill, Everett, Antrobus and Selborne. Salisbury was not present; Chamberlain was on holiday.
175. F.O. 27/3339, Monson to Salisbury, Sept. 5, 1897, no. 262, Africa (most confidential).
176. Ibid.
177. J.C.P. (Imp. Affairs. Nig. Negos.), Selborne to Chamberlain, Sept. 8, 1897 (confidential).
178. F.O. 27/3371, Note by Bertie to Salisbury, Sept. 2, 1897; see also F.O. 800/2 (Sanderson Papers), Sanderson's and Salisbury's Minutes of Sept. 13, 1897; Sanderson to Salisbury, Sept. 18 and 21; Salisbury to Sanderson, Sept. 28; Sanderson to Salisbury, Nov. 19; Salisbury to Sanderson, Nov. 20; Sanderson to Salisbury, Nov. 22; and Same to Same (n.d.)—for F.O.'s views of Goldie's attitude. By this time Salisbury and Sanderson had decided to revoke his company's charter when the moment was opportune.
179. Ibid., Salisbury's Minutes on above.
180. Ibid., Selborne to Hill, Sept. 8, 1897 (written at Hatfield).

181. F.O. 27/3372, Salisbury to McCallum, Sept. 28, 1897.
182. Ibid., C.O. to F.O. Oct. 15, 1897, encl. dispatches to and from Lagos.
183. Ibid.
184. Ibid., F.O. Minutes on Same.
185. Ibid., Memo by Salisbury, Oct. 26, 1897; "Arrest of Messengers and Documents passing thro' Br. territory from the French Commander at Dahomey."
186. Ibid.
187. Ibid., Attorney General to Sanderson, Oct. 27, 1897.
188. F.O. 27/3343, Salisbury to Monson, Sept. 23, 1897 (Tel.) no. 9 Africa; Ibid., Monson to Salisbury, Sept. 16, 1897 (most confidential) no. 15 Africa, Tel.

CHAPTER VI

1. The reference here was to the Tunis Negotiations which were also in progress, and not to the Niger Negotiations.
2. S.P. (Chamberlain), Chamberlain to Salisbury, June 6, 1897; Garvin, *Chamberlain*, 3, p. 204.
3. J.C.P. (Salisbury), Salisbury to Chamberlain, June 7, 1897 (private).
4. S.P. (Chamberlain), Chamberlain to Salisbury, June 8, 1897.
5. J.C.P. (miscellaneous), Salisbury to Chamberlain, Aug. 13, 1897.
6. S.P. 92 (Colonial Office, 1895–1900), Chamberlain to Selborne (copy), Interlaken, Sept. 12, 1897 (secret), no. 17; cf. J.C.P. (Imperial Affairs. Niger Negotiations), Same to Same, Sept. 12, 1897 (secret) for original.
7. J.C.P. ibid., Selborne to Chamberlain, Sept. 8, 1897 (confidential).
8. Ibid., Same to Same, Sept. 15, 1897 (confidential). Lord Selborne was married to one of Salisbury's daughters and often acted as a go-between to Salisbury and Chamberlain.
9. F.O. 800/2 (Sanderson Papers), Salisbury's Minutes of Sept. 13, 1897.
10. S.P. 92 Chamberlain to Selborne, Sept. 12, 1897 (secret).
11. Idem. M. Andre Lebon was the French chauvinistic colonial minister.
12. J.C.P. (Salisbury), Salisbury to Chamberlain, Sept. 17, 1897 (confidential).
13. J.C.P. (Salisbury), Salisbury to Chamberlain, Sept. 17, 1897 (confidential). Salisbury was willing to invest Chamberlain with the title of special commissioner if he was determined on that course. The precedent referred to concerned Prince Menschikoff's mission just before the Crimean War.
14. S.P. (Chamberlain), Chamberlain to Salisbury, Sept. 19, 1897 (private).

15. J.C.P. (Niger Negos.) Chamberlain to Selborne, Sept. 29, 1897.
16. Ibid. (Salisbury), Salisbury to Chamberlain, Oct. 23, 26, 1897 (private); S.P. (Chamberlain), Chamberlain to Salisbury, Oct. 25, 1897 (private).
17. J.C.P. (Niger Negos.), Monson to Sanderson, Sept. 19, 1897 (private copy).
18. Ibid., Marginal comment by C.O. on above.
19. Ibid., Comment by Salisbury on same.
20. F.O. 27/3372, C.O. to F.O., Sept. 27, 1897.
21. See F.O. 800/2, Salisbury to Sanderson, Sept. 28, 1897; ibid., Salisbury's Minutes on Sanderson to Salisbury, Sept. 28, 1897.
22. S.P. 115, Monson to Salisbury, Oct. 8, 1897, no. 79.
23. Ibid., Same to Same, Oct. 12, 1897, no. 80.
24. F.O. 27/3372, Memo on meeting at F.O. on Oct. 16, 1897 to discuss West African questions (most confidential copy).
25. F.O. 27/3340, Monson to Salisbury, Oct. 9, 1897, no. 310 Africa and encl.; cf. ibid., Same to Same, Oct. 12, 1897, no. 314 Africa and encl.; Same to Same, Oct. 19, 1897; no. 322 Africa encl.; Monson to Hanotaux, Oct. 19, 1897. Hanotaux wished to use the occasion of Lebon's absence—he was on a visit to W. Africa—to settle the question and therefore claim the sole credit at the expense of the ebullient colonial minister, see, S.P. 115, Monson to Salisbury, Oct. 12, 1897, no. 80.
26. It will be noted that, contrary to the interpretation placed on this phrase, Salisbury was referring to the region north of the 1890 line accepted to be French by treaty. It was the same region that a few years earlier, he had dismissed as "light soil."
27. S.P. 119, Salisbury to Monson, Oct. 19, 1897, no. 17; cf. F.O. 27/3343, Same to Same, Oct., 1897 (Tel.) no. 11 Africa.
28. They were unable to meet on the 20th because Hanotaux was slightly indisposed.
29. F.O. 27/3340, Monson to Salisbury, Oct. 22, 1897, no. 330 Africa, encl. *Report;* S.P. 115, Same to Same, Oct. 22, 1897, no. 81.
30. Ibid., Same to Same, Oct. 22, 1897 (most confidential), no. 334 Africa.
31. Ibid., Same to Same, Oct. 24, 1897 (confidential), no. 338 Africa; cf. F.O. 27/3336, Salisbury to Monson, Oct. 26, 1897, no. 324 Africa.
32. F.O. 27/3340, Monson to Salisbury, Oct. 24, 1897 (confidential) no. 338 Africa; and no. 344 Africa, Oct. 28, 1897.
33. F.O. 27/3336, Salisbury to Monson, Oct. 27, 1897, no. 328a Africa; see also F.O. 27/3343, Same to Same, Oct. 21, 1897 (Tel.) no. 25 Africa and Minutes.
34. S.P. 115, Monson to Salisbury, Oct. 27, 1897 (Tel.)—reporting conversation with Hanotaux (made official).
35. Britain was represented by Mr. Martin Gosselin (later Sir Martin) of the French Embassy; he was assisted by Col. Everett of the Intel-

ligence Division of the W.O. The C.O. was not represented. The French delegation was led by M. Le Comte, Assistant Director of the F.A. Ministry; he was assisted by Col. Binger, Political Director of the Colonial Ministry.

36. F.O. 27/3340, Gosselin to Salisbury, Oct. 30, 1897 (confidential) no. 345 Africa, *Report.*

37. F.O. 27/3336, Bertie to Gosselin, Nov. 2, 1897 (private copy); ibid., Chamberlain's Minutes (secret) of Oct. 31, 1897, ibid., Wingfield to Sanderson, Nov. 1, 1897; F.O. 27/3343, Salisbury to Gosselin, Nov. 2, 1897 (Tel.).

38. F.O. 27/3340, Gosselin to Salisbury, Nov. 5, 1897, no. 353 Africa, *Report.*

39. Ibid., Same to Same, Nov. 5, 1897, no. 354; Bertie to Gosselin Nov. 7, 1897 (private & confidential) Tel.; Gosselin to Bertie, Nov. 9, 1897.

40. F.O. 27/3373, C.O. to F.O., Nov. 12, 1897 (secret). Salisbury undertook to discuss these proposals privately with Chamberlain, and no doubt impressed on him the necessity of continuing the talks.

41. S.P. 115, "Memo (by Gosselin) reporting conversation with M. Hanotaux on the Niger Negotiations," Nov. 6, 1897, no. 86.

42. F.O. 27/3340, Gosselin to Salisbury, Nov. 12, 1897, no. 366 Africa, *Report.*

43. F.O. 27/3343, Same to Same, Nov. 10, 1897 (Tel.), no. 33 Africa.

44. F.O. 27/3340, Monson to Salisbury, Nov. 14, 1897 (confidential), re Everett's "Summary," no. 368 Africa. For Everett's memo see C.O. 879/50, African (West) no. 539.

45. F.O. 27/3340, Gosselin to Bertie, Nov. 14, 1897 (private); F.O. 27/3343, Monson to Salisbury, Nov. 13, 1897 (Tel.) no. 34 Africa.

46. F.O. 27/3340, Monson to Bertie, Nov. 14, 1897 (private); cf. F.O. 800/160 (Bertie Papers), Monson to Salisbury, Dec. 3, 1897 (private).

47. S.P. 115, Monson to Salisbury, Nov. 14, 1897, no. 87; see also J.C.P. (Niger Negos.), Same to Chamberlain, Nov. 14, 1897 (private). London agreed to reject *general* arbitration, but there was a disposition toward arbitration upon *special* questions of title. Cf. J.C.P. (Salisbury), Salisbury to Chamberlain, Nov. 17, 1897 (private); S.P. (Chamberlain), Chamberlain to Salisbury, Nov. 18, 1897 (private); F.O. 27/3343, Salisbury to Monson, Nov. 25, 1897 (very confidential) Tel. no. 15 Africa.

48. F.O. 27/3372, C.O. to F.O., Nov. 22, 1897 (secret) 7 pp. typed; see also J.C.P. (Niger Negos. Documents 1897–98) for original.

49. S.P. (Chamberlain), Chamberlain to Salisbury, Nov. 17, 1897 (private).

50. F.O. 27/3336, Salisbury to Monson, Nov. 26, 1897, no. 374 Africa; cf. F.O. 27/3340, for F.O. Minutes on Monson's no. 368 Africa, Nov. 14, 1897.

51. S.P. 115, Monson to Salisbury, Nov. 23, 1897, no. 89.

52. F.O. 27/3336, Salisbury to Monson, Nov. 23, 1897, no. 367 Africa: "Copy of draft dictated by Salisbury."
53. The idea was to give the W.A.F.F. time to become effective.
54. J.C.P. (Salisbury), Salisbury to Chamberlain, Nov. 17, 1897 (private).
55. S.P. 115, Monson to Salisbury, Nov. 28, 1897, no. 90; see also F.O. 27/3340, Same to Same, Nov. 28, 1897 (confidential) no. 398, Africa; F.O. 27/3336, Salisbury's nos. 367 and 374 Africa of Nov. 23 and 26, 1897, respectively as well as the *Very Confidential* Tel. of Nov. 26, 1897.
56. F.O. 27/3340, Monson to Salisbury, Nov. 27, 1897, no. 393 Africa, encl. *Report:* Ibid., Same to Same, Nov. 27, 1897 (urgent) no. 394 Africa, and Nov. 28, 1897, no. 400 Africa.
57. S.P. 115, Monson to Salisbury, Nov. 19, 1897, no. 88.
58. F.O. 27/3340, Monson to Sanderson, Nov. 28, 1897 (private).
59. Ibid., Salisbury's Minutes of Nov. 29, 1897.
60. F.O. 27/3374, "Niger Negotiations. Memo by Salisbury," Nov. 30, 1897; cf. F.O. 27/3343, Salisbury to Monson, Nov. 29, 1897 (sent from Hatfield) Tel. no. 16 Africa.
61. F.O. 27/3340, Hill's Minutes of Nov. 29, 1897.
62. F.O. 27/3374, C.O. to F.O., Dec. 2, 1897 (secret), encl. memo by Chamberlain (secret); see also J.C.P. (Niger Negos. Docs. 1897–98). Garvin described this memo in a marginal pencil note in J.C.P. as a very able and important letter on the whole Niger question. The memo is also substantially quoted in Garvin, *Life of Chamberlain*, 3, pp. 212–13; see also J.C.P. (Niger Negos.), Selborne to Chamberlain, Dec. 2, 1897 (secret), offering support to his chief, and Chamberlain to Selborne, Dec. 1, 1897; F.O. 27/3340, Bertie's Minutes of Nov. 28, 1897; S.P. (Chamberlain), Chamberlain to Salisbury, Dec. 31, 1897 (private). Chamberlain also produced some detailed arguments for his own department which would enable them to answer any question from the F.O. relating to the Niger question; see J.C.P. (Niger Negos. Docs.), Memo by Chamberlain, Nov. 30, 1897. Instruction to the department.
63. F.O. 27/3374, C.O. to F.O., Dec. 2, 1897 (secret).
64. F.O. 27/3374, Memo by Chamberlain, Dec. 26, 1897; Ibid., F.O. Minutes of C.O. to F.O. of Dec. 27, 1897 (immediate, secret); F.O. 27/3336, Salisbury to Monson, Dec. 30, 1897, no. 438, Africa.
65. Those interested in the examination of these treaties may consult F.O. 27/3341, 3342; F.O. 27/3410, 3411, 3412, and 3413. Altogether, forty-six meetings were held in the final stage.
66. F.O. 27/3341, Hill's Minutes of Dec. 11, 1897.
67. F.O. 27/3410, Monson to Salisbury, Jan. 12, 1898, no. 16 Africa, reporting conversation with Hanotaux; cf. G. P. Gooch and H. Temperley, ed., *British Documents on the Origins of the War 1898–1914*, 1, no. 161, p. 136 (henceforward, *B.D.*)
68. F.O. 27/3341, Salisbury's and Bertie's Minutes of Nov. 11, 1897;

cf. S.P. 116, Monson to Salisbury, Jan. 14, 1898, no. 1; F.O. 27/3408, Salisbury to Monson, Mar. 7, 1898.

69. F.O. 27/3410, Monson to Salisbury, Jan. 20, 1898, no. 31 Africa and encl. (26 pp. typed); Prof. Louis Renault, of the Law Faculty Paris University and Legal Adviser to the French Foreign Ministry, gave a decision against the British treaties. Hill observed: "I am afraid there is force in the argument that our Fergusson treaties were not meant as treaties of protection, but as bringing the Chiefs to us, whilst leaving us free. . . ." Salisbury agreed. Cf. F.O. 27/3410, Monson to Salisbury, Jan. 11, 1898, no. 13 Africa, attaching Renault's decision, and F.O. Minutes.

70. Cab. 37/46 Niger Negotiations. Memo by Chamberlain, Jan. 25, 1898 (confidential) 11 pp.; cf. J.C.P. (Niger Negos. Docs.) for original.

71. F.O. 27/3416, Salisbury to Monson, Jan. 28, 1898 (Draft in Salisbury's hand) Tel. no. 4 Africa; *B.D.*, 1, no. 163, p. 139.

72. F.O. 27/3411, Monson to Salisbury, Feb. 1, 1898, no. 41 Africa, encl. *Report.*

73. F.O. 27/3411, Same to Same, Feb. 20, 1898 (confidential) no. 75 Africa; F.O. 27/3410, Same to Same, Jan. 31, 1898, no. 39 Africa; *B.D., no.* 164, pp. 139–40.

74. Ibid., Same to Same, Feb. 25, 1898, no. 92 Africa, Feb. 28, 1898 (confidential), no. 93 Africa, encl. Memo by Gosselin re conversation with Hanotaux.

75. F.O. 27/3411, Same to Same, Feb. 28, 1898, no. 93 Africa, and encl.

76. Seven out of ten of the deputies to the chamber were returned by agricultural constituencies. Idem. For the nature of French tariffs, see, F.O. 27/3437, F.O. Memo on "French Duties in West Africa" Feb. 22, 1898.

77. F.O. 27/3412, Monson to Salisbury, Mar. 6, 1898 (very confidential) no. 103 Africa and encl.

78. F.O. 27/3373, C.O. to F.O., Nov. 12, 1897 (secret); F.O. 27/3437, C.O. to F.O., Mar. 12, 1898 and Minutes; F.O. 27/3408, Balfour to Monson, nos. 145 and 150 Africa, Mar. 12, 1898; F.O. 27/3438, F.O. to C.O., Mar. 19, 1898; S.P. 92 Memo. by Chamberlain, Feb. 14, 1898.

79. F.O. 27/3411, Monson to Salisbury, Feb. 1, 1898, no. 41 Africa, encl. *Report.*

80. F.O. 27/3408, Salisbury's Minutes to Bertie of Jan. 11, 1898; see also *B.D.* no. 159, 135; F.O. 27/3416, Bertie to Gosselin, Jan. 11 (?), 1898 (confidential and private); ibid., Salisbury to Monson, Jan. 27, 1898 (Tel) no. 3 Africa (Draft in S's hand).

81. F.O. 27/3408, Salisbury to Monson, Feb. 15, 1898, no. 87 Africa; Cabinet Print, Feb. 11, 1898; *B.D.* no. 165, pp. 140–42.

82. F.O. 27/3412, Monson to Salisbury, Mar. 11, 1898, no. 107 Africa,

encl. *Report* of meeting held at Binger's house (because Binger was indisposed). See also accompanying Minutes.

83. Hanotaux's "Projet de Convention" is one of the enclosures in Monson to Salisbury, Mar. 16, 1898 (private), S.P. 92; Cab. 37/46, Mar. 19, 1898 (Proposals for Settlement of the Niger Question), 5 pp. F.O.
84. Ibid., Chamberlain's Cabinet Memo of Mar. 19, 1898; cf. J.C.P. (Niger Negos. Docs.), Mar. 19, 1898.
85. S.P. 92 Monson to Salisbury, Mar. 16, 1898, no. 29.
86. Idem.; cf. F.O. 27/3412, Monson to Salisbury, Mar. 16, 1898 (private); S.P. 116, Monson to Balfour, Mar. 19, 1898 (Tel.) no. 24.
87. Idem., Encl. no. 3; "Observations on the sketch of the Convention for the settlement of the West African Question, drawn up by M. Hanotaux. . . ."
88. Ibid., Chamberlain's Cabinet Memo of Mar. 19, 1897.
89. F.O. 27/3416; "Sketch of the communication which might be made by Sir E. Monson or the commissioners on presenting the counter-draft (confidential)"; see also, F.O. 27/3408. This dispatch bears the date of Mar. 24 and is enclosed in Balfour to Monson, Mar. 28, 1898; S.P. 119, Balfour to Monson, Mar. 18, 1898 (Tel.) no. 25; *B.D.* no. 176, pp. 149–52.
90. F.O. 27/3408, Balfour to Monson, Mar. 28, 1898. This dispatch grew out of a memo by Balfour which was settled in conjunction with Chamberlain; cf. *B.D.* no. 175, pp. 148–49, Balfour Papers, B.Mus.Add.Mss., no. 49746, Monson to Balfour, April 2, 1898.
91. F.O. 27/3416; (British Draft Counter-Project as given to Mr. Gosselin for communication), Apr. 4, 1898 (confidential); cf. Balfour Papers (Sanderson) B.Mus.Add.Mss. 493739, Sanderson to Balfour, April 9, 1898 (Enclosing copy of a memo he (Sanderson) had sent to Salisbury on West Africa).
92. F.O. 27/3408, Balfour to Monson, Mar. 29, 1898 (private).
93. F.O. 27/3413, Monson to Salisbury, May 1, 1898, no. 154 Africa, encl. *Report; B.D.* no. 177, pp. 152–53.
94. F.O. 27/3409, Salisbury to Monson, May 6, 1898, no. 225 Africa; F.O. 27/3416, Same to Same, June 4, 1898 (Tel.) no. 17 Africa; cf. F.O. 27/3340, C.O. to F.O., June 7, 1898 (secret and immediate); *B.D.* 178, pp. 153–54.
95. F.O. 27/3412, Salisbury's Minutes of April 25, 1898.
96. F.O. 27/3413, Monson to Salisbury, May 19, 1898, no. 178 Africa. Hanotaux said that "it would be a bitter disappointment to him if he did not sign" the Convention personally; cf. also ibid., Same to Same, May 23, 1898 (most confidential) no. 186 Africa; S.P. 116, Same to Same, May 20, 1898, nos. 30 and 31.
97. Ibid.
98. S.P. 116, Monson to Salisbury, May 20, 1898, no. 31.
99. Ibid., Same to Same, May 15, 1898, no. 29; F.O. 27/3409, Salis-

bury to Monson, May 29, 1898, no. 268 Africa and Minutes. The
F.O. draft agreement with France re the Niger Transit Trade can
be found in F.O. Print enclosed in original draft by Mr. H. Farnall
(an assistant clerk at the F.O.); and Mr. Lovell (in charge of the
Lagos Customs) of April 30, 1898, see F.O. 27/3438. Messrs.
Farnall and Lovell were sent to Paris for this purpose, and specifically to assist the Br. commissioners on technical points.

100. F.O. 27/3409, Salisbury to Monson, May 16, 1898, no. 240 Africa;
F.O. 27/3416, Same to Same, May 19, 1898 (Tel.) no. 12 Africa;
J.C.P. (Niger Negos. Docs.), Salisbury to Monson, May 29, 1898
(confidential); Cab. 37/47 (Niger Negos.) 3 pp. F.O., June 2,
1898.

101. Cab. 37/47 (Niger Negos.) 3 pp. F.O., June 2, 1898.

102. S.P. 116, Monson to Salisbury, June 3, 1898 (Tel.) no. 33; J.C.P.
(Imp. Aff. Niger Negos. Monson), Same to Same, June 1, 1898 (Tel.
sent 7:25 a.m.).

103. F.O. 27/3340, C.O. to F.O., May 23, 1898 (immediate, secret);
F.O. 27/3416, Bertie's Minutes of May 22, 1898.

104. S.P. (Chamberlain), Chamberlain to Salisbury, June 3, 1898 (private); F.O. 27/3340, C.O. to F.O., May 25, 1898 (secret, immediate).

105. Ibid.

106. Ibid.

107. Ibid.

108. Hill's Minutes on ibid.

109. Salisbury's Minutes on ibid.

110. F.O. 27/3409, Bertie's note to Salisbury of May 29, 1898; and
Salisbury's note to Bertie of same date.

111. Ibid., Salisbury to Monson, May 29, 1898, no. 268 Africa and
Minutes; F.O. 27/3416, Same to Same, June 4, 1898 (Tel.) no. 16
Africa.

112. F.O. 27/3340, Hill's memo of May 25, 1898.

113. J.C.P. (Salisbury), Salisbury to Chamberlain, June 2, 1898 (private); partly quoted in Garvin, *Life of Chamberlain,* 3, pp. 218–19.

114. S.P. (Chamberlain), Chamberlain to Salisbury, June 2, 1898 (private); Garvin, *Life of Chamberlain,* 3, pp. 219–20.

115. J.C.P. (Salisbury), Salisbury to Chamberlain, June 3, 1898 (private); Garvin, *Life of Chamberlain,* 3, p. 120.

116. S.P. (Chamberlain), Chamberlain to Salisbury, June 3, 1898
(private).

117. F.O. 27/3414, Monson to Salisbury, June 3, 1898, no. 203 Africa.

118. The following are the synopsis of the articles: 1. Delimitation of
the Gold Coast hinterland; 2. Delimitation of territories west of the
Niger; 3. Delimitation of the Niger; 4. Delimitation of the territories east of the Niger; 5. Appointment of commissioners; 6. Treatment of native chiefs; 7. Noninterference in respective spheres;

8. Evacuation of troops; 9. Leases, etc.; 10. Fiscal arrangements; 11. Signatures and annexes.

119. F.O. 27/3414, Monson to Salisbury, June 8, 1898, no. 203 Africa.

120. This line of thought was roundly discredited by the *London Daily Graphic,* an independent organ, in an editorial of Nov. 30, 1897, entitled, "The Government and West Africa."

121. Garvin, *Life of Chamberlain,* 3, p. 203.

122. *Q.V.L., Extract from the Queen's Journal,* Nov. 14, 1897, p. 209.

123. B.Mus.Add.Mss. 49691/2 (Balfour Papers), Salisbury to Balfour, 9, Apr. 9, 1898. But a few months earlier he had told Goschen: "I don't think Chamberlain wants a war," Salisbury to Goschen, Sept. 20, 1897, cited Cecil, *Salisbury,* 5 (draft), p. 240.

124. Garvin, *Life of Chamberlain,* 3, p. 215; Wilkinson to Chamberlain, Mar. 2, 1898. Spencer Wilkinson was Britain's leading writer on foreign relations, politics, and defense.

125. See, for example, S.P. (Queen Victoria), Salisbury to Queen Victoria, Feb. 5, 1898 (Tel.); Same to Same, Feb. 12, 1898 (Tel.); Same to Same, Feb. 23, 1898 (Tel.); Devonshire to Same, Mar. 4, 1898 (Tel.). Between Feb. 5 and Mar. 4, 1898, there were four Cabinets on the Niger question.

126. Whenever Salisbury was away on holiday, or was indisposed, the Cabinet tended to await decisions from him, see, S.P. (Queen Victoria), Devonshire to Victoria, Mar. 4, 1898 (Tel.); F.O. 27/3416, Sanderson to Monson, Mar. 15, 1898 (private tel.).

127. It is surprising that the authors of *Africa and the Victorians* consistently minimized the importance of the West African question (see especially p. 406). Cabinet ministers considered it as of the greatest importance; the public press was of the same view; to Hanotaux it was "la grosse question" (F.O. 27/3410, Monson to Salisbury, Jan. 12, 1898, no. 16 Africa).

128. S.P. (Goschen), Goschen to Salisbury, Sept. 4, 1897. The strike referred to was by engineers in Britain.

129. Ibid., Same to Same, Sept. 10, 1897.

130. Ibid., Same to Same, Sept. 19, 1897; partly quoted in A. D. Elliot, *The Life of Lord Goschen,* 2 (London: Longmans, 1911), p. 211.

131. S.P. (Hicks-Beach), Hicks-Beach to Salisbury, Oct. 1, 1897.

132. F.O. 800/2 (Sanderson Papers), Salisbury's Minutes of Sept. 28, 1897.

133. S.P. (Hicks-Beach), Hicks-Beach to Salisbury, Nov. 1, 1897.

134. See *Nineteenth Century,* 38, no. 223, Sept., 1895, p. 443.

135. *Hansard* (Commons), 4s, 63, Aug. 2, 1898, col. 936. He was Col. Sir H. Vincent, M.P. for Sheffield, Central.

136. *Westminster Gazette,* June 13, 1898, editorial.

137. *Daily Chronicle,* June 13, 1898, editorial.

138. *Daily News,* June 16, 1898, editorial.

139. The truth is that until the outbreak of the Boer War in 1899, the

gulf between the expansionist and antiexpansionist organs had been narrowing toward the advantage of the former since 1895.

140. F.O. 27/3414, Monson to Salisbury, June 11, 1898, no. 206 Africa; Same to Same, June 15, 1898, no. 214 Africa with enclosure; F.O. 27/3415, Same to Same, Aug. 4, 1899 (most confidential), no. 264 Africa.

141. F.O. 27/3414, Monson to Bertie, June 16, 1898 (private) and Minutes.

142. Flint, *Goldie*, p. 293, also holds this view.

143. S.P. 119, Salisbury to Monson, June 17, 1898, no. 26. Gosselin was knighted and promoted to the post of an additional assistant secretary at the F.O.

144. *Times*, June 13, 1898, Leading Article; cf. F.O. 27/3336, Salisbury to Monson, Nov. 23, 1897, no. 367 Africa (copy of draft dictated by Salisbury).

145. Robinson and Gallagher, *Africa and the Victorians*, pp. 379, 402–9. The authors seemed to have hurried over the chapters on West Africa. It may be because, as they consistently held, West African questions were unimportant in their opinion. I do not reject the overriding importance of the Nile question, but I am inclined to the belief that this important issue may have affected the Niger Negotiations no more than did the Transvaal troubles, the difficulties in China, the Newfoundland question, etc.; just as they were, in turn, affected by the West African question.

146. See, for example, F.O. 27/3336, Salisbury to Monson, Dec. 9, 1897, no. 406 Africa; F.O. 27/3341, Monson to Salisbury, Dec. 10, 1898, no. 413 Africa–, re S's no. 406 Africa. Monson instructed Gosselin "to make no reference . . . to the Basin of the Upper Nile"; F.O. 27/3336, Bertie to Monson, Nov. 30, 1897 (private copy); F.O. 27/3408, Balfour to Same, Mar. 28, 1898. In this dispatch, Balfour (Salisbury was on holiday) revealed that he offered to recognize French claims east of Lake Chad, in return for their recognition of British rights in the Nile Valley. The offer was turned down. This is the only concrete proposal we have; and much cannot be made of it; S.P. 115, Monson to Salisbury, Nov. 19, 1897, no. 88; ibid., Same to Same, Dec. 1, 1897, no. 91. In his impressive speech in the Senate supporting the convention, Delcasse made it clear that the Egyptian question in no way affected the Niger Negotiations. Salisbury merely minuted that Delcasse had said nothing new, cf. F.O. 2/219, Monson to Salisbury, June 1, 1899, no. 56 Africa, with encl. and Minutes.

147. S.P. 116, Monson to Salisbury, June 17, 1898, no. 36; cf. F.O. 27/3414, Same to Same, June 15, 1898, no. 212 Africa; *B.D.*, pp. 157–58.

148. See, for example, F.O. 2/218, Salisbury to Monson, Jan. 11, 1899, Apr. 18, 29, 1899; F.O. 2/219, F. H. Newton (H.M.'s Consul at Algiers) to Salisbury, Dec. 31, 1898 (confidential), Monson to

Same, Jan. 8, 1899 (secret), Jan. 12, 1899 (secret), and Jan. 17, 20, 22, 27, 1899, Feb. 17, Mar. 12, 1899, Reginald Lister to Same, Mar. 14 & Apr. 11, 1899 (secret); F.O. 2/221, H. H. Johnston to Same, Mar. 15, 1899 (confidential. tel. from Tunis) and Apr. 22, 1899 (Tel.); L. R. Arthur (H.M. Consul at Dakar) to Same, Feb. 25, 1899 (confidential. tel.); cf. C.O. 879/58, African (West) no. 581, Mar. 1, 1899, and ibid., no. 582, Feb. 28, 1899; see Minutes on C.O. to F.O. June 15, 1898, F.O. 83/1610. Even after ratification, a constant watch was kept over French activities, cf. F.O. 2/218, Salisbury to Monson, June 30, 1899 (copy), and Sept. 8, 1899, and Aug. 26, 1899. F.O. 2/221, Salisbury to Cambon (French ambassador), June 1899.

149. S.P. 116, Monson to Salisbury, Aug. 2, 1898, no. 40; F.O. 2/219, Same to Same, June 1, 1899, no. 56 Africa, encl. speeches in Senate; ibid. Herbert to Same, June 8, 1899, no. 58 Africa with enclosures including the *Journal Officielle* of June 8, 1899, and the Report of the Senate Committee approving the Convention.

CHAPTER VII

1. For details see J. M. Gray, *The British in Mombasa, 1824–1826* (London, 1957).
2. R. Coupland, *East Africa and Its Invaders* (London, 1938), pp. 421–58; idem., *The Exploitation of East Africa 1856–1890* (London, 1939), pp. 134–36.
3. Great Britain, *The Kenya Coastal Strip: Report of the Commissioner*, Cmnd. 1585 (H.M.S.O.; London, Dec., 1961); Coupland, *East Africa*, pp. 14–36.
4. *British and Foreign State Papers*, 57, (1866–67), p. 785.
5. J. M. Gray, "Zanzibar and the Coastal Belt, 1840–1884" in R. Oliver and G. Mathews, eds., *History of East Africa*, 1 (Oxford University Press, 1963), pp. 233–34.
6. Ibid., pp. 234–35.
7. Ibid., pp. 237–38.
8. Richard Burton, *Zanzibar: City, Island and Coast* (London, 1872), 11, pp. 344–47.
9. Gray, "Zanzibar," pp. 238–39.
10. *Parl. Pap.*, 61 (1873), *Corresp. re. Sir Bartle Frere's Mission to the East Coast of Africa.*
11. Cited in Coupland, *Exploitation*, p. 433.
12. Ibid., p. 398.
13. P.R.O. 30/29/144, Gladstone to Granville, Dec. 11, 1884.
14. Coupland, *Exploitation*, p. 394.
15. P.R.O. 30/29/144, Granville to Malet, Jan. 14, 1885; Coupland, *Exploitation*, p. 399.
16. Ibid., Munster to Gladstone, Feb. 6, 1885; Coupland, *Exploitation*, pp. 399–400.

338 *Notes to Pages 149–57*

17. Ibid., Malet to Gladstone, Apr. 28, 1885; Coupland, *Exploitation*, pp. 410–11.
18. Ibid., Same to Same, Apr. 30, 1885.
19. Coupland, *Exploitation*, p. 429.
20. Ibid., Rosebery to Gladstone, Apr. 30, 1885, p. 425.
21. For details of these negotiations see ibid., pp. 448–78.
22. S.P. 44, Salisbury to Malet, Sept. 1, 1885, Tel. no. 14.
23. S.P. 44, Salisbury to Malet, Aug. 24, 1885 (private), no. 13.
24. Ibid., Same to Wolff, Sept. 8, 1885 (private), no. 35.
25. Coupland, *Exploitation*, p. 437.
26. Ibid., Kirk to Salisbury, Sept. 29, 1885, p. 439.
27. Ibid., p. 438.
28. For details of this sordid affair see ibid., pp. 437–39.
29. Cecil, *Salisbury*, 3, p. 230.
30. *Parl. Pap.*, 67 (1885–86), p. 1130.
31. Coupland, *Exploitation*, Iddesleigh to Sultan, Nov. 6, 1886, p. 478.
32. Ibid., p. 484.
33. Ibid., p. 482.
34. S.P. 51, Salisbury to Wolff, Apr. 29, 1887, no. 165.
35. Coupland, *Exploitation*, p. 482.
36. Ibid., p. 481.
37. S.P. 59, Salisbury to Lytton, Feb. 8, 1888, no. 76.
38. F.O. 84/1892, Minutes on Malet to Salisbury, Sept. 26, 1888, Tel. no. 8.
39. S.P. 46, Salisbury to Victoria, Oct. 29, 1888, no. 49; ibid. no. 50 (encl.) Cabinet Print; S.P. 61, Malet to Salisbury, to Nov., 1888, no. 132; Cecil, *Salisbury*, 4, p. 236.
40. Cited J. Iliffe, "Tanzania Under German and British Rule," in B. A. Ogot and J. A. Kieran, eds., *Zamani: A Survey of East African History* (EAPH, 1968), p. 291. For account of this revolt see *Parl. Pap.* C. 5822 (1889), no. 1 Africa.
41. S.P. 80 (to Zanzibar, 1888–92), Salisbury to Portal, Apr. 4, 1889.
42. See the next chapter for a further account of the 1890 agreement.
43. Cecil, *Salisbury*, 4, pp. 234–35.
44. C.A.B. 37/43, memo by Curzon, Dec. 29, 1896, no. 58.
45. For more details of the events leading up to the assumption of the protectorate see L. W. Hollingsworth, *Zanzibar Under the Foreign Office, 1890–1913* (London, 1953), pp. 37–56.
46. S.P. 80, Salisbury to Euan Smith, Nov. 7, 1890.
47. Cited in Cecil, *Salisbury*, 4, p. 304.
48. Ibid., Portal to Salisbury, Sept. 2, 1891, p. 305.
49. S.P. 80, Salisbury to Portal, Dec. 4, 1891, quoted substantially in Cecil, *Salisbury*, 4, pp. 306–7.
50. Ibid., Same to Same, Mar. 8, 1892; Cecil, *Salisbury*, 4, pp. 307–8.
51. C.A.B. 37/43, Memo by G. N. Curzon, Dec. 29, 1896, no. 58.
52. A. R. Tucker, *Eighteen Years in Uganda and East Africa*, 2, (London, 1908), p. 71.

53. P.R.O., C.A.B. 37/43, Memo by Curzon, Dec. 29, 1896, no. 58.
54. Lugard Papers, 40 (Kirk), Kirk to Lugard, Mar. 5, 1896.
55. Ibid., Same to Same, April 22, 1896.
56. F.O.C.P. (6709), "Memo by S. re. the abolition of slavery in Zanzibar," Dec. 16, 1895.
57. Ibid.
58. See, S.P. 92, Memo by Chamberlain: "Slavery in Zanzibar," Dec. 18, 1895 (copy).
59. S.P. 123 (Zanzibar 1895–1900), Hardinge to Salisbury, Jan. 16, 1896, no. 21.
60. F.O.C.P. (6755), "Memo by G. N. Curzon on the proposed abolition of the legal status of slavery in Zanzibar and Pemba," Feb. 5, 1896; F.O. 800/147 (Curzon Papers), for original manuscript.
61. F.O.C.P. (6756), Memo by Sir P. Anderson: "Abolition of legal status of slavery in Zanzibar," Feb. 7, 1896.
62. Cf. A. H. Hardinge, *A Diplomatist in the East* (London, 1928), pp. 131–32.
63. Ibid., p. 119.
64. F.O.C.P. (6756), Memo by Anderson, Feb. 7, 1896.
65. Ibid.
66. Lugard Papers, 40 (Kirk), Kirk to Lugard, July 23, 1896.
67. Tucker, *Eighteen Years*, 2, p. 60. For a good account of this rebellion, see Hollingsworth, *Zanzibar*, pp. 107 ff.
68. Tucker, *Eighteen Years*, 2, pp. 60–62; cf. Hollingsworth, *Zanzibar*, pp. 119–27; F.O. 107/54 and 57.
69. F.O. 107/57, Hardinge to Salisbury, June 21, 1896 (confidential) Tel. no. 4.
70. F.O. 107/54, Cave to Salisbury, Aug. 29, 1896, no. 244.
71. Ibid.
72. Cf. Hollingsworth, *Zanzibar*, p. 127, for reaction of public opinion.
73. *P.M.G.*, Sept. 7, 1895, editorial, Oct. 19, 1895; Oct. 21, 1895.
74. F.O. 800/160, Curzon to Bertie, Aug. 31, 1896.
75. Lugard Papers, 41 (Kirk), Kirk to Lugard, Aug. 28, 1896.
76. F.O. 800/160, Curzon to Bertie, Aug. 31, 1896.
77. F.O. 800/160, Minutes by Bertie, Sept. 1, 1896.
78. F.O. 800/160, Minutes by Salisbury on same.
79. S.P. (Hicks-Beach), Hicks-Beach to Salisbury, Aug. 28, 1896.
80. Lugard Papers, 41 (Kirk), Kirk to Lugard, Aug. 26, 1896.
81. Ibid., Hicks-Beach to Salisbury, Sept. 5, 1896.
82. C.A.B. 37/43, Memo by Curzon, Dec. 29, 1896, no. 58; F.O. 800/28 for original manuscript.
83. Ibid., "Memo by J.C.: Slavery in Zanzibar," Jan. 2, 1897, no. 61.
84. S.P. (Goschen), Goschen to Salisbury, Jan. 11, 1897.
85. S.P. (Hicks-Beach), Hicks-Beach to Salisbury, Aug. 28, Sept. 5, Dec. 30, 1896.
86. Ibid., Same to Same, Mar. 1, 1897.
87. Hardinge, *A Diplomatist*, p. 194.

88. *Hansard,* Commons, 4s., 53, Feb. 10, 1898, cols. 327–31.
89. For details see *Parl. Pap.,* Africa no. 2 (1897), (C. 8433) 62, pp. 707–14.
90. *Hansard,* Commons, 4s., 53, Feb. 10, 1898, cols. 309–17 (Curzon).
91. Ibid. The motion censuring the government's attitude was lost by only 61 votes.
92. Lugard Papers, 41 (Kirk), Kirk to Lugard, Sept. 10, 1897.
93. Ibid., Kirk to Same, Aug. 27, 1897.
94. Tucker, *Eighteen Years,* 2, p. 64.
95. Cf. *Hansard,* Commons, 4s., 50, June 24, 1897, R. Reid (cols. 533–34); Webster (cols. 538–57).
96. S.P., 123, Salisbury to Hardinge, June 29, 1897, Tel. no. 27.
97. *Parl. Pap.* Africa no. 6 (1898), (C. 8858) 60, Hardinge to Salisbury, July 4, and Aug. 1897, pp. 559 ff. But Hollingsworth, *Zanzibar,* p. 145, maintains that, in Zanzibar, every slave was aware of the decree in a matter of weeks, rather than months.
98. Harlow and Chilver, eds., *History of East Africa,* 2, p. 649.
99. Tucker, *Eighteen Years,* 2, p. 71.
100. *The Times,* Sept. 12, 1897.
101. Hollingsworth, *Zanzibar,* pp. 146–53, discusses this question in detail and gives the figures as follows: by 1898, only 2,735 slaves were freed; in 1899, it was 3,659; and in 1900, a bare 1,700. By 1900, therefore, a total of 8,114 slaves had been freed out of a total slave population of 140,000.
102. *Hansard,* Commons, 4s., Feb. 10, 1898, col. 302.
103. F.O. 84/1828, Salisbury's Minutes on Johnston to Salisbury, Oct. 4, 1887, cited in Oliver, *Harry Johnston,* p. 118.
104. S.P. 123, Salisbury to Hardinge, July 15, 1898, no. 33.
105. Cf. Harlow and Chilver, *History of East Africa,* 2, p. 651.
106. Cf. *Parl. Pap.,* 1897 (C. 8683) 60, p. 26.
107. Lugard Papers, 41 (Kirk), Kirk to Lugard, Mar. 10, May 11 and Sept. 17, 1897.
108. Hardinge, *A Diplomatist,* p. 193.
109. Mathews was said to have used Wilde's famous trial and conviction to discredit the humanitarians until Hardinge pointed out the error to him. Ibid.
110. Ibid., p. 194.
111. Ibid.
112. Lugard Papers, 41 (Kirk), Kirk to Lugard, March 10, 1897.
113. *Hansard,* Commons, 4s, 31 (May, 1895), cols. 664 ff.
114. For discussion of the A.S.S. agitation, see Hollingsworth, *Zanzibar,* pp. 132–40.
115. F.O. 107/52, Hardinge to Salisbury, May 4, 1896, no. 144.
116. J.C.P. (Balfour), Chamberlain to Balfour, Dec. 10, 1895.
117. Hardinge, *A Diplomatist,* p. 195.
118. Cf. *Hansard,* 4s., 53, Feb. 10, 1898.
119. Lugard Papers, 41 (Kirk), Kirk to Lugard, Nov. 6, 1896.

120. Ibid., Same to Same, Dec. 22, 1896.
121. F.O. 107/77, Hardinge to Salisbury, Apr. 9, 1897, no. 78. Cf. Lugard Papers, 41 (Kirk), Kirk to Lugard, May 6, 1897.
122. S.P. 123, Hardinge to Salisbury, Mar. 31, 1899, no. 35.
123. Ibid., Same to Same, Mar. 31, 1899, no. 35; Aug. 13, 1898, no. 34.

CHAPTER VIII

1. For these experiences see J. H. Speke, *Journal of the Discovery of the Source of the Nile* (London, 1863); J. A. Grant, *A Walk Across Africa* (London, 1864); S. W. Baker, *Albert Nyanza* (London, 1866); idem, *Ismailia* (London, 1874).
2. Speke, *Journal*, esp. pp. 246–60. Cf. also E. R. Sanders, "The Hamitic Hypothesis; Its Origin and Function in Time Perspective," *J.A.H.*, 10, 4 (1969), pp. 521–32.
3. H. Waller, ed., *The Last Journals of David Livingstone* (London, 1874); G. Masefield, "Livingstone and the Baganda," *Uganda Journal*, 10, 2 (1946), pp. 79–83.
4. J. M. Gray, "Sir John Kirk and Mutesa," *Uganda Journal*, 15 (1951), pp. 1–16.
5. Cited in Coupland, *Exploitation*, p. 328.
6. H. P. Gale, "Mutesa I—Was He a God?" *Uganda Journal*, 20, 1 (1956), p. 83.
7. J. M. Gray, "Ahmed bin Ibrahim, The First Arab to reach Buganda," *U.J.*, 11 (1947); Apolo Kagwa and Henry W. Duta, "Mengo Notes" *U.J.*, 11 (1947), p. 110.
8. R. Rodd, ed., *The British Mission to Uganda in 1893* (London, 1894), pp. 199–200.
9. H. P. Gale, "Mutesa I," *U.J.*, pp. 72–87; J. Roscoe, *The Baganda* (London, 1911), p. 186; R. F. Burton, *The Lake Regions of Central Africa* (London, 1860), pp. 11, 191; Speke, *Journal*, p. 302; cf. D. A. Low, *Buganda in Modern History* (London, 1971), pp. 17–32.
10. Ahmed Katumba and F. B. Welbourn, "Muslim Martyrs of Buganda," *U.J.*, 28, 2 (1964).
11. Gray, "Kirk and Mutesa," *U.J.*, 15 (1951); C. T. Wilson, and R. W. Felkin, *Uganda and the Egyptian Sudan* (London, 1881).
12. H. M. Stanley, *Through the Dark Continent* (London, 1890), p. 206.
13. Low, *Buganda*, p. 25.
14. M. S. M. Kiwanuka, *Muteesa of Uganda* (E. Afric. Literature Bureau, 1967), p. 50.
15. Ibid., pp. 50–56.
16. Ibid., pp. 63–66.
17. Low, *Buganda*, pp. 26–27.

18. Gale, "Mutesa I," *U.J.*, 73.
19. G. N. Uzoigwe, *Revolution and Revolt in Bunyuro-Kitara* (Longmans, 1970); idem, "Kabalega and the Making of a New Kitara," *Tarikh*, 3, 2 (1970), pp. 5–21.
20. The most important ones include F. Faupel, *African Holocaust* (London, 1965); D. A. Low, *Religion and Society in Buganda, 1875–1900, East African Studies* no. 8 (Kampala, n.d.); J. A. Rowe, "The Purge of Christians at Mwanga's Court," *J.A.H.* 4, 1 (1964), pp. 55–71; idem, *Lugard at Kampala* (Longmans, 1969); David Kavulu, *The Uganda Martyrs* (Longmans, 1969); M. S. M. Kiwanuka, "Kabaka Mwanga and His Political Parties," *U.J.*, 33, 1 (1969), pp. 1–16; T. B. Fletcher, "Mwanga—The Man and His Times," *U.J.*, 4, 2 (1936), pp. 162–67; J. M. Gray, "The Year of the Three Kings of Buganda . . . , 1888–1889," *U.J.*, 14, 1 (1950), pp. 15–47; R. P. Ashe, *Two Kings of Uganda* (London, 1890); idem, *Chronicles of Uganda* (London, 1894); C. C. Wrigley, "The Christian Revolution in Buganda," *Comparative Studies in Society and History*, 11, 1 (1959), pp. 33–48.
21. Ashe, *Chronicles*, pp. 67–68.
22. For a more objective study of Mwanga's career see Fletcher, "Mwanga," *U.J.*, 4, 2 (1936); cf. Kiwanuka, "Kabaka Mwanga," *U.J.*, 33, 1 (1969).
23. Kavulu, *Uganda Martyrs*, pp. 19–20.
24. Fletcher, "Mwanga," pp. 163–64.
25. For details see Faupel, *African Holocaust;* Rowe, "Purge of Christians," *J.A.H.*, 4, 1 (1964); Kavulu, *Uganda Martyrs*.
26. Kiwanuka, "Kabaka Mwanga," *U.J.*, 33, 1 (1969).
27. Gray, "Three Kings," p. 18.
28. J. A. Rowe, "The Baganda Revolutionaries," *Tarikh*, 3, 2 (1970), pp. 41–42.
29. According to Kiganda custom the eldest prince was debarred from the throne.
30. Low, *Buganda in Modern History*, p. 33.
31. Rowe, "Baganda Revolutionaries," *Tarikh* 3, 2 (1970), p. 36.
32. For a study of this revolution see Wrigley, *Comparative Studies*, 11, 1 (1959).
33. Rowe, *Lugard at Kampala*, pp. 24–25; cf. Perham, *Lugard: Years of Adventure*, pp. 163–472, for a full account of Lugard's activities in Uganda.
34. M. Perham and M. Bull, eds., *The Diaries of Lord Lugard* (London, 1959), 3, p. 34.
35. For details see Rodd, *British Mission*, pp. 199–200.
36. Entebbe Secretariat Archives (henceforth E.S.A.) A 4/2/1895, Cunningham to Entebbe, July 17, 1895; ibid., Madocks to O.C. Troops, Bunyoro, Aug. 18, 1895.
37. For a thorough study of this agreement see D. A. Low and R. C.

Pratt, *Buganda and British Overrule: 1900–1955* (London, 1960), part I.

38. K. Ingham, *The Making of Modern Uganda* (London, 1958); idem, *A History of East Africa* (Longmans, 1965) 3d. ed., chap. 6; A. D. Roberts, "The Sub-imperialism of the Buganda," *J.A.H.*, 3, 3 (1962), pp. 435–50; H. B. Thomas, "Capax Imperii—The Story of Semei Kakunguru," *U.J.*, 6, 3 (1939), pp. 125–36.

39. See, for example, Robert Rotberg, *Christian Missions and the Creation of Northern Rhodesia, 1880–1924* (Princeton, 1965); R. Oliver, *The Missionary Factor in East Africa* (Longmans, 1965), chap. 3; L. H. Gann, *A History of Northern Rhodesia* (N.Y., 1969) chap. 2; A. J. Wills, *An Introduction to the History of Central Africa*, 2d. ed. (Oxford University Press, 1967).

40. J. D. Omer-Cooper, *The Zulu Aftermath* (Longmans, 1966).

41. T. O. Ranger, ed., *Aspects of Central African History* (London, 1968), p. 85.

42. For evidence of Livingstone's racism see I. Schapera, ed., *Livingstone's Private Journals 1851–53* (London, 1960), pp. 167–68; D. and C. Livingstone, *Narrative of an Expedition to the Zambesi and its Tributaries* (London, 1865), p. 8; *Proceedings of the Royal Geographical Society 1857–58*, p. 126; D. Livingstone, *Missionary Travels and Researches in South Africa* (London, 1857), p. 679; J. P. R. Wallis, ed., *The Zambesi Expedition of David Livingstone 1858–1863* (London, 1956), pp. 11, 416; cf. F. C. Selous, *Sunshine and Storm in Rhodesia*, 2d. ed. (London, 1896), p. 31.

43. Quoted in Gann, *History of Rhodesia*, p. 31; cf. also H. A. C. Cairns, *Prelude to Imperialism: British Reactions to Central African Society 1840–1890* (London, 1965), pp. 192–99 for Livingstone's ideas.

44. Ibid., pp. 24–32; Rotberg, *Christian Mission*, pp. 4–12.

45. Oliver, *Missionary Factor*, p. 70; cf. W. P. Livingstone, *Laws of Livingstonia* (London, 1921), p. 140.

46. Oliver, *Missionary Factor*, p. 69.

47. Quoted in Ranger, *Central African History*, p. 105.

48. Gann, *History of Rhodesia*, p. 38.

49. Ibid., p. 35.

50. Ibid., p. 38.

51. D. Crawford, *Thinking Black* (London, 1913), pp. 324–25.

52. F.O. 84/2052, Johnston to B.S.A.C., July 17, 1890 (copy); cf. Oliver, *Missionary Factor*, p. 128.

53. Quoted in Ranger, *Central African History*, p. 140.

54. Ibid., p. 134; cf. H. A. C. Cairns, *Prelude to Imperialism* for more details.

55. R. Brown, "The Ndebele Succession Crisis 1868–1877" in *Historians in Tropical Africa* (Leverhulme History Conference, 1960), pp. 159–75.

56. This episode of southern Rhodesian history has been thoroughly

studied. See T. O. Ranger, *Revolt in Southern Rhodesia 1896–1897* (London, 1967); idem, *Aspects* . . . , pp. 142–52.

57. Cf. D. Livingstone, *Missionary Travels*, idem and Charles Livingstone, *Expedition to the Zambesi.*
58. Cf. C. W. Mackintosh, *Coillard of the Zambesi* (London, 1907), p. 380.
59. J. Johnston, *Reality Versus Romance in South Central Africa* (London, 1893), pp. 30–39.
60. F.O. 84/2115, Buchanan to F.O. June 10, 1891 cited Rotberg, op. cit., pp. 132–33.
61. For details of this curious evangelism see Rotberg, *Christian Missions*, pp. 33–37.
62. A. J. Hanna, *The Beginnings of Nyasaland and North-Eastern Rhodesia 1859–1895* (Oxford University Press, 1956), p. 135.
63. Cited in A. L. Kennedy, "Fashoda," in *Quarterly Review*, 286, no. 567, April, 1948, p. 146.
64. R. Oliver and A. Atmore, *Africa Since 1800* (Cambridge University Press, 1967), p. 113.
65. Cf. ibid.
66. Cf. ibid.
67. Robinson and Gallagher, *Africa and the Victorians*, p. 223.
68. Ibid., p. 228; cf. Wills, *Introduction . . . Central Africa*, p. 138.
69. Cecil, *Salisbury*, 4, p. 241; cf. S. P. (Holland), Knutsford to Salisbury, Oct. 15, 1888.
70. Robinson and Gallagher, *Africa and the Victorians*, p. 227.
71. F.O. 84/1968, F.O. to Johnston, Feb. 13, 1889 and Mar. 30, 1889.
72. Johnston, *Story*, p. 231.
73. F.O. 2/55, Johnston to Rhodes, Oct. 8, 1893.
74. Oliver, *Johnston*, pp. 150–51.
75. W. P. Livingstone, *A Prince of Missionaries* (London, 1931), pp. 48–52; cf. Oliver, *Missionary Factor*, p. 126.
76. F.O. 84/2051, F.O. to Johnston, Feb. 4, 1890.
77. Hertslet, *Map of Africa*, 111, pp. 1016–26.
78. Oliver, *Missionary Factor*, p. 128.
79. D. A. Low, "The British and Uganda, 1862–1900" (Oxford Ph.D. thesis, June, 1957), pp. 125–26.
80. Cf. ibid., 92, Holmwood to Baring, Sept. 25, 1886.
81. F.O. 403/98, Iddesleigh to Holmwood, Sept. 25, 1886.
82. F.O. 403/142, Salisbury to Malet, June 14, 1890, no. 233 Africa.
83. Roger Louis, "The Anglo-German Hinterland Settlement of 1890 and Uganda," *U.J.*, 27, 1 (1963), pp. 71–73.
84. F.O. 84/2030, Salisbury to Malet, May 5, 1890, no. 140 Africa.
85. This can be inferred from Anderson's Cabinet memo, F.O. 84/2258, Sept. 7, 1892.
86. This memo is quoted substantially in Robinson and Gallagher, *Africa and the Victorians*, p. 191.
87. Low, "British and Uganda," p. 101.

88. F.O. 84/1912, Salisbury to Euan-Smith, Sept. 15, 1888 (Tel.).
89. H. M. Stanley, *Autobiography* (Boston, 1909), p. 447.
90. J. De Kiewiet, "History of the Imperial British East Africa Company 1876–1895" (London, Ph.D. thesis, Oct., 1955), p. 98.
91. S. P. (Goschen), Salisbury to Goschen, April 10, 1890; also Cecil, *Salisbury*, 4, p. 281.
92. *G.D.D.*, 11, Hatzfeldt to Bismarck, Dec. 22, 1889, VIII, p. 6–7.
93. Ibid., "German Note," p. 30.
94. S.P. (Secs. Note Book), Salisbury to Pelly, May 24, 1890.
95. S.P. 63, Malet to Salisbury, Apr. 19, 1890, no. 30.
96. *G.D.D.*, 11, "German Note," p. 30.
97. S.P. 61, Malet to Salisbury, Nov. 10, 1888, no. 132.
98. S.P. 79, Euan-Smith to Same, July 19, 1889.
99. F.O. 84/2030, Salisbury to Malet, May 5, 1890, no. 140 Africa.
100. Roger Louis, *U.J.*, 27, 1 (1963), p. 72.
101. F.O. 84/2031, Anderson to Malet, May 9, 1890, no. 4 (with encl.).
102. Ibid., Malet to Salisbury, May 9, 1890, no. 53 Africa (with encl.).
103. S.P. 63, Same to Same, May 31, 1890, no. 39.
104. Ibid., Swaine to Barrington, July 23, 1892, no. 105; cf. ibid., Trench to Salisbury, July 23, 1892, no. 104.
105. *G.D.D.*, 11, Hatzfeldt to Marschall, May 14, 1890 (private), pp. 32–33.
106. S.P. 61, Salisbury to Malet, July 3, 1889, no. 56.
107. *Parl. Pap.*, 1890 (C. 6043) 51, Same to Same, June 14, 1890, pp. 16–17.
108. Baron von Eckardstein, *Ten Years at the Court of St. James 1895–1905* (London, 1921), p. 99.
109. Ibid., pp. 99–100.
110. F.O. 800/17, Lascelles to Salisbury, Feb. 18, 1898.
111. S.P. 45, Victoria to Salisbury, June 9, 1890 (tel.), no. 88; cf. ibid. 46, Salisbury to Victoria, June, 1890, no. 65; cf. *O.V.L.*, 35, 1, pp. 613–15.
112. See Uzoigwe, "Kabalega and the Making of a new Kitara," *Tarikh*, 3, 2 (1970).
113. F.O.C.P. (6249), memo by Anderson, Sept. 10, 1892 (confidential).
114. Ibid.
115. Cited L. Woolf, *Empire and Commerce in Africa*, p. 297.
116. F.O.C.P. (6249), idem; Kiewiet, "History . . . British East Africa Company," p. 181.
117. For a study of British opinion on this issue see D. A. Low, "British Public Opinion and the Uganda Question, Oct.–Dec., 1892," *U.J.*, 18, Sept., 1954; Low, "British and Uganda," pp. 294–318.
118. For a history of this railway see M. P. Hill, *Permanent Way*, 1 (Nairobi, 1961).
119. G. N. Sanderson, "The Anglo-German Agreement of 1890 and the Upper Nile" in *E.H.R.*, 78, no. 306, Jan., 1963, p. 55.
120. F.O.C.P. (6249), idem; Gardiner, *Life of Harcourt*, 11, pp. 191–93.

121. F.O.C.P. (6249), idem.
122. For the politics of annexation see Robinson and Gallagher, *Africa and the Victorians,* chap. 9.
123. Andrew Roberts, "The Evolution of the Uganda Protectorate," *U.J.,* 27, 1 (1963), p. 95.
124. F.O. 83/1310, Memo by Lugard, Mar. 10, 1894, cf. also A. J. P. Taylor, "Prelude to Fashoda" in *E.H.R.,* 65 (1950), p. 54; W. L. Langer, *The Diplomacy of Imperialism,* pp. 263–68.
125. F.O. 27/3368, Memo by Captain H. H. Wilson, Sept. 25, 1896 enclosure in W.O. to F.O.; Feb. 14, 1897 (secret).
126. Ibid., C.A.B. 37/44, nos. 10 and 18.
127. S.P. 113, Salisbury to Cromer, Nov. 8, 1895 (copy), no. 2.
128. Devonshire Papers, 340. 2697, Salisbury to Devonshire, Oct. 7, 1896 (private).
129. F.O.C.P. (7915), F.O. to C.O. Defense Committee, Nov. 7, 1898 (secret), appendix in no. 16.
130. Ibid., C.O. Defence Committee to F.O., Nov. 22, 1898, no. 16.
131. F.O. 27/3368, W.O. to F.O., Feb. 14, 1897 (secret).
132. Ibid.
133. Ibid., Memo by Major H. Northcote, encl. no. 4 in Same to Same, Feb. 14, 1897 (secret).
134. Ibid.
135. Ibid., Hill's Minutes of Feb. 23, 1897, approved by Salisbury.
136. Ibid., Hill's Minutes of Feb. 24, 1897.
137. Ibid.
138. S.P. 100 (Misc. M-P, 1895–1900), Macdonald to Barrington, Mar. 26, 1897, no. 1.
139. F.O. 2/144, Macdonald to Salisbury, June 17, 1897, no. 3.
140. S.P. 100, Same to Same, Sept. 29, 1897.
141. Ibid.
142. Ibid.
143. A detailed account of the mutiny is contained in F.O. 2/132–4, 144, 154–58, 161 (especially), and 174. Cf. also H. H. Austin, *With Macdonald in Uganda* (London, 1903), pp. 36–37, 90–144; F. Jackson, *Early Days in East Africa* (London, 1930), pp. 304–15; J. P. Barber, "The Macdonald Expedition to the Nile, 1897–1899," *U.J.,* 28, 1 (1964), pp. 1–14 (pedestrian); R. W. Beachey, "Macdonald's Expedition and the Uganda Mutiny, 1897–1898," *Historical Journal,* 10, 2 (1967), based mainly on F.O.C.P.
144. F.O. 2/174, Macdonald to Salisbury, Mar. 16, 1898, no. 25 (with encl.).
145. Ibid., Same to Same, July 18 and 20, 1898 (secret).
146. Ibid., Same to Same, July 27, 1898 (secret), with enclosures.
147. Ibid., Salisbury's Minutes on above.
148. Ibid., Macdonald to Salisbury, Dec. 13, 1898 (confidential), no. 45.
149. Ibid., F.O. Minutes on above.
150. F.O. 2/200, Salisbury to Berkeley, Jan. 27, 1899, no. 12.

151. S.P. 96 (Priv. Secs. Memo, 1895–1900), Barrington to Salisbury, April 5, 1899, no. 86.
152. Ibid., Minutes on above.

CHAPTER IX

1. S.P. 41, Salisbury to Wolff, Sept. 8, 1885 (private), no. 10.
2. For the private correspondence between Salisbury and Wolff re the Constantinople mission see S.P. 41, 42, 44, and 51. See also H. D. Wolff, *Rambling Recollections*, 2 vols. (London, 1908), 2, pp. 309–21; C. L. Smith, *The Embassy of Sir William White to Constantinople, 1886–1891* (London, 1957), pp. 73–86; M. P. Hornik, "The Mission of Sir Henry Drummond Wolff to Constantinople, 1885–87," in *E.H.R.*, 55, 220 (1940), pp. 598–623.
3. See S.P. 113, Salisbury to Cromer, 1896 (confidential), copy, no. 6; S.P. 114, Dufferin to Salisbury, Jan. 16, 1896, no. 24.
4. Cf. S.P. 55, Salisbury to Baring, Dec. 28, 1888 (private), no. 37; Same to Same, Mar. 28, 1890 (private); S.P. 51, Salisbury to Wolff, Windsor, Feb. 23, 1887 (private), no. 149; Earl of Cromer, *Modern Egypt*, 2 vols. (London, 1908), 1, p. 387.
5. Cf. S.P. 51, Salisbury to Wolff, Windsor, Feb. 23, 1887 (private), no. 149; Same to Same, Mar. 23, 1887, no. 155; Same to Same, Apr. 20, 1887, no. 162; S.P. 55, Same to Cromer, Feb. 18, 1887, no. 7.
6. S.P. 51, Salisbury to Wolff, Mar. 9, 1887, no. 153; S.P. 55, Same to Cromer, Jan. 21, Feb. 4 and 11, 1887, nos. 1, 3, and 5 respectively; see also Cecil, *Salisbury*, 4, p. 48; Marquess of Zetland, *Lord Cromer* (London, 1932), p. 149.
7. In June, 1892, created Baron and Viscount in 1899; created Earl of Cromer in 1901.
8. S.P. 54, Baring to Salisbury, Jan. 1, 1892, no. 82.
9. S.P. 59, Salisbury to Lyons, Feb. 5, 1887, no. 63.
10. S.P. 55, Salisbury to Baring, Nov. 21, 1890, no. 60.
11. The Italian danger was removed by the Anglo-Italian agreement of 1891.
12. For an excellent study of British sea power see A. J. Marder, *Anatomy of British Sea Power* (Connecticut, 1964).
13. S.P. 114, Dufferin to Salisbury, Dec. 5, 1895, no. 14.
14. G. N. Sanderson, *England, Europe, and the Upper Nile, 1882–1899* (Edinburgh University Press, 1965).
15. Ibid., p. 249.
16. F.O. 633/7, Rosebery to Cromer, Apr. 5, 1895 (confidential); Zetland, *Cromer*, p. 213.
17. For a similar view see S.P. 55, Salisbury to Baring, Dec. 24, 1890, no. 61.
18. F.O. 633/6, Cromer to Rosebery, Apr. 12, 1895; Zetland, *Cromer*, pp. 213–16.

19. Ibid.
20. Ibid., Same to Same, Apr. 13, 1895.
21. F.O. 633/7, Rosebery to Cromer, Apr. 22, 1895 (secret); F.O. 633/6, Cromer to Rosebery, May 4, 1895.
22. There is no truth in the view that, early in 1895, Salisbury was already contemplating the reconquest of the Sudan, see H. Whates, *The Third Salisbury Administration* (London, 1901), p. 165; Morrison B. Giffen, *Fachoda, the Incident and its Diplomatic Setting* (Chicago, 1930), 25; L. A. C. Raphael, *The Cape to Cairo Dream* (N.Y., 1936), p. 35; Hanotaux, *Fachoda*, pp. 101–2.
23. *Hansard*, Commons, 4s., 36, Aug. 30, 1895.
24. Ibid.
25. Mr. Alonzo Money, an Englishman on his father's side, held a responsible position in Egypt as a financial expert in the *Caisse*.
26. S.P. 109, Cromer to Barrington, Mar. 12, 1896, no. 15 and encls.
27. F.O. 633/5, Cromer to Money, July 1, 1895 (private), no. 619; S.P. 109 (from Egypt, 1896), Cromer to Barrington, Mar. 3, 1896, no. 18 and Minutes.
28. Ibid., Cromer to Barrington, Mar. 18 and 19, 1896, nos. 26 and 27.
29. Ibid., Money to Cromer, Mar. 19, 1896, no. 28; F.O. 633/5, Same to Same, Mar. 19, 1896.
30. Money was openly Francophile. His mother was French; and Cromer believed that he was bent on being mischievous "because he has not been made Sir Alonzo Money."
31. S.P. 109, Cromer to Barrington, Mar. 18 and 19, 1896 and Minutes.
32. S.P. 110, Cromer to Salisbury, Feb. 15, 1897, no. 14.
33. Cab. 37/40, Malet to Salisbury, Aug. 30, 1895 (secret), encl. Cf. F.O. 64/1351, Gosselin to Salisbury, Aug. 30, 1895, no. 194 and encl.
34. Salisbury to Devonshire, Dec. 31, 1895, cited Muriel Grieve, "The Egyptian Policy of Lord Salisbury, 1895–99" (Unpublished Oxford B. Litt. thesis, 1965), p. 75.
35. S.P. (Cavendish), Devonshire to Salisbury, Chatsworth, Dec. 30, 1895.
36. F.O. 407/132 (6802), Rodd to Salisbury, July 19, 1895, no. 93.
37. Ibid., Same to Same, Sept. 3, 1895, no. 114.
38. F.O. 45/732, Salisbury to Edwardes, Aug. 14, 1895 (confidential), no. 131; Grieve, "Egyptian Policy," pp. 99–100.
39. Ibid.
40. Captain Walter represented Egypt; and Lieutenant Miana, Italy.
41. F.O. 407/132 (6802), Rodd to Salisbury, Sept. 3, 1895, no. 114.
42. Ibid., Edwardes to Salisbury, Rome, Oct. 12, 1895, Tel. no. 40.
43. S.P. 104 (Belgium and Holland, 1895–1900), Salisbury's Minutes on Plunket, to Barrington, Aug. 8, 1895, no. 2.
44. Sir Arthur Bigge (afterwards Lord Stamfordham) was Queen Victoria's private secretary.

45. S.P. 85, Salisbury to Bigge, Dec. 7, 1895 (copy), no. 19.
46. Ibid.
47. Ibid.
48. S.P. 85, Salisbury to Bigge, Jan. 17, 1896 (copy), no. 25, Memo.
49. Ibid.
50. F.O. 800/1, Salisbury's Minutes to Sanderson of July 30, 1895.
51. Cited in C. J. Lowe, *Salisbury and the Mediterranean, 1886–1896* (London, 1965), 1; Cecil, *Salisbury*, 4, p. 65.
52. Valentine Chirol was the celebrated Foreign Correspondent of *The Times*.
53. F.O. 800/6 (Sir Frank Lascelles Papers), Chirol to Lascelles, Feb. 11, 1896 (confidential).
54. C. J. Lowe, *Salisbury*, p. 57, believes that by 1890 Salisbury had decided to reconquer the Sudan but lacked the means to do so.
55. S.P. 108, Cromer to Salisbury, Oct. 30, 1895, no. 16.
56. S.P. 113, Salisbury to Cromer, Nov. 8, 1895 (copy no. 2); cf. *Q.V.L.*, 3s., 3, Salisbury to Bigge, Sept. 2, 1896, pp. 72–73.
57. S.P. 108, Cromer to Salisbury, Nov. 15, 1895, Tel. 21.
58. Cromer, *Modern Egypt*, 2, pp. 80–81.
59. Salisbury to Cromer, Nov. 15, 1895; ibid., pp. 81–82.
60. Grieve, "Egyptian Policy," p. 98. If the Cabinet had taken this decision in Oct., as Miss Grieve believes, then Salisbury's letter of Nov. 8 becomes unintelligible—which is, of course, not the case.
61. S.P. 109, Cromer to Salisbury, 1896 (private), Tel. no. 31.
62. S.P. 113, Salisbury to Cromer, Jan. 18, 1896, Tel. no. 5.
63. Ibid., Same to Same, Feb. 20, 1896 (confidential), Copy, no. 6.
64. S.P. 114, Dufferin to Salisbury, Jan. 16, 1896, no. 24.
65. For further French opinion, see for example, F.O. 27/3314, Monson to Salisbury, Feb. 7, 1897 (most confidential), no. 76; S.P. 115, Same to Same, Feb. 12, 1897.
66. For the Porte's initiative and its collapse see F.O. 407/136 (6808), Salisbury to Currie, Feb. 5, 1896 (very confidential), no. 23A; Currie to Salisbury, Feb. 17, 1897, Tel. no. 65; Same to Same, Feb. 18, 1897, Tel. no. 66; Salisbury to Currie, Feb. 18, 1897 (secret), no. 34A; Lascelles to Salisbury, Feb. 26, 1896 (confidential), no. 47; Same to Same, Feb. 28 and 29, 1896; S.P. 125, Ford to Salisbury, Mar. 31, 1896, Tel. no. 11; *G.D.D.*, 2, Marschall to Hatzfeldt, Feb. 27, 1896, 11, p. 145; Hatzfeldt to German F.O., Mar. 4, 1896 (Tel.), 147.
67. For the diplomacy of the Venezuelan Crisis see J. J. Mathews, "Informal Diplomacy in the Venezuelan Crises of 1896," in *The Mississippi Historical Review*, I, no. 2, Sept., 1963.
68. Grenville, *Salisbury and Foreign Policy*, pp. 23 ff.
69. Cab. 37/41, "Resume of Events on the Egyptian Frontiers since 1885 . . . ," Mar., 1896, 2 *PP. W.O.*, no. 22.
70. Ibid. This was perhaps what Cromer meant when he said in his

August report 1895 (Published in Mar., 1896) that the Dervishes were on the defensive.

71. F.O. 407/132 (6802), Cromer to Salisbury, Dec. 17, 1895, no. 150, encl; cf. ibid., Rodd to Salisbury, Sept. 5, 1895, no. 116, encl. Intelligence Report, Egypt, July, 1895.

72. Cab. 37/41, Mar. 31, 1896, no. 22.

73. S.P. 109, Cromer to Salisbury, Dec. 18, 1895 (private), no. 29; F.O. 633/6, Same to Same, Dec. 18, 1895, no. 247.

74. Ibid.

75. Ibid.

76. F.O. 407/136 (6808), Salisbury to Cromer, Jan. 11, 1896, Tel. no. 1; M. Shibeika, *British Policy in the Sudan, 1882–1902* (London, 1952), p. 352.

77. Ibid.

78. F.O. 407/136 (6808), Cromer to Salisbury, Jan. 13, 1896 (confidential), Tel. no. 1.

79. Ibid., Salisbury to Cromer, Jan. 14, 1896, Tel. no. 2.

80. Ibid., Cromer to Salisbury, Jan. 14, 1896, Tel. no. 2.

81. F.O. 800/1, Memo by Sanderson, Dec. 16, 1895.

82. Ibid., Salisbury's Minutes on Sanderson's Memo of Dec. 16, 1895.

83. F.O. 800/6, Sanderson to Lascelles, Dec. 23, 1895.

84. F.O. 407/132 (6808), Sir Clare Ford to Salisbury, Feb. 24, 1896, Tel. 3.

85. Ibid., Salisbury to Cromer, Feb. 24, 1896 (secret), Tel. no. 10.

86. F.O. 78/4986, Memo by Sanderson, Feb. 24, 1896; Shibeika, *British Policy*, p. 353; Robinson and Gallagher, *Africa and the Victorians*, p. 346.

87. F.O. 407/136 (6808), Cromer to Salisbury, Feb. 26, 1896 (secret), Tel. no. 17.

88. Salisbury was not yet in possession of all the facts.

89. F.O. 407/132 (6808), Salisbury to Cromer, Feb. 29, 1896 (secret), Tel., 11; cited with variants in Robinson and Gallagher, *Africa and the Victorians*, pp. 346–47.

90. F.O. 407/136 (6808), Cromer to Salisbury, Feb. 26, 1896, Tel. no. 16.

91. S.P. 109, Same to Same, Feb. 26, 1896, Tel. no. 10.

92. Ibid.

93. There was great rejoicing at Addis Abbaba and Omdurman, the Khalifa's capital, P. Magnus, *Kitchener: Portrait of an Imperialist* (London, 1958), p. 90. Baratieri lost about 200 officers including at least two generals; between 2,000 and 3,000 men were killed; and over 60 pieces of artillery lost; cf. Lugard Papers, 40 (Kirk), Kirk to Lugard, Mar. 5, 1896.

94. F.O. 407/132 (6808), Cromer to Salisbury, Mar. 2, 1896, Tel. no. 22.

95. Ibid., Ford to Salisbury, Mar. 10, 1896, Tel. no. 14.

96. *G.D.D.*, 11, Memo by Marschall, Mar. 4 (approx.), 1896, no. 236, p. 422.
97. Robinson and Gallagher, *Africa and the Victorians*, p. 348.
98. F.O. 407/136 (6808), Salisbury to Cromer, Mar. 12, 1896, Tel. no. 17; F.O. 78/4986, Same to Same, Mar. 12, 1896, Tel. no. 17, contains the original draft of the letter in Salisbury's hand; S.P. 84, Salisbury to Queen Victoria, Mar. 12, 1896, Tel. no. 13; *G.D.D.*, 11, Hatzfeldt to German F.O., Mar. 12, 1896, Tel. no. 241, pp. 422–23.
99. Rodd, *Social and Diplomatic Memories*, 2, p. 86.
100. F.O. 407/136 (6808), Salisbury to Cromer, Mar. 12, 1896, Tel. no. 17; cf. S.P. 84, Same to the Queen, Mar. 12, 1896, Tel. no. 13.
101. *G.D.D.*, 11, Salisbury to Lascelles, Mar. 15, 1896, Tel., 152, p. 423.
102. F.O. 407/136 (6808), Salisbury to Ford, Mar. 12, 1896, no. 24A, and encl.
103. S.P. 113, Salisbury to Cromer, Mar. 13, 1896 (copy), no. 8. The first three sentences of the first paragraph are cited in Robinson and Gallagher, *Africa and the Victorians*, pp. 348–49, and in Zetland, *Cromer*, p. 223; selected sentences of the same dispatch are also cited in Sanderson, *England* . . . , p. 245.
104. *J.C.P.* (Salisbury), Salisbury to Chamberlain, Mar. 18 (?), 1896 (private), no. 65. Garvin, *Chamberlain*, 3, pp. 170–71–his pencil note in *J.C.P.*, dates this letter as Mar. 12–thus creating a confusion. But this letter is a reply to one from Chamberlain dated in *S.P.* as Mar. 17, but which Garvin also, unaccountably, dates as Mar. 11.
105. S.P. 113, Salisbury to Cromer, Apr. 1, 1896, no. 12.
106. This confusion stems from the *Memoirs of Field-Marshall Grenfell* (London, 1925), esp. pp. 124–25.
107. S.P. (Chamberlain), Chamberlain to Salisbury, Mar. 17, 1896. Garvin dates this letter as Mar. 11. But its tone shows clearly that Balfour and Chamberlain were reflecting on the decision already taken, and Salisbury's reply, as already shown, may have been an attempt to reassure Chamberlain. This confusion caused by Garvin has led Sanderson to believe that a Cabinet was held on Mar. 11 (Sanderson, *England* . . . , p. 244). But on that very day, as Salisbury's letter to Ford shows, the Italian ambassador was still urging him to create a diversion in their favor. Moreover, Salisbury did not appear to have sent anyone–not even the Queen–a report of what apparently was an important Cabinet decision.
108. S.P. (Curzon), Curzon to Salisbury, Mar. 31, 1896; *J.C.P.* (Salisbury), Salisbury to Chamberlain, Mar. 18 (?), 1896; S.P. (Hicks-Beach), Hicks-Beach to Salisbury, Mar. 20, 26, 30, 1896.
109. *J.C.P.* (Salisbury), Salisbury to Chamberlain, Mar. 18 (?), 1896 (private), no. 65; cf. also Cab. 37/41, Apr. 28, 1896 for similar views by Lansdowne, the War Minister.
110. Cf. F.O. 633/8, Cromer to Devonshire, May 1, 1896.

111. Cab. 37/41, "Proposed Advance up the Nile," Mar. 24, 1896, 8 *PP.*, *Lansdowne;* S.P. 89, Memo by Lansdowne, Mar. 24, 1896 (secret), no. 10.
112. F.O. 633/6, Cromer to Salisbury, Mar. 27, 1896 (private), no. 251.
113. Idem.; F.O. 407/136 (6808), Same to Same, Mar. 13, 1896, Tel. no. 37.
114. Cab. 37/41, Memo by Lansdowne, Mar. 24, 1896; S.P. 89, Idem (secret).
115. F.O. 45/747, Salisbury to Clare Ford, May 20, 1896; Grenville, *Salisbury and Foreign Policy*, p. 119.
116. S.P. 125, Ford to Salisbury, Mar. 24, 1896, no. 10.
117. For different interpretations see J. D. Hargreaves, "Entente Manquee; Anglo-French Relations, 1895–1896," in *Cambridge Historical Journal*, esp. p. 85. G. N. Sanderson, *England . . .* , p. 249. For German views see, for example, Eckardstein, *Ten Years at the Court of St. James*, pp. 86–88; *G.D.D.*, 2, esp. pp. 420–30; Halevy, *Imperialism*, p. 35. W. S. Blunt, *My Diaries*, 2 vols. (London, 1918–19), 1, p. 272. Muriel Grieve, "Egyptian Policy," pp. 174–75; Rennell Rodd, *Social and Diplomatic Memories, 1894–1901*, 3 vols. (London, 1922–24), 2, p. 87.

CHAPTER X

1. Editorial, Apr. 8, 1896; cf. *P.M.G.;* Apr. 30, 1896, editorial.
2. *National Review*, May, 1898, no. 183, p. 352; for a similar view see Winston Churchill, *The River War* (1933), p. 99.
3. William St. John Broderick (later, Earl of Midleton) succeeded Curzon in 1898 as parliamentary under secretary for foreign affairs; war minister, 1900.
4. *Hansard*, 4s., 67, Feb. 24, 1899, col. 481.
5. Cf. "Diplomaticus" in *Fortnightly Review*, 70, Dec., 1898, p. 1914.
6. Arthur Silva White, *The Expansion of Egypt*, (London, 1899), p. 8.
7. F.O. 800/2 (Sanderson Papers), Salisbury to Sanderson, Apr. 23, 1897.
8. F.O. 633/II (Cromer Papers), Cromer to Salisbury, Feb. 29, 1896; S.P. 109, Same to Same, Feb. 29, 1896, no. 12.
9. F.O. 407/136 (6808), Cromer to Salisbury, Mar. 13, 1896, Tel. no. 27.
10. Cf. Cromer, *Modern Egypt*, 2, pp. 80–81, 83, 85–86; Shibeika, *British Policy*, pp. 356–57, 362–70; Robinson and Gallagher, *Africa and the Victorians*, p. 347; Sanderson, *England . . .* , pp. 246–49.
11. See, for example, Hargreaves, "Entente Manquee," in *Cambridge Historical Journal*, p. 85.
12. Cf. F.O. 407/136 (6808), Ferrero to F.O., Mar. 14, 1896, *Particuliére;* Salisbury to Cromer, Mar. 14, 1896, Tel. no. 20; Ford to

Salisbury, Mar. 14, 1896, Tel. no. 18; Salisbury to Cromer, Mar. 14, 1896, Tel. no. 21.

13. Ibid., Cromer to Salisbury, Mar. 13, 18, 19, 1896 (secret), nos. 30, 41–42, Tels.

14. S.P. 113, Salisbury to Cromer, Mar. 19, 1896, no. 10; Cf. R. Churchill, *Winston Churchill*, 1, p. 441.

15. F.O. 407/136 (6808), Cromer to Salisbury, Mar. 13, 1896, Tel. no. 28; Salisbury to Cromer, Mar. 14, 1896, Tel. nos. 19 and 21.

16. Germany, Austria, and Italy voted for the loan; France and Russia opposed it.

17. F.O. 407/136 (6808), Salisbury to Cromer, Mar. 16, 1896, Tel. no. 23.

18. Cromer, *Modern Egypt*, 2, p. 106.

19. F.O. 407/136 (6808), Cromer to Salisbury, Mar. 23, 1896, Tel. no. 53.

20. Ibid., Same to Same, Mar. 19, 1896 (secret), Tel. no. 44.

21. Cf. Mekki Abbas, *The Sudan Question* (London, 1952).

22. Milner Papers, Vol. 183, Milner to Dawkins, Mar. 1, 1895. Milner was convinced that English public opinion would approve of the operation; that "the European 'colonies'— the most timorous aggregation of human beings in the world" would be too scared to oppose it; that "France might bark (she will not bite)"; that the majority of the Liberal ministers would approve such a course because they were "mortally frightened of being regarded as 'weak' in their foreign policy." He even made out a shadow cabinet—which included Cromer, Kitchener, and Palmer—to take over the Egyptian government after the coup.

23. Mr. C. E. Dawkins was an official in the Ministry of Finance, Cairo.

24. Milner Papers, Vol. 190, Dawkins to Milner, Aug. 16, 1896; see also Same to Same, July 17, 1896.

25. F.O. 407/136 (6808), Cromer to Salisbury, Mar. 18, 1896 (secret), Tel. 41.

26. Milner Papers, Vol. 189, Cromer to Milner, Dec. 5, 1895 (private).

27. F.O. 27/3264, Dufferin to Salisbury, Mar. 17, 1896, no. 90.

28. Idem; F.O. 27/3263, Salisbury to Dufferin, Mar. 23, 1896, no. 42.

29. Ibid.

30. F.O. 27/3264, Dufferin to Salisbury, Mar. 21, 1896, no. 91.

31. Ibid., Same to Same, Mar. 17, 1896, no. 90.

32. Ibid., Same to Same, Mar. 21, 1896, no. 91 (encl.). The conversation was first published in the *Temps* of Mar. 17, 1896.

33. Ibid.

34. Ibid.

35. F.O. 27/3263, Salisbury to Dufferin, Mar. 23, 1896, no. 42; S.P. 114, Dufferin to Salisbury, Mar. 17, 1896, no. 40.

36. F.O. 407/136 (6808), Lascelles to Salisbury, Mar. 28, 1896 (confidential), no. 94—revealed that Count Osten-Sacken (Russian ambassador to Berlin) was more excited over Egypt than M. Herbette

(French ambassador to Berlin); ibid., Same to Same, Apr. 21, 1896 (confidential), no. 3; F.O. 27/3314, Monson to Salisbury, Feb. 7, 1897 (most confidential), no. 76; S.P. 115, Same to Same, Feb. 12, 1897, no. 13.

37. S.P. 114, Dufferin to Salisbury, Mar. 17, 1896, no. 40.

38. Ibid., Same to Same, June 11, 1896, no. 50. Compare Hanotaux's long rope strategy with Salisbury's encouragement of France, in the early nineties, to undertake the conquest of Dahomey for specifically similar reasons.

39. *D.D.F.*, 12, Hanotaux to Courcel, Dec. 9, 1896, no. 39; F.O. 7/ 1244, Milbanke to Salisbury, Dec. 11, 1896 (confidential), no. 396; Grieve, "Egyptian Policy," p. 314.

40. F.O. 800/1, Salisbury to Sanderson, Nov. 2, 1896 (secret and private).

41. Ibid., Cromer to Salisbury, Nov. 2, 1896, Tel.

42. Ibid., Salisbury to Cromer, Nov. 3, 1896, Tel.

43. Devonshire Papers, 340. 2726, Salisbury to Devonshire, Mar. 24, 1897; Kennedy, *Salisbury*, pp. 280–81; Grieve, "Egyptian Policy," p. 332.

44. J.C.P. (Maxse), Admiral Maxse to Chamberlain, Oct. 23, 1897.

45. F.O. 27/3263, Salisbury to Dufferin, June 11, 1896, no. 214–copied to the Queen, Balfour, and Devonshire.

46. Grieve, "Egyptian Policy," pp. 121–22, 317–18, 324. France, in fact, was prepared to fight Germany over the recovery of Alsace-Lorraine rather than fight England over the Nile Valley. In Sept., 1896 the Tsar confided in Salisbury that "he had no objection to our having Egypt," see S.P. 89, Sept. 27, 1896 (very secret), no. 20. It will be remembered that Nicholas I had proposed in 1851 that Britain should have Egypt should the Ottoman Empire be partitioned by the powers. It has also been argued that Russia was unwilling to force England out of Egypt for fear of leaving England free to challenge her in the Far East, see D. S. Crist, "Russia's Far Eastern Policy in the Making," in the *Journal of Modern History*, 14, 1942, pp. 317 ff.; C. N. Spanks, "The Background of the Anglo-Japanese Alliance," in *The Pacific Historical Review*, 8, 1939, pp. 317–37.

47. S.P. 113, Salisbury to Cromer, Beaulieu, Apr. 1, 1896, no. 12.

48. Ibid.

49. F.O. 407/136 (6808), Cromer to Salisbury, Mar. 23, 1896, Tel. no. 53.

50. S.P. 113, Salisbury to Cromer, Mar. 20, 1896, no. 1.

51. F.O. 407/136 (6808), W.O. to F.O., Mar. 26, 1896.

52. S.P. 113, Salisbury to Cromer, Apr. 1, 1896, no. 12.

53. Milner Papers, Vol. 190, Wingate to Milner, Sept. 12, 1896 (private).

54. S.P. 109, Cromer to Salisbury, Apr. 5, 1896, no. 36.

55. S.P. 113, Salisbury to Cromer, Apr. 24, 1896, no. 14; S.P. 84, Salisbury to Victoria, Apr. 27, 1896, Tel. no. 22.

56. F.O. 407/137 (6928), Cromer to Salisbury, Apr. 24, 1896, Tel. no. 122.

57. S.P. 113, Salisbury to Cromer, May 1, 1896, no. 15; F.O. 407/137 (6928), Same to Same, May 1, 1896, Tel. no. 72; cf. also F.O. 633/8, Cromer to Devonshire, May 1, 1896.

58. F.O. 407/137 (6928), Cromer to Salisbury, May 5, 1896, Tel. no. 132.

59. Ibid., F.O. to India Office, May 9, 1896; Salisbury to Cromer, May 11, 1896, Tel. no. 77; S.P. 84, Salisbury to Victoria, May 6, 1896, no. 23; *Q.V.L.*, 3s., 3, p. 43.

60. Cf. Wingate, *Wingate of the Sudan*, p. 196. The troops numbered 2,500.

61. F.O. 407/137 (6928), Memo by Wolseley (dated May, 1896).

62. S.P. 113, Salisbury to Cromer, May 16, 1896, Tel. no. 18. As it turned out, this report was written by Salisbury's son, Lord Edward Cecil, who was Kitchener's A.D.C.; see Lord Edward Cecil, *The Leisure of an Egyptian Official* (London, 1921); Magnus, *Kitchener*, p. 95.

63. F.O. 407/137 (6298), Cromer to Salisbury, June 7, 1896, Tel. no. 162. Ibid., Cromer to Salisbury, June 29, 1896, Tel. no. 187.

64. It has been claimed that the khalifa's plan was to allow Kitchener to penetrate deep into the Sudan and then to destroy him at a major battle to be fought at Omdurman. Robert O. Collins, *The Southern Sudan, 1883–1898* (Yale and London, 1962), p. 171.

65. F.O. 407/138 (6889), Rodd to Salisbury, Sept. 23, 1896, Tel. no. 240.

66. Ibid., Cromer to Salisbury, Sept. 24, 1896, Tel. no. 242. The Dongola expedition claimed only 411 lives (364 of whom died from cholera and other diseases), and cost only £E. 715,000.

67. Milner Papers, Vol. 190, Wingate to Milner, June 28, 1896.

68. F.O. 407/138 (6889), Salisbury to Rodd, June 31, 1896, Tel. no. 107.

69. Milner Papers, Vol. 183, Milner to Balfour, Sept. 19, 1896 (confidential); ibid., Same to Same, Sept. 19, 1896 (confidential); ibid., Milner to Dawkins, Sept. 18, 1896.

70. F.O. 407/138 (6889), Cromer to Salisbury, Sept. 27, 1896, Tel. no. 245.

71. Milner Papers, Vol. 190, Dawkins to Milner, July 17, 1896.

72. This was Kitchener's description of Cromer.

73. Milner Papers, Vol. 190, Dawkins to Milner, July 17, 1896.

74. Ibid., Same to Same, Sept. 25, 1896.

75. Magnus, *Kitchener*, pp. 101–2; Arthur, *Lord Kitchener*, 1, p. 229. The attempted alliance of the khalifa and Menelek failed to materialize. In fact, in May, 1897, Menelek concluded a Treaty with Britain by which he undertook to remain neutral in the Sudan War. The Dervishes and Abyssinians, however, appeared to have remained on friendly terms, see Sanderson, "Contribution from

African Sources to the History of European Competition in the Upper Valley of the Nile," in *J.A.H.*, 3 (1962), pp. 84–86; P. M. Holt, *The Mahdist State of the Sudan, 1881–1898* (Oxford, 1958), pp. 208–10.

76. Magnus, *Kitchener*, p. 102.
77. F.O. 633/6, Cromer to Salisbury, Oct. 30, 1896 (private), no. 264; S.P. 109, Same to Same, Oct. 30, 1896, no. 102.
78. Salisbury to Queen Victoria, Sept. 29, 1896, *Q.V.L.*, 3s., 3, p. 85.
79. Milner Papers, Vol. 190, Wingate to Milner, Nov. 22, 1896 (private).
80. S.P. 113, Barrington to Cromer, Nov. 16, 1896, Tel. no. 30.
81. Created Major-General (Sept. 25), two days after his Dongola victory.
82. Magnus, *Kitchener*, p. 102.
83. S.P. 113, Salisbury to Cromer, Nov. 16, 1896, Tel. no. 31.
84. Ibid., Same to Same, Nov. 17, 1896, no. 32.
85. F.O. 407/139 (6965), Cromer to Salisbury, Oct. 28, 1896, Tel. no. 26; see also Same to Same, Oct. 31, 1896, no. 132; Same to Same, Nov. 11, 1896 (confidential), no. 138, with enclosures. This Egyptian opposition was so serious that they condemned Kitchener's victories. They protested that Christians and Moslems were uniting to overwhelm an entirely Moslem force. They prayed for the Sirdar's defeat; others prayed for a Dervish occupation of Cairo. It has been claimed that the whole Egyptian opposition group was exploiting religious fanaticism for political ends and that they were mainly nationalists rather than religious Messiahs. See Abbas, *Sudan Question*, pp. 42–43.
86. J.C.P. (Salisbury), Salisbury to Chamberlain, Dec. 13, 1896 (private), no. 56.
87. J.C.P. (Balfour), Chamberlain to Balfour, Feb. 2, 1899, no. 81.
88. F.O. 407/139 (6965), Salisbury to Cromer, Oct. 29, 1896, Tel. no. 115.
89. S.P. (Hicks-Beach), Hicks-Beach to Salisbury, Oct. 19 and 23, 1896; Same to Same, Nov. 1, 1897.
90. Ibid., Same to Same, Jan. 2 and 11, 1898.
91. S.P. 113, Salisbury to Cromer, Nov. 27, 1897, no. 34; printed with slight variants in Magnus, *Kitchener*, pp. 102–3.
92. S.P. 113, Salisbury to Cromer, Nov. 27, 1897, no. 34.
93. Cited in Lord Newton, *Lord Lansdowne* (London, 1929), Salisbury to Lansdowne, Oct. 22, 1897, p. 148; cf. Robinson and Gallagher, *Africa and the Victorians*, pp. 358–59.
94. S.P. 84, Salisbury to Victoria, Nov. 25, 1896, Tel. no. 30.
95. F.O. 407/139 (6965), Salisbury to Cromer, Oct. 5, 1896, Tel. no. 112; cf. also ibid., Same to Same, Oct. 5, 1896, Tel. no. 111.
96. Ibid., Cromer to Salisbury, Dec. 2, 1896, Tel. no. 272.
97. Ibid., Salisbury to Cromer, Dec. 2, 1896, Tel. no. 121; Same to Same, Oct. 26, 1896, Tel. no. 114.

98. S.P. 109, Hicks-Beach to Salisbury, Dec. 9, 1896, no. 114.
99. *Hansard*, 4s., 45, Jan. 19, 1897, cols. 20–21.
100. Ibid., cols. 31–32 (Salisbury).
101. Cf., for example, Holt, *Mahdist State*, pp. 225–47; Holt, *History of Sudan*, pp. 105–6.
102. *Hansard*, 4s., 45, Feb. 5, 1897, cols. 1445–49.
103. Ibid., cols., 1450–56 (Morley); cols. 1459–62 (Dilke); cols. 1466–68 (Harcourt).
104. Ibid., Division List, col. 1521. Only 54 M.P.'s voted against it.
105. Ibid., col. 1459.
106. Salisbury was the undisputed master of their docile lordships, and the good natured Kimberley was not the sort of person to cause serious trouble. In fact, he was wont to protest, rather unnecessarily, during these debates: "I am not a little Englander."
107. S.P. (Hicks-Beach), Hicks-Beach to Salisbury, Dec. 22, 1896.
108. Robinson and Gallagher, *Africa and the Victorians*, p. 361.
109. Text of Treaty in Hertslet, *Map of Africa*, 11, no. 99 (1909).
110. Robinson and Gallagher, *Africa and the Victorians*, pp. 359–62.
111. Grieve, "Egyptian Policy," p. 352.
112. S.P. 113, Salisbury to Cromer, Mar. 12, 1897, no. 47.
113. S.P. 114, Dufferin to Salisbury, July 3, 1895, no. 1.
114. S.P. 119, Salisbury to Dufferin, July 26, 1895, no. 1 (copy).
115. F.O. 27/3263, Salisbury to Monson, Dec. 10, 1896, no. 506B; Cab. 37/43, Same to Same, Dec. 18, 1896, "Anglo-French Relations...," 3*PP*, F.O.
116. F.O. 27/3314, Monson to Salisbury, Jan. 10, 1897, no. 15.
117. The loudest were *Echo d'Orient,* which had replaced *Bosphore Egyptien* and was regarded as the organ of the French Agency in Egypt; and *Journal Egyptien,* the recognized organ of M. Deloncle and the French Colonial party.
118. S.P. 115, Monson to Salisbury, Feb. 13, 1897, no. 14. Cf. also F.O. 27/3314, Same to Same, Feb. 7, 1897 (most confidential), no. 76.
119. S.P. 119, Salisbury to Monson, Feb. 2, 1897, no. 9.
120. F.O. 633/9, Cromer to Salisbury, Aug. 9, 1896.
121. F.O. 27/3314, Monson to Salisbury, Feb. 10, 1897 (secret), Tel. no. 12; Same to Same, Feb. 7, 1897 (most confidential), no. 76. But "the Deputies were but little moved by the issue," ibid., Same to Same, Feb. 9, 1897, no. 82.
122. F.O. 407/142 (7091), Rumbold to Salisbury, Feb. 8, 1897 (confidential) Tel. no. 5.
123. S.P. 119, Salisbury to Monson, Feb. 12, 1897, no. 10; for summary reports of this interview with Courcel, see S.P. 113, Salisbury to Cromer, Feb. 12, no. 43; F.O. 27/3312, Salisbury to Monson, Feb. 11, 1897, no. 67.
124. Milner Papers, Vol. 190, Dawkins to Milner, Jan. 16, 1896.
125. F.O. 27/3312, Salisbury to Monson, Feb. 18, 1897, no. 82; cf. also ibid., Same to Same, Jan. 28, 1897, nos. 43A and 43B; Same to

Same, Feb. 2, 1897 (confidential), no. 52; F.O. 407/142 (7091), Cromer to Salisbury, Feb. 2, 1897, Tel. no. 14; Milner Papers, Vol. 183, Milner to Hicks-Beach, Dec. 3, 1896 (confidential); ibid., 88, Same to Same, Dec. 5, 1896 (confidential).

126. S.P. 116, Monson to Salisbury, July 5, 1898, no. 38.

127. F.O. 27/3341, Monson to Salisbury, Nov. 27, 1897 (urgent), no. 394 Africa; F.O. 27/3336, Salisbury to Monson, Dec. 9, 1897, no. 406 Africa (the original in Salisbury's hand). Salisbury stated that the reply was delayed because the points raised had to be considered by the Cabinet. F.O. 27/3341, Monson to Salisbury, Dec. 10, 1897, no. 413 Africa; S.P. 115, Monson to Salisbury, Dec. 1, 1897, no. 91.

128. S.P. 110, Rodd to Salisbury, Addis Abbaba, May 15, 1897, no. 34.

129. F.O. 407/142 (7091), Cromer to Salisbury, Sept. 17, 1896 (secret) Tel. no. 25.

130. C.P. 113, Barrington to Cromer, Feb. 8, 1897, Tel.

131. Ibid., Salisbury to Cromer, Feb. 12, 1897, no. 43.

132. Ibid.

133. F.O. 800/2, Minutes by Salisbury and Sanderson, Mar. 27, 1897.

134. S.P. 113, Salisbury to Cromer, May 7, 1897, no. 48.

135. S.P. 89, Cromer to Salisbury, June 6, 1897 (confidential and private), no. 22, encl.

136. Ibid., Memo by Cromer, June 5, 1897 (confidential and private), no. 24.

137. F.O. 407/144 (7097), Cromer to Salisbury, Oct. 1, 1897, no. 105.

138. Ibid., F.O. to W.O., Oct. 2, 1897; W.O. to F.O., Oct. 4, 1897.

139. Ibid., Salisbury to Cromer, Oct. 5, 1897, no. 166.

140. Ibid., Cromer to Salisbury, Oct. 18, 1897, Tel. no. 114.

141. S.P. 110, Cromer to Salisbury, Oct. 18, 1897, Magnus, *Kitchener*, p. 109.

142. Ibid., Same to Same, Oct. 22, 1897, Tel.; Magnus, *Kitchener*, p. 109.

143. S.P. 89, Cromer to Salisbury, Oct. 22, 1897 (secret and private), no. 25

144. Kitchener to Dawkins, Oct. 6, 1897, cited in Magnus, *Kitchener*, p. 3.

145. Ibid., p. 110.

146. S.P. 113, Salisbury to Cromer, Oct. 29, 1897, no. 56; FitzMaurice and G. Arthur, *The Life of Lord Wolseley* (London, 1924), citing Wolseley to Lansdowne, Oct., 1897, p. 304; cf. also Same to Same, Apr. 2, 1896, p. 301; F.O. 800/2, Sanderson's Minutes to Salisbury of Sept. 18, 1897.

147. S.P. 113, Salisbury to Cromer, Oct. 29, 1897, no. 56; partly cited in Magnus, *Kitchener*, p. 112. Cf. also F.O. 800/2, Salisbury's and Sanderson's Minutes of Sept. 18, 1897; S.P. (FitzMaurice), Lansdowne to Salisbury, Oct. 28, 1897 (secret); Same to Same, Dec. 21 and 28, 1897.

148. S.P. 89, cited in Memo by Cromer and enclosed in Cromer to

Salisbury, Nov. 5, 1897 (private and confidential) no. 28; Cab. 37/
45, "The Soudan Question," 5 *PP*, Nov. 16, 1897 . . . *F.O.*

149. Ibid.

150. Cf. S.P. (FitzMaurice), Lansdowne to Salisbury, Oct. 28, 1897
(secret); Same to Same, Jan. 4, 1898; G. N. Sanderson, "Contributions from African Sources . . ." *J.A.H.*, 3 (1962), pp. 70–71.

151. F.O. 633/6, Cromer to Salisbury, Cairo, Dec. 25, 1897 (private),
no. 293.

152. Sanderson, "Contributions from African Sources . . ." pp. 73–74;
Holt, *Mahdist State*, esp. pp. 217–20. Moreover, between 1896 and
1898 the khalifa had, in addition to the English, the Congolese and
the French to contend with. For the Congo state's activities see
Collins, *Southern Sudan*, pp. 92 ff.; for French activities see
Raphael, *Cape to Cairo*, pp. 340–50.

153. S.P. (Curzon), Curzon to Salisbury, Nov. 12, 1896. Rodd showed
this letter to Curzon who transmitted it to Salisbury.

154. Ibid. Lord Edward Cecil also noted in his diary: "Lord Cromer
was not in favour of a forward Sudan policy, and Kitchener was.
My father's [Lord Salisbury's] support was vital to his whole plan,
and I, by reflected light, became of importance," *Leisure of an
Egyptian Official*, p. 185.

155. S.P. III, Cromer to Salisbury, May 3, 1898, no. 27.

156. F.O. 407/147 (7079), Cromer to Salisbury, Oct. 6, 1897, Tel. no.
107; Salisbury to Cromer, Oct. 7, 1897, Tel. no. 22; Cromer to
Salisbury, Oct. 23, 1897, Tel. no. 116; Same to Same, Oct. 28, 1897,
Tel. no. 121; Salisbury to Cromer, Oct. 28, 1897, Tel. no. 77; Salis-
bury to Sir George Bonhan, Nov. 3, 1897, no. 162; Same to
Cromer, Nov. 3, 1897, Tel. no. 162; F.O. 407/147 (7158), Cromer
to Salisbury, Jan. 19, 1898 (confidential), no. 14, encl. Parsons to
Cromer, Dec. 30, 1897.

157. F.O. 407/147 (7158), Cromer to Salisbury, Jan. 1, 1898, Tel. no. 1;
Same to Same, Jan. 31, 1898, Tel. no. 41.

158. F.O. 407/144 (7097), Cromer to Salisbury, Dec. 22, 1897, Tel. no.
155; F.O. 407/147 (7158), Same to Same, Jan. 1, 1898, Tel. nos.
1 and 3.

159. S.P. (Hicks-Beach), Hicks-Beach to Salisbury, Nov. 1, 1897; cited
in full in Robinson and Gallagher, *Africa and the Victorians*, pp.
363–64. Cf. also S.P. (Chamberlain), Chamberlain to Salisbury,
Dec. 11, 1897; he wrote: "I saw Hicks-Beach yesterday about Egypt,
his view appears to be that our retention of the Protectorate is dangerous."

160. S.P. 113, Salisbury to Cromer, Jan. 4, 1898, Tel. no. 65, transmitting
extract of a letter from Beach. Cf. also F.O. 633/7, Same to Same,
Jan. 4, 1898, no. 503; S.P. 89, Same to Same, Jan. 4, 1898 (private),
Tel. no. 31; Cab. 37/46, "Operations in the Soudan," IP. . . . F.O.,
Jan. 5, 1898, no. 2; S.P. (Hicks-Beach), Hicks-Beach to Salisbury,
Jan. 2, 1898. He did, however, insist in another letter that, after

Khartoum, "we should draw in our horns a little" before proceeding to the Bahr-el-Ghazal. This, he said, was due to administrative and financial difficulties, ibid., Same to Same, Jan. 11, 1898.

161. Ibid.

162. F.O. 633/7, Cromer to Salisbury, Jan. 1, 1898 (private), Tel. no. 501; F.O. 407/144 (7097), Salisbury to Cromer, Dec. 23, 1897, Tel. no. 90.

163. F.O. 407/147 (7158), W.O. to F.O., Jan. 3, 1898.

164. The fear of the strength of the Dervishes still inhibited any decisive action.

165. F.O. 407/147 (7158), Cromer to Salisbury, Apr. 1, 1898, Tel. no. 111; cited in full in Magnus, *Kitchener*, pp. 119–20.

166. Ibid., Cromer to Salisbury, Apr. 2, 1898, Tel. no. 112; ibid., p. 120.

167. Ibid., Salisbury to Cromer, Apr. 2, 1898, Tel. no. 31.

168. Ibid., Salisbury to Cromer, Apr. 3, 1898, Tel. nos. 113 and 114. For the assessment of Kitchener as a General see Magnus, *Kitchener*, p. 123.

169. F.O. 407/147 (7158), Cromer to Salisbury, Apr. 8, 1898, Tel. no. 122.

170. G. Cecil, "Salisbury," 5 (Mss), p. 246.

171. F.O. 407/149 (7219), Rodd to Salisbury, Midnight, Sept. 3, 1898, Tel. no. 214; W.O. to F.O., Sept. 5, 1898, encl. no. 2. Wolseley noted in his Diary: "God be praised. We can once more hold up our heads in the Soudan," cited Maurice and Arthur, *Lord Wolseley*, p. 306.

172. Cf. S.P. 83, Victoria to Salisbury, Sept. 12, 1898, Tel. no. 114.

CHAPTER XI

1. The attempted cooperation with Menelek did not appear to have been seriously executed and did not materialize into an alliance, see Holt, *Mahdist State*, pp. 196–97, 208–10.

2. F.O. 27/3400, Monson to Salisbury, Sept. 7, 1898, Tel. no. 127; F.O. 407/149 (7219), Rodd to Salisbury, Sept. 7, 1898, Tel. no. 220.

3. *The Times*, Sept. 27, 1898; Churchill, *River War* (1899), 2, pp. 311–12. S.P. 100, Sir Edward Malet to Salisbury, Nov. 15, 1898, no. 20, encl. *Hansard*, 4s., 66, Feb. 7, 1899, col. 8.

4. Since 1898 numerous books and articles have been devoted to the Fashoda crisis. In the following passages an attempt will be made to examine very closely Salisbury's handling of this imbroglio and how it compares with his handling of territorial difficulties in West and East Africa.

5. S.P. 55, Salisbury to Baring, Nov. 21, 1890, no. 60.

6. Cf. Langer, *Imperialism*, p. 572.

7. S.P. (Lord Chancellor, 1895–1900), Memo by Salisbury: "Status

of the Khalifa's Dominions if Conquered," July, 1898 (confidential), no. 7.

8. S.P. 89, Memo by Cromer, Nov. 5, 1897 (private and confidential), no. 28.

9. Cf., for example, *Hansard*, 4s., 45, Jan. 19, 1897 (Salisbury): ibid., 53, col. 37 (Salisbury).

10. Victoria Hicks-Beach, *Hicks-Beach*, 2, p. 67.

11. S.P. 55, Salisbury to Baring, Dec. 28, 1888, no. 37; Victoria Hicks-Beach, *Hicks-Beach*, 2, p. 39.

12. *Pall Mall Gazette*, Sept. 13, and Oct. 20, 1898, editorial.

13. *Daily News*, Oct. 19, 1898, editorial.

14. *Scotsman*, Sept. 27, 1898, editorial; cf. also *Daily Graphic*, Sept. 13, 1898; *The Times*, Sept. 29, 1898, Oct. 3, 5, and 10, 1898—editorials.

15. *St. James's Gazette*, Sept. 6 and 13, 1898; *Standard*, Sept. 6, 1898; *Financial Times*, Oct. 11, 1898; *Daily Telegraph*, Sept. 13, 1898, leading articles.

16. *Morning Post*, Sept. 12, 1898.

17. See *Manchester Guardian*, Sept. 6, and Oct. 19, 1898, editorials.

18. *Westminster Gazette*, Sept. 25, 1898, editorial. The *St. James's Gazette*, in dismissing the opposition's argument, also added: "Lord Salisbury has, indeed, made one or two 'graceful concessions' to France; but he has never given any territory without compensation," Oct. 18, 1898, editorial.

19. *Standard*, Sept. 13, 1898, editorial.

20. *Westminster Gazette*, Sept. 20, 1898, editorial; *The Daily Chronicle*, Sept. 27, 1898, editorial; cf. *The Times*, Sept. 27, 1898, leading article.

21. *The Times*, Oct. 13, 1898.

22. Ibid., Oct. 20, 1898, partly cited in Victoria Hicks-Beach, *Hicks-Beach*, 2, pp. 68–69.

23. Ibid., p. 70.

24. Marder, *British Sea Power*, p. 328; *Sheffield Daily Telegraph*, Oct. 21, 1898, editorial; Marder, *British Sea Power*, p. 331.

25. *Daily Graphic*, Oct. 11, 1898 (editorial).

26. Marder, *British Sea Power*, pp. 331–32.

27. Ibid., pp. 328–29.

28. Ibid., p. 332.

29. Robinson and Gallagher, *Africa and the Victorians*, p. 373.

30. Giffen, *Fachoda* . . . pp. 106–7, Marder, *British Sea Power*, p. 332.

31. Marder, *British Sea Power*, p. 321.

32. S.P. 119 Barrington to Salisbury (n.d.) but written on or after Nov. 15, 1898, no. 31.

33. Ibid., Minutes by Salisbury above.

34. Cf. infra, pp. 269, 274–75.

35. Marder, *British Sea Power*, p. 320.

36. Cf. ibid., pp. 320–40 for a good analysis of British and French naval preparations.

37. For this speech see *The Times,* Nov. 5, 1898.
38. *The Times,* Nov. 5, 1898, leading article. Cf. *Pall Mall Gazette,* Nov. 30, 1898, editorial.
39. *The Times,* Nov. 10, and Dec. 17, 1898.
40. *Times,* Nov. 17, 1898.
41. The best account of the Marchand Mission is in Sanderson, *England . . . ,* pp. 269–89. See also Brown, *Fashoda Reconsidered,* op. cit.
42. F.O. 27/3368, "Precis of Events on the Upper Nile and adjacent territories including Bahr-el-Ghazal and Uganda, from 1878 to March, 1898," by Captain Gleichen.
43. F.O. 27/3368, "Precis of events . . . March, 1898."
44. Ibid., W.O. to F.O., Feb. 22, 1897 and encls.
45. F.O. 27/3315, Monson to Salisbury, Feb. 23, 1897, no. 54.
46. F.O. 27/3368, "Precis of events . . . March, 1898"; *Standard,* Dec. 11, 1897.
47. Cf. ibid., for these newspapers whose stories are set down in chronological order. See encl. in F.O. 27/3393, Monson to Salisbury, Feb. 20, 1898, no. 77 Africa.
48. S.P. 100, Barrington to Macdonald, Apr. 8, 1897.
49. S.P. 113, Salisbury to Cromer, Oct. 29, 1897, no. 56; cf. F.O. 800/145, Salisbury to Lansdowne, Oct. 22, 1897 (private); Newton, *Lansdowne,* p. 148.
50. S.P. 115, Monson to Salisbury, Nov. 23, 1897, no. 89.
51. S.P. 119, Salisbury to Monson, Nov. 24, 1897, Tel. no. 19.
52. G. Cecil, *Studies,* pp. 57–58, Penson, *Foreign Affairs under Salisbury,* p. 16; Kennedy, *Salisbury,* p. 276; Robinson and Gallagher, *Africa and the Victorians,* pp. 366–67.
53. S.P. 115, Monson to Salisbury, Dec. 19, 1897, no. 93.
54. Ibid.
55. F.O. 83/1606, note by Hill, Jan. 20, 1898.
56. F.O. 27/3368, "Precis of events on the Upper Nile . . . March, 1898."
57. S.P. (Hicks-Beach), Hicks-Beach to Salisbury, Jan. 11, 1898.
58. F.O. 78/5049, Cromer to Salisbury, Jan. 23, 1898, no. 37; F.O. 78/5050, Same to Same, May 16, 1898, no. 149.
59. Henry John Brinslay Manners, 1852–1925; 8th duke of Rutland (1906) priv. sec. to Salisbury, 1885–86, 1886–88; M.P., Leics., 1885–95.
60. S.P. (Manners), Granby to Salisbury, Apr. 14, 1898.
61. F.O. 407/147 (7158), Salisbury to Cromer, May 15, 1898, tel. no. 41; ibid., Cromer to Salisbury, June 4, 1898 (secret), Tel. no. 163.
62. S.P. 89, Memo by Cromer, June 15, 1898 (private and confidential), no. 32; Cab. 37/47, "Egypt: the future of the Soudan," July 27, 1898, no. 41, *Cromer.*
63. F.O. 78/5050, Salisbury to Cromer, June 3, 1898 (secret), Tel. no. 47.

64. This decision was announced by Beach in the Commons, see *Hansard* 4s., 60, cols. 241–50.

65. F.O. 83/1611, W.O. to F.O., July 22, 1898, with encls.

66. See S.P. 89, Memo by Cromer, June 15, 1898 (private and confidential), no. 32.

67. F.O. 78/5050, Salisbury to Cromer, Aug. 2, 1898 (secret), no. 109; cf. S.P. 89, Memo by Cromer, June 15, 1898 (private and confidential), no. 32; Cab. 37/47, "Soudan," Salisbury to Cromer, July, 1898, no. 60. The final draft was dispatched on Aug. 2. Rodd claimed that these instructions were sent to Kitchener through himself, Rodd, *Memories*, 2, p. 221.

68. F.O. 27/3392, Sanderson's note to Salisbury, Sept. 24, 1898; ibid., Salisbury to Monson, Sept. 27 (secret), no. 340 communicating to him the "secret information."

69. Cf. Kennedy, *Quarterly Review*, p. 149. Kitchener commanded the White Nile flotilla; Hunter followed the Blue Nile; and Rundel took charge at Khartoum.

70. F.O. 407/147 (7158), Rodd to Salisbury, Aug. 18, 1898, Tel. no. 198.

71. Ibid., Same to Same, Aug. 27, 1898, Tel. no. 202.

72. Ibid., Same to Same, Sept. 7, 1898, Tel. no. 221.

73. F.O. 27/3400, Monson to Salisbury, Sept. 7, 1898, Tel. no. 127; F.O. 27/3396, Same to Same, Sept. 6, 1898, no. 438.

74. Marchand and Kitchener first met on Sept. 19; cf. F.O. 78/5051, encl. in Rodd to Salisbury, Sept. 29, 1898 (secret), no. 155; Robinson and Gallagher, *Africa and the Victorians*, p. 370 and fn. 7.

75. F.O. 27/3400, Monson to Salisbury, Sept. 7, 1898, Tel. no. 127; Same to Same, Sept. 18, 1898, Tel. no. 137; S.P. 116, Monson to Same, Sept. 11, 1898, no. 43; Rodd, *Memories*, 11, p. 222.

76. F.O. 27/3400, Monson to Salisbury, Sept. 7, 1898.

77. Ibid.

78. Ibid.

79. F.O. 27/3399, Salisbury to Monson, from Schlucht, Sept. 9, 1898, Tel. no. 57.

80. F.O. 27/3396, Monson to Salisbury, Sept. 12, 1898, no. 449; S.P. 116, Same to Same, Sept. 11, 1898, no. 43; F.O. 27/3400, Same to Same, Sept. 10, 1898, Tel. no. 131.

81. Hanotaux's protest was made on Apr. 5, 1895.

82. F.O. 27/3400, Monson to Salisbury, Sept. 18, 1898, Tel. no. 137; F.O. 27/3396, Same to Same, Sept. 22, 1898, no. 471.

83. For Kitchener's reports see F.O. 407/149 (7219); F.O. 78/4986 (1894–1898–"Proposed cooperation with Italy against the Dervishes").

84. F.O. 27/3399, Salisbury to Monson, Sept. 25, 1898, Tel. no. 95.

85. F.O. 407/149 (7219), Salisbury to Rodd, Sept. 25, 1898, Tel. no. 83.

86. F.O. 27/3400, Monson to Salisbury, Sept. 26, 1898, Tel. no. 147.

87. Ibid., Same to Same, Sept. 27, 1898, Tel. no. 151.

88. F.O. 27/3399, Salisbury to Monson, Sept. 28, 1898, Tel. no. 206.

89. Ibid., Same to Same, Oct. 3, 1898, Tel. no. 213.

90. *Pall Mall Gazette,* Oct. 10, 1898, editorial.

91. This resentment was summarized in an editorial headline in *Le Matin* of Oct. 5, 1898, which read: "NON!" "La seule Response Digne De La France," encl. no. 1 in F.O. 27/3397, Monson to Salisbury, Oct. 5, 1898, no. 499.

92. F.O. 27/3400, Monson to Salisbury, Sept. 28, 1898 (secret), Tel. no. 154; cf. F.O. 27/3397, Same to Same, Sept. 29, 1898, encl. Extract from an article in the *Temps* of Sept. 29, no. 488.

93. For a good account of these negotiations see Grenville, *Salisbury and Foreign Policy,* pp. 177–98. The original documents can be consulted in F.O. 63/1359: "1897–1898: England and Portugal in S. Africa; Portuguese Loans (Private Corresp. and Minutes)"; F.O. 64/1466–67; "Anglo-German Agreement. Africa. Portuguese Loan, 1897–Dec., 1898"; *B.D.* I, chap. 2, sec. 2; Cab. 37/40–48. The private correspondence on this question is very useful. See S.P. 92, nos. 16, 34–46; S.P. 96, nos. 46–47, 49–54, 56, 63–64, 67; J.C.P. (Balfour); Balfour Papers, B.Mus.Add.Mss., no. 4977 (Chamberlain).

94. F.O. 27/3400, Monson to Salisbury, Sept. 30, 1898 (secret). Tel. no. 160; S.P. 116, Same to Same, Sept. 30, 1898, no. 45; J.C.P. (Foreign Affairs, 1885–99), Same to Same, Sept. 30, 1898 (secret) no. 9.

95. S.P. 116, Same to Same, Sept. 30, 1898, no. 45.

96. F.O. 27/3397, Same to Same, Oct. 1, 1898 (secret) no. 491.

97. F.O. 407/149 (7219), Salisbury to Rodd, Oct. 1, 1898 (secret). Tel. no. 92; cf. ibid., Cromer to Salisbury, Oct. 1898, Tel. no. 260; F.O. 78/50–51, Sanderson's Minutes on Rodd to Salisbury, Sept. 29, 1898, Tel. no. 252; S.P. 119, Salisbury to Monson, no. 27; J.C.P. (Foreign Affairs, 1885–99), Salisbury to Rodd, Oct. 1, 1898 (secret) Tel. no. 10.

98. S.P. 116, Monson to Salisbury, Oct. 2, 1898, no. 46.

99. F.O. 407/149 (7219) Salisbury to Cromer, Oct. 7, 1898, Tel. no. 105.

100. Ibid., Cromer to Salisbury, Oct. 9, 1898, Tel. no. 267.

101. S.P. 116, Monson to Salisbury, Oct. 4, 1898, no. 47 and encl.

102. F.O. 27/3392, Salisbury to Monson, Oct. 6, 1898, no. 355A; F.O. 407/149, Salisbury to Cromer, Oct. 5, 1898 (secret), Tel. no. 98.

103. F.O. 27/3397, Monson to Salisbury, Oct. 7, 1898, no. 500.

104. Ibid.

105. F.O. 407/149 (7219) Salisbury to Cromer, Oct. 7, 1898, Tel. no. 106.

106. Ibid., Cromer to Salisbury, Oct. 8, 1898, Tel. no. 264.

107. F.O. 27/3397, Monson to Salisbury, Oct. 9, 1898, no. 504, enclosing article in *Matin* of Oct. 9, 1898.
108. Ibid., Same to Same, Oct. 10, 1898, no. 505, encl. article in *Matin*, Oct. 10.
109. F.O. 343/13 (Malet Papers), Malet to Salisbury, Potsdam, July 31, 1895 (private and secret), no. 8.
110. F.O. 27/3397, Monson to Salisbury, Oct. 10, 1898, no. 505. Cf. ibid., Same to Same, Oct. 7, 1898, no. 501, with encl.
111. F.O. 27/3400, Monson to Salisbury, Oct. 11, 1898 (secret and most confidential), Tel. no. 169. A very long interview on the 12th between Salisbury and Courcel produced no results either, cf. F.O. 27/3392, Salisbury to Monson, Oct. 12, 1898, no. 369.
112. Ibid.
113. F.O. 27/3397, Same to Same, Oct. 11, 1898, no. 508 (encl.).
114. S.P. 116, Same to Same, Oct. 14, 1898, no. 52.
115. F.O. 27/3397, Same to Same, Oct. 14, 1898 (most confidential), no. 517.
116. Grieve, "Egyptian Policy," pp. 515–16.
117. Middleton, *Records & Reactions,* pp. 108–9.
118. F.O. 27/3399, Salisbury to Monson, Oct. 12, 1898, Tel. no. 223. Already he was discussing Marchand's route of return, and was insisting that "he must return by the way he came and could not decend the Nile." Ibid.; Devonshire Papers, 340.2783, Salisbury to Devonshire, Nov. 7, 1898.
119. F.O. 27/3400, Monson to Salisbury, Oct. 21, 1898 (secret), Tel. no. 175; cf. S.P. 116, Same to Same, Oct. 21, 1898, no. 54.
120. Fitzroy, *Memories,* entry on Oct. 1, 1898, 1, pp. 1–2. Sir Almeric was one of the few contemporaries who really understood Salisbury's methods and principles. The mistaken impression that Salisbury needed much prodding in imperial matters is still fashionable.
121. S.P. 116, Monson to Salisbury, Oct. 21, 1898, no. 54.
122. F.O. 27/3400, Same to Same, Oct. 21, 1898 (secret), Tel. no. 175.
123. For British war preparations see Marder, *British Sea Power,* pp. 322 ff. French warships were closely watched, and by Oct. 26 British war strategy had been drawn up.
124. F.O. 27/3397, Monson to Salisbury, Oct. 24, 1898, no. 539, encl. extract from *Matin* of Oct. 23.
125. S.P. (FitzMaurice), Lansdowne to Salisbury, Oct. 15, 1898 (secret).
126. Newton, *Lansdowne,* pp. 152–53.
127. Cf. Marder, *British Sea Power,* p. 324.
128. F.O. 27/3400, Monson to Salisbury, Oct. 24, 1898 (secret and most confidential) Tel. no. 185. Monson said that he got this information from an "entirely trustworthy" source. Cf. S.P. 89 (cab. memo 1895–1900), Same to Same, Oct. 25, 1898 (secret and most confidential), Tel. no. 44; Cab. 37/48, "Anglo-French Relations in Egypt," Oct. 26, 1898, *IP,* F.O., no. 79. Muraviev had a rotten

reputation among British and German diplomats as well as among the press who, indeed, left him in no doubt about their views.

129. *Q.V.L.*, 3s., 3, Victoria to Salisbury, Oct. 28, 1898, Tel.

130. S.P. 84, Salisbury to Victoria, Oct. 29, 1898, Tel. no. 92; *Q.V.L.*, 3s., 3, p. 303.

131. S.P. 83, Victoria to Salisbury, Balmoral, Oct. 29, 1898, Tel. no. 124. Queen Victoria was not quite happy about Monson's appointment to Paris, perhaps because she considered Lady Monson unsuitable there, S.P. 85, Bigge to Salisbury, Aug. 20, 1895, no. 9.

132. Ibid., Same to Same, Oct. 2, 3, and 8, 1898, Tel. nos. 119, 120, and 122 resp.

133. *Q.V.L.*, 3s., 3, Same to Same, Oct. 30, 1898, Tel. no. 305–6.

134. See F.O. 27/3399, Salisbury to Monson, Oct. 22, 1898, requesting information re the rumors that France was seriously mobilizing. Delcasse denied that that was the case, cf. Grenville, *Salisbury and Foreign Policy*, pp. 228–29.

135. *Q.V.L.*, 3s., 3, Salisbury to Victoria, Oct. 27, 1898, pp. 298–99; cf. S.P. 119, Salisbury to Monson, Oct. 27, 1898, Tel. no. 29. The following day the Cabinet's decision was published in the *Pall Mall Gazette* under the heading: "England and France. Attitude of British Government." This information, predictably believed by some to have been leaked by Chamberlain, was rightly described by Barrington as a "cruel indiscretion," see S.P. 89, Minutes by Barrington, no. 46 and encl.

136. Cited in Grieve, "Egyptian Policy," p. 487.

137. Garvin, *Chamberlain*, 3, p. 229, n. i.

138. Curzon to Chamberlain, Oct. 26, 1898, ibid., p. 229.

139. Ibid., p. 230; Marder, *British Sea Power*, p. 332.

140. Sanderson, *England . . .* , p. 350.

141. J.C.P. (Lansdowne), Lansdowne to Chamberlain, Oct. 28, 1898.

142. At this time Sir Almeric Fitzroy was the Queen's clerk of the council in succession to Eddy Hamilton who had retired because of poor health.

143. Fitzroy, *Memories*, 1, p. 4.

144. Ibid., p. 4.

145. F.O. 27/3397, Monson to Salisbury, Oct. 25, 1898, no. 546; Robinson and Gallagher, *Africa and the Victorians*, p. 375.

146. Ibid., Same to Same, Oct. 26, 1898 and encl.; Grenville, *Salisbury and Foreign Policy*, p. 228.

147. F.O. 27/3399, Salisbury to Monson, Oct. 30, 1898 (confidential), Tel. no. 255; Cab. 37/48, "French interests in the Upper Nile," Oct. 31, 1898, no. 80; F.O.S.P. 119 Memo by S., no. 72.

148. S.P. 119, Barrington to Salisbury, Oct. 28, 1898, no. 74.

149. Ibid., Salisbury's Minutes on Barrington's note of Oct. 28.

150. F.O. 27/3397, Monson to Salisbury, Oct. 28, 1898 (secret and most confidential) no. 554.

151. Ibid.

152. F.O. 407/149 (7219), Cromer to Salisbury, Oct. 30, 1898, Tel. no. 296.
153. Ibid., Salisbury to Cromer, Oct. 30, 1898 (secret), Tel. no. 122.
154. F.O. 27/3397, Monson to Salisbury, Oct. 29, 1898 (most confidential), no. 558.
155. Ibid.
156. F.O. 407/149 (7219), Salisbury to Cromer, Nov. 2, 1898, Tel. no. 126.
157. F.O. 27/3400, Monson to Salisbury, Nov. 2, 1898, Tel. no. 199.
158. J.C.P. (Salisbury), Salisbury to Chamberlain, Dec. 26, 1898 (secret), no. 104.

CHAPTER XII

1. For details see Brown, *Fashoda Reconsidered,* op. cit.
2. S.P. 116, Monson to Salisbury, Jan. 21, 1898, no. 2.
3. F.O. 27/3393, Same to Same, Feb. 26, 1898, no. 109; cf. J.C.P. (Niger Negos. Docs.), Same to Same, Feb. 26, 1898 (most confidential), Cabinet Print, Mar. 2, 1898.
4. Ibid.
5. F.O. 78/5051, Minutes on a report of Oct. 20, 1898.
6. Cf. S.P. 119, Salisbury to Monson, Aug. 19, 1898, no. 33.
7. See S.P. 83, Victoria to Salisbury, Nov. 5, 1898, Tel. no. 45; *Q.V.L.* 35, 3, p. 309.
8. *St. James Gazette,* Nov. 7, 1898, editorial.
9. *Daily News,* Nov. 10, 1898, editorial.
10. *Q.V.L.,* 3s., 3, Extract from the *Queen's Journal,* p. 311.
11. F.O. 27/3397, Monson to Salisbury, Nov. 10, 1898, no. 596.
12. S.P. 116, Same to Same, Nov. 8, 1898, no. 63.
13. For this speech see *The Times,* Nov. 10, 1898.
14. S.P. 116, Monson to Salisbury, Nov. 11, 1898, no. 64.
15. F.O. 27/3397, Same to Same, Nov. 11, 1898, no. 598.
16. All these views were printed in the *Pall Mall Gazette* of Nov. 11 and 12, 1898 for the benefit of the British public.
17. S.P. 116, Monson to Salisbury, Nov. 13, 1898, no. 65.
18. Ibid., Same to Same, Nov. 18, 1898, no. 67.
19. Ibid., Same to Same, Nov. 25, 1898, no. 68.
20. S.P. 116, Monson to Salisbury, Nov. 25, 1898, no. 68.
21. F.O.C.P. (7915), "Colonial Defences, 1896–1901," F.O. to Colonial Defence Committee, Nov. 7, 1898 (secret), appendix in no. 16.
22. Ibid., Colonial Defence Committee to F.O., Nov. 22, 1898, no. 16 encl. "Memo by the C.D.C. re. neutrality under the Berlin Act of 1885."
23. S.P. 119, Salisbury to Monson, Nov. 15, 1898, no. 30.
24. Ibid.
25. F.O. 27/3397, Monson to Salisbury, Nov. 20, 1898, no. 628, encl.

26. S.P. 116, Monson to Salisbury, Dec. 2, 1898, no. 69.
27. F.O. 27/3398, Monson to Salisbury, Dec. 13, 1898, no. 684, encl. extract from the Report.
28. F.O. 800/2, Salisbury to Sanderson, Apr. 23, 1898, no. 268.
29. Cf. Grenville, *Salisbury and Foreign Policy*, pp. 231–33; Sanderson, *England* . . . , pp. 364–65.
30. Sanderson, *England* . . . ; Marder, *British Sea Power*, pp. 333–36.
31. Cf. ibid.
32. F.O. 27/3454, Salisbury to Monson, Mar. 15, 1899, no. 94.
33. F.O. 27/3455, Monson to Salisbury, Jan. 6 and 8, 1899, nos. 6 and 12 resp.
34. F.O. 27/3455, Monson to Salisbury, Jan. 8 and 13, and Feb. 3, 1899.
35. Marder, *British Sea Power*, pp. 333–34.
36. F.O. 27/3399, Salisbury to Monson, Dec. 19, 1898, Tel.
37. F.O. 27/3454, Same to Same, Jan. 11, 1899 (confidential), no. 2; J.C.P. (foreign affairs), Same to Same, Jan. 11, 1899 (confidential) no. 23.
38. Ibid.
39. For further details see Sanderson, *England* . . . , pp. 368–80.
40. Cf., for example, *Hansard*, 4s., 53, Feb. 24, 1898, cols. 37–44.
41. S.P. (Hicks-Beach), Hicks-Beach to Salisbury, Wednesday, Oct. 12, 1898.
42. F.O. 633/6, Cromer to Salisbury, Nov. 15, 1898 (confidential), no. 304; S.P. 89, Same to Same, Nov. 15, 1898 (confidential), no. 48; Cab. 37/48, "Situation in the Upper Nile," Nov. 28, 1898, no. 86, *F.O.*
43. *B.D.*, I, Cromer to Salisbury, Oct. 9, 1898, no. 207.
44. Sanderson, *England* . . . , p. 369.
45. F.O. 78/5025, Salisbury to Cromer, Feb. 12, 1899, Tel. no. 29.
46. Zetland, *Cromer*, p. 247.
47. F.O. 78/5025, Cromer to Salisbury, Feb. 3, 1899, Tel. no. 41.
48. This referred to the Niger Convention of June 14, 1898.
49. S.P. 113, Salisbury to Cromer, Feb. 3, 1899, Tel. no. 37.
50. Zetland, *Cromer*, p. 247.
51. F.O. 78/5025, Salisbury to Cromer, Feb. 15, 1899, Tel. no. 37.
52. Cf. J.C.P. (Hereford), Chamberlain's Minutes of Feb. 1, 1899; Balfour Papers, B.Mus.Add.Mss. (49773), Chamberlain to Balfour, Feb. 2, 1899.
53. F.O. 27/3454, Salisbury to Monson, Feb. 9, 15, 22, 28 and Mar. 15, 16, 1899.
54. Lord Edward Gleichen, *A Guardsman's Memories* (London, 1932), pp. 180–82.
55. Grieve, "Egyptian Policy," p. 527.
56. J.C.P. (Imp. Affairs, 1896–99), Memo by Salisbury.
57. F.O. 27/3454, Salisbury to Monson, Feb. 15, 1899, no. 47.
58. Grieve, "Egyptian Policy," p. 528.

59. S.P. 84, Salisbury to Victoria, Mar. 21, 1899, Tel. 99.

60. F.O. 27/3459, Monson to Salisbury, Aug. 14, 1899 (secret), no. 382; S.P. 117, Same to Same, May 12, 1899.

61. S.P. 117, Same to Same, no. 20.

62. S.P. 119, Salisbury to Monson, Aug. 19, 1899, no. 33.

63. Sometimes called the Bahr-el-Jebel.

64. Edward Schnitzer; born 1840; popularly known as Emin Pasha.

65. *The Times*, Sept. 20, 1892.

66. Kerckhoven was killed on Aug. 10, 1892, by his gunbearer—ostensibly by accident, but probably by design, since he was very unpopular among his men. He was succeeded by Delanghe.

67. F.O.C.P. (6588), Memo by Sir C. Hill, Apr. 24, 1895.

68. Ibid.

69. For a good analysis of this agreement see M. P. Hornik, "Mission of Sir Henry Drummond Wolff," in *E.H.R.*, pp. 227–44.

70. This account is based on an official report in F.O. 27/3368, "Precis of events on the Upper Nile . . . ," by the W.O., March, 1898.

71. Langer, *Imperialism*, p. 572.

72. F.O. 407/149 (7219), Cromer to Salisbury, Oct. 30, 1898, Tel. no. 296.

73. S.P. (Chamberlain), Chamberlain to Salisbury, Jan. 9, 1899 (private).

74. F.O. 407/149 (7219), Plunkett to Salisbury, Nov. 23, 1898, encl. extracts from the *Independance Belge* (Nov. 23, 1898) and *Petit Bleu* (Nov. 23, 1898).

75. *Fortnightly Review*, 70, Dec., 1898.

76. F.O. 407/151 (7277), "Memo by S. re. the Belgian claims to the Bahr-el-Ghazal," Apr. 7, 1899, no. 12. For similar views see F.O. 403/284 (7382), Plunkett to Salisbury, Oct. 8, 1899, no. 197.

77. S.P. (FitzMaurice), Lansdowne to Salisbury, Dec. 30, 1900.

78. Cf. S.P. (Hicks-Beach), Hicks-Beach to Salisbury, Mar. 20, 26, 1896.

79. Ibid., Same to Same, Oct. 19, 1896.

80. Ibid.

81. Milner Papers, Vol. 190, Dawkins to Milner, Nov. 17, 1896.

82. Ibid., Same to Same, Dec. 4, 1896.

83. Milner Papers, Vol. 183, Milner to Hicks-Beach, Dec. 3, 1896 (confidential).

84. F.O. 407/139 (6965), Salisbury to Cromer, Dec. 3, 1896, Tel. no. 123; cf. S.P. (Chancellor of the Exchequer, 1895–1900), Hicks-Beach to Salisbury, June 22, 1896, no. 34, for a similar view.

85. Obviously Salisbury was not aware of Milner's memo.

86. F.O. 407/139 (6965), Salisbury to Cromer, Dec. 3, 1896, Tel. no. 123.

87. Ibid., Cromer to Salisbury, Dec. 4, 1896, Tel. no. 276 (secret).

88. F.O. 407/147 (7158), Salisbury to Cromer, May 15, 1898, Tel. no. 41.

89. The British and Egyptian flags.
90. F.O. 407/147 (7158), Cromer to Salisbury, June 4, 1898 (secret), Tel. no. 163, in reply to Salisbury to Cromer, Tel. nos. 41 and 47.
91. F.O. 633/7, Cromer to Salisbury, June 5, 1898 (private), Tel. no. 546; cf. S.P. 111, Same to Same, June 5, 1898, Tel. no. 39.
92. Ibid., Salisbury to Cromer, June 6, 1898 (private), Tel. no. 547.
93. S.P. 111, Cromer to Salisbury, June 5, 1898, no. 40.
94. S.P. 89, Memo by Cromer: Cairo, June 15, 1898 (private and confidential), no. 32; Cab. 37/47, "Egypt; the future of the Soudan," July 27, 1898, *Cromer.*
95. F.O. 407/149 (7219), Treasury to F.O., July 5, 1898, no. 92.
96. Ibid.
97. S.P. 90, Memo by Salisbury: "Status of the Khalifa's Dominions if Conquered," July, 1898 (confidential), no. 7.
98. Ibid. This document is particularly interesting because it has not been published before.
99. Ibid., Memo by Halsbury, July, 1898 (confidential), no. 8. Halsbury supports his case with a Privy Council decision in 1834 (Sir Lancellot Shadwell, Mr. Baron Parke, and Mr. Justice Bosanquet formed part of the Court) in which they laid down the rule that a country reconquered from its enemy reverts to the same State to which it belonged before its reconquest.
100. Ibid., Memo by Halsbury, July, 1898 (confidential), no. 9.
101. F.O. 407/149 (7219), Salisbury to Cromer, Aug. 2, 1898 (secret), no. 109.
102. F.O. 78/4957, Cromer to Salisbury, Nov. 10, 1898 (separate and secret) no. 1.
103. Shibeika, *British Policy*, pp. 418–19.
104. For this Agreement see F.O. 407/150 (7292), Cromer to Salisbury, Jan. 28, 1899, no. 14 (with encls.); see also *Parl. Pap.*, Egypt no. 2 (1899) (C. 9134) 112, pp. 958–59; and in most published works.
105. F.O. 78/4957, Cromer to Salisbury, Nov. 10, 1898 (secret and separate), no. 1.
106. But it was challenged later on. See Mekki Abbas, *The Sudan Question.*
107. S.P. 113, Salisbury to Cromer, Dec. 9, 1898, no. 95; Magnus, *Kitchener*, p. 147.
108. F.O. 407/150 (7292), Cromer to Salisbury, Jan. 19, 1899, Tel. no. 19.
109. Mr. Crawford was H.M.'s Sub-Commissioner at Mombasa.
110. F.O. 407/150 (7292), Salisbury to Crawford, Jan. 20, 1899, Tel. no. 8 Africa.
111. Ibid., Cromer to Salisbury, Jan. 22, 1899 (confidential), no. 15, enclosing instructions to Sidar. For Kitchener's rule in the Sudan see Magnus, *Kitchener*, pp. 138–59.
112. Taylor, "Prelude to Fashoda," in *E.H.R.*, p. 80.

Bibliography

I. MANUSCRIPT SOURCES

A. Official Correspondence

1. *The Foreign Office Correspondence,* Public Record Office, London

F.O. (Africa and General, 1825–1905, 985 volumes)

F.O. 2/96; 97; 114; 133; 134; 144; 154–58, 161; 174; 200; 218; 219–20; 221; 222; 558

Note.—Most of the sources above are administrative material; but there are accounts of various expeditions and missions as well as some unexpected and valuable information. To make the best use of this material, thorough examination is recommended.

F.O. 27 (France, 1781–1905, 3,772 volumes)

F.O. 27/3263–68; 3273–77; 3292–93; 3300–3301; 3312–23; 3335–43; 3368–74; 3387; 3392–3400; 3408–17; 3429–30; 3437–42; 3454–61; 3478–79; 3566; 3766–67.

Note.—This class is an exceedingly rich source for West Africa and the Sudan. And in this study a very thorough and exhaustive use has been made of the material between 1896 and 1898.

F.O. 63 (Portugal)

F.O. 63/1359

F.O. 64 (Germany)

F.O. 64/1466–67

F.O. 78 (Turkey)

F.O. 78/4775; 4892–95; 4986; 5049–52

Note.—Classes F.O. 63, 64, and 78 were only used to supplement the documents in the F.O. Confidential Print.

F.O. 83 (Great Britain and General, 1745–1930, 2,480 volumes)

F.O. 83/1367; 1374–87; 1388; 1453; 1540; 1431; 1440–48; 1519–39; 1606–16

Note.—This class has been fully consulted but the yield was moderate and not commensurate with the time and effort lavished on it. Nevertheless it is interesting and contains all sorts of documents ranging from miscellaneous diplomatic documents to Parliamentary and domestic affairs in Britain.

371

F.O. 107 (Zanzibar)
F.O. 107/54; 57

2. *The Colonial Office Correspondence,* Public Record Office, London

C.O. 96 (The Gold Coast)
C.O. 96/258–62

> *Note.*—The C.O. manuscripts have been sparingly used because
> the relevant documents have been extracted from (*a*) the C.O.
> correspondence with the F.O. in F.O. 27 (Africa, various);
> (*b*) The Colonial Office Confidential Print; (*c*) G. E. Metcalfe's
> *Documents of Ghana History 1807–1957;* and (*d*) C. W. New-
> bury's *Select Documents 1786–1874,* for the earlier period.

B. Private Correspondence

1. *The Papers of Robert Arthur Talbot Gascoyne Cecil, third marquess
of Salisbury,* Christ Church, Oxford

The Salisbury Papers are a mine of information regarding
African affairs. Their importance can be seen from the extent of the
use to which they have been put in the text, though perhaps a little
less than half of my notes have been *directly* used. It is fair to say
that they are vital to this study. The range of the documents is so
wide that they serve individual and particular needs. For the purposes
of this book, those documents dealing with Africa—whether they
appear in this text or not—have been thoroughly perused.

These papers are broadly divided into two parts: (*a*) F.O.
Private Correspondence from 1878–1900 (140 vols.). Beautifully
cataloged to coincide with Salisbury's various years at the Foreign
Office, they can be best utilized when used in conjunction with the
strictly official documents at the P.R.O. as well as the private papers
of some of the most important ambassadors. (*b*) The purely personal
correspondence—starting from 1860 to 1902. These are too enormous
to be cataloged. But they are carefully arranged under the family
name of the correspondents, e.g., the letters of Lord Lansdowne to
Salisbury cannot be found under "Lansdowne," but under "Fitz
Maurice"; and those of Selborne are classified under "Palmer," and
so forth. These, too, have been extensively used in the text.

There is also another group of documents which do not fit into
the above groups: those in the Secretary's Note Book and a catalog
and some reprints of Salisbury's articles in the *Quarterly Review* by
Lady Gwendolen Cecil.

The exact and detailed locations of these documents have been
deliberately cited in the text. It is not therefore necessary to repeat
them here.

2. *The Papers of Joseph Chamberlain,* Birmingham University Library
(Heslop Room)

The Chamberlain Papers are second only to the Salisbury Papers in richness and importance. I have used them extensively, directly and indirectly. About a third of my notes are evident in the text.

The contents of these papers are divided as follows: (*a*) Private Correspondence (enormous in bulk); (*b*) Imperial Affairs—containing semi-official and official documents (mostly dealing with South Africa and West Africa); (*c*) Foreign Affairs—containing Miscellaneous Official documents; (*d*) Cabinet Papers 1870–1914 in microfilm; (*e*) Press cuttings cataloged under "Colonial Policy"; and (*f*) some contemporary periodicals carefully preserved.

These broad headings have been used in the text because they make it easier to check references than the official numbering which I find confusing. The cataloging, however, is well done.

3. *The Papers of Arthur James Balfour, first earl of Balfour:* British Museum, Add. Mss., London

These papers are only of moderate value to this study. They contain, however, important documents on South Africa and on the Anglo-German agreements concerning Portugal's African Colonies. The following volumes have been useful:

> Vols. VIII–IX, nos. 49690–91: Correspondence with Lord Salisbury, 1892–1902
> Vol. XCI, no. 49773: Correspondence with J. Chamberlain, 1887–1900
> Vol. LXXXVII, no. 49769: Correspondence with Duke of Devonshire, 1887–1902
> Vol. I, no. 49683: Correspondence with Queen Victoria, March 27, 1898
> Vol. I, no. 49746: Correspondence on Foreign Affairs, 1898
> Vol. I, no. 493739: Correspondence with J. H. Sanderson, 1898

The Balfour Papers are not yet properly cataloged.

4. *The Papers of Sir Charles Wentworth Dilke:* British Museum Add. Mss. (43874–967), London

These papers, which include Dilke's Confidential Political Diaries and "Memoirs," are disappointing. The "Memoirs" are mainly in the handwriting of Dilke's secretary, Sir H. K. Hudson (C.B.E., 1918), with *autographed* corrections and additions by Dilke, and also notes by his biographers, S. L. Gwynn and G. M. Tuckwell. After 1893 the "Memoirs" became very sporadic. However, the following numbers have been useful:

> No. 43915: Dilke's Election Address, July 9, 1895
> No. 43916: Correspondence with H. M. Hyndman, 1898–99
> No. 43941: Memoirs, 1887–1910
> No. 43944: Foreign Affairs, 1898

5. *The Papers of Sir Henry Campbell Bannerman:* British Museum, Add. Mss. (41206–52), London

    Important for the leadership and divisions in the Liberal party at the close of the century. The following numbers have been useful:
No. 41224: Correspondence with Lord Ripon, 1899–1900
No. 41211: Correspondence with Bryce, 1899–1900
No. 41214: Correspondence with J. E. Ellis, 1899–1900
No. 41218: Correspondence with Sir E. Grey, 1900

6. *The Papers of the first earl of Cromer:* Public Record Office (F.O. 633), London

    "The collection in this and in other volumes of correspondence is far more complete. I destroyed a large number of letters which I received, and wrote many letters of importance without keeping copies," F.O. 633/6, note by Cromer, Sept. 13, 1906. Nevertheless, used in conjunction with the Salisbury Papers, they have been useful to this study:

F.O. 633/5, Miscellaneous Letters, 1883–95
F.O. 633/6, Letters to Secretaries of State, 1883–1905
F.O. 633/7, Some printed correspondence with Lord Salisbury, 1883–1905
F.O. 633/8, Miscellaneous Letters, 1896
F.O. 633/11, Miscellaneous Letters, 1896, 1897, and 1902

7. *The Papers of Lord Sanderson (Sir Thomas):* Public Record Office (F.O. 800/1–2), London

    The documents here are primarily official correspondence in the form of F.O. Minutes by Salisbury and Sanderson, with a few important letters from Salisbury. Important source from 1895 to 1897. The period, 1898–1901 is blank. The letters begin again in 1902 and continue until 1922.
F.O. 800/1, General, 1895–96 (part I)
F.O. 800/2, General, 1897 (part II)

8. *The Private Papers of Sir Frank Lascelles:* Public Record Office (F.O. 800/6–20), London

    Limited use for this study since many of the letters here can also be found in the Salisbury papers.
F.O. 800/6, Abyssinia, Africa, etc., 1895–96 (General)
F.O. 800/9, Germany, Vol. 3, 1896
F.O. 800/17, Correspondence with Lord Salisbury, 1895–99

9. *The Papers of George Nathaniel Curzon, the first marquess Curzon of Kedleston,* Public Record Office (F.O. 800/28; 147–58)

    Important to this study for the slavery question in Zanzibar and Pemba.

F.O. 800/28, Memoranda and Memorials, 1896–97
F.O. 800/147–48, ibid, 1895–98

10. *The Private Papers of Sir Francis Bertie (later Lord Bertie of Thame)*, Public Record Office (F.O. 800/159–191), London

Scanty prior to 1900, but useful F.O. Minutes.
F.O. 800/176, Portugal and Miscellaneous, 1896–99
F.O. 800/160, Africa (General), 1896–97

11. *The Papers of Lord Lansdowne*, Public Record Office (F.O. 800/115–146), London

The only important letters are those from Lord Salisbury, most of which have been used by Lord Newton.
F.O. 800/115, Confidential. General. Letters in this volume were discovered in a press in the Map Room in June, 1942. They contain both Lansdowne's and Sir T. Sanderson's personal papers. Hence the volume is officially described as the "Personal Papers of Lord Lansdowne and Sir. T. Sanderson, 1898–1905."
Note.–The class F.O. 800 (*Private Collections: Ministers and Officials Various*), supersedes the previous list of this class and the volumes were renumbered in November, 1965. The Lansdowne, Sanderson, and Lascelles Papers were transferred from the Foreign Office Library, London, in 1965. The Curzon Papers were transferred from the Commonwealth Relations Office, London, at the same time.

12. *The Papers of Sir Edward Malet*, Public Record Office (F.O. 343/1–13), London

These papers contain only thirteen volumes; and only volume thirteen has been found useful.

13. *The Papers of the eighth duke of Devonshire*, Chatsworth, Bakewell, Derbyshire, 340.2606–2853 (1895–1900)

Limited value, though useful letters from Salisbury. Chronologically cataloged.

14. *The Papers of Lord Lugard*, Rhodes House Library, Oxford

Lugard's correspondence with Sir John Kirk, 1896–97 (vols. 40 and 41) has been found most useful in writing the chapter on East Africa, and particularly in treating the slavery issues in Zanzibar and Pemba. The letters are mostly from Kirk to Lugard, and a few to Flora Shaw. They throw a lot of light into the working of the F.O.; and they also give a clear idea of the F.O. personalities.

15. *The Papers of Sir Alfred Milner, Viscount Milner.* Deposited Bodleian Library, Oxford, in 1965

Important for the study of the Sudan question. The following volumes have proved most helpful:

Vol. 183, Letters written by Milner, 1890–96

Vol. 188, Letters received by Milner, 1892–94; and letters to Sir Michael Hicks-Beach and Various, 1896

Vol. 189, Letters received, 1895

Vol. 190, Letters from Philip Gell, and letters to Bertha Synge, 1825–1900

Vol. 442, Memorandum on British and foreign trade and industry, 1903 (ca. 1761)

Vol. 596, Official pamphlets relating to British East Africa, Bechuanaland, Barotseland, and Southern Rhodesia, 1892–98

Vol. 600, Papers relating to non-British territories in Africa, and to British treaties demarcating boundaries, 1894–1912

II. PRINTED SOURCES

A. Primary Sources
Official Correspondence

1. *Foreign Office Confidential Print* (F.O.C.P.)

F.O. 403 (Africa)–P.R.O., London

F.O. 403/224 (6941); 258 (7040); 277 (7212); 291 (7422); 307 (7445)

Note.—These volumes deal mainly with the organization and administration of the Uganda railway. They also contain minutes of the meetings of the Uganda Railway Committee.

F.O. 403/251 (7145); 284 (7382); 297 (7379)

F.O. 407 (Egypt)

F.O. 407/132 (6802); 136 (6808); 137 (6928); 138 (6889); 139 (6965); 142 (7091); 143 (7079); 144 (7097); 147 (7158); 149 (7219); 150 (7292); 151 (7277); 152 (7293)

Note.—These prints contain more variety than the original letters in F.O. 78, with which they have been cross-checked.

F.O.C.P. (6588); (5284); (7915); (7075); (6249); (6401); (6489); (6709); (6755); (6756); (6847)

Note.—These prints contain miscellaneous but important material.

2. *Colonial Office Confidential Print* (C.O.C.P.)

C.O. 879 (Africa), until 1965 C.O. 806 (Africa), P.R.O., London

C.O. 879/42–43; 44; 45; 48; 49; 50; 52; 54; 55; 57; 58; 59; 61; 62; 67

Note.—The F.O. and C.O. Confidential Print are a collection of printed papers containing selected correspondence, memoranda, and other documents for cabinet circulation. Many of them are edited and published as *Parl. Paps.* or Command Papers. Minutes are usually omitted, but everything relevant is included. The materials they contain do not necessarily come from one class of documents. For example, the F.O.C.P. on the Sudan, not only includes extracts from F.O. 78, but also those from F.O. 27, F.O. 45, F.O. 64, and so forth. This is their great importance. They make the researcher see all the dimensions of all the important problems at issue at a glance, as it were.

From 1874 to 1890 some of the original correspondence printed in the C.O.C.P. had been destroyed. For this period therefore the C.P. may supply the only extant source for reference. The new class of C.O.C.P. (879 Africa) contains, mostly between 1862 and 1879, some of the papers which earlier were classified under the *Mediterranean* series (C.O. 883). It also contains some papers previously classified under St. Helena, as well as a few others under the *West Indies* (C.O. 884) and under *Miscellaneous* (C.O. 885).

3. *Cabinet Papers or Cabinet Confidential Print, 1895–1900* (P.R.O. C.A.B. 37), London

The following volumes have been found useful:

C.A.B. 37/39–40, 1895; 41–43, 1896; 44–45, 1897; 46–48, 1898; 49, 1899; 52, 1900.

Note.—The Cabinet Papers are documents which cabinet members considered important enough to be printed and circulated to their colleagues in the form of memoranda either with the aim in view of giving them information or seeking their assent to a measure they proposed to adopt.

Before the formation of the cabinet secretariat in December, 1916, these papers were scattered in various places—both private and official. In the P.R.O. the main source of the Cabinet Papers is the class *Cabinet Office Miscellaneous Records* (Cab. 1)—containing about 800 papers returned to the cabinet office by former ministers or their executors. The F.O. library houses another 1,500, dealing mainly with F.O. affairs from 1900. The rest—a majority—are extant in private papers of ministers all over the country. The Royal Archives, too, have their share. In November, 1962, the P.R.O. undertook the useful task of collecting these papers between 1880 and 1914 under the title: *List of Cabinet Papers, 1880–1914,* which was published by H.M.S.O., London, 1964. The list contains about 3,300 papers, though about 5,000 are said to be extant. The list therefore is not complete, because many of them are still undiscovered. In the "Salisbury Papers," for example, there are still some letters marked: "Cabinet Print," but which are not included in the P.R.O. list, and which I have not seen anywhere else.

Microfilm copies of this list are in "Chamberlain Papers" and can be conveniently used at Birmingham University Library.

4. *Other Collections*

Gooch. G. P., and Temperley, Harold, eds. *British Documents on the Origins of the War, 1898–1914,* 2 vols. *The End of British Isolation,* vol. 1 (London, 1927). Sparingly cited since most of the documents are in the manuscript and original sources where, unlike in these collections, they are unabridged.

Temperley, H., and Penson, L. M., eds. *Foundations of British Foreign Policy: From Pitt (1792) to Salisbury (1902), Or Documents, Old and New* (Cambridge University Press, 1938). Few useful documents in 1898.

Joll, James, ed. *Britain and Europe, 1793–1940* (London, 1961). A collection of important memoranda and political speeches from Pitt to Churchill.

Newbury, C. W., ed. *British Policy towards West-Africa. Select Documents 1786–1874* (Oxford, 1965). Useful pioneer work.

Metcalfe, G. E., ed. *Great Britain and Ghana. Documents of Ghana History, 1807–1957* (London, 1964). Another useful pioneer work.

Dugdale, E. T. S., ed. *German Diplomatic Documents 1871–1914*, 4 vols. (London, 1929). Useful for the Heligoland offer of 1890 and the advance on Dongola.

5. *Parliamentary Papers.* (Parl. Pap.)

West Africa

1865, V(412)	1898, (C. 8854)LX
1890, (C. 5905)LI	1899, (C. 9124)LXIII
1892, (C. 6701)LVI	1899, (C. 9529)LXIII
1893–94, (7108)CIX	1899, (C. 9372)LXIII
1893–94, (C. 7026)CIX	1899, VI(260)
1893–94, (C. 7230)CIX	1899, (C. 9388)LX
1896, (C. 7918)LVIII	1899, (C. 9391)LX
1896, (C. 7977)LIX	1899, (C. 9334)CIX
1898, (C. 8922)LIX	1901, (Cd. 501)XLVIII
1898, (C. 8677)LX	

East Africa

1890, (C. 6043)LI	1896, (C. 7971)XLV
1890, (C. 6046)LI	1897, (C. 8435)LXII
1892, (C. 6560)LVI	1898, (C. 8683)LX
1892, (C. 6555)LVI	1898, (C. 8718, C. 8941)LX
1893–94, (C. 7025)LXII	1898, (C. 9027)LX
1893–94, (C. 6847, C. 6848,	1898, (C. 8942)LX
C. 6853, C. 7109)	1899, (LI 108)
1894, (C. 7303)LVII	1899, (C. 9123)LXIII
1895, (C. 7646)LXXI	(C. 9232, C. 9503)
1895, (C. 7708)LXXI	1899, (C. 9331,
1895, (C. 7833)LXXI	C. 9333)LXIII
1896, VII (Bill 305)	1899, (C. 9125)LXIII
1896, (C. 8274)LIX	1900, (V, Bill 182)
1896, (C. 8049)LIX	1900, XLVII (109)

1900, (Cd. 256, Cd. 361)LVI   1901, (Cd. 674)XLVIII
1900, (Cd. 97, Cd. 355)LVI

Zanzibar

1897, (C. 8374)LXII   1899, (C. 9502)LXIII
1897, (C. 8433)LXII   1900, (Cd. 96)LVI
1898, (C. 8858)LX   1901, (Cd. 593)XLVIII

General

1897, (C. 8449)LX   1899, (C. 9223)LXIII
1903, (Cd. 1635)XLV

Egypt/Sudan

1898, (C. 9054)CXII   1899, (C. 9134)CXII
1898, (C. 9055)CXII   1899, (C.9231, C. 9332,
1899, (C. 9133)CXII   C. 9424)CXII
1899, (C. 9242)CXII

Unofficial Sources

1. *Hansard's Parliamentary Debates*, 4th Ser. 1895–1900

August 15, 16, 22, 30, 1895   May 6, 1898 LVII
   XXXVI   June 10, 1898 LVIII
February 11, 28, 1896 XXXVII   June 24, 1898 LX
March 12, 16, 20, 1896   February 7, 1899 LXVI
   XXXVIII   February 24, 1899 LXVII
March 27, 1896 XXXIX   March 10, 1899 LXVIII
May 8, 1896 XL   April 10, 1899 LXIX
June 5, 12, 1896 XLI   Commons and Lords, June 5, 8,
July 2, 1896 XLII   1899 LXXII
July 27, 1896 XLVIII   July 3, 1899 LXXIII
Lords, August 10, 13, 1896   July 26, 28, 1899 LXV
   XLIV   Lords, October 17, 1899
Lords and Commons, January   LXXVIII
   19 and February 5, 1897   Lords, January 30, 1900
   XLV   LXXVIII
April 2, 20, 1897 XLVIII   Lords, February 15, 1900
Lords, May 24, 1897 XLIX   LXXIX
June 22, 1897 L   March 15, 1900 LXXX
July 19, 1897 LI   Lords, June 21, 1900 LXXXIV
February 8, 10, 24, 1898 LIII   December 6, 1900 LXXXVIII
March 3, 1898 LIV

2. *Journals, Letters, Diaries*

Blunt, W. S. *My Diaries. Being a Personal Narrative of Events, 1888–
   1914*, 2 vols. (London, 1918–1919).
Brett, M. V., ed. *Journals and Letters of . . . Viscount Esher*, vol. I
   (London, 1934).

Buckle, G. E., ed. *The Letters of Queen Victoria.* 3d series. vol. 3 (London, 1932).

Colson, Percy, ed. *Lord Goschen and His Friends.* (*The Goschen Letters*) (London, 1946)

Gwynn, Stephen, ed. *The Letters and Friendships of Sir Cecil Spring Rice 1859–1918—A Record,* vol. 1 (London, 1929).

Healy, T. M. *Letters and Leaders of My Day,* 2 vols. (London, 1928).

Hutchinson, H. G., ed. *Private Diaries of Sir Algernon West* (London, 1922).

Lucy, H. W. *A Diary of Two Parliaments. The Disraeli Parliament, 1874–1880* (London, 1885); *A Diary of the Salisbury Parliament, 1886–1892* (London, 1892); *Peeps at Parliament* (London, 1903). Covers the period 1893–July, 1895; *Later Peeps at Parliament* (London, 1905). Covers the period Dec., 1896–Dec., 1902; *A Diary of the Unionist Parliament, 1895–1900* (London, 1901).

Lutyens, Mary, ed. *Lady Lytton's Court Diary 1895–1899* (London, 1961).

Zetland, Marquis of, ed. *The Letters of Disraeli to Lady Bradford and Lady Chesterfield, 1873–1881,* 2 vols. (London, 1929).

3. *Memoirs, Memories, Autobiographies*

Asquith and The Earl of Oxford. *Memories and Reflections 1852–1927,* 2 vols. (London, 1928); *Fifty Years of Parliament,* 2 vols. (London, 1926).

Asquith, Margot. *Autobiography,* 2 vols. (London, 1920–1922).

Balfour, A. J. *Chapters of Autobiography,* ed. Mrs. Edgar Dugdale (London, 1930).

Balfour, Lady Frances. *Ne Obliviscaris,* 2 vols. (London, 1930).

Barclay, Sir Thomas. *Thirty Years: Anglo-French Reminiscences, 1876–1906* (London, 1914).

Cecil, Alice Cecily (A. S.) *A Memory, 1887–1947* (1950, deposited Bodleian Library, Oxford, 1964). A memory of James Edward Hubert Cecil, 4th Marquess of Salisbury 1861–1947 and of life at Hatfield; *Hatfield 1887–1903.* Typed. Deposited Bodleian Library, Oxford, 1964.

Cecil, Lord Edward. *The Leisure of an Egyptian Official* (London, 1921).

Cecil, Viscount, of Chelmwood. *All the Way* (London, 1949).

Channing, F. A. *Memories of Midland Politics, 1885–1910* (London, 1918).

Churchill, Winston S. *My Early Life. A Roving Commission* (London, 1930).

Cook, A. R. *Uganda Memories, 1897–1940* (Kampala, 1945).

Dugdale, Blanche E. C. *Family Home Spun* (London, 1940).

Eckardstein, Baron Von. *Ten Years at the Court of St. James 1895–1905* (London, 1921).

Fitzroy, Sir Almeric. *Memoirs,* 2 vols. (London, 1925).

Gladstone, Viscount. *After Thirty Years* (London, 1929).

Gleichen, Lord Edward. *A Guardman's Memories* (London, 1932).

Gooch, G. P. *Under Six Reigns* (London, 1958).

Grenfell, Lord. *Memoirs of Field-Marshall Lord Grenfell* (London, 1926).

Grey, Viscount of Fallodan. *Twenty-Five Years 1892–1916,* 3 vols. (London, 1928).

Hamilton, Lord George. *Parliamentary Reminiscences and Reflections, 1886–1906* (London, 1922).

Haldane, Richard Burdon. *An Autobiography* (London, 1929).

Hardinge, Sir Arthur. *A Diplomatist in the East* (London, 1928).

Helier, Lady St. *Memories of Fifty Years* (London, 1909).

Jackson, Sir F. *Early Days in East Africa* (London, 1930).

Johnston, Sir Harry. *The Story of My Life* (London, 1923).

Lyttleton, General Sir Neville. *Eighty Years* (London, 1927).

Midleton, Earl of. *Records and Reactions 1856–1939* (London, 1939).

Milner, Viscountess. *My Picture Gallery, 1886–1901* (London, 1951).

Morley, Viscount. *Recollections,* 2 vols. (London, 1917).

Neville, Ralph, ed. *The Reminiscences of Lady Dorothy Neville* (London, 1906).

Newton, Lord. *Retrospection* (London, 1941).

O'Connor, T. P. *Memoirs of an Old Parliamentarian,* 2 vols. (London, 1929).

Penshurst, Lord Hardinge, of. *Old Diplomacy* (London, 1947).

Ponsonby, Sir Frederick. (1st Lord Sysonby). *Recollections of Three Reigns* (London, 1951).

Raymond, E. T. *Portraits of the Nineties* (London, 1921).

Rodd, Sir James Rennell. *Social and Diplomatic Memories,* 3 vols. (London, 1922).

Smith-Dorrien, General Sir H. *Memories of Forty-Eight Years' Service* (London, 1925).

Smith, Goldwin. *Reminiscences* (New York, 1910).

Spender, J. A. *Life, Journalism and Politics,* 2 vols. (London, 1927).

Tucker, Alfred R. *Eighteen Years in Uganda and East Africa,* 2 vols. (London, 1908).

Wolff, Sir Henry Drummond. *Rambling Recollections,* 2 vols. (London, 1908).

4. *Newspapers and Periodicals*

A deep, careful, and most rewarding study of these sources has been made, particularly of the years between 1895 and 1903. Over 35 newspapers and periodicals, representing all shades of opinion, and in the case of the former, from representative parts of the country, have been consulted. With the exception of *The Times* and the *Daily Graphic*—which are in the Bodleian Library, Oxford—all the newspapers were read at the Colindale Library of the British Museum,

London. All the periodicals cited here are in the Bodleian or Rhodes House Library, Oxford. Foreign newspapers and periodicals, of which some considerable use has been made, are not included here. They come under the category of the F.O. class series in which they are enclosed. Throughout this study the author has tried very hard to ascertain contemporary opinions; in a study of this nature what people said or did is more important than the sophisticated interpretations put on their actions by historians.

Below is the list of these newspapers and periodicals. The details of the articles and the authors cited are too numerous to be recounted here. The documentation in the text has been deliberately full.

Newspapers, 1895–1903

The Times. Independent and imperial.

The *Daily Telegraph.* "Popular" paper. Claimed to have the "largest circulation in the world." Unionist and imperial. Turned Unionist over the Home Rule issue. Faithfully supported by the *Petite Bourgeoisie.*

The *South Wales Daily News.* Vigorous provincial Liberalism. Anti-Tory. Dislike of Chamberlain. Judged imperial issues on their merits. Some of the copies between 1897 and 1899 destroyed during World War II.

The *St. James' Gazette.* Pro-Salisbury and pro-Disraeli. Appealed to the "cultivated British audience."

The *Morning Post.* "Classical" paper. Right wing conservative, landed *Whig,* and imperial.

The *Daily News.* Largest circulation of Liberal papers. Level-headed, sober. Supposed to be chief Liberal party organ. But in this period hardly anti-expansionist. Edited by E. T. Cook, 1896–1901. Originally more Gladstonian than Gladstone himself.

The *Pall Mall Gazette.* Skeptical Tory. Devout jingo.

The *Westminster Gazette.* Liberal Imperialist, "cultivated" audience.

The *Financial Times.* Conservative and imperial, level-headed.

The *Yorkshire Post.* Conservative and imperial. Some copies in this period destroyed during the last war.

The *Daily Graphic.* Non-party, but imperial.

The *Daily Mail.* Exuberant jingoism. Over a million copies a day. Imperial.

The *Standard.* Chief Tory organ. "Classical" paper. Imperialist, but level-headed.

The *Daily Chronicle and Clerkenwell News.* Appealed to the "small shop-keeper." Supposed to be Liberal-Unionist—but tended to support the Liberal Imperialists.

The *Manchester Guardian.* Perhaps the only authentic anti-imperialist paper. Opponent of Salisbury's foreign policy.

The *Scotsman.* Deserted the Liberals over the Home Rule issue. Strongly Unionist and imperial.

The *Birmingham Daily Post.* Strongly Unionist and imperial. Some copies in this period destroyed during the last war. Deserted the Liberals over the Home Rule issue.

The *Birmingham Daily Mail.* Strongly Unionist and imperial. Many copies destroyed during the last war.

The *Evening News.* Imperialist and jingoistic.

The *Glasgow Herald.* Unionist and imperialist. Deserted the Liberals over the Home Rule issue.

The *Globe.* Conservative and imperialist.

The *Northern Echo.* Provincial radicalism. Anti-imperialist.

Periodicals, 1895–1903

Brittania. Monthly magazine for United Empire Loyalists.

The *British Empire Review.* The organ of the British Empire League. Monthly magazine.

Annual Register. Review of public events at home and abroad.

The *Edinburgh Review,* or *Critical Journal.* Monthly magazine. Nonpartisan.

Blackwoods Magazine. Monthly. Tended to support Salisbury's imperial policies.

The *Fortnightly Review.* Excellent periodical. Balanced. All opinions printed.

The *Nineteenth Century and After.* Monthly review. Allowed all shades of opinion to be printed.

The *Quarterly Review* (1860, 1863, 1883, 1895–1903, 1948). Tory organ.

The *National Review* (1894–1908, 1934). When Leo Maxse acquired the *Review* in 1893 from Alfred Austin, he was made to undertake to keep it "Unionist and Imperial." The *Review* was originally launched in 1883 by a collection of 1,000 subscribers at the Carlton.

The *Monthly Review.* First number appeared in October 1900. Independent.

The *Review of Reviews.* Unreliable.

The *Contemporary Review.* All opinions printed—but inclined to be moderate. Excellent monthly.

The *Spectator.* Watch-dog of Tory principles. Unionist and Imperial.

Africa. Pamphlets etc. Liverpool Chamber of Commerce Publications.

Westminster Cartoons. A parody of political events.

Miscellaneous

Publications of the Conservative Central Office, 1895–1900.

Lord Rosebery on Salisbury. Speech at Oxford Union Society printed in Oxford Miscellaneous. *Report of Proceedings and Speeches.* Bodleian Library, Oxford (Oxon., 8715).

B. Secondary Sources

Biographies

1. *Biographies of, and important works on, Salisbury*

Aitken, W. F. *The Marquess of Salisbury* (London, 1901).

Cecil, Algernon. "Salisbury" in *British Foreign Secretaries 1807–1916.* (London, 1927).

————. "Lord Salisbury" in *Queen Victoria and Her Prime Ministers* (London, 1953).

Cecil, Lady Gwendolen. *Life of Robert Marquis of Salisbury,* 4 vols. (London, 1921–32).

————. "Life of Robert Marquis of Salisbury," vol. 5 (Draft). Deposited at Christ Church Library, Oxford.

————. *Biographical Studies of the Life and Political Character of Robert, Third Marquis of Salisbury* (Printed for private circulation).

Ellis, Rev. J. J. *The Marquis of Salisbury* (London, 1892).

Forshaw, C. F., ed. *Poetical Tributes to the Memory of the late Most Hon. The Marquess of Salisbury* (London, 1904).

Grenville, J. A. S. *Lord Salisbury and Foreign Policy* (London, 1964).

How, F. D. *The Marquis of Salisbury* (London, 1902).

Jeyes, S. H. *The Life and Times of the Marquis of Salisbury,* 4 vols. (London, 1895).

Kennedy, A. L. *Salisbury, 1830–1903: Portrait of a Statesman* (London, 1953).

Lowe, C. J. *Salisbury and the Mediterranean 1886–1896* (London, 1965).

Low, Sidney. "Lord Salisbury," in *Fortnightly Review,* vol. 80, Oct., 1903.

Mee, Arthur. *Lord Salisbury: The Record Premiership of Modern Times* (London, 1901).

Penson, Lillian. *Foreign Affairs Under the Third Marquis of Salisbury* (London, 1962).

————. "The Principles and Methods of Lord Salisbury's Foreign Policy" in *Cambridge Historical Journal,* vol. 5 (1935).

Pulling, F. S. *Life and Speeches of the Marquis of Salisbury,* 2 vols. (London, 1885).

Smith, W. B. *Lord Salisbury* (London, 1903).

Taylor, A. J. P. "Lord Salisbury" in *From Napoleon to Stalin* (London, 1953).

Trail, H. D. *The Marquis of Salisbury,* 2nd ed. (London, 1892).

Whates, H. *The Third Salisbury Administration, 1895–1900* (London, 1900).

2. *Other Biographies*

Arthur, Sir George. *Life of Lord Kitchener,* 3 vols. (London, 1920).

Beach, Lady Victoria. *Life of Sir Michael Hicks-Beach* (Earl St. Aldwyn), 2 vols. (London, 1932).

Chilston, Viscount. *Chief Whip: The Political Life and Times of Aretas Akers-Douglas 1st Viscount Chilston* (London, 1961).

Churchill, Randolph. *Winston S. Churchill. Youth, 1874–1900* (London, 1966).

Dugdale, Blanche. *Arthur James Balfour, First Earl of Balfour, 1848–1905* (London, 1939).

Elliot, Arthur. *The Life of Lord Goschen, 1831–1907* (London, 1911).

Flint, J. E. *Sir George Goldie and the Making of Nigeria* (Oxford University Press, 1960).

Fraser, Peter. *Joseph Chamberlain: Radicalism and Empire, 1868–1914* (London, 1966).

Gardiner, A. G. *The Life of Sir William Harcourt*, 2 vols. (London, 1923).

Garvin, J. L. *The Life of Joseph Chamberlain*, 3 vols. (London, 1932–34).

Guedalla, Philip. *Mr. Churchill: A Portrait* (London, 1941).

Gwynn, S. and Tuckwell, G. M. *The Life of Sir Charles W. Dilke*, 2 vols. (London, 1918).

Holland, B. *The Life of Spencer Compton, Eighth Duke of Devonshire*, 2 vols. (London, 1911) 2d ed.

James, R. R. *Rosebery: A Biography of Archibald Philip, Fifth Earl of Rosebery* (London, 1963).

Jenkins, Roy. *Sir Charles Dilke, A Victorian Tragedy* (London, 1958).

Longford, Elizabeth. *Victoria R. I.* (London, 1964).

Magnus, Philip. *Kitchener: Portrait of an Imperialist* (London, 1958).

Monypenny, W. F. and Buckle, G. E. *The Life of Benjamin Disraeli: Earl of Beaconsfield*, 2 vols. (London, 1929).

Newton, Lord. *Lord Lansdowne: A Biography* (London, 1929).

Oliver, Roland. *Sir Harry Johnston and the Scramble for Africa* (London, 1957).

Perham, Margery. *Lugard: The Years of Adventure, 1858–1898* (London, 1956).

Ronaldshay, Earl of. *The Life of Lord Curzon*, vol. 1 (London, 1928).

Spender, J. A. *The Life of . . . Sir Henry Campbell-Bannerman*, vol. 1 (London, 1923).

Spender, J. A. and Asquith, Cyril. *Life of Lord Oxford and Asquith*, vol. 1 (London, 1932).

Trevelyan, G. M. *Grey of Fallodan* (London, 1937).

Wingate, Sir Ronald. *Wingate of the Sudan . . .* (London, 1955).

Young, Kenneth. *Arthur James Balfour . . . 1848–1930* (London, 1963).

Zetland, Marquess of. *Lord Cromer* (London, 1932).

Contemporary Works

Alford, H. S. L. and Sword, W. D. *The Egyptian Soudan: Its Loss and Recovery* (London, 1898).

Ashe, R. P. *Two Kings of Uganda* (London, 1890).

———. *Chronicles of Uganda* (London, 1894).

Austin, H. H. *With Macdonald in Uganda* (London, 1903).

Baker, S. W. *Albert Nyanza* (London, 1866).

———. *Ismailia* (London, 1874).

Burton, R. F. *The Lake Regions of Central Africa* (London, 1860).

Churchill, W. S. *The River War,* 3d ed. (London, 1933).

Cromer, Earl of. *Modern Egypt,* 2 vols. (London, 1908).

Dilke, Sir Charles W. *Greater Britain,* 2 vols. (London, 1868).

———. *Problems of Greater Britain,* 2 vols. 2d ed. (London, 1890).

Eliot, Sir Charles. *The East Africa Protectorate* (London, 1905).

Gleichen, Count. *With the Mission to Menelik, 1897* (London, 1898).

Grant, J. A. *A Walk Across Africa* (London, 1864).

Gregory, J. W. *The Foundation of British East Africa* (London, 1901).

Hertslett, Sir E. *Map of Africa by Treaty,* 3 vols. (London, 1909) 3d ed.

Hobson, J. A. *Imperialism: A Study* (London, 1902).

Johnston, H. H. *The Uganda Protectorate,* 2 vols. (London, 1902).

Kingsley, Mary. *West African Studies* (London, 1899).

Livingstone, David. *The Last Journals of David Livingstone,* ed. H. Waller (London, 1874).

Lugard, F. D. *The Rise of Our East African Empire,* 2 vols. (Edinburgh and London, 1893).

Masterman, C. F. G., ed. *The Heart of the Empire* (London, 1901).

McDermot, P. L. *British East Africa. Or I.B.E.A.* (London, new ed., 1895).

Macdonald, J. L. *Soldiering and Surveying in British East Africa* (London and New York, 1897).

Milner, Viscount. *England in Egypt* (13th ed., London, 1920).

Morel, E. D. *The Affairs of West Africa* (London, 1902).

Pasha, Slatin. *Fire and Sword in the Sudan . . . 1879–1895* (London, 1896).

Rodd, R., ed. *The British Mission to Uganda in 1893* (London, 1894).

Speke, J. H. *Journal of the Discovery of the Source of the Nile* (London, 1863).

Stanley, H. M. *Through the Dark Continent* (London, 1890).

Vandeleur, S. *Campaigning on the Upper Nile and Niger* (London, 1898).

White, A. S. *The Expansion of Egypt Under Anglo-Egyptian Condominium* (London, 1899).

Wingate, F. R. *Mahdism and the Egyptian Sudan* (London and New York, 1891).

Later Works

Anene, J. C. *Southern Nigeria in Transition, 1885–1906* (Cambridge University Press, 1966).

Barber, J. P. "The Macdonald Expedition to the Nile, 1897–1899," *Uganda Journal*, 28, 1 (1964).

Beachey, R. W. "Macdonald's Expedition and the Uganda Mutiny, 1897–1898," *Historical Journal*, 10, 2 (1967).

Benians, E. A., ed. *Cambridge History of the British Empire*, vol. 3 (Cambridge University Press, 1959).

Bennett, G., ed. *The Concept of Empire: Burke to Attlee 1774–1947* (London, 1953).

Berard, V. *British Imperialism and Commercial Supremacy* (London, 1906).

Bodelsen, C. A. *Studies in Mid-Victorian Imperialism* (New York, 1925).

Brown, Roger Glenn. *Fashoda Reconsidered: The Impact of Domestic Politics on French Policy in Africa, 1893–1898* (Johns Hopkins Press, 1970).

Bullock, A. and Shock, M., eds. *The Liberal Tradition: From Fox to Keynes* (London, 1956).

Cairns, H. A. C. *Prelude to Imperialism: British Reaction to Central African Society 1840–1890* (London, 1965).

Cole, G. D. H. *A Short History of the British Working-Class Movement, 1789–1947* (London, 1947).

Collins, R. O. *The Southern Sudan, 1883–1898: A Struggle for Control* (Yale and London, 1962).

Cook, A. N. *British Enterprise in Nigeria* (Philadelphia, 1943).

Coupland, R. *Kirk on the Zambesi* (Oxon. 1928).

―――――. *East Africa and its Invaders* (Oxon. 1938).

―――――. *The Exploitation of East Africa 1856–1890* (London, 1939).

Crowder, Michael, ed. *West African Resistance: The Military Response to Colonial Occupation* (London, 1971).

Dike, K. O. *Trade and Politics in the Niger Delta 1830–1885* (Oxon. 1956).

Dunbabin, J. P. D. "Parliamentary Elections in Great Britain, 1858–1900: A Psephological Note," in *E.H.R.*, 81, no. 318 (Jan., 1966).

Fieldhouse, D. K. *The Colonial Empires: A Comparative Survey from the Eighteenth Century* (London, 1966).

―――――. "Imperialism: An Historiographical Revision," *E.H.R.*, 2d Ser., 14 (Dec., 1961).

Fieldhouse, D. K., ed. *The Theory of Capitalist Imperialism* (London, 1967).

Flecter, T. B. "Mwanga—The Man and His Times," *Uganda Journal*, 4, 2 (1936).

Fyfe, C. *A History of Sierra Leone* (Oxford University Press, 1962).

Gale, H. P. "Mutessa I . . . Was he a God?", *Uganda Journal*, 20, 1 (1956).

Gann, L. and Duignan, P., eds. *Colonialism in Africa, 1870–1960*, vol. 1 (Cambridge University Press, 1969).

Geary, N. M. *Nigeria Under British Rule* (London, 1927).

Gifford, P. and Louis, R., eds. *Britain and Germany in Africa* (New Haven, 1967).

————. *France and Britain in Africa, Imperial Rivalry and Colonial Rule* (New Haven, 1971).

Gillard, D. R. "Salisbury's African Policy and the Heligoland Offer of 1890," in *E.H.R.*, 75, no. 297, Oct., 1960.

————. "Salisbury's Heligoland Offer: The Case Against the 'Witu Thesis,'" in *E.H.R.*, 80, no. 316, July, 1965.

Gray, J. M. "The Year of the Three Kings of Buganda . . . 1888–1889," *Uganda Journal*, 14, 1 (1950).

Grenville, J. A. S. "Great Britain and the Isthmian Canal, 1898–1901," in the *American Historical Review*, 61, no. 1, Oct., 1955.

————. "Goluchowski, Salisbury, and the Mediterranean Agreements," in *The Slavonic and East European Review*, 36, no. 87, June, 1958.

Halevy, E. *Imperialism and the Rise of Labour* (2d ed., London, 1951).

Hargreaves, J. D. *Prelude to the Partition of West Africa* (London, 1963).

————. "*Entente Manquee:* Anglo-French Relations 1895–1896," *Cambridge Historical Journal*, 11, no. 1 (1953).

————. "Toward a History of the Partition of Africa," *Journal of African History*, 1, no. 1 (1960).

Harlow, V. and Chilver, E. M., eds. *History of East Africa*, 2 (Oxon. 1965).

Hayes, C. J. H. *A Generation of Materialism, 1871–1900* (New York, 1941).

Hill, M. F. *Permanent Way: The Story of the Kenya and Uganda Railway*, 1 (Nairobi, 2d ed., 1961).

Hollingsworth, L. W. *Zanzibar Under the Foreign Office, 1890–1913* (London, 1953).

Holt, P. M. *The Mahdist State of the Sudan, 1881–1898* (Oxon. 1958).

Ingham, K. *The Making of Modern Uganda* (London, 1958).

————. *A History of East Africa* (London, 1962).

Jones, Kennedy. *Fleet Street and Downing Street* (London, 1920).

Kanya-Forstner, A. S. *The Conquest of the Western Sudan: A Study in French Military Imperialism* (Cambridge University Press, 1969).

Kavulu, David. *The Uganda Martyrs* (Longmans, 1969).

Kimble, D. *A Political History of Ghana, 1850–1928* (Oxon., 1963).

Kiwanuka, M. S. M. "Kabaka Mwanga and His Political Parties," *Uganda Journal*, 33, 1 (1969).

————. *Muteesa of Uganda* (Nairobi, 1967).

Koebner, R. "The Concept of Economic Imperialism," *Economic History Review*, 2 ser., 2, no. 1 (1949).

Koebner, R. and Schmidt, H. D. *Imperialism* . . . (Cambridge University Press, 1964).

Langer, W. L. *The Diplomacy of Imperialism* (2d ed., New York, 1956).

Lenin, V. L. *Imperialism: The Highest Stage of Capitalism* (London, 1916).

Lewis, Roger. "Sir Percy Anderson's Grand African Strategy, 1883–1893", *E.H.R.*, 81, no. 319, April, 1966.

Low, D. "British Public Opinion and the Uganda Question, October–December, 1892," *The Uganda Journal*, 18, 2 (1954).

Low, D. A. *Buganda in Modern History* (London, 1971).

_____. *Religion and Society in Buganda, 1875–1900* (Kampala, n.d.).

Lowe, C. J., ed. *The Reluctant Imperialists: British Foreign Policy, 1878–1902*, 2 vols. (London, 1967).

Lugard, F. D. *The Dual Mandate in British Tropical Africa* (Edinburgh and London, 1922).

Maccoby, S. *English Radicalism, 1886–1914* (London, n.d.).

Mansergh, Nicholas. *The Coming of the First World War: A Study in the European Balance, 1878–1914* (London, 1949).

Marder, A. J. *Anatomy of British Sea Power* (Connecticut, 1964).

Moon, P. T. *Imperialism and World Politics* (New York, 1927).

Newbury, C. W. "Victorians, Republicans and the Partition of West Africa," *J.A.H.*, 3, no. 3 (1962).

Obichere, Boniface I. *West African States and European Expansion* (New Haven, 1971).

Ogot, B. A. and Kieran, J. A., eds. *Zamani: A Survey of East African History* (EAPH, 1968).

Oliver, R. *The Missionary Factor in East Africa* (London, 1952).

Oliver, R. and Matthew, G., eds. *History of East Africa*, 1 (Oxon., 1963).

Penson, L. M. "The New Course in British Foreign Policy, 1892–1902," *Transactions of the Royal Historical Society*, 4s., 25 (March, 1942).

Ranger, T. "The Last Word on Rhodes?," *Past and Present*, no. 28 (July, 1964).

Ranger, T. O., ed. *Aspects of Central African History* (London, 1968).

Ranger, T. O. *Revolt in Southern Rhodesia, 1896–1897* (London, 1967).

Raphael, L. A. C. *The Cape-To-Cairo Dream: A Study in British Imperialism* (New York, 1936).

Roberts, A. D. "The Sub-imperialism of the Baganda," *J.A.H.* 3, 3 (1962).

Robinson, R. and Gallagher, J. "The Partition of Africa," *New Cambridge Modern History*, XI.

————. "The Imperialism of Free Trade," *Economic History Review*, 6, no. 1 (1953).

Robinson, R., Gallagher, J. with Denny, A. *Africa and the Victorians* (London, 1961).

Roscoe, John. *The Baganda* (London, 1911).

Rostow, W. W. *British Economy of the Nineteenth Century* (Oxon., 1948).

Rotberg, Robert. *Christian Missions and the Creation of Northern Rhodesia, 1880–1924* (New Jersey, 1965).

Rowe, J. A. *Lugard at Kampala* (Longmans, 1969).

————. "The Purge of Christians at Mwanga's Court," *J.A.H.* 4, 1 (1964).

Sanderson, G. N. "The Anglo-German Agreement of 1890 and the Upper Nile," *E.H.R.*, 77, no. 306, Jan., 1963.

————. "Contributions from African Sources to the History of European Competition in the Upper Valley of the Nile," *Journal of African History*, 3, 1 (1962).

————. *England, Europe and the Upper Nile, 1882–1899* (London, 1965).

Schumpeter, Joseph A. *Imperialism and Social Classes* (Harvard University Press, 1951), trans. by Heinz Norden, ed. by Paul M. Sweezy.

Scott-James, R. A. *The Influence of the Press* (London, 1913).

Shibeika, M. *British Policy in the Sudan, 1882–1902* (Oxford University Press, 1952).

Spender, J. A. *The Public Life,* 2 vols. (London, 1925).

Stanley, H. M. *Autobiography* (Boston, 1909).

Taylor, A. J. P. "Prelude to Fashoda: The Question of the Upper Nile, 1894–1895," *E.H.R.*, 65, no. 254 (1950).

Thomas, H. B. and Scott, R. *Uganda* (Oxford University Press and London, 1935).

Thomson, D. *England in the Nineteenth Century, 1815–1914* (London, 1964).

Thornton, A. P. *Doctrines of Imperialism* (New York and London, 1965).

Tuchman, Barbara W. *The Proud Tower: A Portrait of the World Before the War, 1890–1914* (New York, 1966).

Uzoigwe, G. N. "Kabalega and the Making of a New Kitara," *Tarikh*, 3, 2 (1970).

————. *Revolution and Revolt in Bunyoro-Kitara* (Longman, 1970).

Ward, A. W. and Gooch, G. P., eds. *The Cambridge History of British Foreign Policy*, 3, 1866–1919 (Cambridge University Press, 1923).

Ward, Barbara. *The International Share-Out* (London, 1958).

Webb, Beatrice. *Our Partnership* (London, 1948).

Webster, J. B. and Boahen, A. A. *The Revolutionary Years: West Africa Since 1800* (London, 1967).

Woolf, L. *Empire and Commerce in Africa: A Study in Economic Imperialism* (London, no date).

Wrigley, C. C. "The Christian Revolution in Buganda," *Comparative Studies in Society and History*, 2, 1 (1959).

Young, G. M. *Victorian England: Portrait of an Age* (Oxford University Press, 1960).

Unpublished Theses

Aderibigbe, A. A. B. "Expansion of the Lagos Protectorate 1863–1900" (London, Ph.D. thesis, 1959).

Flint, J. E. "British Policy and Chartered Company Administration in Nigeria, 1879–1900" (London, Ph.D. thesis, 1957).

Gertzel, C. "John Holt: A British Merchant in West Africa in the Era of Imperialism" (Oxon. Ph.D. thesis, 1959).

Grieve, M. "The Egyptian Policy of Lord Salisbury, 1895–1899" (Oxon. B.Litt. thesis, 1965).

de Kiewiet, M. J. "History of the Imperial British East Africa Company, 1876–1895" (London, Ph.D. thesis, 1955).

Low, D. A. "The British and Uganda, 1862–1900" (Oxon. Ph.D. thesis, 1957).

Nwafor, M. O. E. "Anglo-French Relations with Special Reference to West Africa, 1898–1904" (London, M.A. thesis, 1958).

Index